THE FRONTIER IN AMERICAN DEVELOPMENT

Essays in Honor of Paul Wallace Gates

Paul Wallace Gates

The Frontier in
American Development

ESSAYS IN HONOR OF PAUL WALLACE GATES

EDITOR

David M. Ellis

ASSOCIATE EDITORS

Lee Benson
Allan G. Bogue
Margaret Beattie Bogue
Harry N. Scheiber
Mary E. Young

Cornell University Press

ITHACA AND LONDON

First published 1969

Library of Congress Catalog Card Number: 69–18209

PRINTED IN THE UNITED STATES OF AMERICA
BY KINGSPORT PRESS, INC.

Prefatory Note

In 1962 a group of his former students, wishing to honor their professor upon his retirement, decided to prepare a *Festschrift* for Paul Wallace Gates. They chose a board of editors: Lee Benson, of the University of Pennsylvania; Allan G. Bogue, of the University of Wisconsin; David M. Ellis, of Hamilton College; Harry N. Scheiber, of Dartmouth College; and Mary E. Young, of Ohio State University. Western development was selected as the theme, and David Ellis was appointed chairman of the board and editor of the volume.

We are especially indebted to Dr. Frederick Merk, Professor Emeritus of Harvard University, for his illuminating appraisal of the work of his student. Gould Colman of Cornell University deserves our thanks for assembling the bibliography.

The editing of this book has been truly a cooperative enterprise of the graduate students of Professor Gates, and the editors wish to thank all who assisted them. We are also indebted to the staff of Cornell University Press for their skill in making more uniform the style and form of this work.

DAVID M. ELLIS

Clinton, New York
September 1968

Contents

Contents

Foreword

In the eighteenth and nineteenth centuries the federal government of the United States acquired title to land in most of the vast territory between the Appalachian Mountains and the Pacific Ocean. It acquired title to most of the Old Northwest and Old Southwest and to all the Louisiana Purchase, the Florida cession, the area gained by the Oregon Treaty, and the cession from Mexico, except those portions alienated to private individuals prior to the cessions. It acquired no land title east of the Appalachians, since the states, after the American Revolution, gave up only their western claims. It acquired no land in Kentucky, little in Tennessee, none in Texas. Of its huge acquisitions, it distributed approximately four-fifths to individuals, corporations, and states during the century and a half between the formation of the Union and the adoption of the Taylor Grazing Act of 1934.

This divestiture was the greatest real estate transaction in modern history, with respect to the extent of the land distributed and, even more, the value of the distribution. What the government distributed was the best of its holdings. What it retained was picked-over land, mountain land too rough for farming, land of low or marginal fertility, grazing land either arid or semi-arid, forest land that was of lower productivity in general than what had been disposed of. The retained land was of high social value. It was important for watershed protection, for the preservation of the land itself against wind or water erosion, and for the protection of the people on it against a deteriorating standard of living. It was essential also for recreation. Few, if any, national transactions in this century and a half transcended in importance this disposal of the federal domain. Yet not until it had been all but completed did it attract detailed attention from historians.

In 1893, Frederick Jackson Turner read his essay that was destined to become famous and to draw the notice of the academic world to the meaning of this process. The essay, entitled "The Significance of the Frontier in American History," was deliberately general—it presented a hypothesis intended to direct study to the effect of three centuries of distribution of free, or nearly free, land upon the institutions, the national character, the sectional politics, and the economic and social life of the nation. It was a preliminary appraisal of the meaning and result of an advance of pioneers seeking land across a savage wilderness and was designed to focus the sights of historical scholars upon that untilled field. It accomplished its purpose, though in the end it drew fire upon itself. Its generalizations have become a battleground for American historians and for historians of frontiers on other continents.

Studies of public-land disposal stimulated by the essay were at first chiefly political. They were accounts of agitation for the liberalization of land laws, precedents (colonial and state), debates in Congress, differences between sections over legislation, bargains bridging the differences, pressures for congressional grants in aid of internal improvements, lists of the amounts of land distributed under the more important acts, and the relationship of land sales to the ups and downs of the economy. Notable studies of this sort were those of A. C. Ford, P. J. Treat, L. H. Haney, B. H. Hibbard, R. G. Wellington, and G. M. Stephenson. The later and fuller treatment of land policy by R. M. Robbins continued that tradition. The focus of these studies was the interrelation of land policy with other political issues: treasury surpluses, proposals to distribute the lands or their proceeds to the states, currency issues, tariff adjustments, constitutional interpretations, or the question of warrants as rewards for military service. The emphasis was on the making of the land laws; the functioning of the laws was less closely examined.

Toward the end of the 1920's attention was turned increasingly to the administration of the land laws. The question was, How had the laws worked in practice? The newer trend was signaled by a notable teacher in the field of western history, James B. Hedges. Hedges was interested especially in the role of land-grant railroads in the distribution of lands obtained from Congress, and in their activity as colonizers of the West. He attracted to this subject an enthusiastic disciple, Paul Wallace Gates.

In 1934, Gates published an initial study, *The Illinois Central Railroad and Its Colonization Work*. In it he combined old themes and new. An old theme appeared in the early chapters, in which the history of the first railroad land grant by Congress was traced, including the maneuverings of Whigs to reverse Andrew Jackson's policy of resistance to congressional aid for internal improvements. The Whig triumph opened the way for lavish grants to railroads east and west of the Mississippi River. A fresher portion of the book was the second half, in which discussion turned to the gradual sale of the granted lands, the modes of attracting settlers, American and foreign, to the lands, the services rendered by the company to settlers in the form of extended credits—which the federal government did not give convenient means of access to markets, and stimulation of improvements in farming. Standards were set in this portion of the volume for all later studies of railroad land grants and their disposal. The book gave a balanced account of speculators' activities in Illinois. It dispassionately described townsite promotion and speculation by insiders in the company, contrary to Illinois law.

The period in which the volume appeared—the early 1930's —was a time of distressed agriculture and of alarming disturbances of nature in the United States. It was a time remembered as the "black thirties." Evidences of errors in the past distribution and use of land troubled the public: deterioration of soil in once rich farm areas; ravages by gulleying in hill and upland country that was once productive; dust storms of unprecedented severity on the Great Plains; clogging of river channels with soil carried off by dust storms and floods; impairment, through overuse, of grazing areas in the Far West; floods of record height and destructiveness; and the emergence of blighted areas of submarginal living in the cut-over lands of the northern Great Lakes region, in the basin of the Tennessee River, and in much of the southern Appalachians. The increase in farm tenancy in areas of the nation's best soil was brought to public notice. It seemed to reformers to mark the withering of the Jeffersonian ideal of ownership of the soil by the tillers of it. These problems, or elements of them, were the province of the Land Policy Section of the Agricultural Adjustment Administration, of which L. C. Gray, a socially minded economist and historian, was head.

In 1934, Gates was called to this staff. During a year's leave of absence from Bucknell University he served with it, examining the historical origins of some of these problems and their relationship to public-land disposal. He had been aware, in the course of his researches, of discrepancies between the intent of federal laws and their operation. In the New Deal atmosphere of reappraisal of the administration of the laws, he dwelt increasingly on overlapping legislation, on lax administration by the Land Office, on frauds perpetrated on the frontier by speculators, large and small, upon an absentee government, and on the consequent growth of great land holdings.

An early product of the new visions and convictions was a study (1935), "Recent Land Policies of the Federal Government," in *Certain Aspects of Land Problems and Government*, part of the report of the National Resources Board. The study described "roots of maladjustment" in land policy, evils arising from them, and changes needed to correct them. A major "root of maladjustment" was the decision of Congress in 1862 to permit an older system of land disposal to remain in operation, with a new one of different aim merely superimposed upon it. The old system emphasized cash sales in unlimited amounts (either at public auctions or as "private entries" at land offices after land had been offered at auction), pre-emption rights to squatters on the public domain, grants to states for education, grants to them of "swamp lands" for drainage and flood control, and land warrants (which were made transferable) to veterans of past wars. The new system superimposed on the old one provided for free homesteads—donations to settlers of quarter sections of agricultural land on condition merely of improving them. The results of the merging of the two systems were an encouragement of speculation and a limitation of the effectiveness of the donation policy. An example of the merging was the commutation principle in the Homestead Act which permitted converting a homestead claim into a pre-emption claim that could be bought at the minimum price and later sold.

Lax administration was another major "root of maladjustment." This had opened the gates to fraud before the two systems were developed, and it did so increasingly afterward. Speculators, great and small, consistently took advantage of failures in the enforcement of the conditions of homesteading, of the commutation privilege, and of such special legislation as the Timber Culture Act of 1873. That act had been adopted as an encouragement to tree planting in sparsely timbered areas. It contained no adequate protection against frauds, and it greatly facilitated the engrossment of public land by speculators. The combined effect of the merging of the two systems and of lax administration was the building up of large speculative holdings in timber, mining, and agricultural land—a subject of special interest to Gates.

The "Recent Land Policies" article was followed in 1936 by a survey in the *American Historical Review:* "The Homestead Law in an Incongruous Land System." In this a challenge was thrown at the old belief that the homestead law, in departing from preceding legislation, had opened wide to settlers the doors of opportunity. The law was shown to have been, by reason of its competition with earlier laws, more limited in its use by actual settlers than had been supposed. Settlers always had to compete with speculators and engrossers who appeared early in freshly opened areas and who were adept at acquiring the best lands and the best locations. Speculators had untiring energy, adequate capital, inside knowledge of newly opened districts, and practice in combining elements of the two systems. Homesteaders were left with only a choice between picked-over land in good locations and better land at a costly distance from convenient markets.

The incongruity between the two systems was well known before historians discovered it. It had been the subject of controversy in congressional debates. Every session of Congress from 1876 to 1891 was a battle between land reformers and vested interests, especially over the issues of cash sales in unlimited amounts and the abuse of pre-emption rights. But the *status quo* long remained unchanged. Curbs on cash sales in unlimited amounts came only in 1889 and 1890, and the pre-emption law was not repealed until 1891.

In his seminal early articles Gates laid out a field for subsequent investigation. The field was as wide as the area of land disposal, and the intensive cultivation of it was possible only in segments. The segments were often regional and topical, but their central theme was clear—the handicaps settlers found in a system supposedly designed for them and the opportunities speculators found in a system that did not sufficiently guard against them.

The growth of farm tenancy in the northern prairie states of the Union became a major concern of Gates. It had come into public notice dramatically in the 1920's and 1930's because of its spread across the best soils of the region. Its spread in the southern states was less startling, because its main roots had been planted there during the revolution in agriculture which attended the emancipation of the slaves in 1865. Tenancy on the northern prairies became the topic of a series of important articles by Gates, in which he showed that it had its roots in frontier days and that it had developed in considerable part from the building of great estates through legitimate cash purchases of public domain.

Some of these holdings had been built up for purely speculative reasons by wealthy men from all sections. Others had been built up as agricultural estates tilled by tenants on the English model. Others grew out of the operations of the "cattle kings" that were a stage in the development of the beef-producing economy centering in Ohio and Indiana in the 1850's and extending into Illinois in the 1860's. Fodder for the cattle was at first the native prairie grasses. Later corn was raised in increasing amounts to supplement the grasses. In the 1880's cattle were imported from the Great Plains for a final period of fattening. Estates, in the meantime, were divided into tenant farms to increase corn production. The core of tenancy prevalence shown on the maps of the 1920's and 1930's was in the areas owned by earlier "cattle kings."

Two factors favoring the development of and increase in tenancy were the ease with which capitalists had been able to acquire extensive estates at low prices, improve them, and pass them on to heirs, and the difficulties which settlers encountered in the high costs of creating prairie farms. The breaking, draining, and fencing of prairies were expensive, and on the frontier money could be borrowed only at usurious interest. In periods of economic stress foreclosures occurred and equities of settlers were wiped out. A settler was likely to become a tenant on land transferred to a mortgage holder.

On some northern frontiers a factor in building up extensive holdings was, as Gates has showed, the removal of Indians from reservations. He pointed this out, with reference to the Indiana prairie region, in an introduction to the *John Tipton Papers*, published in three volumes in 1942. Tipton was an Indiana politician who, in the 1830's, was agent to the Pottawatomie and Miami tribes. The lands of these Indians lay north of the Wabash River and were remnants of the possessions of those tribes when they had been the terror of American frontiersmen in the era of the American Revolution. The removal of the tribes resulted in part from debts to white traders residing among them, incurred in the purchase of supplies, firearms, and whiskey. Debts grew with the advance of white settlement, inasmuch as purchases could no longer be balanced by sales of furs. The traders expected the ultimate discharge of debts from the sale of tribal lands to the federal government. Land-sale treaties arranged in collaboration with traders usually contained provisions for the discharge of debts. Treaties made with the Pottawatomie and Miami tribes late in the 1830's had such provisions.

In these treaties special allotments of land were reserved for tribal chiefs and headmen. The lands so reserved were of particular attractiveness, in location or otherwise. They became, by treaty, the private property of the chiefs or headmen. As a result of arrangements made before the conclusion of such treaties, the lands had already virtually passed into the hands of creditors and land speculators. Some were even acquired by the government Indian agent who had assisted in the preliminaries. In this way, Gates shows, valuable lands in the regions east of the Mississippi passed by hundreds of thousands of acres to speculators, without ever having been part of the federal domain. Tipton was a speculator who saw no wrong in taking profit as an Indian agent from treaties he helped to negotiate. He became a person of wealth—a United States senator from Indiana.

In Kansas the transfer of Indian lands to whites in bypass of the public domain was open and extensive. It occurred in the attractive eastern portion of the territory. In this portion were the reservations of the "intruded" Indians, those who, as in the case of the Miami and Pottawatomie, had given up land east of the Mississippi for land west of it. Their reservations, like those in Oklahoma, were definitely bounded and were to be theirs "forever," as was declared in treaties made in the 1830's. But "forever" was a word taken less seriously by whites than by Indians.

Most of the Kansas lands of the intruded Indians passed to whites in two series of treaties, the first in 1854–1855; the second, from 1859 to 1868. The treaties, numbering nearly a score, established four categories of lands: (1) allotments to individual Indians, (2) lands ceded "in trust" by the Indians, (3) lands unconditionally ceded and put under control of the Land Office, and (4) "diminished reserves." Allotments to individual Indians, limited in size, went to them in fee simple. The idea was that the Indians under Indian Office supervision would become land-owning farmers. The lands in the ceded-in-trust category were to be surveyed as soon as possible and sold for the benefit of the Indians by the Indian Office. The sales were to be at auction, the starting price to be an appraised price (but not less than $1.25 an acre), and the lands were not to be open to pre-emption. The unconditionally ceded lands were to be disposed of under the general land laws. Diminished reserves— lands left after a cession had been made—were to remain tribal properties.

By 1860 allotments, "trust lands," and unconditionally ceded lands, of the first series of treaties, had virtually all passed to whites. Allotments had passed by reason of Indian debts or alleged tax delinquency—though the taxes were later held to have been illegal. Trust lands had been sold to speculators and to settlers. Unconditionally ceded lands, available under the general land laws, had gone in the same way as soon as they were surveyed.

By 1859 new treaties were in demand, and the second series was negotiated. In these, allotments were again created, but diminished reserves and hitherto untouched reserves were the prime subject matter of the negotiations. The treaties provided, in general, for the sale, intact, of reservations or remainders of reservations, with the sales to be directed by the Indian Office.

More often than not, the treaties named prospective purchasers and set the conditions and price of purchase. The purchasers were railroad groups. They found the reserves more attractive than congressional land grants, since reserves were not affected by the alternate-section provision of the land grants. The railroad groups—some based in Kansas, others absentee-owned—vied for influence with the Indian Office in the treaty negotiations and for influence in the Senate for ratification. Among treaties earmarked for specific railroads were those with the Pottawatomie, with the Kickapoo, and with the Cherokee for their so-called Neutral Tract. In the case of the Cherokee treaty the price paid the Indians was $1.25 an acre, and the price obtained from settlers soon afterward was double this amount, or more.

One of the most attractive of the reservations was the Osage. A treaty was made in 1865 providing for the sale, for the benefit of the tribe, of part of it at a minimum price of $1.25 an acre. The treaty was no sooner ratified than negotiation was begun by the Indian Office for the remainder. A commission rigged in favor of a railroad dominated by an aggressive Detroit promoter, James F. Joy, proceeded to the Osage in 1868 and concluded a treaty under which all remaining Osage lands were to be sold to the railroad at twenty cents an acre. The treaty produced an outcry in Congress and from the public. As a result it was withdrawn by President Grant, and in 1871 Congress passed a law ending forever the system of Indian cessions arranged through the Indian Office and ratified as "treaties" by the Senate. Congress thereafter assumed authority for all acquisitions of Indian lands and for their disposal to settlers.

The story of this alienation of Indian lands in Kansas is told in detail by Gates in his *Fifty Million Acres*. The title refers to the extent of the Kansas land surface. Of this total acreage, the amount disposed of without regard to general land laws (in the sales of Indian lands described above, and by congressional grants to railroads and to the state of Kansas) was 47 per cent. This went largely to speculators and corporations. Even of the remaining 53 per cent subject to the general land laws, much passed to speculators, large and small, in the course of the normal operation of the laws.

The significance of this parceling of the soil of Kansas is believed by Gates to have been political as well as economic. Clashes between settlers and speculators and protests by settlers against premature government land sales contributed to the excitement in Kansas before the Civil War and to the movement for homestead legislation. The feeling against railroads on account of their engrossment of land and their control of the Indian Office persisted through the Civil War and into the discontent of the seventies, eighties, and nineties. The year 1871, which marked the end of the system of dealing by treaty with Indians, marked also the ending of congressional land grants to railroads. But railroads already possessed a fifth of Kansas, while settlers in search of homesteads were obliged to seek them in areas of deficient rainfall west of the ninety-seventh meridian. These were background elements in Kansas for the antimonop oly storm of the era of Populism.

A case study in the functioning of federal land policy in a different part of the country appears in Gates's volume *The Wisconsin Pine Lands of Cornell University*, which deals with the Morrill Act of 1862. The act was predicated on the belief that agriculture in the United States should be made more scientific and that the federal government should help achieve this end by donating public lands for education. The measure authorized donations to states in proportion to their representation in Congress. Any state lacking federal lands within its own borders would receive scrip representing the number of acres to which it was entitled—the scrip to be located in the public-land states. The act was opposed in the western public-land states and in the South. It was approved only after the southern states had with-

drawn from Congress during the Civil War. New York, by reason of its large population, was especially fortunate in the amount
of scrip it received. Its use of the scrip seemed to Gates to illustrate the opportunities and the risks inherent in speculation in the
wilderness lands of the West.

A new university, Cornell, was created by the state legislature
to benefit from the state's sale of its scrip. The state sold the bulk
of it to Ezra Cornell, a wealthy and public-spirited resident of
Ithaca who was interested in education. The state thus obtained
funds for the establishment and immediate needs of the new
university. In purchasing the scrip, Cornell proposed to donate
to the University all the profits (over his costs plus 7 per cent)
he would make from the ultimate sale of lands that he would
acquire with the scrip. He invested the scrip in the late 1860's,
chiefly in a half-million acres of the pinelands of the Chippewa
Valley, in Wisconsin. They were held for years, until they had
increased in value. Then they (or their stumpage) were sold by
Cornell University to lumbermen. The University realized a
profit of five million dollars in the operation.

In his book Gates discusses the hazards as well as the profits of
the transaction. Among the hazards were state and local taxes
that were levied on absentee-owned land. University agents
were vigilant and fought off discriminatory taxes of this kind.
The total tax cost proved ultimately to be less than 10 per cent
of the gross-sale income from the lands. Loss of timber from
depredations against absentee-owned lands and from fire was
another hazard. Cornell lands were better guarded against these
dangers than were federally owned lands, but protection was an
additional item of cost.

The success of Cornell illustrates the general conclusions of
Gates. One is that speculation in the public domain could be
very profitable. Another is that the speculator had definite advantages over the ordinary settler. Ezra Cornell had, besides
scrip in large amounts, the means to employ a skilled timber
cruiser for locating the best pine and the means to guard against

discriminatory taxes, theft, and fire. Also, the University could wait until time had produced what was essentially unearned increment. Experienced agents of the University knew the right time for the selling of timberland or stumpage. Cut-over lands passed to speculators and, though of dubious promise for farming, were sold to unwary settlers. Other states that had Morrill Act scrip profited less than did New York. In most instances other states sold their scrip—in a depressed market—to dealers in land scrip, in an effort to create agricultural-college "land funds." Speculators with the wisdom and means of Ezra Cornell and Cornell University reaped high profits but left the University far from popular in Wisconsin. Two other areas of land speculation, examined in articles by Gates, were state lands in California (both agricultural and timber) and federal timberlands in the Gulf states after the repeal of the Southern Homestead Act in 1876.

On the perimeters of the United States the bounty intended by Congress for settlers was limited to a great degree by large estates originating from grants made by the governments antecedent to the United States in these areas. The grants had been made in the Louisiana Purchase region (including Missouri) by the French or Spanish, in the Floridas by the Spanish or British, and in the region ceded at the close of the Mexican War by Spanish or Mexican authorities. Some of the grants were of dubious legality; many, especially those that had passed to assignees, were under contest. Gates discusses grants in several of the areas of claims, giving special attention to California.

In California approximately eight hundred grants had been made before American jurisdiction was established in 1848. Their extent was thirteen million acres or more of the most desirable California land. They had been made for grazing purposes to intimates of California's authorities. Their boundaries were vague and overlapping, and in many cases conditions had not been fulfilled. Some families held multiple claims, resting on grants or on assignments of grants. Thomas O. Larkin, former consul of the United States at Monterey, held, for instance, five such claims, of which four (whose boundaries were ultimately confirmed) totaled 164,000 acres.

A sudden massive migration to California by American gold seekers and land seekers followed the cession of Guadalupe Hidalgo. They were a strenuous element, in search of riches. They were accustomed to squatters' rights, pre-emption, and purchase from the government at minimum prices. They came into a confused situation for which Congress had made no adequate preparation. In this respect California was a predecessor of Kansas. The donation of land to settlers which Congress had voted for the Oregon Territory had not been extended to California. Squatting on land that looked unoccupied was instinctive among American pioneers. In California it occurred even on land that was recognized to be claimed and occupied. Bitter clashes with holders of old titles took place.

Congress was tardy in intervening, because it was busy with its own clashes over the organization of the newly acquired territories. Moreover, it was torn by strife between those wishing a vigorous testing of the claims of "old Californians" (or of their assignees) and those wishing an indulgent testing. Among those who wished a strict testing was California's Senator Gwin, of the Judiciary Committee of the Senate, who represented the views of the settlers. Among those wishing an indulgent testing was Thomas H. Benton, who had been a champion of claimants to old grants in Missouri. Benton's son-in-law, John C. Frémont, who held a major claim in California with great mining possibilities, was also among those wishing an easy testing. A bill which the Gwin committee reported to the Senate in 1851 was based on a half-century of congressional and judicial experience in dealing with such claims. It provided for a Land Commission before which holders of claims were to make their case for validation of title. Appeals were permitted to the federal courts from decisions of the commission. Claimants who were successful were to have their tracts surveyed at their own expense. The bill became law.

The Land Commission proved to be a fairly efficient sifter of claims. The tendency was to confirm claims that showed at least a minimum compliance with the conditions of grants. The federal courts were even more tolerant of questionable claims carried to them from the rulings of the commission. But the commission's rulings and its mode of dealing with the problem became in its day targets for violent attack by disappointed claimants and their attorneys—attacks echoed in writings by later California historians. Gates's study, which rests on the most thorough examination yet made of the California claims, is a valuable contribution, not merely to an understanding of the claim question itself, but also to an understanding of the delay in extending the federal land system to California.

One ingredient in the California controversy was the question of "rights of occupancy." Occupancy laws existed in many American states. Under them settlers who had occupied wilderness land which later proved to be owned by others could be evicted only after being reimbursed for improvements they had made in the period of their occupancy. Settlers in California sought similar protection with respect to improvements made by them on lands which were later shown to be within the limits of grants obtained in the Mexican period. They asserted that evidence of private ownership had been missing at the time of their occupation. In 1856 the California legislature, in response to pressure from the public, adopted a right-of-occupancy law. In the following year the law was voided by the California Supreme Court on the ground that it violated the contract clause of the federal constitution. The clash over the law and its reversal is described by Gates in an article, "California's Embattled Settlers."

The issues of the California controversy are given an eastern setting by Gates in a study tracing the evolution of occupancy rights. Kentucky was the center of the evolution. The state had suffered from land conveyances as loose and lavish as those afflicting California. Enough rights to Kentucky lands had been issued to cover the state four times over. The ensuing confusion had led to conflicting claims on an extensive scale. Occupiers with some sort of claim later found that they had been making improvements on lands belonging to others. To protect settlers' equities, the Kentucky legislature had passed statutes in the era from 1797 to 1830 providing for reimbursement to an evicted settler for improvements, with the value of the improvements to be set by a local jury and not to be offset by rent charges. A seven-year uncontested occupancy was to be considered sufficient in itself for title. Claimants who might prove their legal right to disputed tracts were made subject to legal hindrances before they could eject occupiers. Such protection was given only to occupiers who could advance at least a "color of title" to a claim. In other states of the union, notably in Vermont and in Tennessee, where confusion of title existed, laws of this character had also been adopted.

In 1821 all such laws had been challenged by a decision of the United States Supreme Court in the case of *Green* versus *Biddle*, which held that the Kentucky legislature had violated the contract clause of the federal constitution. The court invoked the harshness of the common law regarding contracts, unsoftened by equity jurisdiction or by the remedial measures of the state legislature, against the occupancy laws. The decision was defied by the Kentucky legislature and by others. In more than a dozen states and territories rights-of-occupancy laws were passed and enforced, some of them increasing the protection to occupiers beyond what it had been in 1821.

The California statute of 1856 giving protection to occupiers was more sweeping than those of other states. It protected settlers who had intruded, without even a "color of title," on lands of others. It did so in response to the popular feeling against claimants under old grants. This was one reason for the resurrection of the outmoded principle of *Green* versus *Biddle* by the California Supreme Court in its reversal of the law. The reversal and the security it gave to old claimants were elements, Gates believes, in the building up of great holdings in California.

The story of the occupancy laws in their eastern origins, their spread despite the *Green* versus *Biddle* case, the significance of the California reversal, and the adoption of a congressional act allowing occupancy rights in cases that reached federal courts is told by Gates in "Tenants of the Log Cabin," his presidential address to the Mississippi Valley Historical Association in 1962. This address, as a study of one phase of the progress of land reform in the United States, is a major contribution to land-policy history.

Outside the domain of land policy Gates has made two valuable contributions to agricultural history. One is *The Farmer's Age;* the other, *Agriculture and the Civil War. The Farmer's Age* is a survey of the period 1815 to 1860. It compares favorably with such studies as *History of Agriculture in the Northern United States, 1620–1860,* by Percy Bidwell and J. I. Falconer, and *History of Agriculture in the Southern United States to 1860,* by L. C. Gray. Its organization is similar, and likewise its treatment of individual crops. It examines such subjects as markets, transportation, labor, scientific advances, improvements of animal and plant species, and education. Its emphasis on education is greater than that in the other volumes, as is its emphasis on the effect of federal policies on land tenure. It exhibits an unequaled familiarity with the vast contemporary printed literature on the subject, including books on crops and livestock and farm journals that were read by farmers. Gates has a feeling of kinship with the farmer. Harry J. Carman, another notable scholar in the field of American agriculture, once modestly described himself as a "farmer gone wrong." Paul Gates, as a scholar, is in the same tradition.

Agriculture and the Civil War carries the story of the preceding volume forward. The book gives the first full-scale history of the impact of the Civil War and agriculture upon each other. It traces the sectional pattern of northern and southern crops and describes the diversification of crops in the North in a search for substitutes for withdrawn southern crops, especially for cotton and sugar, and the opposite tendency in the South—a concentration, increasingly, on food production owing to the shutting off of foreign markets for cotton, sugar, and tobacco and to the need to compensate for the withdrawal of northern food supplies and the ravages of the war. The book tells of the steady diminution of southern food resources in the latter years of the war, as invading Union forces sliced segment after segment from Confederate territories and left widening belts of desolation in their rear, or as the Confederacy conscripted more and more able-bodied men into its armies, or as farm implements wore out. The South was brought near to starvation, Gates believes, in the closing period of the war. The North, in the meantime, was growing stronger and richer from its exports of wheat and meat.

In this book Gates describes four congressional measures adopted in the second year of the war which are significant in his fields of land policy and agriculture. Discussions of two of them —the Morrill Act and an act setting up an independent Department of Agriculture—also round out chapters in *The Farmer's Age*. The third was a congressional grant to the first of the transcontinental railroads, an outgrowth of the policy initiated in the Illinois Central grant. The fourth was the Homestead Act, which Gates credits in this volume—as he does in his articles published in connection with the Homestead Act centennial— with more favorable results than he had in his earlier writings. He discusses the act as having been of benefit to settlers in areas open to homesteading east of the Mississippi and in those west of the river that were suited for farming units of 160 to 320 acres. He holds that the act served settlers well until about 1880. That judgment is the product of newer studies by himself and others. The book takes rank among the best scholarly achievements of the Civil War's centennial years.

In describing agricultural progress, Gates has given proper recognition to several important reformers. One of these is Charles Lewis Fleischmann, a German-born American citizen, who was an early advocate of agricultural education and of soil conservation, to whom he has devoted an entire article, as well as several pages in *The Farmer's Age*. Another is Ulysses Prentiss Hedrick, a noted horticulturist and historian of farm life, for whose republished *History of Agriculture in the State of New York* Gates has written an illuminating introduction. Henry L. Ellsworth, as head of the agricultural work of the Patent Office and as a benevolent landlord in Indiana, appears in his pages in true dimensions. George W. Julian's role as a land reformer is no longer hidden behind his roles in other reforms.

In all the writings of Gates his reliance on manuscript sources is evident. The manuscripts in the National Archives in all their vast volume have been ransacked, including, for example, the valuable and little used Record of Proclamations of Land Sales, 1857–1875 (useful for the timing of land sales), and abstract books showing when and where entries were made by holders of military warrants and land scrip.

But Gates wished to work especially on the unforeseen results of ill-considered legislation and lax administration and in the dark places of perversion and violation of laws. His search for such evidence has led him to the discovery and exploitation of types of source material his predecessors had left untouched, much of it outside of Washington. Examples of his finds are manuscripts of old census schedules still lying in dusty local archives, useful for land and agricultural information omitted from even the most detailed of the printed census volumes; records of federal district courts containing information on the adjudication of private land claims; county-court records, revealing the size of land holdings through contests over the division of estates; deed and mortgage records, important for evidence of early tenancy; private correspondence of public officials, especially those in the Land Office and Indian Office;

private correspondence of land speculators with their agents in public-land states; the correspondence of land companies, of railroad land departments, and of law firms engaged in land-claims cases; unpublished letters of governors of Confederate states, revealing conditions of southern agriculture during the Civil War; and archives of universities that were the beneficiaries of the Morrill Act. A trail has been blazed to these depositories for other scholars.

Gates has also made imaginative use of printed sources, some well known, others less so. National newspapers such as the *National Intelligencer* and the *New York Tribune* were useful, for example, for information about the market prices of military land warrants, while the *Tribune* was a major source for his books on agriculture. Even more widely used by him were the newspapers of the public-land states, where accounts of land auctions were reported. Advertisements in local newspapers of agricultural land for rent were an important source for the prevalence of tenancy prior to the taking of tenancy statistics. Advertisements in local papers (inserted by moneylenders, absentee or local) revealed the exorbitant rates of interest on loans to squatters, especially in the face of imminent land sales. Local papers also revealed the wages of farm laborers, while aroused local sentiment on land or credit issues found expression in local editorial columns and in letters of anonymous farmers.

The printed volumes of state historical collections, the transactions of state agricultural societies, county histories, and biographies of leading county personalities (who usually possessed land-based wealth) were also rich sources. Local maps of land ownership were instructive in showing concentrations of land ownership, especially where private land claims going back to an earlier sovereignty had been confirmed. Comparisons of plat-book maps of original entries with later concentrations of ownership on county maps provided clues to the extent of foreclosures.

Closeness to his sources has given Gates concreteness in his writing. Some of the concreteness comes from the use of statistics, often his own compilations gathered from scattered portions of the federal censuses or from scattered Land Office records. Some of his concreteness comes from a candid use of personal letters (many not yet published) and from an eye for the printed letters of obscure individuals submitted to newspapers or farm journals. Excerpts from frontier reporting of "land deals" add to the sense of contemporaneousness. Concreteness has also been achieved as a result of extensive travels into agricultural country to examine land, topography, and farm buildings, and to visit the stately town houses of the "cattle kings" of the prairies, often still in the possession of their descendants, whom he interviewed. Vividness is achieved in other ways. Gates chooses apt but not too lengthy quotations. His own language is evocative —and provocative.

Challenging questions are asked by Gates. Granted that large private land holdings were built up in the United States in the nineteenth century, what were the methods by which this was achieved? What was the relative reliance upon purchase from government land offices by cash, by military warrants, by agricultural-college scrip? To what extent were large holdings the result of purchases from railroad land offices, of purchases from state land offices, of purchases of Indian land through one or another of the types of sales conducted by the Indian Office? To what extent were large holdings the result of the fraudulent use of the settlement laws? What proportion of the applicants for homesteads under the act of 1862 perfected title to their claims? What did the failures to do so mean? How many farmers were themselves engaged in land speculation?

Gates is determined to find what has been overlooked and to inject truth into stereotyped views of American land policy. He notes to what extent the sale of state lands has been overlooked in studies of the building up of large holdings, and how the sales of Indian lands by the Indian Office contributed to the same result. He shows how much the extensive grants to states for education, internal improvements, and drainage limited the amount of land the federal government could offer for sale or for other forms of entry and that, therefore, the government never realized the "double-the-minimum" price which it was supposed to have received for the reserved sections within railroad land grants.

His methods in writing explain also the success of Gates as a teacher. Stimulating in the lecture hall, he has been in his graduate seminars a "producer of producing scholars." His twenty-three Ph.D.'s, as of July 1967, have written twenty-one excellent books, to say nothing of their many valuable articles. Furthermore, his students have won numerous honors and prizes: the John H. Dunning Prize, the Albert J. Beveridge Award, Fulbright fellowships, and Social Science Research Council Post-Doctoral fellowships. They hold positions in many major institutions, from the London School of Economics to the University of Wisconsin. Not least among the number of producing scholars inspired by him is his wife, Lillian Francis Cowdell Gates, whose publications include several articles in the *Canadian Historical Review* and a volume, *Land Policies of Upper Canada*, recently published by the University of Toronto Press.

The writings of Paul Gates and of his followers have added a new dimension to land-policy history and, indeed, to western development. Of this greater scope the present volume of essays is an illustration. The vigor of the essays and the unabated productivity of the leader who gave them inspiration offer promise of a future synthesis of the history of American public-land disposal more meaningful than any published in the past.

FREDERICK MERK

Cambridge, Massachusetts
August 1967

PART I

THE DISPOSITION OF PUBLIC LANDS

The Historian as Mythmaker: Turner and the Closed Frontier

❧〇❧

LEE BENSON

Histories make history. More precisely, historians significantly influence men's conceptions of the past, and men's conceptions of the past significantly influence their present behavior. If we accept these assumptions, the making of histories is responsible work that historians should perform responsibly. A truism? Of course. But a truism that historians would do well to dust off constantly, particularly when they report their findings and present their conclusions.

Ideally, historians reconstruct the past accurately; they "tell it like it was," to restate Ranke's nineteenth-century credo in contemporary idiom. Sometimes, however, historians unwittingly function as mythmakers; i.e., they invent legends or myths that gain credence and influence behavior. Frederick Jackson Turner, this essay contends, functioned as a mythmaker when he popularized Achille Loria's "free land" theory of history and applied it to America in the form of the "frontier thesis." [1]

[1] I showed, at least to my own satisfaction, that Turner took over the Lorian system in an article, first published in 1950, "Achille Loria's Influence on American Economic Thought: Including His Contributions to the Frontier Hypothesis." It is reprinted in my *Turner and Beard: American Historical Writing Reconsidered* (New York, 1960), 1–40. All citations below are to this edition. Additional information, particularly a letter to Turner from Loria cited below, and more reflection have strengthened my conviction that the "Turner frontier

3

Why label Turner a mythmaker? Why not simply write that the frontier thesis is wrong, or unfounded, or invalid? I do not claim that Turner consciously helped to invent a myth. I do claim that we can better understand Turner's influence on American historiography if we recognize that the remarkably uncritical acceptance of the frontier thesis for several decades and its uncanny ability to survive logical and empirical refutation neatly fit the "sociological" definition of "myth": "a collective belief that is built up in response to the wishes of the group rather than an analysis of the basis of the wishes." [2]

Briefly summarized, the Loria-Turner thesis assumed that, as Turner paraphrased Loria in 1893, "The existence of an area of free land, its continuous recession, and the advance of American settlement westward explain American development." In 1892, he had expressed the same basic proposition in slightly different form: "In a sense, American history up to our own day has been colonial history, the colonization of the Great West. This ever retreating frontier of free land is the key to American development." [3] Commenting upon those sentences, Fulmer Mood significantly observed, "In this reference to free land,

thesis" is better characterized as the "Loria-Turner free-land thesis." American historians may resist the idea that the "frontier thesis" essentially is Turner's version of Loria's version of Karl Marx's theory of historical development. But it now seems clear to me—contrary to my 1950 observation that "Loria was a Lorian; he was *sui generis*"—that Loria served as the major medium for the transmission of Marx's ideas, although in distorted form, to American historiography. That claim, which I hope to develop at length in a book analyzing economic determinism in American historiography, is strengthened by a letter (in my possession) I received in 1951 from Walter Prescott Webb. Webb's letter explicitly acknowledges that his ideas came directly from Lindley M. Keasbey, the American translator of Loria's *Economic Foundations of Society*. (See my article on Loria.)

[2] As defined in C. J. Barnhart, ed., *The American College Dictionary* (New York, 1959), 805.

[3] Fulmer Mood, ed., *The Early Writings of Frederick Jackson Turner* (Madison, Wis., 1938), 72, 186. The first quotation, of course, comes from Turner's famous essay, "The Significance of the Frontier in American History," which was first read as a paper in 1893 and published in 1894. This edition, in my judgment, is by far the most

4

Turner for *the first time in print* [italics added] put his finger upon the material cause, the fundamental economic factor, that he was to stress in his interpretation of our history." [4]

Since the young provincial professor had simply extended in greater detail Loria's own application of his "Landed System of Social Economy" to American history, upon publication of "The Significance of the Frontier in American History," he naturally sent a copy to the world-famous Italian theorist whose books had been extravagantly praised by leading American scholars and whose theory had been summarized at length in the June 1892 issue of the *Political Science Quarterly*.[5] Just as naturally, Loria delightedly responded in February 1894 that he had read Turner's lecture with "the very greatest interest" and found in it "many documents important in support of *my* [italics added] economic theses." [6] Had the title of the lecture literally conveyed the essence of Loria's "economic theses," however, we would know it as "The Significance in American History of Unoccupied Land Which Can Be Cultivated and Possessed without Capital." As both Loria and Turner made clear and contemporaries recognized, that is what free land meant, not simply unoccupied land.[7]

---

useful one extant, since it contains an appendix that compares differing versions of the essay as Turner changed it in various reprintings.

[4] *Ibid.*, 37–38.

[5] Historians who resist recognizing that Turner took over the Lorian system also seem to resist reading Loria's writings and the reviews of, and articles about, his work in the leading American scholarly journals, beginning in December 1890. See my discussion in *Turner and Beard*, 10–20; better yet, read the items cited in those pages.

[6] Loria to Turner, Feb. 17, 1894, in Turner Papers, Henry E. Huntington Library, San Marino, Calif. (quoted by permission of The Huntington Library). Loria wrote in French, and I have tried to keep the original tone.

[7] Ray Billington unfortunately has misread Loria and defined "free land" as meaning only "unoccupied land." He has also failed to recognize that Loria's theory about "the economic foundations of society" explicitly claimed that the presence or absence of free land determined a nation's culture and society. Instead, Billington asserts that Turner "learned" this concept from Henry George. He seems to dismiss the

Turner, in his *text,* explicitly emphasized that the "most significant thing about it [the American frontier] is that it lies at the hither edge of free land." [8] In his *title,* however, he focused attention on the census concept of a "frontier line" of population density rather than on Loria's concept of free land. As a result, as Turner popularized the application of Loria's "economic theses" to American history, they came to be known as the "frontier thesis." Thus their economic determinist character was blurred by association with the romantic myths of "noble savages" and primitive unspoiled "virginal nature" that seem to have been so powerful in the American imagination after the eighteenth century.[9]

---

statement he quotes from a letter Turner wrote in 1931: "I never saw his [George's] earlier essays and think that I never read his *Progress and Poverty* before writing the 'Frontier.'" Wilbur R. Jacobs, in my judgment, also tends to overestimate George's influence on Turner. After observing that the "notes which Turner made on Loria refer frequently to the importance of 'free land' in American history," Jacobs wrote, "Henry George, as well as Loria, provided basic ideas for Turner's frontier hypothesis. Upon discovering in Loria's *Analisi* a quotation from *Progress and Poverty* translated into Italian, Turner jotted down the reminder: 'Be sure to get this quotation from George.'" Surely this shows that George influenced Turner by way of the former's incorporation into Loria's system. See Wilbur R. Jacobs, ed., *Frederick Jackson Turner's Legacy* (San Marino, Calif., 1965), 15. Systematic comparison of Loria's writings and the "Frontier" essay demonstrates that the basic ideas in the latter work, with one exception, are all integral parts of the Lorian system that had been summarized in the June 1892 issue of the *Political Science Quarterly.* My article on Loria showed that Turner's ideas prior to 1892 radically differed from those presented in the "Frontier" essay. As Loria's 1894 reply to Turner shows, he regarded the latter's work as merely documenting Loria's "economic theses." Compare the discussion of "Frederick Jackson Turner's Debt to Loria," in my *Turner and Beard,* 21–34, and Ray Billington, *America's Frontier Heritage* (New York, 1966), 10–11, and 239–240, n. 29.

[8] *Early Writings,* 187.

[9] The growth of Romanticism and the celebration of the "natural man" are commented upon in Merle Curti, *The Growth of American Thought* (3d ed.; New York, 1964), 230–233, 362–363.

Loria had emphasized that the experiences of seventeenth-century Britons transported to a "virgin region" like Pennsylvania or Virginia, where land was available to everyone without capital, demonstrated that a "rebirth of mankind" takes place under those conditions. But as free land disappeared in the erstwhile virgin region, society proceeded "to pass through the stages of economic evolution." The entire historical process, he argued, could be discovered by using the comparative method to observe its repetition in a land such as America. There we can "read in the book of the present, pages torn from social history." The East exhibited a society which had evolved into the advanced stage characterized by "the New York factories," while the West simultaneously exhibited a society in the primitive stage characterized by "the Dakota fields." [10]

Turner, echoing Loria, affirmed:

American development has exhibited not merely advance along a single line [of social evolution] but a return to primitive conditions on a continually advancing frontier line, and a new development for that area. American social development has been continually beginning over again on the frontier. This perennial rebirth, this fluidity of American life, this expansion westward with its *new opportunities* [italics added], its continuous touch with the simplicity of primitive society, furnish the forces dominating American character. [11]

"Perennial rebirth" could only occur, however, if "virgin land" were cost-free land freely available to anyone dissatisfied with conditions in settled regions. Given this premise, from the observation that "never again will such gifts of free land offer themselves" to Americans now that "the frontier has gone," Turner logically deduced that with its going "has closed the first period of American history." Clearly, the Loria-Turner thesis was economic determinist in character, despite the romantic

[10] See the translation of Loria's chapter "The Historical Revelation of the Colonies," in my *Turner and Beard,* 35–36, 39–40.

[11] *Early Writings,* 187.

metaphors and symbols used to state and support its propositions.[12]

If the thesis were valid, so long as free land existed, American
society and culture would differ radically from contemporary
European societies and cultures. Once men who lacked capital
could no longer move west to take up and possess unoccupied
land, America's uniqueness must disappear. When that stage was
reached, Loria claimed, America would have recapitulated all
the stages of European history, including the present "era of
capitalist production relations." [13] It is crucial to recognize that
Turner explicitly and unequivocally endorsed Loria's "recapitulationist concept" (my term). "America has the key to the
historical enigma which Europe has sought for centuries in
vain," Loria asserted, "and the land which has no history reveals
luminously the course of universal history." Commenting upon
this sentence, Turner just as flatly asserted: "He is right. The
United States lies like a huge page in the history of society." [14]

Suppose, however, that despite the continued existence of free
land, basic changes occurred in American society and culture,

---

[12] *Ibid.*, 228–229. Ray Billington has recently presented a "frontier
hypothesis" about the development of American society and culture
that avoids economic determinism and is likely, in my judgment, to
prove more fruitful than the Loria-Turner thesis, although I do not
agree with all its propositions. His book presents and defends what is
most accurately called the "Billington frontier hypothesis." My discussion in the present essay is restricted to the Loria-Turner thesis. See
Billington, *America's Frontier Heritage*, 3, 23–46, 219–235, and *passim*.
Subsequent research and greater maturity led Turner later to say that he
had merely presented "an hypothesis." If one reads them as originally
published, however, his early essays of 1892, 1893, and 1896 do not have
this tentative character. They make such sweeping and self-assured
claims that I cannot read them as merely presenting a tentative hypothesis for systematic exploration.

[13] Benson, *Turner and Beard*, 5–9.

[14] *Early Writings*, 198. I have quoted Turner's translation of Loria's
sentence; it differs slightly from the translation provided me. In 1895,
Turner reaffirmed his belief in Loria's recapitulationist thesis in an
unpublished lecture. See Jacobs, ed., *Turner's Legacy*, 155–156.

changes that made contemporary America increasingly resemble contemporary Europe. The Loria-Turner thesis then would be demonstrably invalid, for its postulates required that so long as free land existed, America must experience "perennial rebirth" and remain basically different from Europe.

If we brush aside the romantic metaphors and symbols beclouding the frontier thesis and perceive its rigid economic determinism, we can better understand why Turner found it necessary in 1896 to claim that the rise of Populism was due to the end of free land. Basic changes were occuring in American society and culture—Populism was only one expression of them, according to Turner—because America no longer possessed the *material* basis for continued social and cultural rebirth.

In the remoter West, the restless, rushing wave of settlement has broken with a shock against the arid plains. The free lands are gone, the continent is crossed, and all this push and energy is turning into channels of agitation. *Failures in one area can no longer be made good by taking up land on a new frontier* [italics added]; the conditions of a settled society are being reached with suddenness and with confusion. . . . Now the frontier opportunities are gone. Discontent is demanding an extension of governmental activity in its behalf. In these demands, it finds itself in touch with the depressed agricultural classes and the workingmen of the South and East.[15]

Turner treated Populism as confirming Loria's proposition that the presence or absence of free land was the basic determinant of American society and culture. Contrary to his assumptions, however, free land, as noted below, continued to exist for several decades after 1890. It follows, therefore, that the frontier thesis is demonstrably invalid, and that the Loria-Turner thesis should not have gained credence among historians, for it is based on antihistorical postulates and substitutes superficial assertions for systematic research on the complex interactions of economic and noneconomic phenomena.

[15] Frederick Jackson Turner, *The Frontier in American History* (New York, 1962 printing), 219–220.

To show that free land never actually operated in America as Loria and Turner claimed would require a lengthy paper.[16] For our purposes, rather than presenting such a paper or assembling the data to show that no essential differences existed in the availability of free land before 1890 and during at least three decades thereafter, it is only necessary to cite some relevant passages from Ray Billington's book, *Westward Expansion.*[17]

Turner opened his famous essay by quoting the observation from the *Census Bulletin* that there "can hardly be said to be a frontier line of settlement." He went on to describe this brief official statement as marking the "closing of a great historic movement."

Billington explicitly tried "to follow the pattern that Frederick Jackson Turner might have used had he ever compressed his voluminous researches on the American frontier within one volume." [18] But he knew that subsequent research had demolished Turner's claim that free land had ended around 1890. He conceded, therefore, that "the economic impact of the passing of the frontier was comparatively slight, largely because the westward movement continued after 1890 as before. Good land still waited newcomers in the West, for despite the pronouncement of the Census Bureau, only a thin film of population covered that vast territory." [19]

[16] In my judgment, apart from the fallacious assumption that "free land" was generally available in America, the most glaring error in the "free land thesis" is the assumption that raw land operated as a constant in world and American history. Even if we restrict attention to American experience, the assumption seems untenable. Not "free land" but "fee simple" has been the key characteristic of land in influencing the development of American economy and society. Unlike European societies, neither American law nor culture inhibited the treatment of land as a commodity to be bought and sold for profit.

[17] New York, 1949. Citations below are to the second edition, published in 1960.

[18] *United States Census, 1890: Distribution of Population According to Density, 1890, Extra Census Bulletin 2* (Washington, April 20, 1891), hereafter cited as *Census Bulletin;* Billington, *Westward Expansion,* vii.

[19] Billington, *Westward Expansion,* 751.

How could Billington make so sweeping a concession and not go on to the necessary conclusion that the frontier thesis was demonstrably invalid? He invoked the concept that truth in history is not only what actually happened but also what men *believed* had happened.

The great mass of the people in the 1880's still looked to a rosy future of continuous expansion. To them the announcement of the Superintendent of the Census in 1890 that the country's "unsettled area has been so broken into by isolated bodies of settlement that there can hardly be said to be a frontier line" remaining, came as a distinct shock. Since that time they have been adjusting themselves —economically, psychologically, and politically—to life in a nonexpanding land. . . . Continued expansion into the Canadian Northwest and the submarginal lands of the American Far West softened the impact of the frontier's closing on the nation's economy but had little influence on the popular mind. The *psychological effects* [italics added] of the dramatic Census Bureau announcement of 1890 far outweighed the material. Suddenly, unexpectedly, the nation realized that its age of expansion was over, its age of adjustment to closed boundaries at hand. To thousands of thinking citizens the implications seemed staggering. Overnight they must answer a dozen difficult questions. . . . [Examples are given.] Little wonder that the *American people* [italics added] . . . succumbed to a panicky fear that helped transform their rural economy, their foreign policy, and their theories of government.[20]

Given the "psychological" closed frontier hypothesized by Billington, both Turner's explanation of Populism and the general thesis from which it derived might be retained. The motivating force in American life after 1890 would no longer be the sudden disappearance of free land; it would be the sudden "panicky fear" created by "the dramatic Census Bureau announcement of 1890." To put it another way, while writing an epitaph for the myth Turner invented about the *material* closed frontier,

[20] *Ibid.*, 751–753. I have spliced together statements on different pages but have kept them in sequence.

Billington raised it from the dead to be reborn in the form of a myth of the *psychological* closed frontier.

Nothing indicates the power of the frontier myth in American historiography so well, in my judgment, as Billington's gallant attempt to prevent its demise. Though his long and distinguished scholarly career has been characterized from the start by excellent command of source materials and intensive research, in this instance he cited no evidence to support his claims about the remarkable impact of the *Census Bulletin* on American public opinion.[21] Like Turner in the 1890's, Billington acted as though it were unnecessary to test his claims before asserting them. Billington's hypothesis supports the proposition that once myths created by historians gain professional acceptance by satisfying some emotional deep-seated psychological need or ideological premise, they take on a life of their own.

What warrant do I have for so negative—and so confident—an assessment of the psychological closed-frontier hypothesis? For one thing, the *Census Bulletin* simply did not have the connotations attributed to it by Billington; it made no dramatic announcement of structural changes in American society. For another, it is extremely unlikely that more than a minuscule fraction of the American public ever saw the *Census Bulletin*, or even heard about it indirectly via Turner's essays, until late in 1896, when Populism had reached, or perhaps passed, its high point of popular appeal. It follows that American public opinion could not possibly have experienced the "distinct shock" hypothesized by Billington.

The *Census Bulletin* was not issued by the Superintendent of the Census in 1890; it was anonymously published in Washington and dated April 20, 1891. By that date, of course, Populism was well developed. Therefore, the *Bulletin* could not have

[21] Though critical of what I regard as Billington's misguided attempt to save the Loria-Turner thesis, I have high regard for, and have profited heavily from, his many and varied contributions to American historiography.

caused the diverse movements conveniently grouped under the generic term "Populism." Moreover, far from making any dramatic announcement, that much cited and little-read publication consisted of four pages whose contents were in all respects routine, except for the brief observation couched in matter-of-fact language that there "can hardly be said to be a frontier line of settlement." [22] Its anonymous author did not draw any implications about American development from that observation.

No evidence has ever been presented, and no reason exists to think, that the *Census Bulletin* was distributed to any individuals or institutions other than those on the mailing list for that class of census publication. As late as November 1892, when the Populist candidate received over one million votes, Turner could not be numbered among the select few who might have read it.

On November 4, 1892, Turner published an article in the student newspaper of the University of Wisconsin. He called it "Problems in American History" and later noted that it was "the foundation" of his 1893 essay.[23] He did not refer to the *Census Bulletin* or to the end of the frontier. On the contrary, as Rudolf Freund perceptively observed some time ago, internal evidence shows that he had not seen the *Bulletin* before he wrote the article; he explicitly referred to the "new frontier line" which would be shown on the population map for the 1890 census. Moreover, Turner sent a copy of the article to Woodrow Wilson, who followed its argument closely in a book review published in December 1893. Since the review assumed the continued existence of the frontier, we can reasonably infer that Turner made no marginal comment about the frontier's alleged demise on the copy he sent to Wilson.[24]

I do not have "hard" evidence to fix the date when Turner first saw the *Census Bulletin*. But a reasonable speculation is that

[22] *Census Bulletin,* 4.

[23] *Early Writings,* 185, n. 1.

[24] The argument that Turner had not seen the *Census Bulletin* before writing "Problems in American History" is developed in my *Turner and Beard,* 21–24.

it occurred after March 20, 1893. That date's issue of the National Geographic Society's magazine contained an article entitled "The Movements of Our Population." Written by Henry Gannett, the probable author of the *Census Bulletin,* the article reviewed the findings of the 1890 census on population density and specifically commented on the significance of the passing of the frontier line of settlement. Turner apparently did not belong to the Society and did not therefore automatically receive a copy of the issue. Professor Charles Van Hise, one of his colleagues, did, and he probably brought the article to the attention of his younger colleague.[25]

Internal evidence supports the conclusion that by 1893 neither the 1890 *Census Bulletin* nor Gannett's later article had significantly influenced Turner's thinking. Except for the "Frontier" essay's highly dramatic opening and closing paragraphs, it could have stood as written, whether or not free land had ended in 1890.[26] Moreover, in direct contradiction to the position Turner subsequently took in his 1896 essay, "The Problem of the West," in 1893 he explicitly attributed Populism to the *existence* of a frontier society, not to its *disappearance.* The inference seems reasonable that he had not become acquainted with the *Census Bulletin* in time to recast his thinking before he published

[25] Henry Gannett, "The Movements of our Population," *National Geographic Magazine,* (March 20, 1893), 26. Pages vi and lxiv of that volume of the *Geographic* provide the information that it was regularly sent to all members and that Van Hise was a member. His friendship with Turner is mentioned in a note printed under the title "Turner's Autobiographic Letter," in *Wisconsin Magazine of History,* XIX (Sept. 1935), 101. The speculation that Gannett probably was the author of *Census Bulletin* is based on a comparison of it and his *Geographic* article, as well as on information supplied to me by Fulmer Mood. Mr. Mood, of course, should not be held responsible for any of my claims, but I happily take this opportunity to acknowledge my indebtedness to him for information about Gannett and the *Census Bulletin* in particular, and Turner's activities in general.

[26] One sentence is an exception to this statement, but its brevity and tone actually reinforce the point (*Early Writings,* 185–186, 196, 228–229).

"The Significance of the Frontier in American History." By
1896, however, Populism had taken on such a character and
scope that Turner now apparently recognized that it could not
be dismissed as simply another instance of the "paper-money
agitation" recurrent in American history. As noted above, he
then explicitly attributed Populism to the end of free land rather
than, as he had in 1893, to the "lax financial integrity" characteristic of the "primitive society" re-created on "successive
frontiers."[27]

Once we become aware that Turner himself was unac-
quainted with the *Census Bulletin* until 1893, it surely becomes
unlikely that its publication in 1891 produced sudden "panicky
fear" among "the great mass of the American people." Contrary
to the hypothesis advanced by Mr. Billington, the claim then
becomes reasonable that, at least until August 1896, when Turner's essay "The Problem of the West" was in print,[28] the *Census
Bulletin* had no significant effect upon either "mass" or "thinking" public opinion.

To test my hypothesis, I made a systematic content analysis of
five periodicals widely read from 1890 through 1896, including
the monthly *Review of Reviews*, which regularly abstracted
articles from forty other magazines.[29] I went through the table of
contents of every issue and then read every article that either

[27] *Ibid.*, 222. Internal evidence suggests that Turner's 1896 interpretation of Populism derived from his close study of the July 1894 issue of
the *Review of Reviews*, pages 30–46. Compare his comments on Senator William V. Allen and Populism with Albert Shaw's sketch of Allen
and Professor J. Willis Gleed's letter on Western discontent, printed
under the title "Bundle of Western Letters," Turner Papers.

[28] The essay was published in the September issue of the *Atlantic
Monthly*. A letter from its editor, Walter Hines Page, to Turner,
August 22, 1896, indicates that the issue was in print before that date.
For information on the article's origins and reception that suggests the
extent to which it reflected Turner's "present-mindedness," see my
Turner and Beard, 88–89.

[29] The other magazines were *Arena, Atlantic Monthly, Forum,* and
North Atlantic Review.

from its author or title might be expected to refer to the *Census Bulletin* directly or indirectly. For the seven years I found a total of *three* references to the end of the frontier that can reasonably be attributed to knowledge of the *Census Bulletin*.[30] The first, in July 1895 by Woodrow Wilson, clearly derived from Turner's 1893 essay; the second, in September 1896, was by Turner; the third, in October 1896, was an editorial based on Turner's article of the month before.[31] Thus he was the direct source or inspiration of all references to the end of the frontier found in five magazines that can be treated as good indicators of what the "thinking public" read. Hence Billington's assertions about the "psychological" closed frontier caused by a dramatic announcement about the census of 1890 have as little factual basis as Turner's assertions about the "material" closed frontier.

To my knowledge, no one has systematically studied the impact of the closed-frontier myth upon American opinion *after* August 1896. To the extent that it took hold of educated or popular opinion, it seems reasonable to say that Turner, not the author of the *Census Bulletin*, bears the prime responsibility.[32]

During the early 1890's a wide variety of special-interest groups did try to influence American opinion by using some variant of the argument that the arable public domain was "exhausted." Probably the most widely publicized version of the

[30] It is possible, of course, that the method used did not uncover every reference. It would have taken exhaustive research to find other references, however, and they certainly could not, therefore, have had a strong impact on public opinion over the period of six years from 1891 to 1896 inclusive. (The periodicals for 1890 were searched, since references to the census findings might have been made in advance of formal publication.)

[31] "The Proper Perspective of American History," *Forum*, XIX (July 1895), 547; Frederick J. Turner, "The Problem of the West," *Atlantic Monthly*, LXXVIII (Sept. 1896), 296–297, and "The Political Menace of the Discontented," *ibid.*, LXXVIII (Oct. 1896), 450

[32] For a brief but informative survey of the reception given to the "frontier hypothesis," see Billington, *America's Frontier Heritage*, 13–15, and notes for those pages.

argument was advanced by C. Wood Davis, a self-taught disciple of Malthus. But he boasted no scholarly credentials, carried the stigma that was then attached to proponents of Malthusianism, and had the misfortune fatal to prophets of making a flat prediction subsequently discredited by events. Convinced that the public domain was virtually exhausted and that food shortages would therefore soon appear, in 1891 Davis confidently predicted two-dollar-per-bushel wheat and a price of "one hundred golden dollars" for an acre of good farm land "not later than 1895." Alas for prophecy: grain prices and land values continued to drop to disastrous lows. As a result, Davis was assailed by "an army of critics" who ridiculed his claims and ideas on grounds subsequently confirmed by the historical research summarized by Billington. For example, numerous invitations were extended to Davis to come and see for himself that there was "plenty of land out West," and Canadians particularly ridiculed the "hoary nonsense" of his "Malthusian ideas," pointing to the immense Canadian prairies awaiting cultivation.[33]

Davis and other spokesmen for special-interest groups that emphasized "land exhaustion" used clumsy arguments and had transparent objectives that induced distrust and opened them to effective ridicule from men opposed to the policies they advocated. Unlike them, when Turner published the 1896 version of his "Frontier" essay in the *Atlantic Monthly*, he could and did invest himself with the aura and authority of a professional historian whose explanation of the present "problems of the west" derived from disinterested scholarly study. His magisterial survey of American history, though actually based on superficial, impressionistic, and limited research,[34] and his definitive

[33] See my essay "The Historical Background of Turner's Frontier Essay," published in *Agricultural History*, XXV (April 1951), 50–82, and reprinted in my *Turner and Beard*, 41–91—particularly 58–63.

[34] That Turner's research had been extremely limited until then, and that he had not even yet done systematic research on the West, is evident from Turner's letter to Walter Hines Page, August 30, 1896 (Turner Collection, Harvard University). The letter reveals that, at

pronouncement that the end of free land caused the contemporary political agitation and demands for governmental action apparently were taken as the products of responsible and authoritative scholarship by men in positions to influence public opinion. Thus the editor of the *Atlantic Monthly* wrote to him from the East, "The newspapers here are at once taking up your article for discussion—very favorably." Turner quickly replied that he was sending the editor a copy of an editorial in the Chicago *Tribune* "giving a western version of my Atlantic paper." Numerous other contemporaries must have commented on it, for Turner later noted that he had collected copies of "reviews, letters, editorials on this article." [35]

Clearly, the frontier thesis has functioned as the most influen-

---

best, Turner can be said to have done something like systematic research only on the Old Northwest. His 1892, 1893, and 1896 essays, nevertheless, purported to explain all American history. And in 1893, the young man who had not yet published even one article in a scholarly journal directed to professional historians grandly confirmed Loria's intrinsically antihistorical "thesis" that American history recapitulated and thereby revealed "the course of universal history." Critically analyzed, the "Frontier" essay consists of a series of remarkably sweeping assertions supported by a hodgepodge of selective and sporadic quotations from scattered primary sources, travel accounts, and secondary works. Given the sketchiness of his research, the self-assured tone adopted by Turner in his early essays cannot be justified. It can be *explained*, perhaps, by recognizing that the basic ideas came from Loria, then receiving acclaim from leading scholars throughout the western world, and that Loria claimed to have derived his general theory especially from "researches in the economic development of the United States." In this connection, see my *Turner and Beard*, 10–17. My unflattering estimate of Turner's early research is supported by Stull Holt's assessment of the doctoral dissertation Turner had written, "The Character and Influence of the Indian Trade in Wisconsin," printed in 1891. See W. Stull Holt, review of *Early Writings*, in *Journal of Southern History*, V (Aug. 1939), 387–388.

[35] Benson, *Turner and Beard*, 88–89, n. 105. In that note, I regretted my inability to locate the folder Turner referred to as containing the "copies." Ray Billington subsequently found it in the Turner Papers at the Huntington Library after they were opened to researchers in 1960. See his *America's Frontier Heritage*, 241, n. 41.

tial set of ideas yet presented in American historiography. By significantly influencing American thinking it has influenced American history. If my claim that it is best viewed as a myth rather than a thesis has merit, the observation seems warranted that historians ought constantly to remind themselves that making histories is responsible work.

Senators, Sectionalism, and the "Western" Measures of the Republican Party

~⌐(⌐~

ALLAN G. BOGUE

"A study of votes in the federal House and Senate from the beginning of our national history reveals the fact," wrote Frederick Jackson Turner, "that party voting has more often broken down than maintained itself on fundamental issues; that when these votes are mapped or tabulated . . . a persistent sectional pattern emerges."[1] Thus Turner indicated the importance of sectionalism in Congress, and few academic specialists in American history since his time have failed to use the concept of sectionalism or its related term "the frontier" to some degree, at least in explaining our national politics. A study of the role of sectionalism in a Congress which passed four major "western" laws, authorizing homesteads, a system of land-grant colleges, a federal department of agriculture, and a transcontinental railroad, is particularly appropriate in a book dedicated to Paul Wallace Gates. The Thirty-seventh Congress, the first of the Civil War, was unusual in that most of the southern representatives were missing. But although the empty seats rendered this and the next Congress exceptional in the history of national legislative behavior, Earle Ross and others have argued that

[1] "The Significance of the Section in American History," *Wisconsin Magazine of History*, VIII (Mar. 1925), 270.

20

sectionalism, particularly as it affected East and West, continued to influence the behavior of legislators during the Civil War.[2]

In discussing the politics of the Civil War, historians have usually emphasized other factors than sectionalism. We are all familiar with the interpretation that presents a beleaguered Lincoln struggling to maintain his leadership against the determined onslaughts of the radical faction that dominated his party and the Congress. Recently, David Donald has argued that historians have overstressed the differences between radical and moderate Republicans and has suggested that the importance of party bonds should be emphasized instead.[3] T. Harry Williams, however, continues to believe that the distinction is an important one.[4] Professor Donald has also suggested that the congressional constituency played a major part in influencing the votes of members of the House of Representatives when they were considering reconstruction legislation.[5] In other words, historians have stressed the importance of factionalism, party, and constituency in determining the behavior of legislators during the Civil War. This paper examines the influence of sectionalism on the voting of senators during the second session of the Thirty-seventh Congress, the relation of sectionalism to other voting determinants, and its particular role in the debates and votes on the great western measures.

Certainly the sectionalism of East against West colored senatorial oratory at times, as when James W. Grimes of Iowa argued: "We [of the Northwest] are the only portion of all the

[2] Earle D. Ross, "Northern Sectionalism in the Civil War Era," *Iowa Journal of History and Politics*, XXX (Oct. 1932), 455–512; Jacque Voegeli, "The Northwest and the Race Issue, 1861–1862," *Mississippi Valley Historical Review*, L (Sept. 1963), 235–251.

[3] "Devils Facing Zionwards," in Grady McWhiney, *Grant, Lee, Lincoln and the Radicals: Essays on Civil War Leadership* (Evanston, Ill., 1964), 72–91.

[4] "Lincoln and the Radicals: An Essay in Civil War History and Historiography," in McWhiney, *Grant, Lee, Lincoln and the Radicals*, 92–117.

[5] *The Politics of Reconstruction: 1863–1867* (Baton Rouge, La., 1965).

loyal States that feel the effect of this war oppressively. . . . Whilst men who own the railroads in the Northwest are making fortunes out of this war by the transportation of our produce, we are receiving nothing in fact from it." [6] Later in the session, John Ten Eyck of New Jersey spoke for the East when he queried, "Now what inducement is there for a senator from an Atlantic State to vote an appropriation of large sums of money, even in the shape of a loan to construct a variety of [rail] roads for the advantage of the Western States?" [7] But oratorical flourishes can be deceiving; in the end it was the votes of the senators that counted. And what do the votes tell us of the sectionalism of East and West, or of North and South?

I

This research began as an analysis of the substantive votes that were concerned with slavery and confiscation measures (both broadly defined), the tariff and the internal-revenue tax bills, legal tender, the four western laws, northern civil liberties, and the general conduct of the war, as well as a few important procedural votes that seemed related to such measures. Most of the votes fell into one of three broad categories. Eighty-seven dealt with the confiscation of rebel property or the status of slavery; fifty-one resulted from the debate on the internal revenue act of 1862; and the debates on other major economic legislation of national interest produced thirty-five votes, including those on the western measures. During the course of the research the scope of the study broadened to include 368 roll calls of this session; only those were excluded that related to appointments. [8] These votes are the major source for the scholar seeking evi-

[6] *Cong. Globe*, 37 Cong., 2 sess., 114, 1862. References to the *Globe* hereafter are to this Congress and session.

[7] *Ibid.*, 2805.

[8] Included were votes in the Senate proper, in committee of the whole, and in executive session. Tallies used were those in the *Senate Journal*, supplemented occasionally by those in the *Congressional Globe*.

dence of sectional groupings or other patterns in the voting of the thirty-one Republicans, eleven Democrats, five border Unionists, and one northern Unionist who sat in the Senate during most of the second session of the Thirty-seventh Congress.

In the following pages, a few simple devices are used to describe legislative behavior in quantitative terms.[9] An index number of cohesion shows, on a scale running from 1 to 100, the extent to which a political party or group was united in a particular roll call. Similarly, an index number of agreement or likeness measures the degree to which the members of two parties or groups voted alike on a proposal, and the obverse of such a number can be called an index of disagreement. Thus, if Democrats and Republicans agreed on a particular vote to the extent of 40 per cent of the maximum degree of agreement that would have resulted if all Republicans and all Democrats voted alike, the index of likeness would be 40, and the index of disagreement 60.

If we record the number of times that each legislator voted in the same way as every other legislator, we can find groups of like-minded individuals by fitting the pair-agreement scores into a matrix, with the highest agreement scores in the upper left corner. Legislative groupings derived by this process are often called cluster blocs.

The Guttman scale deals with association among the senators in a different way. In effect this type of scaling procedure isolates a roll call in which a small group of legislators voted against the

[9] These devices are described in more detail in Lee F. Anderson *et al.*, *Legislative Roll-Call Analysis* (Evanston, Ill., 1966) and in Samuel C. Patterson, *Notes on Legislative Behavior Research* (University of Iowa, The Laboratory for Political Research, Iowa City, *Report 1*, 1965). An index of cohesion may be calculated by subtracting the percentage of yeas in a party's vote (if the smaller) from the percentage of nays (if the larger), or vice versa. When 83 per cent of the Republicans voted yea and 17 per cent voted nay on a bill, the index number of cohesion is 66, i.e., 83 minus 17. If 75 per cent of the Democrats and 50 per cent of the Republicans voted yea in a roll call, the index of likeness or agreement is 75, i.e., 100 minus the difference between 75 and 50.

rest of the chamber and then adds to this roll call others, in which the members of the small group continued to agree in their voting but were joined, roll call by roll call, by other legislators, who continued to vote with the original minority on the votes added subsequently. Since they could find few who shared their opinion in the anchor roll call, the members of the original small group are assumed to have held an extreme or radical position in that particular division. The added roll calls indicated increasingly moderate views on the same subject of legislation, or a related one, until the last roll call showed perhaps only a small group in opposition to the minority in the anchor roll call—a remaining group composed of members who were utterly opposed to any legislative concession on the matter under debate. Roll calls arranged in this way therefore form a scale which ranks legislators according to their attitude on legislative proposals dealing with a particular issue or related subjects.

In examining the roll calls of the Senate, I assumed that a disagreement index of 40 or more represented substantial disagreement between eastern and western Republicans. Western Republican senators included all those from Ohio or states to its west, and eastern Republicans comprised those from the states east of Ohio. The states represented by Democrats were few and widely spread apart; Democratic votes were therefore not used in the search for roll calls that revealed the sectionalism of East and West. According to these definitions, substantial sectional disagreement between eastern and western Republican senators appeared in 46 of the 368 roll calls of the second session. In comparison there were 58 roll calls during this session in which disagreement between radical and moderate Republicans reached a comparable level, and 159 votes in which the members of the Republican and Democratic parties recorded a disagreement index of 40 or more.[10]

[10] I discuss the division of Republicans into moderates and radicals in my article "Bloc and Party in the United States Senate, 1861–1863," *Civil War History*, XIII (Sept. 1967), 221–241.

The sectionalism of East and Wext appeared most frequently in voting on economic measures of national significance.[11] In the original selection of 87 roll calls relating to slavery and confiscation and of 86 that were linked to major economic legislation, only 7 per cent of the slavery and confiscation roll calls showed substantial sectional disagreement among the Republicans, in comparison to 22 per cent of the roll calls on economic policy. Consideration of all 368 roll calls does not change the generalization. Among the votes on economic legislation we find a division between eastern and western Republicans in 8 roll calls during the debates on the internal revenue bill, in 8 during the discussion of the land-grant college bill, in 3 concerning United States notes, in 3 during the Pacific railroad debates, and in 2 bearing on the tariff. Sectionalism appeared also in 3 roll calls relating to the judiciary, 3 concerning appropriations for the armed forces, and 5 on miscellaneous matters.

Eastern Republicans were more united in their approach to certain categories of legislation than were their colleagues from the West. The average voting agreement among all western senators was 61 per cent in the roll calls on the great economic program and 59 per cent in the votes on the internal revenue bill.[12] In contrast, the mean agreements among eastern Republicans were 76 and 65 per cent. Six New England senators—Daniel Clark (New Hampshire), James Collamer (Vermont), William Fessenden (Maine), Solomon Foot (Vermont), LaFayette Foster (Connecticut), and Lot Morrill (Maine)—were in particularly strong agreement in the voting on economic legislation. Minimal mean agreement among these men was 73 per cent, and Clark and Fessenden voted together in 97 per cent of the roll calls on the great economic program. There was no western

[11] Of course much of the legislation passed or proposed concerning the South was "economic" in both its short-run and long-run implications, but for the sake of convenience I will distinguish between laws dealing with slavery on confiscation and national economic legislation.

[12] Absences were disregarded in calculating these percentages.

group comparable either in numbers or in the strength of agreement among its members.

Among the 368 roll calls of the second session there were 91 in which the cohesion indices of eastern and western Republicans differed by as much as 40 points. In 59 of these roll calls it was the easterners who showed the greater solidarity. Of the 105 ballots in this session that were apparently related to economic measures of national interest, 35, or 33 per cent, showed a marked difference in the cohesion of eastern and western Republicans.[13] Of 120 roll calls linked to slavery, confiscation, and the general conduct of the war, only 18, or 15 per cent, revealed a similar pattern. Clearly, eastern Republicans were more united in voting on economic issues than were western Republicans, and this particular kind of voting pattern was more apparent in divisions on economic issues than on slavery and confiscation measures.

Was there any relation between the sectionalism of East and West and the disagreement between radicals and moderates in the Republican party? The application of cluster-bloc analysis and Guttman scaling to the original 87 roll calls on slavery and confiscation issues suggests a division of the 31 Republican senators into two groups, or blocs, in the second session—a radical bloc of 17 and a moderate group of 14:

Republican radicals	*Republican moderates*
Chandler (Mich.)	Anthony (R.I.)
Clark (N.H.)	Browning (Ill.)
Foot (Vt.)	Collamer (Vt.)
Grimes (Iowa)	Cowan (Pa.)
Hale (N.H.)	Dixon (Conn.) [14]
Harlan (Iowa)	Doolittle (Wis.)

[13] These ballots include the original selection, with the addition mainly of various procedural roll calls, taken while economic measures were under discussion.

[14] There are grounds for arguing that Dixon of Connecticut voted a radical pattern during this session, but I have for various reasons included him among the moderates.

Howard (Mich.)
King (N.Y.)
J. H. Lane (Kan.)
Morrill (Me.)
Pomeroy (Kan.)
Sumner (Mass.)
Trumbull (Ill.)
Wade (Ohio)
Wilkinson (Minn.)
Wilmot (Pa.)
Henry Wilson (Mass.)

Fessenden (Me.)
Foster (Conn.)
Harris (N.Y.)
Howe (Wis.)
H. S. Lane (Ind.)
Sherman (Ohio)
Simmons (R.I.)
Ten Eyck (N.J.)

If the Republican radicals were primarily either eastern or western in constituency, roll calls showing a high sectional disagreement between eastern and western men should also have a high index of disagreement between radicals and moderates. Ten roll calls are included in both the list of forty-six in which eastern and western Republicans differed substantially and the group of fifty-eight that showed substantial disagreement between radicals and moderates. As Table 1 shows, slightly more than half of

Table 1. Sections, radicals and moderates *

Republican senators	Radicals		Moderates	
Eastern (17)	8	(47%)	9	(53%)
Western (14)	9	(64%)	5	(36%)

* The contingency coefficient gamma is −.34

the eastern Republicans were moderates and that a somewhat larger proportion of western Republicans were radicals.

Antislavery sentiment in the West is sometimes linked to eastern origins, and Table 2 presents place of birth as a possible variable. For what it is worth, the Republican senator most apt to be extreme in his views toward the South and its institutions was a western senator of eastern origins; seven of the nine

Table 2. Birth, radicals and moderates *

Republican senators	Radicals		Moderates	
Of eastern birth (26)	15	(58%)	11	(42%)
Of western birth (5)	2	(40%)	3	(60%)

* Gamma is .34

senators who fitted this description were radicals (78 per cent). The senator most apt to be a Republican moderate, on the other hand, was a western senator of western birth; three out of five, or 60 per cent, in this category were moderates. But given the relatively small numbers of men involved, the percentage differences that support a sectional interpretation of the disagreement between radicals and moderates are rather small.

The fact that there were proportionately more radicals in the West has sometimes made it difficult for historians to decide whether the sectionalism of East and West or the division between radical and moderate Republicans most influenced a particular vote. A few years ago Jacque Voegeli argued persuasively that anti-Negro sentiment was particularly strong in the northwestern states during the early years of the Civil War and that the Republican senators of that region led the movement to include colonization provisions in the emancipation act for the District of Columbia and in the confiscation law which the members of the second session of the Thirty-seventh Congress approved.[15] The northwestern senators received aid from the senators of the Middle Atlantic states in these efforts, according to the author, and encountered opposition mainly from their colleagues from New England. Certainly the rhetoric of the debates in this session does support a sectional interpretation to some degree, but voting analysis weakens the argument.

Professor Voegeli emphasized the results of a "key" roll call in the Senate on April 3, 1862, when thirteen Republican senators from the Northwest and the middle states supported the coloni-

[15] "Northwest and the Race Issue," 235–251.

zation amendment and only three opposed it.[16] But he excluded
Kansas from his northwestern region, and that state's Senator
Samuel Pomeroy voted against the amendment; nor did he note
that Morton Wilkinson of Minnesota announced his opposition
to the amendment during the roll call, explaining that he was
paired with his Democratic colleague, Senator Henry Rice.[17]
Western Republicans were therefore divided, 9 to 5, in favor of
the amendment. On the other hand, the four senators from the
Middle Atlantic states who voted in this division all favored the
colonization amendment. See Table 3. If the votes of a section's

Table 3. Republican senators and the
"key" confiscation vote *

Region	Yea		Nay	
Western states	9	(70%)	4	(30%)
Middle Atlantic states	4	(100%)	–	–
New England states	5	(45.5%)	6	(54.4%)

* Excluding Wilkinson

senators reflect the public opinion of that section, the people
of the Middle Atlantic states apparently feared the freedman
and favored colonization more than did the residents of the
West.

When we test the sectional interpretation of the colonization
amendment by comparing the western vote (plus Wilkinson's
preference) with that of New England, we find the index number of disagreement to be 19.[18] But if we divide the Republican
senatorial vote on the amendment into moderate and radical
categories, as is done in Table 4, we find 36 to be the index num-

[16] *Ibid.*, 244, n. 21.

[17] *Cong. Globe*, 1522–1524; *Sen. Journal*, 37 Cong., 2 sess., 368, 1862.

[18] See Joel Silbey, "The Civil War Synthesis in American Political
History," *Civil War History*, X (June 1964), 130–140, and *The Shrine
of Party: Congressional Voting Behavior, 1841–1852* (Pittsburgh, 1967),
for a warning about the danger involved in overemphasizing sectionalism in these years.

Table 4. Radicals, moderates, and the
"key" vote on colonization *

Senators	Yea		Nay	
Moderates	10	(83%)	2	(17%)
Radicals	8	(47%)	9	(53%)

* Including Wilkinson

ber of disagreement. Neither number reveals substantial disagreement according to our definition. The division of the senators into moderates and radicals, however, goes further toward explaining the voting than did the sectional analysis, and this explanation is strengthened when we discover that two earlier votes on the colonization amendment produced considerable disagreement between radicals and moderates, reflected in index numbers of 65 and 42. Arranging the preferences of the New England senators and of the western Republicans (including Wilkinson) in the "key" roll call in a four-fold table we find a contingency coefficient of .37; the coefficient of a similar table in which the Republican senators are divided into radicals and moderates is .7. Disagreement over the colonization amendment apparently is more properly considered a part of the conflict between radical and moderate Republicans than an example of differences between eastern and western constituencies.

II

Let us follow the great western measures through Congress.[19] On April 17, 1862, James Simmons opened the debate on House

[19] Limitations of space prevent discussion of the treatment of individual bills, but there are a number which are of particular interest. See Paul W. Gates, "Western Opposition to the Agricultural College Act," *Indiana Magazine of History,* XXXVII (June 1941), 103–136; John Y. Simon, "The Politics of the Morrill Act," *Agricultural History,* XXXVII (April 1963), 103–111; and Wallace D. Farnham, "The Pacific Railroad Act of 1862," *Nebraska History,* XLIII (Sept. 1962), 141–167. See also Earle D. Ross, *Democracy's College: The Land Grant Movement in the Formative Stage* (Ames, Iowa, 1942) and "The Civil War Agricultural New Deal," *Social Forces,* XV (Oct. 1936), 97–104.

Bill 269, to establish a department of agriculture, and during May and June the senators also debated and approved the homestead bill, the land-grant-college bill, and the Pacific-railroad bill.

As sent to the Senate floor by the Patents Committee, H.R. 269, to establish the agricultural division of the Patent Office as a separate department under the direction of a commissioner, provided merely for a change in administrative organization and little else. It was, said Simmons, "simply a compliment to the great leading interest of industry," a "little boon" for the agriculturists who constituted "the pillar of the national strength." [20] But a northern Unionist and former Democrat, Joseph Wright of Indiana, moved to substitute his own bill, which outlined a considerably more elaborate organization than the plan for a continuing force of clerks that the original bill prescribed. He proposed to pay the commissioner $5,000 per year rather than $3,000 and to organize four bureaus within the department, and he particularly stressed the importance of the unit charged with gathering and disseminating production and marketing statistics. A generation ahead of his time, Wright could find only eleven other senators who were willing to support his amendment.

Next the senators considered an amendment from Foster of Connecticut which was also a substitute for the House bill. In some respects Foster's bill represented middle ground between Wright's bill and the original one. Foster too emphasized the collecting of agricultural statistics and proposed to make the decennial census a responsibility of the new agency. But Foster visualized a bureau within the Department of the Interior rather than an independent department. The Foster amendment failed in the committee of the whole by a vote of 18 to 18. When its sponsor reintroduced it in the Senate, the vote was exactly the same, although two men changed their positions. The final vote on the bill was 25 yeas and 13 nays.

In support of his amendment Wright was joined by Henry S.

[20] *Cong. Globe,* 1690.

Lane, by John Hale, and by nine Democrats or border Unionists. Seven of the same men supported Foster's amendment also. Lane, Benjamin Stark of Oregon, and Wright carried their opposition to the House bill to the point of voting against it, and several Democrats and border Unionists failed to vote in the final balloting. The Wright amendment attracted strong support from the Democrats; the index number of party disagreement on the vote is 66, in contrast to the minor disagreement between the parties on the other three roll calls. The disagreement between the senators from the slave and from the free states also reached 40 per cent in the voting on the Wright amendment and in the final vote.

Table 5 shows the four ballots on the Department of Agriculture bill arranged as a scalogram. James McDougall, Waitman Willey, and Robert Wilson voted "yea" in all of the roll calls and clearly stand at the opposite extreme from Edgar Cowan and Preston King, who voted "nay" on each occasion. The views of the senators between these two groups represented intermediate positions on the agricultural-department legislation. But the roll calls on this bill result in a poor scale, with more deviations from pattern, or errors, than the social scientist is willing to tolerate. Although the Wright and the Foster amendments scale well together, the vote on the bill does not scale well with the amendments. Eleven of the thirteen opponents of the bill in the final balloting had supported one or the other of the major amendments. The scale does show that the senators who seemingly most favored a strong, independent department of agriculture were Democrats and Border Unionists; those most firmly opposed were Republicans. Were the Democrats and Border Unionists trying to embarrass the Republicans by presenting themselves as greater friends of agriculture than the party of Lincoln?

Of the thirteen senators who voted against the Department of Agriculture bill, eleven were Republicans. From the West came Orville Browning, James Doolittle, James Harlan, and Henry

Table 5. Department of Agriculture bill voting patterns *

Senator	Party	State	Type	1 Y	2 Y	3 Y	4 Y	1 N	2 N	3 N	4 N
Henderson	D	Mo.	0	+	+	−	+			x	
McDougall	D	Calif.	0	+	+	+	+				
Willey	BU	Va.	0	+	+	+	+				
Wilson, R.	BU	Mo.	0	+	+	+	+				
Lane, H. S.	R	Ind.	0	+	+	+	−				x
Stark	D	Ore.	0	+	+	+	−				x
Wright	NU	Ind.	0	+	+	+	−				x
Davis	BU	Ky.	1		+	+	+	+			
Howe	R	Wis.	1		+	+	+	+			
Morrill	R	Me.	1		+	−	+	+		x	
Browning	R	Ill.	1		+	+	−	+			x
Clark	R	N.H.	1		+	+	−	+			x
Collamer	R	Vt.	1		+	+	−	+			x
Doolittle	R	Wis.	1		+	+	−	+			x
Fessenden	R	Me.	1		+	+	−	+			x
Foster	R	Conn.	1		+	+	−	+			x
Harlan	R	Iowa	1		+	+	−	O			x
Lane, J. H.	R	Kan.	1		+	+	−	O			x
Wade	R	Ohio	2			+	+	+	O		
Foot	R	Vt.	2			+	+	+	+		
Hale	R	N.H.	3	x			+	−	+	+	
Saulsbury	D	Del.	3	x			+	−	+	+	
Chandler	R	Mich.	3				+	+	+	+	
Anthony	R	R.I.	3				+	+	+	+	
Dixon	R	Conn.	3				+	+	+	+	
Powell	D	Ky.	3				+	+	+	+	
Simmons	R	R.I.	3				+	+	+	+	
Sumner	R	Mass.	3				+	+	+	+	
Wilkinson	R	Minn.	3				+	+	+	+	
Harris	R	N.Y.	3				+	O	+	+	
Kennedy	BU	Md.	3				+	O	+	+	
Pomeroy	R	Kan.	3				+	O	+	+	
Ten Eyck	R	N.J.	3				+	O	+	+	
Trumbull	R	Ill.	3				+	O	+	+	
Cowan	R	Pa.	4					+	+	+	+
King	R	N.Y.						+	+	+	+

* + = pattern vote; −, x = deviant vote (error); O = absent
Voting key: 1 Wright amendment
 2 Foster amendment
 3 Foster amendment
 4 Vote on the bill
Coefficient of reproducibility = .896. Senators who voted in fewer than 50 per cent of the scaled roll calls are not included in this or the following scales.

and James Lane, who were joined by Wright of Indiana and Stark of Oregon; from the East came Clark, Collamer, Fessenden, Foster, Cowan, and King. Long a champion of the farmer, Wright may have considered the bill a meaningless gesture and perhaps he carried his colleague Henry S. Lane with him. The New Englanders—Fessenden the most vocal among them—opposed the bill, they explained, because they believed that an independent department would cost the Treasury dearly in the future. They did support the Foster amendment, which retained the agricultural division within the Department of the Interior. Voting against any change whatsoever, Cowan and King are enigmas, although at the time King retained some of his old Democratic prejudices about enlarging the scope of government, and Cowan was concerned about the letter of the Constitution and state rights.

Party and sectional alignments only partially explain the voting patterns in the Department of Agriculture debate. Although Republican cohesion was high on the Wright amendment, it was low in the divisions on the Foster amendment and the bill itself. The sectionalism of East and West was not apparent, but there was a substantial difference between the voting of northern and southern senators in the balloting on the Wright amendment and on the bill. Certainly the Republican party could not take sole credit for the law establishing the Department of Agriculture; had five of the border-state and Democratic senators changed their votes, the bill would have been lost.

Of the western measures, the homestead bill was to have the briefest debate. Brought to the floor by Benjamin Wade on April 30, 1862, this bill provided 160-acre homesteads for adult males or heads of families and also cash bounty payments to veterans as well. The amendments from the Committee on Public Lands eliminated the bounty features and added a commutation clause, allowing the homesteader to buy 160 acres for $1.25 on acre after six months' residence and certain improvements. The senators accepted these alterations without any call for the yeas and nays. John Carlile of Virginia then moved to substitute a bill which provided that members of the armed forces could request homesteads on the public domain in lieu of a federal bounty of one hundred dollars in cash. This proposal substituted the familiar system of military bounties for the homesteads to which the members of the Republican party were committed.

With Carlile's amendment before the Senate, there ensued a debate on the homestead bill, such as it was. Carlile, suffering as he explained "with a very severe pain," spoke briefly in support of his amendment and in effect summarized his position in two sentences when he described the homestead bill as "a general giving away and disposition of the public domain; squandering, in other words, the means of the Government, which at this particular time of all others should, . . . be husbanded. It is perfectly consistent with the policy that would destroy, strike out of existence at one blow, two billions of dollars of personal property subject to taxation." [21]

In making the only major oration of the homestead debate, Pomeroy argued that the public lands had already repaid their costs and that the products of the settlers from their homesteads would expand the market for imported goods and generate more revenue in added customs duties than might be lost to the Treasury by a free-land policy. He rang the changes on the theme of the small independent husbandman: "Real [national] strength consists in the hearts, the bones, the sinews of an independent, loyal, free yeomanry, who have the comforts of a home, the fear of a God, the love of mankind, and the inspiration of a good cause." As a veteran of the Kansas troubles of 1956, Pomeroy demanded the bill to "secure a country to freedom, forever" and to develop the great West. In retrospect Pomeroy was an incongruous spokesman for the honest western yeoman, but to the party faithful—their memory of "bleeding Kansas" still fresh—

[21] *Ibid.*, 1916.

his paean to " 'free homesteads for free men' " seemed particularly fitting.[22]

Carlile's amendment was lost by a vote of 28 to 11; its supporters were recruited solely from the ranks of border Unionists and Democrats, with the addition of Wright. In the vote for the bill Wright joined the Republicans, as did Anthony Kennedy, McDougall, John Henderson, and Robert Wilson of Missouri, leaving James Bayard, Carlile, Garret Davis, Lazarus Powell, Willard Saulsbury, Stark, and Willey to cast their votes against free land. Two Democrats from the Pacific coast, Milton Latham and James Nesmith, later announced in the Senate that they would have voted for the homestead bill if they had been present. As the vote was actually recorded, party disagreement and North-South disagreement amounted to 83 and 79 per cent on the Willey amendment, and 67 and 65 per cent on the bill itself. The cohesion index of the Republicans was 100 in both roll calls. Of the slave state senators only Kennedy of Maryland and the Missourians voted for the bill. Both the major speakers on the bill, Pomeroy and Carlile, linked it to the slavery problem—it had become a symbol of the sectional conflict. We have, therefore, in the votes a relic of voting patterns from the years immediately prior to the war, when most southerners were ranged against the homestead principle. Some of the votes against earlier homestead measures came from the northeastern states. Of this pattern there was no remaining trace in the voting on the homestead bill in the Senate of the Thirty-seventh Congress.[23]

Six substantive votes on the land-grant-college bill fit together to make a good scale as shown in Table 6. The arrangement of the thirty-nine senators shows a sharp division between East and West. The six roll calls in the scale include the final balloting on the bill, four limiting amendments, and a successful motion to

[22] *Ibid.*, 1938–1939.

[23] Fred A. Shannon, "The Homestead Act and the Labor Surplus," *American Historical Review*, XLI (July 1936), 642–644.

Table 6. Land-grant-college bill voting patterns *

Senator	Party	State	Type	10 N	7 Y	6 N	8 Y	5 Y	9 Y	10 Y	7 N	6 Y	8 N	5 N	9 N
Doolittle	R	Wis.	0	+	+	+	+	+	+						
Grimes	R	Iowa	0	+	+	+	+	+	O						
Howe	R	Wis.	0	+	+	+	+	+	+						
Lane, H. S.	R	Ind.	0	O	+	+	+	+	O						
Lane, J. H.	R	Kan.	0	+	+	+	+	+	+						
Wilkinson	R	Minn.	0	+	+	+	+	+	+						
Wright	NU	Ind.	0	+	+	+	+	+	+						
Pomeroy	R	Kan.	1		+	+	+	+	+	+					
Harlan	R	Iowa	1		+	+	O	+	+	+					
Latham	D	Calif.	1		+	−	O	+	+	+		x			
Nesmith	D	Ore.	1		+	+	O	+	+	+					
Stark	D	Ore.	1		+	+	−	+	+	+			x		
Trumbull	R	Ill.	2			+	+	+	−	+	+				x
Browning	R	Ill.	2			+	+	+	+	+	+				
Chandler	R	Mich.	2			+	+	−	+	+	+		x		
McDougall	D	Calif.	3				+	+	+	+	+	O			
Howard	R	Mich.	3				+	+	+	+	+	+			
Dixon	R	Conn.	4					+	−	+	+	+	+		x
Davis	BU	Ky.	4					+	+	+	+	+	+		
Sumner	R	Mass.	5						+	+	+	+	+	+	
Ten Eyck	R	N.J.	5						+	+	+	+	+	+	
Wade	R	Ohio	5						+	+	+	+	+	+	
Wilson, H.	R	Mass.	5						+	+	+	+	+		
Kennedy	BU	Md.	6		x			x		+	+	+	−	+	+
Rice	D	Minn.	6	x				x		+	−	+	+	−	+
Anthony	R	R.I.	6							+	+	+	+	+	+
Carlile	BU	Va.	6							+	+	+	+	+	+
Clark	R	N.H.	6							+	+	+	+	+	+
Collamer	R	Vt.	6							+	+	+	+	+	+
Cowan	R	Pa.	6							+	+	+	+	+	+
Fessenden	R	Me.	6							+	+	+	+	+	+
Foot	R	Vt.	6							+	+	+	+	+	+
Foster	R	Conn.	6							+	+	+	+	+	+
Hale	R	N.H.	6							+	+	+	+	+	O
Harris	R	N.Y.	6							+	+	+	+	+	+
King	R	N.Y.	6							+	+	+	+	+	+
Morrill	R	Me.	6							+	+	+	+	+	+
Simmons	R	R.I.	6							+	+	+	+	O	+
Willey	BU	Va.	6							+	+	+	+	+	+

* + = pattern vote; −, x = deviant vote (error); O = absent

Voting key: 10 Final vote on the agricultural-college bill
 7 Wilkinson amendment to postpone operation of the bill until January 1, 1864
 6 Dixon motion to reconsider 5
 8 Grimes amendment to limit the total acreage to be located in any territory
 5 Pomeroy amendment, requiring that assignments be recorded on the face of the scrip and forbidding assignment of scrip in units of more than 640 acres
 9 Howe amendment requiring yearly reports from governors on the disposition of scrip

Coefficient of reproducibility = .966

reconsider Pomeroy's amendment. Westerners sponsored all of the restrictive amendments: Timothy Howe moved that reports on the sale of scrip be submitted yearly by the governors; Pomeroy required that assignments of scrip be noted on the face of the paper and forbade assignment in units larger than 640 acres; Grimes suggested that the amount of scrip located in any one territory be limited; and Wilkinson proposed to set the effective date of the bill at January 1, 1864. Seven westerners form a scale type, or voting bloc, whose members voted against the bill and supported all of the restrictive amendments. Six other westerners voted for the bill but supported all of the restrictive amendments. At the other end of the scale, a solid bloc of fourteen senators, mostly from the Northeast, opposed the intransigent westerners in every division. The land-grant-college bill shattered party lines and provided the most striking illustration of the sectionalism of East against West in the voting of the Republican senators during this session. The index of disagreement ranges from 42 to 92 on the six substantive roll calls, and two efforts to call up the bill provoked substantial sectional disagreement as well.

To the student of economic development in the United States, the debate on the land-grant-college bill is an extremely interesting one. It is sometimes thought to have reflected a revolt of the West against eastern land speculators, and the western senators did indeed say a great deal about the baneful effects of land speculation. Morton Wilkinson was typical of the westerners when he predicted that "the scrip authorized by this bill will pass into the hands of speculators, a remorseless class of vampires, who care little for the common prosperity of the country; and still less for the cause of education." Where, he queried, would the young veterans find their homesteads at war's end if this bill was passed? The western Vesuvius, James H. Lane, predicted the "ruin" of his state if the bill was passed, and the gentle Wright of Indiana demanded that the measure be postponed until the next session, because "there is a country and section called the West, and they will have twenty-one more votes in the House six months hence than they have now." [24]

The speculator argument inadequately explains the delays and the barrage of amendments that marked the debate. At that very time most of the westerners were planning to vote generous land subsidies to western railroads, and such grants would be no less subject to speculation than would the agricultural lands. And it is doubtful that anyone was seriously impressed by Jim Lane's contention that the act would deprive the railroads of lands needed for their grants. Apparently the westerners saw little usefulness in the agricultural-college grants, while easterners were attempting to seize a final opportunity to derive immediate benefit from the public domain before the homestead law revolutionized the public-land system. The *New York Tribune* described the measure as a "small requital" for the homestead law, and eastern insistence may also have reflected the fact that the need for agricultural improvement was more generally acknowledged and the sentiment in favor of industrial colleges stronger there than in the new-land states. [25]

The debate on the Pacific-railroad bill was both long and sharp; we can do no more here than discuss its major features and the basic voting patterns. McDougall, chairing the special Senate railroad committee, was for so long frustrated in his efforts to bring the bill to the floor that he accused other senators of trying to kill it. But the culprits argued that other bills were more pressing and that the bill should be brought to the floor when there was ample time for discussion. They objected to McDougall's attempts to bring it up in the morning hour and to have it made a special order for debate. These men were Republicans who were pledged to support of the Pacific railroad by the terms of the national party platform of 1860. They were not obliged, however, to support any particular form of the project,

[24] Wilkinson's comments appear in *Cong. Globe*, 2395; see the remarks of Lane and Wright in *ibid.*, 2275 and 2441.

[25] June 21, 1862.

and the debates of June 1862 suggest that it was the details of the House bill that roused opposition in the Senate.

The House bill provided for a single railroad, connecting the eastern boundary of California with a point on the one-hundred-and-second meridian of longitude, then the western boundary of the state of Kansas. Connections were planned with the Central Pacific in the West, and with branches at the eastern end running from the mouth of the Kansas River, from Leavenworth, from St. Joseph, from Omaha, and from Sioux City when that community should have a connection with the East. The government was to aid both the main line and the branches with land grants and loans of government bonds to the roads. The Leavenworth, Pawnee, and Western Railroad Company was to build the major line through Kansas, although it had not constructed any track in the years since the Kansas legislature had bestowed a charter upon it. McDougall emphasized that the House bill was very much a compromise. Those "railroad interests" that controlled the roads stretching westward from Philadelphia and Baltimore through Cincinnati and the Ohio Valley and thence to Missouri, those other interests with lines along the Great Lakes to Chicago and with termini in New York, as well as hopeful local groups in Minnesota, Wisconsin, Iowa, Kansas, and Missouri, all had their representatives in the lobbies and their champions on the floors of Congress. Members of the House committee decided, as a result, to share the benefits of the transcontinental system among most of the interests rather than to make any group the sole custodian of transcontinental traffic. The product of compromise is not necessarily logic, but it was acceptable to a majority of the representatives.

In the upper house the senators evidently suspected that the House of Representatives had favored the connecting lines through Kansas by fixing the terminus of the main line on the one-hundred-and-second meridian, and some believed as well that the aid to the branch lines was excessive. Compromise prevailed in the committee, and most of its members agreed on an amendment that fixed the hundredth meridian as the terminus of the transcontinental trunk, considerably shortening the length of the feeders and thereby diminishing the land and bond aid. Since some senators believed that Congress had no authority to charter a corporation that would operate within the boundaries of a state, it was also agreed that the line must run through Nebraska Territory. The northern margin of the Platte and the southern edge of the Republican River valleys served as the outer limits within which the grant could be located.

The long-suffering McDougall brought these major amendments and numerous minor ones before the Senate from his committee representing, as they did, a major victory for those who wished the main line to have its most direct eastern connection through Iowa. McDougall found his colleagues generous both in irony and in the number of amendments that they proposed. This "Colossus of roads," said the senators, had "as many heads as a hydra" and was "many pronged" and "almost a centipede." Howe compared the system to a sprinkler, designed to distribute the benefits of transcontinental traffic to almost every portion of the midwestern and northern states, and Pomeroy considered the proposal to begin the eastern trunk in the middle of the plains country rather like starting to build the Washington Monument at the top.[26]

Ostensibly the Senate debate focused on the problem of rationalizing the system. But the reader finds it difficult to detect where the search for economy and efficiency ended and the quest for local advantage began. As McDougall explained, the Senate committee was twice enlarged in an effort to have all views represented among its members. But of the group neither Clark nor Harlan, a late appointee, felt obliged to support all of the committee recommendations.

Senators, mostly from the northeastern states, shaped the railroad debate by their efforts to eliminate or reduce government

[26] *Cong. Globe,* 2752, 2784, 2785, 2809, 2810.

aid to all but one of the eastern branches. After some initial success they failed but continued the task of making the arrangements between the federal government and the railroads as "businesslike" as possible by providing that a portion of the bond aid to the roads be withheld until construction was finished, by clarifying the mortgage arrangement that was to secure the government loans, by amending the recapture clause, by fighting a committee amendment that would have eliminated the government's right to alter, amend, or repeal the charter, and by providing that the bylaws of the corporation be worked out in a meeting of the shareholders rather than by the directors.

McDougall and Latham of California, Harlan of Iowa, Lane and Pomeroy of Kansas, and Wilson and Henderson of Missouri were the major champions of the bill and of the committee's amendments, but never such stalwart defenders that they ignored opportunities to improve the interests of their own states. Most prominent among the rationalizers was Clark of New Hampshire, who led the effort to eliminate the western branches and who summarized his objections to the bill forthrightly:

I do not mean to be bound by the bill as reported by the committee, because it is not just; it is a scheme to get the Government money to build five railroads to the starting point, because you cannot agree where to start. I am willing to build a Pacific railroad; I am willing to start near Fort Kearny, or at some proper point, and build it through the deserts and over the mountains, so as to give a national road; but I am not willing to give the Government's money to aid the people in particular States to build branches to it.[27]

From the fourteen roll calls on the Pacific-railroad bill there emerges a voting scale that was shaped by the conflict over rationalization. See Table 7. Actually only seven of the fourteen ballots of the railroad debate scale well together, but these include all but one of the substantive roll calls generated by the efforts of the rationalizers. The rest were either procedural in

[27] *Ibid.*, 2752.

Table 7. Pacific-railroad bill voting patterns *

Senator	Party	State	Type	6 Y	2 Y	11 Y	5 Y	3 Y	13 Y	14 Y	6 N	2 N	11 N	5 N	3 N	13 N	14 N
Davis	BU	Ky.	o	+	−	+	+	O	+	+	x						
Howe	R	Wis.	o	+	+	+	+	+	+	−							x
Clark	R	N.H.	o	+	+	+	+	+	+	+							
Collamer	R	Vt.	o	+	+	+	+	+	+	+							
Fessenden	R	Me.	o	+	+	+	+	+	O	O							
Foot	R	Vt.	o	+	+	+	+	+	+	+							
Foster	R	Conn.	o	+	+	+	+	+	+	+							
Hale	R	N.H.	o	+	+	−	O	O	+	+			x				
King	R	N.Y.	o	+	+	+	+	−	+	−			x				x
Lane, H. S.	R	Ind.	o	+	+	+	+	+	−	+				x			
Morrill	R	Me.	o	+	+	+	+	+	+	+							
Ten Eyck	R	N.J.	o	+	+	+	+	+	+	O							
Trumbull	R	Ill.	o	+	−	+	+	O	−	+	x		x				
Wilson, H.	R	Mass.	o	+	+	−	+	+	+	+			x				
Wright	NU	Ind.	o	+	+	+	+	−	+	−			x				x
Chandler	R	Mich.	1		+	+	+	+	−	+	+					x	
Grimes	R	Ia.	1		+	−	+	+	+	+	x						
Sumner	R	Mass.	1		+	−	+	+	+	+	x						
Anthony	R	R.I.	2			+	+	+	+	+	O	O					
Howard	R	Mich.	2		+	+	+	+	+	+	+						
Sherman	R	O.	2		+	O	−	+	+	O	+		x				
Harris	R	N.Y.	3				+	O	+	+	O	+	+				
Wilmot	R	Pa.	3				+	+	+	+	+	+	+				
Harlan	R	Ia.	3				x	+	−	+	+	−	+			x	
Dixon	R	Conn.	4					+	−	+	+	+	+	+		x	
Lane, J. H.	R	Kan.	4					+	−	+	+	+	+	+		x	
Pomeroy	R	Kan.	4					+	−	+	+	+	+	+		x	
Wade	R	O.	4					+	−	+	+	O	+	O		x	
Doolittle	R	Wis.	4				x	+	−	+	+	−	+	+		x	
McDougall	D	Cal.	4					+	+	+	+	+	+	+			
Wilkinson	R	Minn.	4					+	+	−	+	O	+	O			x
Browning	R	Ill.	5						+	+	+	+	+	+			
Powell	D	Ky.	5	x					+	O	−	+	O	+	+		
Cowan	R	Pa.	5						+	+	O	+	O	O			
Henderson	D	Mo.	5						+	+	+	+	+	+	+		
Latham	D	Cal.	5						+	+	+	+	+	+			
Nesmith	D	Or.	5						+	+	+	+	+	+			
Rice	D	Minn.	5						+	+	+	+	+	+	O		
Stark	D	Or.	5						+	+	+	+	+	+			
Willey	BU	Va.	5						+	+	+	+	O	+			
Kennedy	BU	Md.	5			x			+	+	O	+	+	−	+		

* + = pattern vote; −, x = deviant vote (error); O = absent

Voting key:
6 Clark amendment to strike out the Sioux City branch
2 Harlan amendment to fix the eastern terminus at Fort Kearney
11 Trumbull amendment to build a single line to the Missouri
5 Clark amendment to strike out the Leavenworth branch
3 To concur in committee amendment to route the St. Joseph connection through Atchison
13 Henderson amendment to strike the Atchison requirement under certain conditions
14 Vote on the bill
Coefficient of reproducibility = .901

nature or subregional in interest—for instance, Doolittle's amendment that would have given land-grant aid to the Northern Pacific project.

Of the eastern senators, Collamer, Morrill, and Ten Eyck, in addition to Clark, were particularly critical of the branches.

Many of the votes in support of their cause came from northeastern Republicans, but a number of midwestern senators opposed aid to the branches—most notably Lyman Trumbull. At one end of the railroad scale stand fifteen senators, of whom ten represented northeastern or Middle Atlantic states. These men supported five rationalizing amendments and then, their cause lost, voted to free the St. Joseph connection from the restriction of an earlier amendment which had forced it to swing its route southwest to Atchison over the Platte Valley road. This relocation saved the government the cost of some twenty-five miles of aid. Most members of this bloc supported the amended bill. At the other end of the scale we find a group of ten: Browning, Cowan, and eight Democrats and border Unionists, who voted consistently in defense of the branches and of the bill.

Clark and his allies won their greatest victory when they eliminated aid to a branch connection between Leavenworth and Lawrence. Of this line Clark remarked, "You might as well . . . give a man money to build a line to his cow pasture. . . . It is a grand scheme to get thirty miles of road built in that vicinity for Kansas." [28] They failed when they supported Harlan's effort to fix the eastern terminus at Fort Kearney, and more crucially when Clark tried to strike out the Sioux City branch. At this point Trumbull introduced an amendment providing for a single road to strike the Missouri River at a point to be designated by the President between 40 and 43 degrees north latitude. Eighteen senators supported the amendment, and twenty-five opposed it. Yet the vote is instructive. Sixteen Republicans supported Trumbull's amendment, and only eleven opposed it. Democratic and Unionist votes prevented such a drastic revision of the bill that the House might well have refused to accept it. And Harlan's effort to fix the eastern terminus of the road at Fort Kearney drew the votes of seventeen Republicans and failed because of the votes of Democrats and border-state men. In the end three

[28] *Ibid.*, 2805.

western Republicans, King of New York, and Wright voted against the railroad bill. The railroad scale does reflect the sectionalism of East and West to a considerable degree, but the alignment was less sharp than in the voting on the land-grant-college bill. Nor does the railroad scale include all of the substantive roll calls in the railroad debates.

The four western measures of the second session of the Thirty-seventh Congress did not provoke identical responses from the senators. Only the balloting on the homestead law revealed high Republican-cohesion and low party-likeness scores. The sectionalism of North against South welded together a mixed opposition of Democrats and Border Unionists. Although party majorities were ranged in opposition to each other in seventeen of the twenty-six major divisions on the four bills, it was only in the voting on the homestead law that a majority of Democrats failed to join the Republicans in favor of the amended bill. Indeed the Democrats and border Unionists could apparently have defeated the Department of Agriculture bill, and they insured the defeat of an amendment to the Pacific-railroad bill that might well have made it unacceptable to the House of Representatives. Party likeness was reasonably high and sectionalism little apparent within the Republican party in the voting on the Department of Agriculture act. Most unlike the voting on the homestead bill were the roll calls on the land-grant-college act in which the western senators ranged themselves against their eastern colleagues. The motivations of its opponents were apparently mixed in nature. Although some votes on the railroad bill revealed disagreement between eastern and western legislators, the differences were less sharp than those in the voting on the land-grant-college legislation. Party likeness was low in a number of the railroad roll calls, because Republicans were splintered on subregional lines and a bloc of Democrats and border Unionists held firm in defense of the committee's version of the bill.

Despite the impressive majorities with which the senators approved the western laws, we oversimplify if we emphasize the ease with which they passed through Congress in the absence of the southern cadres.[29] Nor did these laws dovetail neatly into the expression of a grand "free-soil" philosophy. In retrospect provision for the democracy's colleges may seem to have supplemented the homestead law; the idea, however, eluded many Republican senators at the time. Rather, these measures won approval after considerable interplay of party and sectional influence, subregional or constituency pressures, and personal conviction. Although significant, sectionalism was only one of a number of important voting determinants that were apparent during this session of the senate. And if these determinants seem to provide a warp and a woof of explanation for congressional behavior, we must remember that they were in part the expression of various political values and assumptions: for instance, the belief of American politicians that campaign pledges must be met if possible, that rewarded legions are loyal legions, and that the search for party recruits must never end. It was no accident surely that the two western laws which evoked the least Republican opposition in the final roll calls were the Homestead Act and the Pacific-railroad law, both of which had been promised in the Republican platform of 1860. The doctrinaire Hale scoffed that the department-of-agriculture bill was not desired by the men who leaned "upon their plow-handles; but . . . the men who want them to take their hands off the plow-handle and vote for them at the ballot-box." [30] The more practical politicians of the new party prevailed; the Thirty-seventh Congress left its mark on American agriculture and the development of the West as have few other congresses.

[29] Gladys L. Baker, Wayne D. Rasmussen *et al.*, *Century of Service: The First 100 Years of the United States Department of Agriculture* (Washington, 1963), 11.

[30] *Cong. Globe,* 2014.

The Homestead Clause
in Railroad Land Grants

DAVID M. ELLIS

Our incongruous land policy has received its sharpest analysis in the writings of Paul Wallace Gates.[1] In abundant and convincing detail he has presented the competing and sometimes contradictory measures by which the government disposed of the public domain. Alexander Hamilton's original objective of raising revenue from land sales was soon undermined by gifts of lands to veterans, states, and private agencies. After two generations of agitation Congress passed the Homestead Act of 1862, which offered free a quarter section (160 acres) of land to citizens and would-be citizens who settled upon and improved it.

The homestead principle was thus "grafted upon a land system to which it was ill-fitted and incongruous."[2] In particular the policy of granting over one hundred million acres of land to railroads after 1861 undermined the principle of free home-

[1] His early article "The Homestead Law in an Incongruous Land System," *American Historical Review*, XLI (July 1936), 652–681, established Professor Gates as a major historian of the West. His interpretation became part of the canon of frontier historiography. But in 1963 he felt obliged to expand upon his earlier views, because his analysis had unwittingly discounted the importance of the Homestead Act. See his "The Homestead Act: Free Land Policy in Operation, 1862–1935," in *Land Use Policy and Problems in the United States*, ed. Howard Ottoson (Lincoln, Neb., 1963), 33.

[2] *Ibid.*, 30.

steads. This conflict was plainly visible to contemporaries both in the press and in Congress. To be sure, men like Stephen A. Douglas and Daniel Webster denied that there was any incompatibility and endorsed both a homestead law and grants to railroads. The famous platform of the Republican party in 1860 called for both. On the other hand, a small group, mainly southerners, opposed both policies as contributing to the expansion of small freeholdings in the west and thus to "free-soil" commonwealths. Some free-soil groups, however, were skeptical of efforts to adopt the two policies in tandem.[3]

The sponsors of railroad land grants tried to meet homestead objections in two ways. First of all, the railroads were not to receive solid tracts of land but alternate sections. Secondly, the various acts provided that the alternate sections retained by the government could be occupied under the Pre-emption Act or, after 1862, under the Homestead Act. Under the latter law the settler could secure only eighty acres within the limits of the railroad land grant, a limitation which sent many settlers farther afield. Sponsors of land grants pointed out that the government could charge $2.50 an acre for its own sections, because proximity to the railroad track made the lands more valuable. The settlers promptly countered that doubling the price of land was in effect a 100-per cent tax on settlers.

The same Congress that authorized the homestead law made huge land grants to the Union Pacific and Central Pacific railroads. Congress, in the eight years following the passing of the Homestead Act of 1862, granted five times as much land to railroads as it had previously donated, following its first grant to the Illinois Central Railroad in 1850.

The charter of the Union Pacific Railroad, however, included a new and unusual provision, which reflected homestead sentient. This clause stated that three years after the completion of the road, all lands not sold "shall be subject to settlement and

[3] *New York Tribune*, March 20, 1852.

preëmption, like other lands at a price not exceeding one dollar and twenty-five cents, to be paid to said company." [4] Clearly Congress wanted the railroad officials to get rid of the land quickly. Most of the major grants—Union Pacific, Central Pacific, Denver Pacific, and Northern Pacific—were to have a variant of this homestead clause in their charters. This clause provided for what is usually called the contingent right of preemption.

Railroad land grants often conflicted with the interests of homesteaders. First of all, forty out of some eighty-odd subsidized roads did not construct their lines within the time limit (usually ten years), including extensions. Consequently the railroad and, usually, the government could not sell the land along the route of the uncompleted road. Furthermore, some railroads failed to patent lands along their constructed lines, either because the government failed to conduct surveys on time or because the railroads hoped to avoid local taxes.

Most aggravating of all was the uncertain status of land within the "indemnity" or "lieu" limits, that is, lands in the zone beyond the primary zone bordering the track. Sometimes the railroad would find that settlers had already taken much land in the primary zone which would otherwise have gone to the railroad. As compensation, the Illinois Central Railroad, for example, had the right to take in lieu thereof land in the indemnity zone between six and fifteen miles farther from the line. The Secretary of the Interior withdrew the indemnity lands of many railroads for over thirty years. This action seemed necessary in order to protect the railroads from losing their rights to indemnity, or lieu lands. But settlers and speculators rushed to locate land within the indemnity limits and resisted the efforts of the railroads to select the companies' sections. In fact, the Department of the Interior recognized the rights of squatters to land within the indemnity limits, even though it was clear that the

[4] U.S., *Statutes at Large*, XII, 489.

railroads would not get the total acreage which they expected. Sometimes a railroad tried to oust genuine homesteaders who had made their selections before the railroad had located its route.

In 1887, Congress passed a law whereby the Secretary of the Interior was directed to adjust land grants. The process of adjustment involved endless difficulties: the disputed claims of bona fide settlers; the attempts of speculators to use the Preemption Act and other devices to claim part of the land; delays in the Land Office, especially in making surveys.[5]

Other railroad abuses, such as high rates, discrimination, tax evasion, and political skulduggery led to strong antirailroad sentiment throughout the nation. This feeling was intensified in the public-land states by the irritation caused by the land-grant policy. In the years after the Civil War the movement to regulate railroads paralleled the crusade to safeguard the public domain from further grants. Farmers in the Old Northwest, laboring men concerned with corporate monopolies, and land reformers brought tremendous pressure on Congress to cease "Squandering the National Patrimony," as an editorial in *The Nation* phrased it.[6] The ground swell of public feeling swept up from the minor parties and influenced both the Democratic and, finally, the Republican parties.[7] The Liberal Republicans in 1870 and 1872 opposed further land grants to railroads. The Democratic party in 1868 and again in 1872 called for a disposition of the public domain under the pre-emption or homestead laws that would guarantee the land to actual settlers. Of course, the westerners usually failed to distinguish between "actual settlers" and speculators, but that is another story. Even President Grant felt

[5] Leslie E. Decker, "The Railroads and the Land Office: Administrative Policy and the Land Grant Patent Controversy, 1846–1896," *Mississippi Valley Historical Review*, XLVI (March 1960), 679–699.

[6] April 16, 1865, I, 305.

[7] See Kirk Porter, *National Party Platforms* (New York, 1924), 67, 73, 83; and Fred E. Haynes, *Third Party Movements since the Civil War* (Iowa City, 1916), 47.

impelled in December 1870 to oppose further grants to railroads. If Congress were to make any more grants, he urged it to protect the "rights of the settlers." [8]

The homestead, or settler's, clause was an interesting effort to effect a compromise between the homestead principle and aid to railroads. The provision in the Union Pacific grant cited above was too weak. It went into operation only after the completion of the road and applied only to lands not sold. Therefore on July 24, 1868, the House of Representatives passed a much more stringent resolution:

All lands hereafter granted in aid of railways be sold by State or corporation to actual settlers, in quantities no greater than one quarter section, to any one person, and at a price to be fixed by the company which shall build the road, not exceeding $2.50 per acre.[9]

This homestead, or settler's, clause did not win the support of all land reformers. Perhaps the most determined foe of the current land policy was Congressman William Holman of Indiana. In 1869, Holman pushed a resolution calling for the end of all land grants, but Congressman George W. Julian, who was to spearhead land reform forces for two decades or more, moved a substitute:

Resolved that no more public lands should be granted to aid in the construction of railroads except on condition of actual settlement in quantities not greater than one hundred and sixty acres to one purchaser and for a fixed maximum price.[10]

Holman declined to accept the amendment, and the resolution was tabled. A year later Holman's resolution passed the House, declaring that the United States should hold the public domain "for the exclusive purpose of securing homesteads to actual settlers under the homestead and preëmption laws." [11]

[8] *Sen. Journal*, 41 Cong., 3 sess., 23, 1871.
[9] *Cong. Globe*, 40 Cong., 2 sess., 4429, July 24, 1868.
[10] *Ibid.*, 40 Cong., 3 sess., 424, Jan. 18, 1869.
[11] *Ibid.*, 41 Cong., 2 sess., 2095, March 21, 1870.

Meanwhile, on April 10, 1869, Congress provided for the homestead clause and time extensions for three railroads which had failed to build their lines within the original limit.[12] One of these companies was the Oregon Central, later taken over by the Oregon and California Railroad Company. A second was the Selma, Rome, and Dalton Railroad Company, a venture in Alabama which later forfeited its grant. The third was the Little Rock and Fort Smith, in which James Blaine, the Speaker of the House, had more than a Platonic interest. Julian, the chairman of the House Committee on Public Lands, in 1870 helped repeal its homestead clause. He explained that the clause had injured the credit of the enterprise and that Congress could not impose a further limit on the grant in which the company had a "vested right."[13] Congress in 1869 also placed a similar clause in the grant to the Coos Bay Wagon Road Company, which was chartered to build a military road from Coos Bay to Roseburg, in Oregon.[14]

The struggle over the Northern Pacific land grant presents the most interesting and significant testing of the relative strength of the homestead forces and railroad promoters. This huge grant of over forty million acres became the battlefield for all kinds of interests: homesteaders, speculators ranging from small farmers to huge lumber concerns, businessmen in terminal points, and government officials such as those in the Forest Service and the General Land Office. Land reformers, politicians, bankers, and lobbyists were to fight over every line of the legislation authorizing the railroad's construction.

Congress in 1864 awarded an imperial domain, larger than New England, to the Northern Pacific, the brain child of Josiah Perham and his New England partners.[15] The original grant was

---

[12] U.S., *Statutes at Large*, XVI, 47; *Cong. Globe*, 41 Cong., 1 sess., 588, April 7, 1869.

[13] *Cong. Globe*, 41 Cong., 2 sess., 1698, March 4, 1870.

[14] U.S., *Statutes at Large*, XV, 340.

[15] An old but adequate account is available in Eugene V. Smalley, *History of the Northern Pacific Railroad* (New York, 1883).

of odd sections within a limit of twenty miles on each side of the track in the states, and double that width in the territories. If the railroad found that certain of its sections had already been taken up by homesteads, government reserves, or other purchases, it could select "lieu" sections within an indemnity strip ten miles wide on each side of this primary limit. Moreover, the railroad could not select "mineral lands," but in lieu of them the company could choose agricultural land within fifty miles of the right of way.

By 1866 the Northern Pacific project had passed into the hands of the "Vermont clique," so named because most of its members lived in the Green Mountain State. Governor J. Gregory Smith, who was also president of the Vermont Central, became president, and Thomas Canfield, of Burlington, later became general agent. This coterie planned to build the railroad by getting a federal subsidy in addition to the land grant. They proposed that Congress guarantee the interest on Northern Pacific bonds for twenty years. Imagine their dismay when they found Congress overawed by the mounting antirailroad sentiment, and their anger when they discovered the covert opposition of the Union Pacific and Central Pacific group.[16] The officers and the lobbyists saw the scheming of Oakes Ames of the Union Pacific behind every maneuver in Congress. When it became obvious that Congress would boggle over a money subsidy, Smith hastened to settle for an extension of the time limit during which the Northern Pacific could complete its road.[17]

[16] Smith described his foes as "almost without exception professional swindlers and expert at that" (J. G. Smith to A. E. Smith, March 11, 1866, J. Gregory Smith Papers, Vermont Historical Society, Montpelier).

[17] Few legislative acts have left behind more "inside" accounts than the struggle over the Northern Pacific grant, 1864–1870. See Theodore L. Nydahl, ed., *The Diary of Ignatius Donnelly, 1859–1884* (Minneapolis, 1941). Donnelly's reports to Jay Cooke, as well as Henry Cooke's reports, are available in the Jay Cooke Papers, Historical Society of Pennsylvania, Philadelphia. The Thomas Canfield Papers are in the Vermont Historical Society, in Montpelier, Vermont. But the most interesting Canfield letters are those discovered in the Northern Pacific

Governor Smith and his partners pushed hard for a federal subsidy. On January 10, 1867, they signed an agreement pledging themselves to secure aid from Congress, and each subscriber agreed to pay assessments to provide for a lobby in Washington.[18] Smith brought in several men of influence from outside of New England in order to exert more pressure on Congress. Among the new associates were William Ogden, president of the Chicago and Northwestern; J. Edgar Thomson, president of the Pennsylvania Railroad; William Fargo, vice-president of the New York Central; and Robert Berdell, president of the Erie Railroad. These men had a wealth of railroad experience and powerful connections, but they were not willing to invest substantial funds in a transcontinental railroad. They appointed a first-rate chief engineer, Edwin Johnson, to make the surveys along the route.

Further efforts to secure funds from Congress ran into a stone wall. At the last minute, in June 1868, Thomas Canfield secured another two-year extension of the time for commencing work on the road, while the date of completion was extended to July 4, 1877.

Meanwhile, Jay Cooke in the summer of 1868 visited Duluth in order to inspect lands bought for him by his agents.[19] The scenery and the resources of the area aroused so much enthusiasm in him that he bought a controlling interest in the Lake Superior and Mississippi Railroad, a local project that hired Ignatius Donnelly to lobby for a federal land grant. When the

---

offices in St. Paul and printed in *Northern Pacific Land Grants, Hearings before the Joint Congressional Committee on Investigation of the Northern Pacific Railroad Land Grants* (18 parts; Washington, 1925–1928), Pt. VIII, 4272–4273. Hereafter this document will be cited as *Joint Hearings.*

[18] An account book in the J. Gregory Smith Papers of the Vermont Historical Society lists the various assessments levied by the association.

[19] Ellis Paxson Oberholtzer, *Jay Cooke, Financier of the Civil War* (Philadelphia, 1907), II, 106–108.

bankers of London, Paris, and Frankfort spurned the bonds for this railroad, Cooke peddled them to the American public in much the same way he had disposed of United States bonds during the Civil War. He rehired Samuel Wilkeson, whose lyrical pen had helped sell war bonds. Wilkeson agreed also to win over Horace Greeley and to set President Ulysses S. Grant straight about the Northern Pacific. Grant, however, was taking a firm position against further grants of money, bonds, or credit to railroads.[20]

In 1869 the Northern Pacific won permission to mortgage its railroad and telegraph lines, but the act giving permission failed to mention the land grants. Therefore the company had to go back to Congress the next year for permission to mortgage the land grant. Of course the railroad's supporters were hoping for an outright subsidy, but the mood of Congress discouraged their efforts.

The Northern Pacific clique cultivated Jay Cooke diligently. If they could not get money from Congress, perhaps the wily banker from Philadelphia could supply them with the money. They sent him the report of Johnson's inspection of the route. Johnson's careful report persuaded Cooke that the project was feasible; so by May 1869 he was ready to throw his talents behind it, provided his own experts approved the route and the prospects. Cooke sent out his brother Henry and Thomas Canfield to look over the western half of the route. Their reports glowed with enthusiasm. At the same time Cooke sent William Moorhead, a senior partner, to approach the Rothschilds and other bankers to suggest participation in the venture. Moorhead, himself skeptical of the enterprise, had no luck in convincing the bankers of Europe. Money was exceptionally tight, because the relations between Germany and France were reaching a breaking point. Besides, a surfeit of American railroad bonds, some of them of dubious value, discouraged further investment.

[20] Wilkeson to T. Canfield, Feb. 1, 1869, in *Joint Hearings*, VIII, 4276.

Canfield meanwhile was marshaling Northern Pacific forces in Washington. Speaker Blaine in October predicted a subsidy, but he warned Henry Cooke not to sign a contract with the Northern Pacific before Congress had acted. If congressmen suspected that Cooke would undertake the venture on his own, they would not make further concessions to the company.[21]

Governor Smith reported to Canfield in December 1869, "Cooke talks as if he is prepared to put in the necessary funds to carry it through at all hazards."[22] But Cooke wanted the right to mortgage the land grant and to build a branch line across the Cascades where he pleased, and also additional indemnity lands. He complained that thousands of settlers had taken up land along the proposed route since 1864, thus depriving the company of much land.

The Northern Pacific lobbyists had to make deals with other groups seeking favors from Congress.[23] Ben Holladay wanted a land grant for his railroad from Portland to Astoria. Another group wanted to build a railroad from Salt Lake City on the Central Pacific to Oregon. To the south, General John Frémont wanted assistance for the Atlantic and Pacific. Smaller roads were also pressing for all kinds of favors, from time extensions to new grants. The competing projects surreptitiously knifed rival ventures, because they realized that Congress was not likely to endorse several of the land grants. Henry Cooke reported to his brother, "The Central Pacific is treacherous, malignantly hostile & inspires all this opposition."[24] No doubt Collis P. Huntington

[21] Henry Cooke to Jay Cooke, Oct. 16, 27, Nov. 13, 1869. Jay Cooke Papers. Hereafter, letters referred to are in the Cooke Papers, unless otherwise indicated.

[22] *Joint Hearings*, VIII, 4277.

[23] Joseph Gaston, writing to Henry Villard, Nov. 10, 1899, recalls the events of 1870 (Villard Papers, Houghton Library, Harvard University), H. Cooke to J. Cooke, Jan. 27, 1870.

[24] H. Cooke to J. Cooke, March 1, 1870. I am grateful to the Historical Society of Pennsylvania for permission to quote from the Jay Cooke Papers.

of the Central Pacific was seeking to kill off a rival road to the Pacific.

Each railroad had to face the hurdle of the settler's clause. Henry Cooke spoke to Congressman Julian and reported that Julian would push the homestead clause, but somewhat half-heartedly.[25] Ignatius Donnelly reported that Julian suggested a compromise: a $2.50 price for agricultural land but a $10.00 top for timberland.[26] Henry Cooke discounted the homestead amendment of Senator James Howell, which applied to new lands granted to the railroad. He wrote:

Virtually the $2.50 clause is inoperative, for there are a dozen ways by which we can get around it; sell our lands to a Land Company or to purchasers of our own choosing & etc. As to the actual settlers, we would of course be willing, for the development of the Country and the business of the Road, to let all who would actually settle along the line have their land at $2.50; that is, our native preemptors.

Howell's resolution neither affects our present grant nor any amendment thereto, except probably the grant from Portland to Puget's Sound.[27]

But Jay Cooke replied at once that Henry Cooke must fight Howell's resolution. He was afraid that there was "no way by which the lands can be properly taken from the railway company, & taken hold of by a land company." [28] Moreover the Northern Pacific had to oppose the settler's clause if it wanted to retain the support of the other groups seeking land grants.[29] When Senator Allen Thurman of Ohio proposed that the $2.50 clause apply to the sale of all Northern Pacific land, he was firmly repulsed. Senator Henry Wilson of Massachusetts (later

[25] H. Cooke to J. Cooke, Jan. 29, 1870.
[26] I. Donnelly to J. Cooke, Feb. 3, 1870.
[27] H. Cooke to J. Cooke, March 2, 1870.
[28] March 3, 1870.
[29] Donnelly noted, "Other parties seeking land grants and supporting us demand that we shall not yield that point" (Donnelly to J. Cooke, April 9, 1870).

named in the Crédit Mobilier investigation) skillfully presented an amendment to Thurman's proposal, limiting the clause to new lands granted in 1870. The railroad forces voted in Wilson's amendment but then voted down the amended amendment.[30]

The struggle in the House was closer. Henry Cooke was not above distributing "discreetly" twenty cases of Catawba wine and a thousand cigars. Representative William Wheeler, chairman of the Committee on Pacific Railroads and floor manager of the bill, tried to bulldoze the bill through the House on May 5 without allowing any amendments, but the enemies were able by delaying motions to force it back to the floor within a week. There Representative John Hawley proposed the homestead clause, which led to retorts by railroad spokesmen. Representative Austin Blair of Michigan claimed that the homestead clause would attract a swarm of land "bummers" who would spy out the best tracts and grab them. Wheeler insisted that settlers had plenty of cheap land available in addition to the government sections available at $2.50 an acre. For a time it seemed that the advocates would force acceptance of the clause, but Governor Smith made an appearance to rally his lobbyists.[31] He insisted on no compromise, and the House voted down Hawley's amendment, 78 to 106.[32]

The Northern Pacific forces made no real objection to the inclusion of the contingent right of pre-emption clause similar to that imposed on the Union Pacific in 1862. Since the language of this section was fought over phrase by phrase in the twentieth century, it would be wise to quote it in full.

That all lands hereby granted to said company which shall not be sold or disposed of or remain subject to the mortgage by this act

[30] The more important references to this debate in the Senate are found in *Cong. Globe*, 41 Cong., 2 sess., 2483, April 7, 1870, and 2581, April 11, 1870.

[31] S. Wilkeson to T. Canfield, May 13, 1870, *Joint Hearings*, VIII, 4282; H. Cooke to J. Cooke, May 18, 1870.

[32] *Cong. Globe*, 41 Cong., 2 sess., 3797–3798, May 25, 1870.

authorized, at the expiration of five years after the completion of the entire road, shall be subject to settlement and pre-emption like other lands, at a price to be paid to said company not exceeding two dollars and fifty cents per acre; and if the mortgage hereby authorized shall at any time be enforced by foreclosure or other legal proceeding, or the mortgaged lands hereby granted may be executed, be sold by the trustees to whom such mortgage may be executed, either at its maturity or for any failure or default of said company under the terms thereof, such lands shall be sold at public sale, at places within the States and Territories in which they shall be situate, after not less than sixty days' previous notice, in single sections or subdivisions thereof, to the highest and best bidder.[33]

The Supreme Court was later to accept the contention of the Northern Pacific that Congress intended that this $2.50 clause apply only to *new* lands conveyed in the joint resolution of 1870, namely, the lands in the second indemnity zone and those along the route from Portland to Tacoma.

President Smith awarded contracts on both the eastern and western sections of the Northern Pacific Railroad. With his land grant in hand, Jay Cooke began to sell Northern Pacific bonds and stock. Cooke raised over $30,000,000, but in 1872 sales fell off, and the next year his famous banking house had to close its doors. As a result construction came almost to a halt. The Northern Pacific Railroad Company went into bankruptcy in 1875 but passed its land grant to a reorganized company in a manner which ignored the terms of the charter and smacked of fraud.

As 1877 approached, the question of another extension of the time limit became pressing. Would Congress forfeit the grant, as many land reformers and antirailroad champions were urging? The Supreme Court in the Schulenburg case had ruled in 1874 that land grants were "*in praesenti*, immediately transfering title, although subsequent proceedings might be necessary to give

---

[33] U.S., *Statutes at Large*, XVI, 378.

precision to the title." [34] Only Congress could take advantage of the failure of the railroad to fulfill its obligations. If Congress failed to act, the railroad companies could continue to construct their lines and presumably "earn" the land patents along the constructed portion. They could feel confident that Congress would not take away their "earned" lands.

The movement to forfeit railroad land grants which began in earnest in the 1870's was closely associated with the demand of land reformers to secure more land for homesteaders. When Congress carried out in 1876 one of the first forfeitures of a grant, namely, that to the Leavenworth, Lawrence, and Galveston, it insisted that the lands be thrown open only under the homestead law.[35]

The major land grants—to the Union Pacific and its ally the Central Pacific, the Texas Pacific, and the Northern Pacific—had the watered-down version of the homestead clause known as the contingent right of pre-emption. The courts had to interpret this clause in the 1870's when the Union Pacific sought to avoid state and local taxes on the ground that it was an agency of the federal government. The Supreme Court ruled that the contingent right of pre-emption did not exempt the railroad from the taxation of its patented lands.[36] It observed that the purchaser of a parcel of land from the railroad had to feel assured that he had a clear title.

Secretary of the Interior Carl Schurz in 1878 threw open to pre-emption all the unsold lands of the Union Pacific Railroad.[37]

[34] Schulenburg v. Harriman, 21 Wallace 44 (1875).

[35] *Cong Record*, 44 Cong., 1 sess., 4355, July 1, 1876. For an extended treatment of the forfeiture movement, see David Maldwyn Ellis, "The Forfeiture of Railroad Land Grants," *Mississippi Valley Historical Review*, XXXIII (June 1946), 27–60.

[36] Union Pacific Railroad Company v. McShane, 22 Wallace 444 (1875).

[37] *Speeches, Correspondence and Political Papers of Carl Schurz*, ed., Frederic Bancroft (New York, 1913), IV, 168–181. Schurz blamed Julian for his failure to tighten the wording of the homestead clause.

Later he boasted that his ruling had forced six land-grant rail-roads to open up their lands at the government price of $2.50 an acre, except the Union Pacific, which was directed by its charter to charge $1.25 an acre. Railroad officials rushed a case to the Supreme Court when William Platt tried to exercise the right of pre-emption on the Nebraska lands of the Union Pacific. The Supreme Court ruled that the land-grant mortgage "was a dispo-sition of the lands mortgaged within the meaning of the statute, and, consequently, that the tract of land claimed by the com-plainant was not open to pre-emption." [38] In brief, the lien of the mortgage holder superseded that of the prospective pre-emptor. The Platt decision seemed to safeguard railroad land grants from the contingent right of pre-emption, since all the companies had mortgaged their lands.

The Oregon and California Railroad Company had to accept on April 10, 1869, a "strong" homestead, or settlers', clause. To repeat, this clause stipulated that the lands should be "sold to actual settlers only, in quantities not greater than one quarter section to one purchaser, and for a price not exceeding $2.50 per acre." Prior to 1895 the railroad sold most of its land in small parcels to settlers who wanted to farm along the right of way in the valley bottoms.[39] But in the 1890's agents for lumber compa-nies in the Lakes states began to increase their holdings in the Pacific Northwest. Stumpage prices rose far above $2.50 an acre, especially for the fine Douglas fir. The land department of the Oregon and California was delighted to find eager buyers at advancing prices, but in January 1903 it discontinued land sales. A chorus of criticism swept up and down the Willamette Val-ley, because local businessmen believed that the railroad was

[38] Platt v. Union Pacific Railroad Company, 9 Otto 48 (1879). The most searching analysis of the contingent right is in Leslie Edward Decker, *Railroads, Lands, and Politics: The Taxation of the Railroad Land Grants 1864–1897* (Providence, 1964), 15 ff.

[39] For a documented study, see David Maldwyn Ellis, "The Oregon and California Land Grant, 1866–1945," *Pacific Northwest Quarterly*, XXXIX (Oct. 1948), 253–283.

freezing the development of the region and because the lumber-men wanted more lumber. Edward Harriman, president of the Southern Pacific Railroad, which had secured control of the Oregon and California, put the matter bluntly: "The agricultural land we will sell, but the timber-land we will retain, because we must have ties and bridge timbers, and we must retain our timber for future supply. . . . Yes, we will sell to settlers, but speculators will get none." [40]

Meanwhile an antiquarian-minded citizen in Portland had discovered the "homestead" clause in the charter of the Coos Bay Wagon Road Company, which had received a grant of about one hundred thousand acres. Local officials of the railroad in 1904 warned their superiors that they could expect a similar attack on the O. and C. grant. The general public disliked high rates and discrimination among shippers. They were greatly disturbed when Harriman and other railroad magnates created in 1901 the gigantic holding company, the Northern Securities Company, which had a monopoly on transportation in the Northwest.

A. C. Dixon of the Booth-Kelley Lumber Company of Detroit, which owned 70,000 acres, spearheaded the campaign against the O. and C. Small speculators joined in the hue and cry. After all, with good stumpage going for upward of $10.00 an acre, what easier way was there to make money than to offer the railroad $2.50 an acre? The Oregon legislature no doubt reflected state-wide opinion when it sent in 1907 a memorial to Congress asking relief from continued violation of the clause. After some debate Congress passed a joint resolution directing the attorney general to enforce compliance and to recover the grant. It based its right to act on the authority of the Schulen-burg decision.

Attorney General George Wickersham began the long, tortuous legal proceedings which have filled so many volumes of

[40] Quoted in *ibid.*, 261.

court records and proved a bonanza to scores of lawyers. Counsel for the government contended that the homestead clause was in the nature of a condition subsequent and therefore failure to fulfill the terms operated to forfeit the grant. The company held that the clause was a simple covenant and not a condition subsequent. It held that the clause was so ambiguous that it was impossible to put it into effect. The company also argued that the main purpose of the original grant, to help in the construction of the road, took precedence over other provisions. Moreover, the government had waived its rights to protest by recognizing deeds of record and issuing patents to the company from 1871 to 1906. The company correctly asserted that speculators would benefit most from enforcement.

Congress in 1912 provided that certain bona fide purchasers who had bought from the railroad about 400,000 acres before 1904 in tracts of more than 1,000 acres could go to court, pay $2.50 an acre, and receive new patents. This payment would nullify the government's claim. No legal action was taken against purchasers of tracts of under 1,000 acres, since no one wished to deprive several thousand small purchasers of their rights.

When the district court in 1913 forfeited the grant, the company took an appeal to the Supreme Court. The justices reversed the forfeiture but held that the clause was an enforceable covenant. The court thus threw the problem to Congress, which was directed to make sure that the railroad received a sum equivalent to $2.50 an acre for the entire grant, less the amount it had already received. If Congress should fail to act, the court declared it would order the company to dispose of the remaining land according to the original terms. Meanwhile some fourteen thousand to fifteen thousand applications for land flooded the land department of the O. and C. Professional promoters were advertising in papers across the nation that they would "locate" homesteads for citizens.

Representatives of many groups descended on Congress in

order to influence its decisions. Railroad lawyers, land speculators, lumber companies, county officials fearful of having the
lands off the tax rolls, businessmen who opposed the establishment of more national forests—all testified before the
congressional committees. Congress presented and adopted a
compromise act in 1916. It returned about 2,891,000 acres of
unsold land to federal ownership. Congress directed the Secretary of the Interior to classify them as power-site, timber, or
agricultural land. It authorized him to sell the timber as rapidly
as reasonable prices could be obtained, then open the timber
lands, as well as those classified as agricultural, to homestead
entry at a price of $2.50 an acre. Congress set up the Oregon and
California Land Grant Fund, which would receive the income
from both timber sales and homestead fees. The first charge to
this fund was the payment to the O. and C. of an amount
sufficient to bring its receipts up to the $2.50 an acre specified
in the Supreme Court ruling.

The fate of the Coos Bay Wagon grant deserves brief mention. It contained the homestead clause, but with no mention
about sales to actual settlers. The Attorney General in 1908,
with Congressional approval, brought suit to forfeit 96,000 acres
sold in violation of the terms. The United States Circuit Court
of Appeals upheld the government's position and in 1919 some
93,000 acres of unsold lands were reconveyed to the government. The Treasury paid the owners of the Coos Bay Wagon
Road a sum equivalent to the amount of the total acreage multiplied by $2.50, less the income the company had already re-
ceived and the back taxes due. The government did not disturb
the purchasers of land from the company.

The fate of the recovered lands can only be sketched here.
Although the Department of the Interior reclassified the land as
open to homesteading, few of the cut-over lands were ever
occupied, for the simple reason that they were unsuitable for
farming. Congress authorized the sale of the revested lands, but
few persons wanted these lands aside from those who wanted the

timber on them. As a result county officials began to complain to Washington about the loss of tax revenues. Consequently, in 1937 Congress drew up a law that was much more generous to the counties. Fifty per cent of the income, and another twenty-five per cent after unpaid claims were taken care of, were to go to the counties.

The most important feature of the 1937 act was its directive to the Interior Department to administer the revested lands on a sustained-yield basis.[41] Secretary Harold Ickes established the Oregon and California Revested Land Administration, with twelve forestry units. His advisory board, after an inventory, authorized an annual cut of 500,000,000 feet, a figure that was gradually raised to 1,127,000,000 feet by 1961. During World War I the demand for and the price of lumber shot upward. Subsequently the construction boom underwrote an increasing demand. The average price per thousand feet rose to $28.25 from 1958 to 1962, twelve times that of the period from 1916 to 1937. The rise in income meant bulging coffers for Oregon counties, which received $277,000,000 between 1937 and 1962.

The homestead clause in the O. and C. grant thus had far-reaching consequences. It stirred up the citizenry of Oregon, forced congressional action, led to complicated legal proceedings, and stimulated rivalries between local government units and the national government. Unexpectedly, the federal government after a false start adopted the intelligent principle of developing the recovered timber lands on the sustained-yield basis. The principle of preserving the public domain for the public welfare, which had been the intent of the land reformers of 1869, was thus achieved some three-quarters of a century later in a way somewhat different from the one the land reformers had intended.

The controversy over the O. and C. lands spread to the

---

[41] The most recent summary is David Mason, "The Effect of O & C Management on the Economy of Oregon," *Oregon Historical Quarterly*, LXIV (March 1963), 55–84.

huge Northern Pacific grant, always the favorite target for anti-railroad leaders, homesteaders, and particularly speculators. Speculators hoped to acquire valuable timber lands along the Northern Pacific route for only $2.50 an acre. Some two thousand individuals made application for homesteads at the land office in Vancouver, Washington. Melvin Heath on May 11, 1908, applied for a homestead, but the local register rejected it because it conflicted with the claims of the railroad. On appeal to Washington, the Secretary of the Interior upheld the register.[42]

Heath claimed that the railroad had violated the terms of the grant in that it did not open its lands to entry five years after the road was completed. The foreclosure of 1875 was attacked as tainted, since it did not meet the conditions spelled out in the resolution of 1870. He asserted that the land department had the authority to issue regulations providing for entry. Secretary James Garfield rejected these arguments, holding that the land did not revert from the company until either the courts or Congress ordered such a forfeiture. Since the $2.50 clause was a condition subsequent, the Interior Department could not take any action in the absence of a specified act of Congress. This firm stand dismayed prospective homesteaders.

The Northern Pacific grant, however, came under another legal assault after World War I. Once again the homestead clause provided the opening. Ironically, the railroad company's efforts to enlarge its holdings boomeranged, and eventually the Northern Pacific was to lose additional land, as well as its claim to government land.

The Northern Pacific in 1904 had applied for 5,681 acres in the Gallatin National Forest, on the ground that these lands were within the indemnity limits of its grant. But the Secretary of the Interior turned down its selection of unsurveyed lands, adhering to well-established rules of the Land Office. On April

[42] Heath v. Northern Pacific Railroad Company, 38, *Land Decisions of the Secretary of the Interior*, 77–84.

5, 1905, after the temporary withdrawal order but before the presidential proclamation setting up a forest reserve, the railroad filed its claim for lands within the indemnity limits. In June 1909 the Land Office erroneously issued patents for this acreage, but some five years later the government sought to recover the land. When the Northern Pacific refused to comply, the government brought suit against it, and the case finally reached the Supreme Court on April 11, 1921.[43] The Court held that the right of the United States to create forest reserves was limited if a deficiency in the indemnity limits was ascertained. It estimated that the total extent of the grants of 1864 and 1870 was the aggregate of the odd-numbered sections within the place limits, except where the line of another railroad with a prior claim crossed the route. It referred the matter to the Secretary of the Interior for the purpose of having the acreage accurately recounted.

Preliminary estimates ran as high as 3,900,000 acres, with the timber worth upward of $25,000,000. The Secretary of the Interior later cut the first figure to 2,672,268.57 acres.[44] The Forest Service was appalled, because the Supreme Court decision would take away land which had been under its jurisdiction and protection for over two decades. It assigned four clerks to the General Land Office to assist in the compilation of the figures, a task which took the better part of two years.

Meanwhile, D. F. McGowan, counsel for the Forest Service, made a separate inquiry into the Northern Pacific grant in order to determine whether the railroad had complied with the provisions of its legislative contract with the United States. McGowan drew up a list of twenty-two points on which the Northern Pacific had violated the stipulations of the grants of 1864 and 1870.[45] Among them were the failure to dispose of the land at prices not exceeding $2.50 an acre, the erroneous selection of

[43] 256 U.S. 51 (1921).

[44] *Joint Hearings*, Pt. IV, 2008.

[45] A summary of the legal developments is given in the first section, *ibid.*, I, 1–20.

1,300,000 acres within the second indemnity limits, the patenting of excess acreage in Washington, and illegalities connected with the bankruptcy proceedings in 1875 and 1896. Secretary of Agriculture Henry Wallace became convinced that the matter should go before Congress. He won over Secretary of the Interior Hubert Work, and in a joint letter to N. J. Sinott, chairman of the Committee on Public Lands of the House of Representatives, they urged an investigation. President Calvin Coolidge, on February 23, 1924, recommended to Mr. Sinott that Congress investigate the claims of the company and the rights of the government. Perhaps the Teapot Dome affair made the Coolidge administration ultrasensitive to possible charges of being influenced by large corporate interests.

Both the House and Senate Committees on Public Lands held preliminary hearings in 1924. The government lawyers and witnesses drew up a long list of grievances and charges. The failure of the Northern Pacific to live up to the contingent right of pre-emption was a major weapon in the government's case. Mr. McGowan declared that the company

was entitled only to $2.50 per acre for all lands sold after July 4, 1884 [five years after the date of acceptance by the government of the main line]. The Northern Pacific did not dispose of its lands after July 4, 1884 for $2.50 an acre. It sold the land in the open market for what it could get, and what it did receive through the sale of the lands exceeded by many millions of dollars the maximum Congress intended it should have. It further violated the terms of the law by disposing of many acres of the lands to large lumber companies instead of under settlement and pre-emption as the law provided.[46]

Lawyers for the railroad opposed bringing up again the history of the grant and urged the government to hand over the acreage at once. Charles Donnelly, the president of the Northern Pacific Railroad, issued a pamphlet, *Facts about the Northern*

[46] *Ibid.*, I, 41.

Pacific Land Grant, which tried to refute the charges leveled against his company. He denied that the homestead clause had ever been operative. But Congress refused to heed his appeal and on June 5, 1924, called for a thorough joint investigation by both houses of the respective rights of the company and the government.

The hearings during the next three years covered a large number of subjects, some of them highly technical aspects of land administration and some of them explorations of the rights of both parties in equity. The government lawyers stressed equity and the company's delinquencies. The Northern Pacific lawyers relied more on narrow legal rights, although they too appealed to equity.

The homestead clause came in for much attention. Skimming rapidly over the foreclosure of 1875, attorneys for the railroad claimed that the reorganization of 1896 amounted to a disposition of the property. Thereafter the Northern Pacific Railway Company, the legal successor of the Northern Pacific Railroad Company, was relieved of this limitation on its freedom of action. Mr. Britten, who led the battery of high-priced lawyers, declared, "The entire grant was sold out, the franchise was lost, the organized corporation bought these lands in under the mortgage, and it owned them just the same as I would have owned them if I had bought them in." [47] He insisted that the requirement in the resolution of 1870 of obtaining the highest and best price showed Congress' intent that a clear title should pass to the new owner. Otherwise, who would buy bonds, if anyone could come and secure title by offering $2.50 an acre? Furthermore, since Congress had repealed the Pre-emption Act in 1891, no one had the right to go on land, because of the contingent right of pre-emption.

Government lawyers showed how the company had evaded the requirements of the original agreement in the foreclosure

[47] *Ibid.,* I, 304. For more extended treatment, see Pt. III, 1248–1291, and VIII, 4668–4682.

proceedings of both 1875 and 1896. Indeed fraud characterized both transactions, it was asserted. The lawyers held that the successor company was subject to all the obligations, including the homestead clause. The decision in the Oregon and California case was cited in the hope of overruling the decisions in the Platt and Heath cases relied upon by the Northern Pacific. Realizing the crucial importance of the O. and C. ruling, Charles Bunn, a lawyer for the Northern Pacific, made several distinctions:

The Northern Pacific act contains the following features not in the Oregon and California act: (a) Provision for mortgage against the lands; (b) Five years after the completion of the entire road given the company before the requirement attaches; (c) requirement not to attach so long as the lands remain subject to mortgage by the act authorized; (d) provision for mortgage sale, in single sections or subdivisions, to the highest and best bidder.[48]

The report of the joint congressional committee unanimously agreed that the Northern Pacific had not complied with the terms of the grant.[49] It directed the Attorney General to begin proceedings to ascertain the respective rights of the United States and the company. It declared that all lands within the indemnity limits of the grant and within the exterior limits of the national forests should be retained by the government. The Forest Service was delighted that it had won the case, at least in the minds of congressmen. Furthermore, the committee held forfeit all unsatisfied indemnity selection rights claimed by the company and called on the attorney general to institute suit for a full accounting. In effect Congress retained the land but agreed to pay for it if a court found the railroad claims valid.

The Attorney General brought suit in the United States District Court of the Eastern District of Washington. The suit dragged on for years and years, since dozens of witnesses testi-

[48] *Ibid.*, I, 438.
[49] *Sen. Report*, 5, 71 Cong., 1 sess. April 29, 1929.

fied in the hearings held before a Special Master. His report was filed in federal district court July 27, 1937.[50] It found that the government had confiscated about 2,400,000 acres. The district court returned to the government about 1,363,000 acres, while the railroad received approximately the same number.[51]

The decision following appeal to the Supreme Court in 1940, however, upheld most of the contentions of the United States, although the justices remanded the suit to the district court for a redetermination.[52] Justice Owen Roberts declared that the evidence was such that the government might prove fraud of such character and extent as would disentitle the railroad to any award, even though the fraud did not affect an acreage equal in amount to that taken back by the act of 1929. Looking at the settler's clause, the Court instructed the government to "prove the damages suffered by it" as a result of the company's breach.

The Northern Pacific decided to surrender. No doubt its officers feared the threat of conviction for fraud. Perhaps the prospect of another decade of law suits made them eager to close the books. Moreover, by settling the case, the Northern Pacific could qualify for benefits under the Transportation Act of 1940.

The final terms ran as follows: The Northern Pacific gave up claims to compensation for 1,453,016 acres of withdrawn lands, the court having already denied the road's claim to the remainder of the approximately 2,900,000 acres in question. The company surrendered its claims to approximately 363,000 acres of the 428,986.68 acres for which it had been awarded patents by the district-court decree of June 27, 1939, which the Supreme Court had affirmed. It agreed to pay $300,000 for land erroneously patented and turned back scrip permitting it to select another 50,000 acres.

[50] A summary is given in *Railway Age*, CIII (Aug. 7, 1937), 176.
[51] *Ibid.*, CVII (July 1, 1939), 46.
[52] U.S. v. Northern Pacific Railway Company *et al.*, 311 U.S. 317 (1941).

After consulting with the Secretary of Agriculture, Attorney General Robert Jackson approved the terms.[53] The final settlement represented a striking victory for the government. Its lawyers had not only saved the national forests from railroad assault but had also recovered much additional land for the public domain. The value of this land in the years following World War II exceeded $100,000,000.

The land reformers of the 1860's sought to prevent land monopoly by including a homestead clause in several land grants. The weaker version, the contingent right of pre-emption, was tacked onto the Union Pacific grant of 1862 and onto most major grants thereafter. The promoters of the transcontinental railroads regarded this clause as a pious gesture to the land reformers. The more stringent version, like that attached to the Oregon and California land grant in 1869, was intended to control the sale of land from the outset. Neither had any discernible effect on the land offices of the railroad companies. They had confidence that no Congress would make them forfeit their lands. They felt certain that the courts would protect their holdings from any assault.

Various groups—speculators eager to secure timber lands, country and state officials in Oregon, conservation champions in and out of the government, congressmen, and judges—took a hand in reinterpreting the homestead clause. As a result the Oregon and California Railroad lost almost three million acres, because it had clearly violated the provision directing it to sell land in small tracts to actual settlers at not more than $2.50 an acre.

The greed of the Northern Pacific for timber lands within the national forests backfired. Citing the company's violations of the contingent right of pre-emption to illustrate the wanton misbehavior of the railroad, government lawyers won the moral support of Congress and impressed the Supreme Court.

[53] For a copy of this agreement, see *Sen. Doc.* 48, 77 Cong., 1 sess., 1941.

Admittedly yeoman farmers derived practically no benefit from the homestead clause in the nineteenth and twentieth centuries. A further irony is that the original limitations on the grants were ultimately effectual *because* they were irrelevant to the needs of the homesteaders. Although the homesteaders and two of the largest land holders failed to achieve their objectives, the general public won. Today the Forest Service and the Oregon and California Revested Land Administration safeguard these national resources for the benefit of the American people.

Congress Looks West: Liberal Ideology and Public Land Policy in the Nineteenth Century

~⌘~

MARY E. YOUNG

The developing frontier has always served Americans as a metaphor of their nation's unique potentialities. As recently as the second President Johnson's 1965 State of the Union address, with its Horatio Alger biography of an arid patch of Texas, the emergence of opulent civilization out of the pioneer's contest with nature has been read as a portent of the Great Society.

Several historians have taken as their theme this national "image" of the West in the nineteenth century, when Americans spanned and populated their share of the North American continent in what many still acknowledge to be the greatest spatial achievement of the pre-Sputnik era. As yet, however, no one has attempted a thorough analysis of the views of well-defined groups of Americans who had a measure of responsibility for what was going on in the West.[1]

[1] Henry Nash Smith, *Virgin Land: The American West as Symbol and Myth* (New York, 1957) makes extensive use of the debates. Focusing on those myths exploited in common by the creators of literature and subliterature and by congressmen, Smith is so thematically selective as to be somewhat misleading. He emphasizes the mythopoeic elements in the debates, concentrates on agrarian themes to the exclusion of other themes, and at times implicitly equates myth with error or with deliberate attempts to mislead on the part of those

74

The American Congress constitutes such a group. Congressmen were responsible for serving the needs of a varied constituency in relation to western problems and for persuading each
other and their constituents that they were doing the job properly. Debates over public-land policy in particular represent a
crucial point of intersection between ideas and practice with
respect to the West, its problems, and its prospects.

The views of congressmen on public issues are packaged conveniently in the records of their debates. But in analyzing the
debates, it is important first to examine what *kind* of document
they are. They are not the sort which permits the historian to
determine from internal evidence whether one or another party
to the debate is "correct" in his representation of the "the facts"
or in his predictions. These congressional records have, rather,
posed the questions and defined the controversies which historians for more than seventy years have attempted to resolve. Their
scholarly task has entailed an exacting blend of muckracking,
econometrics, and Monday-morning quarterbacking; and it is
not yet finished. Nor can one determine from the debates the
precise function of a given view or constellation of images in
forwarding the particular interest of a particular congressman or
his constituents. Congressmen were often moved to attribute

---

representing "the interests." Such an analysis gives too little credit to
the complexity, variety, and scope of congressional views and may be
quite simplistic with respect to their function. Other explorations
include Loren Baritz, "The Idea of the West," *American Historical
Review*, LXVI (April 1961), 618 ff.; Arthur E. Bestor, Jr., "Patent
Office Models of the Good Society: Some Relationships between Social
Reform and Westward Expansion," *ibid.*, LVIII (April 1953), 505 ff.;
Arthur K. Moore, *The Frontier Mind: A Cultural Analysis of Ken-
tucky Frontiersmen* (Lexington, Ky., 1957); Charles L. Sanford, *The
Quest for Paradise: Europe and the American Moral Imagination* (Ur-
bana, Ill., 1861); and Rush Welter, "The Frontier West as Image of
American Society: Conservation Attitudes before the Civil War,"
Mississippi Valley Historical Review, XLVI (March 1960), 593 ff. A
historiographical approach is Earl S. Pomeroy's, in "Rediscovering the
West," *American Quarterly*, XII (Spring 1960), 20 ff.

motives to one another; to discover whether or not they were right would be the work of several hundred atypically skeptical and thorough biographers.

What most congressmen say is rationalization—they want to justify policies they prefer and to discredit those their opponents defend. If we combine the patterns of rationalization implicit in the debates with what is already known about the development of the West and the administration of land policies, we may arrive at very general notions about the function of ideology in the formulation of policy. Furthermore, the terms in which policy is rationalized, especially those basic assumptions about what is desirable and about the way society is likely to work that are shared by opposing parties, may tell the historian much about the values and perspectives which condition both outlook and policy. Such values and perspectives have an interest of their own, and it is on them that this analysis of the debates will concentrate. For those who prefer to take their history simply, as a record of crime and folly, the center of interest will be the anatomy of hypocrisy rather than the physiology of venality.[2]

[2] In reviewing the debates, I shall follow the convention of defining "nineteenth century" elastically, to include the period up to America's involvement in World War I. The terminal date is chosen not so much to contrast the egocentric with the international outlook as to include the discussion of the last major homestead legislation, which was passed in 1916. I shall not, however, attempt to recapitulate the excellent work of Samuel P. Hays, *Conservation and the Gospel of Efficiency: The Progressive Conservation Movement, 1890–1920* (Cambridge, Mass., 1954), and Elmo Richardson, *The Politics of Conservation: Crusades and Controversies, 1896–1913* (Berkeley, 1962), in analyzing the controversies over conservation. Legislative histories of the period under discussion include Benjamin H. Hibbard, *A History of the Public Land Policies* (New York, 1924); E. Louise Peffer, *The Closing of the Public Domain: Disposal and Reservation Policies, 1900–1950* (Stanford, Calif., 1951); Roy M. Robbins, *Our Landed Heritage: The Public Domain, 1776–1936* (Princeton, 1942); George M. Stephenson, *Political History of the Public Lands from 1840–1862* (Boston, 1917); Payson J. Treat, *The National Land System, 1785–1820* (New York, 1910); and Raynor G. Wellington, *The Political and Sectional Influence of The Public*

Ever present before the eyes of congressmen in their consideration of the public lands was an image of the West as a
storehouse of potential wealth. In much of their persuasive
communication, statesmen presented themselves as strategists of
economic development. Most spokesmen for revision of the land
laws, at whatever period, tended to equate the disposal of land to
small holders with settlement, and settlement with development.[3]
Occasional disagreement arose over the optimal pace of settlement; but more often argument centered about the measures most
likely to encourage it.

Congressmen—like subsequent students of land policy—often
spoke of a conflict between the "revenue principle" and the
"settlement principle." Actually, nearly all of them agreed that a
well-conceived system of land disposal would augment the
public revenues. They differed over whether more money might
be raised by charging higher prices for land or by charging
lower prices, encouraging settlement, and enjoying the revenues
arising indirectly from the ensuing economic growth. Western
congressmen were especially concerned to increase local tax
bases by getting land into productive private ownership, while
easterners lamented the diversion of specific revenues and grants
of land from general funds to projects directly benefiting the
public-land states alone.

Probably the most intricate arguments over developmental
policy were those employed in discussion of the proposal to
reduce or "graduate" the price of lands in proportion to the time
they had been on the market. Senator Thomas Hart Benton of
Missouri introduced this proposal in 1824, elaborated his first

Lands, 1828–1842 (Cambridge, Mass., 1914). Useful summaries of the
principal laws may be found in Richard Morris, ed., *Encyclopedia of
American History* (rev. ed.; New York, 1961), 436 ff.

[3] Critics of "settler-oriented" policy questioned the equation of disposal to small holders with settlement. Thomas H. LeDuc, "Public
Policy, Private Investment and Land Use in American Agriculture,
1825–1875," *Agricultural History*, XXVII (Jan. 1963), 3 ff., questions
both equations.

77

defense of it in 1826, kept it before the attention of Congress for thirty years, and saw it enacted into law in 1854. By February 1845, Representative George F. Houston of Alabama could assert, "Indeed, so plain was it, and so often brought before the public mind, that there was scarce a boy in all the West that could not make a pretty good argument for graduation." [4]

Benton's major premise was that only the best lands the government had to offer could command the $1.25 per acre minimum price the land offices charged. He attributed the huge quantity of unsold land on the market to the fact that most of it was not "worth" what the government charged for it. A reduction in price, he argued, would stimulate land sales, increase revenues, and pay off the federal debt. If graduation were accompanied by donations of "refuse" lands to pauper settlers and ultimately followed by the cession of long-unsold lands to the states, the federal government could eventually eliminate the administrative costs that currently absorbed an estimated one-third of the public-land revenues. [5]

The federal debt was less reliably burdensome in his century than in ours, and Benton came to place major emphasis on the economic benefits of rapid and compact settlement. Settlers, he predicted, would raise exportable crops; more exports would pay for larger quantities of imported goods; customs revenues would be increased. More compact settlement would enlarge local tax bases, would lead to the building of roads and schools,

[4] *Cong. Globe*, 28 Cong., 2 sess., App., 206, Feb. 2, 1845. Ninian Edwards of Illinois had introduced an amendment to the bill for revising the public-land laws in February 1819, calling for a graduation of price in proportion to the size of tract purchased, with lesser prices for smaller sizes (*Annals of Congress*, 15 Cong., 2 sess., 241, Feb. 18, 1819). The revised law of 1820, providing only for the public auction of land and subsequent private sale—both at a minimum price of $1.25 per acre—remained in effect until 1889, though subsequent legislation established many alternative ways of selling or donating land.

[5] *Register of Debates in Congress*, 19 Cong., 1 sess., 720–745, May 16, 1826; *ibid.*, 20 Cong., 1 sess., IV, 23–28, Dec. 24, 1827.

and would enable settlers to enjoy the benefits of cooperative labor on their own homes.[6]

Benton's opponents contended that the large quantity of unsold public land was a direct consequence of the government's policy of dumping more land on the market than was required for cultivation. Senator Samuel A. Foote's famous resolution looking toward the cessation of survey and offering of new land was thus an appropriate retort to the Bentonian school of political economy.[7]

A labor theory of value was implicit in all arguments favoring lower prices to settlers. As applied to land policy, this theory stipulated that land in its natural state was unproductive and hence worthless; only the settler's labor gave it economic value. Since settlers built roads, schools, churches, and courthouses, as well as barns and fences, their labor gave "value" to land outside the limits of their individual farms.[8]

Benton's opponents were no more concerned than was Benton himself with the contradiction between the assertion that the price of wild land should vary in proportion to the time it had been on the market and the assumption that no unoccupied or uncultivated land could have value. Instead, they offered their own, more complex, theories of land value. Henry Clay of Kentucky, Benton's most vocal contemporary rival in the field of developmental analysis, enumerated the determinants of land value as follows: "the fertility of the soil, the natural advantages

---

[6] *Cong. Globe*, 25 Cong., 2 sess., App., 292–293, April 12, 1838.

[7] Cf. Sen. David Barton (Mo.), *ibid.*, 19 Cong., 2 sess., 45, Jan. 9, 1827, and *ibid.*, 20 Cong., 1 sess., IV, 484–493, March 25, 1828; Sen. Samuel Vinton (Ohio), 21 Cong., 2 sess., VII, 471–472, Jan. 12, 1831; and Sen. Henry Clay (Ky.), *Cong. Gobe*, 25 Cong., 2 sess., App., 563, April 11, 1838. Debate on Foote's Resolution as it relates to land policy may be found in *Register*, 21 Cong., 1 sess., VI, 3–7, Dec. 30, 1829; 15, Jan. 13, 1830; 22, Jan. 18; 29–35, Jan. 19; 144, Feb. 8; 180, Feb. 24; 196–197, Feb. 26; 224, March 4; 250–251, March 15; 442, May 20; and 452, May 22.

[8] Sen. John A. McClernand (Dem., Ill.), *Cong. Globe*, 28 Cong., 2 sess., App., 40, Dec. 27, 1844.

of the tract, its capacity to yield a profitable return for the capital and labor expended on it." [9]

Opponents of graduation and other schemes to reduce land prices insisted that the demand for agricultural land was relatively stable and that the combination of excessive offering and low price would simply encourage speculation.[10] To counter them, the Bentonians, argued that as long as the government remained the country's greatest land monopolist, its own offerings should be sufficient to keep prices as low as the government cared to make them.[11]

As the subject of debate shifted from cheap land to free land, and as labor reformers lent free-homestead proposals their political support, increasing emphasis was placed on western lands as a safety valve—a means of keeping wages high by providing alternatives to factory employment.[12] Land reformers did not even agree among themselves on precisely how the safety valve was to work. Some anticipated that tenants, the unemployed, and poorly paid workingmen would move west to free land.[13] Others expected eastern wages to remain high because *potential* competitors for factory jobs—the sons of eastern farmers—might move

[9] *Ibid.*, 25 Cong., 2 sess., App., 138, Jan. 29, 1838. In 1838 the Committee on Public Lands (Senate) proposed a method for valuation by federal officials. Benton's supporters then argued that there was *no* sure way of determining land values, and talked of bureaucracy (Rep. Clement C. Clay [Dem., Ala.], *ibid.*, 293, April 9, 1838).

[10] Cf. Clay's speech, cited in N. 9, with Sen. Barton, *Register*, 20 Cong., 1 sess., IV, 486, March 25, 1828; and Rep. George O. Rathbun (Dem., N.Y.), *Cong. Globe*, 29 Cong., 1 sess., App., 773, July 9, 1846.

[11] Sen. Elias K. Kane, 20 Cong., 1 sess., IV, 497–504, March 25, 1828; Sen. John McKinley (Dem., Ala.), *ibid.*, 507–508, 521, March 27, 1828.

[12] For the land-reform movement, see Helen S. Zahler, *Eastern Workingmen and National Land Policy, 1828–1862* (N.Y., 1941).

[13] Thomas Hart Benton, *Register*, 21 Cong., 1 sess., VI, 406–407, May 3, 1830; Rep. Cyrus L. Dunham (Dem., Ind.), *Cong. Globe*, 32 Cong., 1 sess., App., 408, April 6, 1852; Rep. Joseph A. Chandler, (Whig, Pa.), *ibid.*, 32 Cong., 1 sess., 1022, April 8, 1852; Sen. Lewis Cass (Dem., Mich.), *ibid.*, 33 Cong., 1 sess., 1706, Jul. 12, 1854; Sen. Andrew Johnson (Dem., Tenn.), *ibid.*, 36 Cong., 1 sess., 1654, April 11, 1860.

westward rather than cityward. The opposition was equally divided. Some argued that the poor could not use the safety valve and that the comfortable had no need for it. Others contended that subsidizing the diversion of labor into agriculture was unwise and uneconomic.[14]

Actually, the argument that free land would drain free labor from the factory was more frequently attributed to opponents of land reform than acknowledged by them. A more common fear involving interregional competition was that subsidizing rapid settlement of the west would depress land prices in states adjacent to those being settled.[15] To counter such fears, champions of cheaper land argued that national wealth depended on the productivity of labor rather than on its location. Self-employed labor on fresh land was of course the most productive.[16] To reassure the supposedly anxious manufacturer, they presented the frontiersman as a consumer and spoke enticingly of the home market.[17]

Though proponents of free lands expended hours of eloquence in praise of agriculture, decrying the evils of urban

[14] Rep. Charles Skelton (Dem., N.J.), *ibid.*, 32 Cong., 1 sess., App., 381, March 30, 1852; Rep. W. K. Smith (Dem., Ala.), *ibid.*, 514. Cf. Henry Clay, 22 Cong., 1 sess., VIII, 1113, June 20, 1832; Sen. Thomas Ewing, (Ohio), 22 Cong., 2 sess., IX, 169, Jan. 21, 1833; Rep. John Welch (Whig, Ohio), *Cong. Globe*, 32 Cong., 1 sess., App., 687, July 12, 1852; Sen. Robert M. Charleton (Ga.), *ibid.*, 32 Cong., 2 sess., App., 206–207, Feb. 24, 1853, and Sen. John Bell (Whig, Tenn.), *ibid.*, 33 Cong., 1 sess., App., 1104, July 10, 1854.

[15] Cf. Sen. Samuel F. Vinton, *Register*, 21 Cong., 2 sess., VII, 471–472, Jan. 12, 1831; Clay, *Register*, 22 Cong., 1 sess., VIII, 1101, 1107–1108, June 20, 1832; Sen. Ewing (Ohio), *ibid.*, 1141, June 8, 1832, and *ibid.*, 22 Cong., 2 sess., IX, 164, 167, 169, Jan. 21, 1833. It should not be forgotten that, until well into the century, various eastern states were selling their own public lands in competition with the federal government.

[16] Sen. John Black (Dem., Miss.), *Register*, 22 Cong., 2 sess., IX, 107–108, Jan. 16, 1833.

[17] *Ibid.*, 111; Rep. Johnson, *Cong. Globe*, 31 Cong., 1 sess., App., 950, July 25, 1850; Sen. Isaac P. Walker (Dem., Wis.), *ibid.*, 1572, July 13, 1850, and App., 78, Jan. 14, 15, 1851.

poverty and the horrors of technological unemployment, they also emphasized the reciprocity of agricultural interests with those of commerce and manufacturing. For Benton, the farmer might be the only producer of "real" wealth, but his product nevertheless could be expected to filter profitably through the hands of the merchant, the banker, and the manufacturer.[18]

Later in the century, champions of subsidized settlement rested their case, not only on the reciprocity of interest between agriculture and industry, but on the variety of western resources and the West's own potential for urbanization. Asked why the federal government should encourage irrigationists and dry-land farmers when there were already farmers and products to spare, spokesmen for the arid domain were quick to reply that figs, lemons, and alfalfa did not compete with corn and wheat.[19] Furthermore, mining, lumbering, railroads, and cities would follow the plow; food supplies grown on dry-land farms and irrigated acres would be entirely absorbed by the nonagricultural occupants of the Far West.[20] The last pioneers of the shrinking public domain were represented as consumers of cultivated taste, who borrowed money if necessary to supply themselves with plows, pans, and musical instruments produced by eastern toil.[21]

A common criticism of post–Civil War policy was that its agrarian bias was ill-adapted to the development of any but

[18] For Benton, see especially *Cong. Globe*, 25 Cong., 2 sess., App., 292, April 12, 1838. Cf. Rep. John L. Dawson (Dem., Pa.), *ibid.*, 33 Cong., 1 sess., App., 185, Feb. 14, 1854; Rep. William R. Sapp (Whig, Ohio), *ibid.*, 33 Cong., 1 sess., App., 179, Feb. 16, 1854; and Rep. Galusha Grow (Free Soil, Pa.), *ibid.*, 523, March 2, 1854.

[19] Rep. Charles W. Ray (Rep., N.Y.), *Cong. Record*, 57 Cong., 1 sess., 6685, June 12, 1902; Rep. Francis E. Warren (Dem., Wyo.), *Cong. Record*, 52 Cong., 1 sess., 6489, July 21, 1892; Sen. Henry C. Hansbrough (Rep., N.D.), *ibid.*, 57 Cong., 1 sess., 1383–1385, Feb. 6, 1902.

[20] Hansbrough, *Cong. Record*, 57 Cong., 1 sess., 1383–1385, Feb. 6, 1902, and 58 Cong., 2 sess., 3363, 3667, March 25, 1904.

[21] Rep. James V. McClintic (Dem., Okla.), *ibid.*, 64 Cong., 1 sess., 1122, Jan. 15, 1916. Cf. Rep. Wesley L. Jones, (Rep., Wash.), *Cong. Record*, 57 Cong., 1 sess., 6751, June 13, 1902.

agricultural resources and that the 160-acre homestead unit was too small to accommodate the needs of dry-land agriculture. Nonmineral lands that had been offered for sale prior to the passage of the Homestead Act in 1862 remained available in unrestricted quantity at $1.25 per acre until private cash sale was terminated by law in 1889. The auction system of offering newly surveyed lands to the highest bidder, again in unrestricted quantities, was not formally abandoned until 1891. But following the passage of the Homestead Act, the General Land Office seldom offered new lands at auction. Hence most of the territory of the United States settled after 1862—and this includes almost the entire area between eastern Kansas and the Rockies, as well as much of the Pacific Coast was closed to unrestricted cash sale. Legislation of the 1870's permitted the limited acquisition, in certain states, of land allegedly valuable only for timber, timber culture, or irrigation. But the unrelenting pressure of the advocates of homes for the homeless insured that even such purchases must be limited to amounts ranging from 160 to 640 acres. In the more newly settled areas of the West, therefore, sawmill operators, ranchers, and irrigation companies had no legal means of getting title to public lands in quantities suitable for their large-scale operations.

Contemporary criticism of the maladaptation of federal land policy to nonagricultural lands and to "modern" conditions is exemplified in the debate over what was to become the Timber Cutting Act of 1878. In 1876, when the bill permitting westerners of the Pacific Coast states to purchase timber lands in quantities of up to 160 acres was discussed in the Senate, John Sherman of Ohio asserted that a modern sawmill could cut the timber on a quarter section in six months:

The old-fashioned sawmills which cut a few logs a day are among the myths of the past. The saw-mill now devours a forest, and it requires thousands of acres of land to keep one of those great gang-mills running for a year or two. Therefore, if this land is to be utilized for timber, as a matter of course it will get into the hands of corporations and great companies who will devour the forest for lumber and cut a thousand acres probably in a single year.

Sherman, however, expressed no serious concern for the fate of the lumberman. He predicted that by using agents who would contract to sell the timber rather than the land, "a speculator [could] ride through this bill with a coach and four without any difficulty." [22]

With reference to the range-cattle industry, congressional discussions implied to an even greater degree that large users of nonagricultural resources were generally content to employ dummy entrymen under the "settlement" laws or simply to use public lands as their own, rather than actively to seek revision of the land laws.[23] Ordinarily, these "leviathan squatters" protested the anachronistic bias of the law and the general "misunderstanding" of their special needs only when overzealous inspectors from Washington interfered with the working arrangements (otherwise known as "corruption") by which local land officials permitted adaptation of the "agrarian" system to nonagricultural requirements.[24]

It is open to question whether limitations on land acquisition reflect preoccupation with the needs of petty agriculture or simply bias in favor of small units of ownership, whatever the enterprises involved. The debates over revision of the special homestead legislation imposed on the conquered South suggest

[22] *Cong. Record*, 44 Cong., 1 sess., 1105, Feb. 16, 1876.

[23] Rep. Horace F. Page (Rep., Calif.), *ibid.*, 47 Cong., 1 sess., 5910, July 11, 1882; Rep. Pleasant B. Tully (Dem., Calif.), *ibid.*, 48 Cong., 1 sess., 4775, June 3, 1884; Rep. George W. Cassidy (Dem., Nev.), *ibid.*, 4776; Rep. Bishop W. Perkins (Rep., Kan.), *ibid.*, 4896, June 7, 1884; Rep. John Lind (Rep., Minn.), *ibid.*, 58 Cong., 3 sess., 3676, Feb. 28, 1905.

[24] See, for example, debates in *Cong. Record*, 46 Cong., 2 Sess., 1564–1565, March 15, 1880; 3577–3579, May 20, 1880; 3627–3629, May 21, 1880; 51 Cong., 1 sess., 10087–10088, Sept. 16, 1890; and 54 Cong., 2 sess., 1409, Feb. 1, 1897. The phrase "leviathan squatter" is used by Rep. Charles B. Lore (Dem., Del.), in *ibid.*, 48 Cong., 1 sess., 4794, June 3, 1884.

that the latter bias was sometimes the more important. From 1866 to 1876, only homestead entries were permitted in the South. The system was abandoned largely at the insistence of those interested in exploiting southern pine-timber resources. Yet land reformer William Holman of Indiana argued that timber lands themselves would be appropriate grants to the landless if nothing "better" were available.[25] The timber baron, suggested Congressman Poindexter Dunn of Arkansas in 1884, might just as well buy his logs from the homesteader.[26]

Perhaps the most amusing instance of the adaptation of "agrarian" premises to the disposal of nonagricultural land is found in the consideration by Congress of mineral-land legislation. The gold and silver miners of California and Nevada enjoyed their discoveries on the public domain unimpeded by federal regulation for eighteen years after the incident at Sutter's mill. Notoriously, the miners' associations worked out their own methods for defining and transferring individual claims to this public property. Their activity has often been held to demonstrate the American pioneer's genius for self-government. When, following the Civil War, the government's concern for paying off the war debt coincided with the miners' interest in establishing greater security for their growing capital investment, laws were finally enacted (in 1866 and 1872) for the "disposal" of the well-worked mines. Senator William A. Stewart of Nevada imported the labor theory of value and the complementary notions of squatters' rights, undamaged by earlier debates on the farmer's right to pre-emption, into the discussion of the miner's right to his claim. Squatters on mineral lands went

[25] *Cong. Globe,* 44 Cong., 1 sess., 2604, April 19, 1876. On small cattle ranchers, see Rep. Poindexter Dunn (Dem., Ark.), *Cong. Record,* 48 Cong., 1 sess., 4781, June 3, 1884. For the Southern Homestead Act and its repeal, see Paul W. Gates, "Federal Land Policy in the South, 1866–1888," *Journal of Southern History,* VI (1940), 303 ff. It is of course possible to argue that in a society replete with small farmers the farm supplied the model of petty individual enterprise.

[26] *Cong. Record,* 48 Cong., 1 sess., 4893, June 7, 1884.

the squatters of Iowa one better, since they ware able to translate their own methods of defining claims into federal law.[27]

The major developmental legislation besides subsidies to settlers was that granting land for "internal improvements." The national legislature donated millions of acres to finance the building of canals and railroads, drainage, irrigation, the education of western children, and the education of citizens of all the states in agriculture and the mechanic arts. Unhappily, Congress did not publicly consider the petition of Leonard Jones and Henry Banta of Kentucky, "representing themselves subjects of endless life, who had made important discoveries connected with the morals, religion, and eternal existence of man, and asking for a grant of land for the purpose of enabling them to extend and propagate their discovery." [28] But only President Pierce's constitutional scruples inhibited the legislators from what a skeptical southern physician-turned-congressman described as an attempt to "cure insanity with land" by granting ten million acres to the states to support institutions for the "indigent insane." [29]

Congress was most generous with its donations in the generation between the passage of the Pre-emption Act of 1841 and the granting of the last transcontinental subsidy in 1871. This was also the period of the allegedly settler-oriented Graduation Act

[27] For debates on mineral-land legislation, see *Cong. Globe*, 36 Cong., 1 sess., 1754–1795, April 17–19, 1860; *ibid.*, 38 Cong., 2 sess., 684–686, Feb. 9, 1865; *ibid.*, 39 Cong., 1 sess., 3225–3236, June 18, 1866; 3451, June 28, 1866; 4021–4022, July 21, 1866; 4050–4054, July 23, 1866; and *ibid.*, 41 Cong., 2 sess., 2028–2029, March 17, 1870. A useful recent treatment of mineral-land laws and their operation is Rodman W. Paul, *Mining Frontiers of the Far West, 1848–1880* (N.Y., 1963).

[28] *Register*, 22 Cong., 2 sess., IX, 98, Jan. 14, 1833.

[29] Rep. Thomas H. Averett (Dem., Va.), *Cong. Globe*, 32 Cong., 1 sess., 1019, April 1, 1852. Averett added primly, "The power to cure insanity is not expressed in the Constitution." For his background, see James L. Harrison, ed., *Biographical Directory of the American Congress, 1774–1949* (Washington, 1950), 797. In general, first names and party designations are derived from this source. Pierce's message of May 3, 1854, is quoted in *Cong. Globe*, 35 Cong., 2 sess., 717, Feb. 1, 1859.

(1854) and the Homestead Act (1862). A question which greatly agitated congressmen, as it has interested historians, was the degree of congruity between the developmental subsidies to states and corporations and the developmental subsidies to "actual settlers." [30] Most supporters of the grant legislation argued analogously with supporters of settlement laws that the work expended by the grantees in improving the land would not only increase the national product, but also enhance the cash value of the government's adjacent property.[31] Several of the early homestead proposals called for donations to settlers according to the alternate-section, checkerboard pattern characteristically employed in grants to canals and railroads.[32]

The bitterest debates over the congruity of grants to states and corporations with grants to settlers centered about the railroads, both during the period when grants were being given and during the later period when forfeiture of unearned grants was being considered. Critics of the donations to railroads contended

[30] Cf. Paul W. Gates, "The Homestead Act in an Incongruous Land System," *American Historical Review*, XLI (July 1936), 652 ff., and "The Homestead Act: Free Land Policy in Operation, 1862–1935," in Howard W. Ottoson, ed., *Land Use Policy and Problems in the United States* (Lincoln, Neb., 1963).

[31] This argument was a convenient way of getting around constitutional scruples about federal donations for internal improvements. The ingenious reasoning was that if the improvement doubled the value of the alternate sections not granted, the government lost nothing and had therefore given nothing. Like a prudent proprietor, it was merely investing in the improvement of its estate. See Sen. Cass (Dem., Mich.), *Cong. Globe*, 33 Cong., 1 sess., App., 1087, July 18, 1854. On the question of congruity, see for example debates of March 16–18, 1852, *ibid.*, 32 Cong., 1 sess. 765; and Rep. S. C. Foster (Rep., Me.), *ibid.*, 36 Cong., 1 sess., App., 244–245, April 24, 1860. Foster included the "suppression of polygamy" along with the Homestead Act and the Pacific Railroad Bill as "three measures of Republican policy which admirably harmonize with each other."

[32] The comparison is made explicit by Rep. John L. Dawson (Dem., Pa.), in his defense of the Homestead Act (*Cong. Globe*, 33 Cong., 1 sess., App., 180, Feb. 15, 1854), and by Andrew Johnson (*ibid.*, 35 Cong., 1 sess., 2266–2267, May 20, 1858).

that they encouraged land speculation rather than railroad construction, and that grants, in any case, were unnecessary to secure construction. Several champions of the settler implicitly rejected the notion that railroads *had* a developmental function, insisting that settlement prior to construction would create both demand and support for the iron rails.[33] Congressmen from the Far West betrayed understandable exasperation over the reformers' assumption that settlement was likely to precede the railroad in areas remote from any other sort of cheap transportation.

The discussion of a proposed grant to the Portland and Astoria Railroad, in April 1870, provides a comprehensive illustration of the dilemmas involved. In the course of the debate, Representative William S. Holman of Indiana described the threat of railroad monopoly to the actual settler in darkest terms. Representative Thomas A. Fitch of Nevada artfully deflected the argument from the utility of land grants to the utility of railroads.[34] He declaimed:

A settler who objects to railroads! Sir, there is no such settler in reality.

Hence, horrible shadow! Unreal mockery, hence!

Sir, there are millions upon millions of acres of rich lands all over the United States . . . through which no railroad passes or is projected. If there be those in Ohio or New York or New England or Indiana who contemplate immigration to some place where they cannot market the fruits of their industry; if there be those who

[33] Rep. Timothy L. Jenkins (Dem., N.Y.), *Cong. Globe*, 32 Cong., 1 sess., App., 429–430, April 14, 1852; Sen. George E. Pugh (Dem., Ohio), *ibid.*, 35 Cong., 1 sess., 2240, May 19, 1855 (Pugh predicted that by the grant system "you will never make a railroad until the afternoon of the day of judgment"); Sen. Albert G. Brown (Dem., Miss.), *ibid.*, 35 Cong., 2 sess., 329, Jan. 18, 1854; Rep. Holman, *ibid.*, 41 Cong., 2 sess., App., 311, April 29, 1870.

[34] Holman's speech is in *Cong. Globe*, 41 Cong., 2 sess., App., 310–312, April 29, 1870; Fitch's is in *ibid.*, 41 Cong., 2 sess., 3105–3107. The speech of Sargent, seconding Fitch, is on page 3104 of the same volume. For Sargent's connections, see R. F. Radebough to J. W. Sprague, Feb. 3, 1882, Henry Villard Papers, Houghton Library, Harvard University.

prefer to toil over the sandy desert or the muddy prairie in stage or wagon rather than be whirled along by a monopoly on an iron road . . . they can obtain the amplest opportunity for the gratification of their fancies. I do not believe there are a hundred such men in the country. I do not think there are five.

Like most champions of the iron horse, Fitch saw the railroad as opening up far more than an avenue of commerce or a "fee simple empire" of small farmers. For him, agriculture was but one aspect of the potential of virgin lands:

The forests of Oregon, and Washington, and Eastern California; the pastures of Nevada, and Utah, and Colorado, and Wyoming; the prairies of Kansas, and Nebraska, and Dakota, and New Mexico, and Arizona [*sic*]; the mineral wealth of the Sierras and Rocky mountains—all these are spread out in unclaimed and unavailable affluence. There are beds of salt and soda, and lakes of borax and sulphur, and mountains veined with silver and gold and copper and lead. There is opportunity for almost indefinite expansion of all the industrial pursuits of man. Virgin fields and home markets await the husbandman. Unused powers and equable climate invite the manufacturer. The Indies and the northern seas open untried ventures to the merchant. New combinations of metals demand the assayer's crucible. The application of new remedies to old diseases and old principles to new conditions challenge physician and lawyer. Yosemite defies the artist's pencil. Shasta woos the poet's lyre. The ruins of empire puzzle the antiquarian's research, and the promise of empire fires the philosopher's thought.

Representative Aaron A. Sargent, a San Francisco attorney closely allied with Collis P. Huntington in both business and politics, seconded Fitch by making explicit the assumptions on which they justified deflecting the discussion from the usefulness of grants to the usefulness of railroads: "Unless railroads are a curse any means to secure them that does not cripple our resources or oppress our people should be employed." Limiting the price railroads might charge for land was a more realistic way to protect the settler than refusing grants to railroads altogether.

The Portland and Astoria controversy has additional interest because in one respect Holman and Fitch were rarities in the annals of Congress. They were virtually the only legislative spokesmen of their period to question explicitly the prevalent assumption that policies truly designed to enhance the nation's wealth would fail to promote the social and economic equality of its citizens and strengthen its political institutions.

Holman acknowledged that in some instances rapid railroad-building *might* lead to more rapid accumulation of wealth. But he insisted that if inequality accompanied economic development, such development was unhealthy and should be avoided. Not the size of the national product but its equal division was the test of a good society.

Fitch, on the other hand, included in his defense of the railroad a defense of "monopoly" unique in the congressional land debates of his era. "Whether in social or political life, it is true that 'in union there is strength.' There seems no adequate way of centralizing human power so as to effect development or accomplish great results without more or less of monopoly. If this be the disease of an advanced civilization, there should be some better and more philosophical remedy than to kill the patient in order to get rid of the complaint."

This exchange recalls us to a second major theme of the debates. Congressmen were not merely economists; they were *political* economists; for them wealth was the substratum upon which to erect a republican polity of equal, independent, and prosperous citizens.

Congressional statesmen spoke of empire; yet the structure they would raise with western materials was not an empire in the bad old tradition which had afflicted Europe since the demise of republican Rome. Rather, the liberal utopia that congressmen projected for the West was conceived as being in polar opposition to what they perceived as the social, political, and economic institutions of the Old World. Their debates on land policy echo the timeless rhetorical contest of American liberalism with the ghosts of monarchy, aristocracy, and feudalism.[35]

In their capacity as statesmen, the legislators assessed the issue in the public-land debates as nothing less than the role American republicanism was to play in the drama of world history. Their perspective was at once sweeping and selective. They found their usable past in certain favored locations. To the Jews and the Spartans they occasionally accorded the character of philosophers teaching by example.[36] Homestead advocates of the 1850's, especially, made use of the pseudo history of man's natural right to property and the transformation of this natural right into a civil prerogative of man-in-society.[37] But Rome and feudal Europe, together with England and Ireland past and present, supplied the main historical frame of reference.

When the Thirty-second Congress took up the homestead bill, the reputation of the Gracchi became a living issue.[38] Representative Richard J. Bowie, a Maryland Whig, pronounced that agrarian reforms looking to the equal division of lands had led to the decay of the Roman Republic. With much flourishing of Barthold Niebuhr's *Lectures on Roman History*, defenders of free homesteads and of Roman reformers insisted that the at-

---

[35] Cf. Louis Hartz, *The Liberal Tradition in America: An Interpretation of American Political Thought since the Revolution* (New York, 1955).

[36] Sen. Richard M. Johnson (Dem., Ky.), *Register*, 20 Cong., 1 sess., IV, 573, April 1, 1828; Benton, *ibid.*, 21 Cong., 1 sess., VI, 22, Jan. 18, 1830; Sen. John Pettit (Dem., Ind.), *Cong. Globe*, 33 Cong., 1 sess., 930, April 18, 1854.

[37] Sen. Isaac P. Walker, *Cong. Globe*, 31 Cong., 1 sess., 1570, Aug. 18, 1850; Rep. Joseph Cable (Dem., Ohio), *ibid.*, 32 Cong., 1 sess., App., 297, March 10, 1852; Rep. Grow (Free Soil, Pa.), *ibid.*, 427, March 30, 1852. Reformer Gerrit Smith (Abolitionist, N.Y.) asserted that man had no natural right to property in land, only to its use (*ibid.*, 33 Cong., 1 sess., App., 208, Feb. 21, 1854). Smith was one of the largest landowners in New York.

[38] *Cong. Globe*, 32 Cong., 2 sess., App., 479–492, April 26, 1852.

tempt of the Gracchi to revive the Licinian laws by dividing land among the plebs might, if it had been successful, have saved the decadent republic. The failure of the Gracchi portended the fall of Rome, for patricians monopolized the land, and the plebeians, having no stake in the country, refused to defend it from its enemies.

Congressmen already knew that the fall of the Roman Empire had brought no relief to the dispossessed, for the feudal system which succeeded it was but "a cunningly devised scheme to rob the great body of the people of their just and legitimate interest in the landed estate of the country, and thereby build up an aristocracy upon the ruins of popular liberty." Even yet, asserted Missouri Democrat and historian James B. Bowlin in 1844, the feudal land system "constitutes the props to uphold the monarchies of the Old World." [39]

Fortunately for mankind, the policy of monarchs in dealing with their New World possessions was "diametrically opposed to the system of policy adopted at home." To encourage emigration and settlement, feudal autocrats made liberal donations of land to emigrants. "The effect of it," Bowlin asserted," was to inculcate ideas of independence in the great body of the people, elevating their moral sentiments, and arousing their innate love of liberty, until it resulted in stretching a line of republics from the St. Laurence [*sic*] to the Rio de la Plata."

Here in the New World, statesmen could perpetuate both republican liberty and the republic itself only by continuing to follow a policy "diametrically opposed" to that of the Old World monarchs on their home ground. Representative Orlando B. Ficklin of Illinois expanded this theme:

It is a cardinal and sound principle of political economy, that, in a republican government, the people, the masses, should, as far as possible, be encouraged in their laudable desires to become owners of the soil. The relation of landlord and tenant is not favorable to

[39] *Ibid.*, 29 Cong., 1 sess., 1059–1062, July 6, 1846.

the growth or maintenance of free principles. The constant aim of monarchies is to build up a landed and moneyed aristocracy; to accumulate wealth and power in the hands of the few; to create distinctions and orders in society; to make the poor laborer a mere serf of his wealthy employer: and a policy precisely opposite to that should be adopted by us. The claim of the general government to the lands within the limits of the respective States should be extinguished as speedily as is practicable, and sound policy requires that they should pass at an early day in the hands of the actual settler. The moment the citizen becomes a freeholder, his ties to his country and its institutions are increased. He has his home, his fireside, and his personal liberty and security, to protect and defend.[40]

Not only would distributing land give the freeholder a stake in society and an urge to defend his country; it would insure his political freedom. Representative Bowlin, our historian of feudalism, argued the case as follows: "It is the inevitable destiny of nations to be controlled by proprietors of the soil, and the government is free or despotic, just in proportion to the number of its rulers, or participants in political privileges. If you wish to preserve and perpetuate its democratic form, you must pursue a policy tending to disseminate the lands amongst the largest possible number of people in the state."[41]

The land-reform movement of the 1840's and 1850's brought proponents of free lands into contact with land reformers from England and Ireland. The Irish famine of 1846 and subsequent Irish emigration to the United States seemed a drastic demonstration of the evils of land monopoly and the opportunity of the New World to counter them. England became the exemplary monarchy of modern times, and Ireland its unexemplary victim. Statistical comparisons of Ireland, England, and the United States with respect to the numbers of freeholders, tenants, and large estates abound in debates on the graduation and homestead acts.

[40] *Ibid.*, 28 Cong., 2 sess., 51–52, Dec. 19, 1844.
[41] *Ibid.*, 29 Cong., 1 sess., 1059–1062, July 6, 1846.

The Democratic platform of 1844 had promised cheap lands along with free trade as part of its republican program. In the year of the great famine, the proposal to graduate the price of lands was introduced into both houses of Congress for the first time as an administration measure. This measure provided the occasion for the historical reflections of Democrats Bowlin and Ficklin, cited above, while Representative John A. McClernand of Illinois, House sponsor of the bill, cited the modern example of the Irish as a warning of the evils of monopoly:

In our own time we have seen that the monopolies and perpetuities of land, aggravated by the evil of non-resident proprietorships, have brought upon Ireland a series of calamities little less desolating than the judgment of heaven denounced against the contumacious Egyptians. . . . Her population is divided by faction and hunted down like wild beasts; her prisons and scaffolds are crowded with victims of despair, and her poorhouses thronged with paupers.[42]

England herself illustrated not only the woes of tenancy, but the exacerbated ills of an industrial society plagued by low wages and unemployment on the one hand and by land monopoly on the other. Stating the case for free homesteads in 1851, Milwaukee Democrat Isaac P. Walker contrasted the situation of the American worker with that of his English counterpart. The American worker displaced by a machine could resort to the public lands; the British wage slave enjoyed no such alternative. In England since the time of Henry VIII, "while machinery has usurped the province of human labor, and cut off that source of human subsistence, legislation and land monopoly have cut off the only other—a resort to the bosom of the earth." [43]

When general access to landed property is equated with lib-

[42] This speech was made in the first session of the Twenty-ninth Congress, July 10, 1846. It is printed in *Cong. Globe*, 29 Cong., 2 sess., *App.*, 33–39.

[43] *Ibid.*, 31 Cong., 2 sess., App., 79, Jan. 14, 15, 1851. Cf. J. L. Dawson (Dem., Pa), *ibid.*, 32 Cong., 1 sess., App., 260, March 3, 1852.

erty, the safety valve of free lands becomes more than a means of elevating the wages of labor. On his own land, the former tenant or laborer can become wealthy and independent. As dependency and tyranny breed rebellion, independence and liberty guarantee public tranquillity. Revolutions in France and strikes in New York alike served to remind statesmen of the importance of making land free to the people. Where it was not, industrialization threatened to result in both poverty and tyranny.[44]

The contrast between America and Ireland, England, or feudal Europe was not drawn merely for the sake of fatuous self-congratulation. "Europe" for Americans was more than a negative reference term; it was a warning and perhaps a portent. If wise policy, "diametrically opposed" to that of historic and contemporary tyrants, could avoid poverty, inequality, tyranny, and rebellion, a foolish policy, analogous to that of the despot, would remake America in the image of Europe. Wisely distributed, the lands of the West might—did—offer history's greatest proving ground for liberal principles. Foolishly squandered, they could become a tragic arena in which the social mechanisms of progress shifted into reverse. The test of foolish policy was the appearance on the scene of monopolists possessed with the evil spirits of feudal autocrats. The "aristocratic" speculator, the railroad or timber "baron," the cattle "king"—all threatened with their relentless avarice to recapitulate the fall of republican liberty under the grasping tyranny of the robber barons of an earlier age.

Democrat Thomas Metcalfe, of Kentucky, pointed out the danger as early as February 1821. Monopolizing of land in Europe had enabled "the few to bind the many in chains of arbitrary and despotic rule . . . . Will not the same causes produce the same effects? And what is the difference, whether your landed domain, this joint inheritance of all, shall be seized upon

[44] Rep. Chandler (Whig, Pa.), *ibid.*, 32 Cong., 1 sess., 1022, April 8, 1852.

by military force, by unjust laws, or by the magic power of cash in hand." [45]

As long as government could compete in the market with lesser monopolists, it could counter Europeanization by making land available to settlers. Once the government's lands had been taken, however, the monopolists could take over. Thus land reformers who wanted to preserve the safety valve anticipated the Superintendent of the Census Bureau by two generations in predicting the end of the "frontier," and class war as a consequence.

Senator Robert J. Walker of Mississippi, presenting the first proposal to restrict the sale of land to "actual settlers" and to them alone, foresaw in 1837 the imminent and fatal disappearance of the frontier:

In vain shall we have struck down the feudal system, with its accompanying relation of lord and vassal, if we create and continue here this worse than feudal vassalage, this system of American landlords, engrossing millions of acres, and regulating the terms of sale or settlement. In vain shall we have abolished the system of primogeniture and entailments, as calculated to create landed monopolies, if we sustain the existing policy, by which a few capitalists may engross in a single year the ownership of States, and control the destiny of millions. . . . Must not this create here a landed aristocracy, without title, but more wealthy and powerful than the sinking nobility of England? . . . It will certainly introduce into the new States the system of landlord and tenant. . . . It will establish a relation of abject dependence on the one hand, and tyrannical power on the other. It will impoverish the many, and enrich the few. It will create a war of capital against labor, of the producer against the non-producer, of the cultivator against the speculator; a war in which this government will be arrayed on the side of the speculator. [46]

By the time free-homestead bills were receiving serious con-

[45] *Annals of Cong.*, 16 Cong., 2 sess., 1231, Feb. 26, 1821.

[46] For versions of Walker's bill, see *Cong. Globe*, 24 Cong., 2 sess., XIII, 204, Jan. 2, 1837; 427, Jan. 14, 1837; and 726, Feb. 7, 1837. For his speech, see *ibid.*, 420–421, Jan. 14, 1837.

gressional attention, champions of the safety valve had decided that the very "system of land traffic" entailed in selling land on the open market had been "imported to this country from Europe." [47] Moreover, since the revolutions of 1848, Europeans were appearing on the scene not merely as possessing spirits, but in person. "The expelled aristocracy of European despotisms are buying up our lands for speculation, while American republicans are *homeless*." [48]

Almost simultaneously, a new and more threatening native monopolist had also entered the picture: the railroad. The convening of the Thirty-first Congress in December 1849 saw the introduction of scores of bills for donating land to railroads. Land reformers regarded the railroad corporations as doubly evil, for unlike individuals, corporations were perpetual. Thus, in their independence from the individual life cycle, they threatened to resurrect the evils of primogeniture and entail. [49] These new monsters did not even compete with the settler in the market place. They secured their princely grants directly, by corrupting Congress itself. "Class legislation and favoritism" seemed to the American democrat still more inexcusable in the United States than in Europe, "for here you *profess* the doctrine of *equality*." [50]

In 1859, after thirteen apparently fruitless years of agitation for free homesteads, Senator Andrew Johnson of Tennessee exploded over the Pacific Railway bill:

[47] Petition presented by Salmon P. Chase (Free Soil, Dem., Ohio), from 1500 citizens of Cincinnati, *Cong. Globe*, 31 Cong., 1 sess., 469, Mar. 5, 1850.

[48] Petition "from citizens of the U.S.," presented by Sen. Isaac P. Walker, *ibid.*, 196, Jan. 21, 1850.

[49] Sen. A. O. P. Nicholson (Tenn.), *ibid.*, 35 Cong., 1 sess., 1223, March 19, 1860; Sen. Allen G. Thurman (Dem., Ohio), *ibid.*, 41 Cong., 2 sess., App., 113, Feb. 19, 1870. For the proposed grants, see *ibid.*, 31 Cong., 1 sess., xix, l–li.

[50] Sen. Isaac P. Walker, *Cong. Globe*, 31 Cong., 2 sess., App., 76, Jan. 14, 15, 1851.

Two thousand miles long and twenty miles wide of the public land, are to go at one single sweep! . . . There is not much difference between monopolies and corporations at home, and foreign powers abroad, especially if they are monarchical. . . . England, proud and potent as she is, . . . has only an area of fifty thousand square miles upon which she operates; but, at a single grant, the Congress is prepared to give away the foundation of an empire to a railroad company.[51]

After Johnson's homestead proposal and his own Agricultural College Act had both been adopted by a generous Republican Congress, Representative Justin Smith Morrill of Vermont was able to protest with a gentler irony. In the discussion of a grant to one of the Wisconsin railroads, he suggested, "In view of the immense extent of the National territory proposed to be given away, I ask the gentleman from Wisconsin whether he has any objection to having a clause inserted providing that slavery or involuntary servitude shall not be allowed therein." [52]

The reporter records that Lincoln's second Congress greeted that good-humored suggestion with appropriate "Laughter." But to postwar critics like Representative George W. Julian of Indiana, the association of railroad grants with slavery was no joke. Having put down the rebellion of the autocrats whose votes and vituperation had for so long frustrated the advocates of free soil for free men, having liberated their slaves and guaranteed them a perpetual republican polity by reserving *southern* public lands exclusively for homesteaders, Julian and his fellow reformers found the lords of the locomotive carrying on in the good old tyrannical tradition of the lords of the lash. Appraising a proposal to restore a prewar land grant to "those rebels" who owned the New Orleans and Opelousas Railroad, Julian quoted this bitter comment from an agent of the Freedmen's Bureau in Louisiana. "It seems to me very inconsistent for a Congress that

[51] *Ibid.*, 35 Cong., 2 sess., 582, Jan. 25, 1859. Cf. Johnson, *ibid.*, 32 Cong., 1 sess., 312, Jan. 23, 1851.
[52] *Ibid.*, 38 Cong., 1 sess., 1887, April 26, 1864.

talked of confiscating plantations for the benefit of freedmen to give away the only available land to a company of speculators under the pretext that northern capitalists are interested in it." [53] Fighting yet another grant to a transcontinental, Julian spelled out the parallel between slaveholding capitalists and railroad capitalists:

The railway, as one of the great forces of American politics, is new; but in this age of marvelous activities and commercial greed it already represents a larger moneyed interest than that through which three hundred thousand slaveholders so long and so absolutely governed the country. It took generations to limit the baron's prerogative by law, but in less than twenty years the law has been made the servant to do the bidding of the railway.[54]

Julian and his fellow Hoosier, William S. Holman, were feudalism's principal foes in the post–Civil War generation. In the sixties, Holman carried his share of the rhetorical burden in the battle against further grants to railroads; in the eighties he led the movement for forfeiture of unearned grants. Born in 1822, Holman had begun his congressional career in 1859 and for forty years served as a Democrat.[55] His imagery recalls that of Andrew Johnson and other early champions of the Homestead Act. He was thoroughly enamored of the allegedly egalitarian and agrarian society of the Mississippi Valley; and his arguments imply that while broad acres determined republican polity in the Midwest, perverse legislation was converting more recent frontiers into an economic base for aristocratic tyranny.

Holman's assumptions are revealed in the 1870 debate over the grant to the Portland and Astoria:

How strangely, sir, does Congress imitate the policy of monarchies! The ruthless conquerors of the middle ages partitioned out countries

[53] *Ibid.*, 40 Cong., 2 sess., 310–311, Dec. 20, 1867.

[54] *Ibid.*, 41 Cong., 3 sess., App., 194, Feb. 23, 1871.

[55] *Biographical Directory*, 1324. Holman's resolutions for forfeiture of unearned grants and reserving lands to homesteaders are in *Cong. Record*, 48 Cong., 1 sess., 546, Jan. 21, 1884.

and principalities to their favorites. . . . Shall America, the last and only hope of free government upon God's green earth, in the mad zeal for amassing wealth, imitate the feudalism by which Europe has been crushed for fifteen centuries, which in the monopoly of lands has built up the stately palace to frown down upon millions of huts, the abodes of misery and poverty? . . . The common safety was the specious arrangement of the old monopolists; the speedy development of countless wealth is the delusive argument of the new.

. . . The great states of the Allegheny mountains, the great states extending from the Wabash and the Mississippi rivers, were in the main built up under a different policy—the policy of individual enterprise. I venture to say that a very casual observation will convince any gentleman that a country so settled shows more equal distribution of land and wealth and a more substantial body of citizens, each cultivating his own homestead, than can be found in those sections of the country further west and northwest which have been settled under the influence of great monopolies.[56]

In praise of tradition, Holman followed the convention of the fifties in citing not only the unhappy history of Rome, "so familiar to us all in our boyhood," but the words of that "grand old Republican of the last age," Andrew Jackson: " 'It is not in a splendid Government, supported by powerful monopolies and aristocratic establishments that our people will find happiness or their liberties protection, but in a plain system, void of pomp, protecting all and granting favors to none.' "[57]

To keep government true to republicanism, Holman advocated not only the forfeiture of railroad grants, but the confining of the public lands to homesteaders and the repeal of all laws—including the Pre-emption Act, the Desert Land Act, and the Timber Culture Act—which permitted the acquisition of non-mineral land by anyone by any other means than homesteading. Characteristically, he pictured the corporations and other specu-

[56] *Cong., Globe,* 41 Cong., 2 sess., App., 311–312, April 24, 1870.

[57] Cf. Andrew Johnson, *Cong. Globe,* 31 Cong., 1 sess., 1449, July 25, 1850; Grow, *ibid.,* 35 Cong., 2 sess., 613, Jan. 26, 1859, and 36 Cong., 1 sess., App., 129, Feb. 29, 1860.

lators as shutting off the safety valve of free lands: "We seek year after year to exhaust the public domain, as if unconscious that we but hasten on that period which is to test the permanency of our own free institutions." [58]

Holman's was assuredly an "agrarian" ideology as well as a liberal one; some of his speeches appear to imply that land unfit for agriculture is fit for nothing. Some of the railroad forfeitures he advocated received support from owners of roads that were competitors of the roads he intended to punish.[59] In this context, one might agree with Henry Nash Smith that agrarian ideology was employed to serve special interests other than those of the farmer. Reformers and special pleaders sometimes shared objectives; it does not prove that agrarian ideology served exclusively to inhibit land reform. Holman was in his own view and in the view of his contemporaries a land reformer, an enemy rather than a champion of the "interests." On occasion, his archaic ideology—which was both agrarian and petty-bourgeois—rendered him an unwitting tool of one set of special corporate interests against another. But one might also speculate that the principal comfort Hoosier constituents could draw from their congressmen's ceaseless mental fight with commercial feudalism was the shared conviction that the center of that liberal utopia to which all the world aspired was located somewhere between Aurora and Centerville, Indiana.[60]

By the 1880's, evidence that conspirators had nearly succeeded in closing the safety valve lay everywhere at hand. While immigrants crowded the East and strikes increased and multi-

[58] *Cong. Record*, 47 Cong., 2 sess., 3136–3137, Feb. 22, 1883.
[59] See, for example, editorials in the Seattle *Weekly Chronicle*, Feb. 3, 1882, and the Albany *Argus*, Feb. 10, 1882, in Henry Villard Papers.
[60] For praise of Indiana, Illinois, and Ohio, see *Cong. Record*, 38 Cong., 1 sess., 2035, May 2, 1864. Holman represented Aurora; Julian, Centerville (*Biographical Directory*, 310). Julian did apparently offer his services to the Northern Pacific in 1881; perhaps ungratefully, they informed him that he was not needed. See Henry Villard to Hon. George W. Julian, May 23, 1881, Villard Papers.

plied, railroads and cattle kings battled squatters, lumber barons defeated the reserving of southern pinelands for the home-steader, and irrigation companies threatened monopoly of the water on which small farmers of the arid region must wholly depend. In 1880, the superintendent of the Census Bureau for the first time published statistics on tenancy throughout the country, adding urgency to the belief that America was degen-erating into "almost European conditions." Congressmen quoted Henry George, whose testimony before the Senate Committee on Education and Labor in 1883 reiterated the assertions of his *Progress and Poverty* and confirmed congressional notions of the interdependence of landlordism and exploitation.[61] Now the oft-told tales of Ireland's woes were accompanied, not by self-congratulatory estimates of the proportion of freeholders in the American population, but by gloomy statistics of alien landhold-ings and the burgeoning of bonanza estates: "With all the curses we have heard heaped upon the land system of England, and the land monopoly of England and Wales, it is no comparison to our own. The great landholders of England are mere 'pygmies' when compared with our 'giants.' " [62]

A sense of the comprehensive encroachment on freedom by monopoly that was associated with the demise of the public domain and the Europeanization of American institutions was expressed also by congressmen of the eighties who coupled the

[61] John J. O'Neill (Dem., Mo.), *Cong. Record*, 48 Cong., 2 sess., 867, Jan. 20, 1885 (O'Neill was arguing on behalf of opening the Indian Territory); Rep. James H. Hopkins. (Dem., Pa.), *ibid.*, 48 Cong., 2 sess., App., 52, Feb. 18, 1885; Sen. Henry W. Blair (Rep., N.H.), *ibid.*, 49 Cong., 1 sess., 6000–6002, June 22, 1886. Compare the more sanguine evaluation of statistics on landholding and tenancy by Sen. Henry M. Teller (Rep., Colo.), *ibid.*, 49 Cong., 1 sess., 5956–5957, June 21, 1886, and the reply by Sen. Wilkinson Call (Dem., Fla.), *ibid.*, 590.

[62] Rep. Strother M. Stockslager (Dem., Ind.), *ibid.*, 48 Cong., 2 sess., App., 136–139, March 2, 1885. Stockslager became Assistant Commis-sioner of the General Land Office, and in 1888–1889, Commissioner (*Biographical Directory*, 1869). Cf. Rep. Charles B. Lore (Dem., Del.), *Cong. Record*, 48 Cong., 1 sess., 4794, June 3, 1884.

cattle and railroad kings with the robber barons of industry and finance. In June 1884, Congressman Poindexter Dunn of Arkansas supported the bill to suppress illegal fencing on the public lands with a desperate appeal for the vanishing safety valve:

Sir, the evil of the day is the tendency of the great associations of wealth to crowd out individual efforts from all the remunerative industries of the country. I know of no life today more inviting or more fascinating and promising to the poor man than to become a cattle-raiser on the great plains of the West, but he is absolutely about to be forced out of it by great associations of wealth now rapidly occupying that whole country. . . .

Already these huge associations of wealth have possessed the whole vast volume of our transportation and commerce, . . . the banking and currency of the country. . . . In the form of manufacturing associations they have possessed themselves of a dangerous power of insensible and stealthy taxation. . . . They have possessed themselves of vast tracts of the public domain, sufficient in extent for an empire, which they hold for speculation or sell slowly on hard and oppressive terms which practically exclude the poor from it. They have possessed themselves of nearly all the precious-metal and other mineral and coal lands in the country, and hold them as in the grip of a giant. They have possessed themselves of nearly all the valuble timber lands of the country, and now comes the last act in the drama in this effort to seize without right or law the vast arid plains of the West. . . . Their all-grasping hands are laid upon the whole earth and all the "riches thereof."

Sir, they have closed and are rapidly closing all the avenues to individual effort and enterprise, and soon there will be left no hope to man except as the tenant, servant, or slave of these insatiate and merciless cormorants. They seek to seize upon the very elements of nature, and would tax the world for the privilege of using them.[63]

Despite their gloomy predictions, most land reformers pictured the closing of the safety valve—just over the horizon. Representative William McAdoo of Jersey City, who asserted in 1890 that "there was no public issue which so much aroused the

[63] Rep. Lore, *Cong. Record*, 48 Cong., 1 sess., 4781, June 3, 1884.

constituencies in the large industrial centers of the United States as the policy of taking back from the railroad companies lands which belonged to the people," and who compared the "lords of the locomotive" to "William the Conqueror in England, Oliver Cromwell in Ireland, the feudal barons in France," nonetheless predicted the closing of the public domain at the "close of the century." [64]

The end of free land was further postponed by the efforts of western congressmen to secure federal grants for irrigation and the enlargement of homesteads to accommodate dry-land farmers and petty stock raisers. Even as they promised that railroads, telephone and telegraph lines, and cities would follow the plow, these advocates exploited the antiurban rhetoric of the safety valve and promised homes for the poor and homeless far from the urban grind.[65] Perhaps they felt that urbanization was somehow sanitized as it moved west of the hundredth meridian, though they do not say this explicitly. It seems plausible that their simultaneous idealization of urban progress and agrarian simplicity represents not so much a cultural tension as a hospitable, if unintellectual, capacity for entertaining two convenient but contradictory ideas simultaneously. In their exploitation of western themes, far more than in Turner's celebrated essay, we may locate the cultural "end of the frontier." As Representative Aston Cokayne Shallenberger of Nebraska champions the Reclamation Act of 1902, we discover the final result of the devolution of the frontier myth from religion to art to sheer ideological eclecticism:

We will build for you broader and better and closer markets than any you can find beyond the seas. We will build up a nation of men

---

[64] *Ibid.*, 51 Cong., 1 sess., 7129, July 10, 1890.

[65] Rep. Thomas L. Glenn (Populist, Idaho), *Ibid.*, 57 Cong., 1 sess., 6748, June 13, 1902; Sen. Francis G. Newlands (Dem., Nev.), *ibid.*, 58 Cong., 2 sess., 3668, March 25, 1904; Rep. Harvey B. Ferguson (Dem., N.M.), *ibid.*, 63 Cong., 2 sess., App., 682–684, June 15, 1914; Rep. Denver S. Church (Dem., Calif.), *ibid.*, 64 Cong., 1 sess., 1130, Jan. 15, 1916.

better than any you can find upon the other side of the world, because they will be white men, men of the mountains and men of the plains, men who will buy your goods and fight your battles for you, men who can ride far and shoot straight.[66]

Representative Shallenberger, whose earlier analysis of the role of irrigation in the economy was in fact quite acute, did not explain how or why reclaimed westerners on their ten-acre irrigated farms would attempt to "ride far and shoot straight."

What of the opponents of land reform? Feudalism found no champions in their midst; monopoly, very few. Occasionally, during the homestead debates, they brought charges of "socialism" against the reformers and discovered their evil spirit in Louis Blanc.[67] Socialism found no defenders either; the reformers indignantly asserted that universal proprietorship was property's best friend and socialism's surest enemy.[68]

As both sides conceived of their own positions, the question at issue was the nature of true liberalism. All agreed that individually owned landed property constituted the foundation of the good society; though some insisted that "mechanical occupations" were both as dignified and as lucrative as farming. Nearly all agreed that the task of republican government was to convert public property into private as expeditiously as was consonant with that property's economic development. Opponents of free homesteads held that republican policy consisted of leaving men to acquire their own property through vocations freely chosen —a situation in which the virtuous, the industrious, and the

[66] *Ibid.*, 57 Cong., 1 sess., 6704. Cf. Rep. Charles Quincy Tirrell (Rep., Mass.), *ibid.*, 6698, June 12, 1902.

[67] Rep. Volney E. Howard (Dem., Texas), *Cong. Globe*, 32 Cong., 1 sess., 1279, May 6, 1852. A favorite term, harking back to Rome, was "agrarian." See for example Rep. Josiah Sutherland (Dem., N.Y.), *ibid.*, App., 738, June 23, 1852.

[68] Isaac P. Walker, *ibid.*, 31 Cong., 1 sess., 1570, Aug. 13, 1850; Sen. Lewis Cass (Dem., Mich.), *ibid.*, 32 Cong., 1 sess., App., 277, March 15, 1852; Rep. Orlando B. Ficklin (Dem., Ill.), *ibid.*, 1183, April 24, 1852.

educated would be successful.[69] Proponents agreed that the government was no almshouse; they simply insisted that donating land, the *means* of getting a livelihood, was not the same as providing a livelihood. Given the initially unequal distribution of income and the hazards of tenancy and unemployment, the blind justice of the market place could not be relied on to reward and develop industry, frugality, and fortitude with land. Government must do this. Dividing the common property of the nation among actual or aspiring cultivators was both the opportunity and the obligation of a republic that wanted to assure its citizens independent prosperity and itself perpetuity.[70]

Opponents of land reform rarely challenged the reformers' basic assumptions; they differed only on their application. The economic case for donations to the cultivator rested on twin assumptions: labor gives property value; private ownership inspires labor. This, in a nutshell, was precisely the defense of the speculator, the railroad, the lumberman, the cattleman, and the irrigation company.[71] "Mere" speculators or monopolists were

[69] Sen. Ewing (Ohio), *Register*, 22 Cong., 1 sess., VIII, 1140–1141, June 28, 1832; Sen. Alpheus Felch (Dem., Mich.), *Cong. Globe*, 31 Cong., 2 sess., App., 111, Jan. 13, 1851. Felch insisted that Americans would not become like Europeans, because of "the spirit and genius of our free government, the nature of our free institutions, the enterprising character of our population and the general legislation of government affecting the public weal." The abolition of primogeniture and entail alone, he insisted, was sufficient to prevent land monopoly. See below, n. 81.

[70] Isaac P. Walker, *Cong. Globe*, 31 Cong., 1 sess., 1570, Aug. 13, 1850; Sen. Felix Grundy (Dem., Ky.), *Register*, 22 Cong., 2 sess., IX, 117, Jan. 17, 1833; Rep. John A. Kelly (Dem., N.Y.), *Cong. Globe*, 35 Cong., 1 sess., App., 434, May 25, 1858.

[71] "Federal dominion over land is a barren sceptre, under which nothing grows; individual ownership is the fruitful sceptre, which makes the soil available for every public and for every private benefit," said Benton on behalf of the graduation bill in April 1838 (*Cong. Globe*, 25 Cong., 2 sess., App., 292). Benton also led the movement for selling rather than leasing reserved lead mines. See n. 77. Cf. Rep. Eben Newton (Whig, Ohio), *ibid.*, 32 Cong., 2 sess., App., 182, Feb. 5, 1853; Sen. R. J. Oglesby (Rep., Ill.), *Cong. Record*, 44 Cong., 1 sess., 1104, Feb.

acknowledged to be bad fellows, though an occasional forth-right Whig pointed out that the land dealers' operations were at least legal, while the squatters' were not.[72]

Before the passage of the Homestead Act, the economic contribution of the land dealer found only an occasional champion.[73] Critics of squatter-oriented policy simply denied that squatters were or would become good citizens. Rather, people who squatted on property not their own, people who had to be bribed and subsidized to go west, were lawless, shiftless, and unreliable. Most likely they themselves were speculators, or stand-ins for speculators.[74] To this assertion, reformers replied either that the actual cultivator had a right to sell the fruits of his *labor* in improved land (speculators of course sold barren land), or that if there were land for all, no one could speculate.[75]

But when the railroad, the cattleman, the lumberman, and the irrigation company were held to represent aristocracy, their defenders could simply allege that transportation, timber, beef, and water were necessities—even for settlers. No one attacked

16, 1876; Rep. Goldsmith W. Hewitt (Dem., Ala.), *ibid.*, 44 Cong., 1 sess., 3288, April 19, 1876; Rep. Cassidy (Dem., Nev.), *ibid.*, 48 Cong., 1 sess., 4776, June 3, 1884; Sen. Francis E. Warren (Rep., Wyo.), *ibid.*, 58 Cong., 2 sess., 4141, April 2, 1904.

[72] During the 1838 debates over pre-emption, Henry Clay's denunciations of the squatters were very strongly worded. His opponents rejoiced, his Whig colleagues in 1840 turned to the rhetoric more favorable to the squatter. For Clay's speeches, see *Cong. Globe*, 25 Cong., 2 sess., App., 137–142, Jan. 27–Jan. 30, 1838. Cf. Benton, *ibid.*, 143, Jan. 30, 1838; and Rep. Hubbard, (Dem., Ala.), *ibid.*, 26 Cong., 1 sess., App., 577, May 24, 1840.

[73] Sen. Ewing (Whig, Ohio), *ibid.*, 24 Cong., 2 sess., XIII, 536–548, Jan. 24, 1837; Sen. John Davis (Whig, Mass.), *ibid.*, 771, Feb. 9, 1837.

[74] Sen. Samuel Bell (N.H.), *Register*, 21 Cong., 1 sess., VI, 8, Jan. 4, 1830; Ewing, (Whig, Ohio), *Cong. Globe*, 24 Cong., 2 sess., XII, 536–548, Jan. 24, 1837. Rep. John Robertson (Whig, Va.), *Cong. Globe*, 25 Cong., 3 sess., App., 307, Feb., 1839; Rep. Isaac E. Morse (Dem., La.), 31 Cong., 1 sess., 1459, July 26, 1850; Sen. Felch, *ibid.*, 31 Cong., 2 sess., 106–109, Jan. 13, 1851.

[75] Sen. James Buchanan (Dem., Pa.), *Cong. Globe*, 25 Cong., 2 sess., App., 132, Jan. 27, 1838; Rep. Caleb Cushing (Dem., Mass.), *ibid.*

the "agrarian myth" so sardonically as did the opponents of land *reforms* designed to confine the West to the homesteader.[76]

Aside from the problem of whether steers and catchment basins could be accommodated on 160 acres, the chief difficulty land reformers faced was the fact that so long as a settler could sell, mortgage, or even lease his land, only the stroke of pen on contract was required to transform him into a speculator and subvert the whole program of confining the national domain to cultivators. Yet how could a group whose careers were dedicated to the eradication of feudalism commit their republican govenment to unfree tenure? They could not, and "radical" proposals to limit alienation, in common with programs for leasing such nonagricultural resources as lead, gold, silver, and the open range, were sooner or later defeated, on the high ground of principle, amid outraged references to entails, federal landlordism, and tyrannical officialdom.[77]

By the 1890's, a few congressmen from the arid states were frank to acknowledge that they preferred water from a monopolistic irrigation company to deserts monopolized by cactus and the federal government.[78] By the time of the Newlands Act of

[76] For a "patient" approach, and a critical but temperate review of the history of United States land policy, see Sen. Stewart, *Cong. Record*, 50 Cong., 1 sess., 3225–3228, April 23, 1888. Compare the treatment of Stewart in Wallace Stegner, *Beyond the Hundredth Meredian: John Wesley Powell and the Second Opening of the West* (Boston, 1962). See also Sen. James F. Wilson (Rep., Iowa), *Cong. Record*, June 3, 1884, 49 Cong., 1 sess., 4779; Rep. Cassidy (Dem., Nev.), *ibid.*; and Del. Smith (Dem., Ariz.), *ibid.*, 52 Cong., 1 sess., 5637, June 29, 1892.

[77] Benton, *Annals*, 17 Cong., 2 sess., 240, Feb. 14, 1823; Benton, *Register*, 19 Cong., 1 sess., 740, 747–748, May 16, 1826; Sen. Samuel McRoberts (Dem., Ill.), *Cong. Globe*, 27 Cong., 2 sess., 300, March 9, 1842; Sen. Felch (Dem., Mich.), *ibid.*, 31 Cong., 2 sess., 109, Jan. 13, 1851; Rep. James C. Dobbin (Dem., N.C.), *ibid.*, 29 Cong., 1 sess., App., 1095, July 7, 1846; Walker, *ibid.*, 31 Cong., 1 sess., 1572, Aug. 13, 1850; Dawson, (Dem., Pa.), *ibid.*, 33 Cong., 1 sess., App., 181, Feb. 14, 1854.

[78] Cf. Sen. J. Dolph (Rep., Ore.), *Cong. Record*, 52 Cong., 1 sess., 5145, June 8, 1892; Smith, (Dem., Ariz.), *Cong. Record*, 52 Cong., 1 sess., 5637, June 29, 1892.

1902 some of them were arguing the case for government monopoly against private monopoly.[79] Their resigning themselves to this state of affairs, as to the Rooseveltian policies of reserving timber and mineral resources, is an important chapter in the intellectual history of progressivism, but it will not be explored here.[80]

An extended discussion of ideologies should not, of course, be taken to imply that congressmen confined their consideration of land policy to mere abstractions. Despite their horror of feudal Europe and modern Ireland, many were quick to cite "successful" European precedents for policies they advocated. The history of irrigation from the beginning of civilization to the latest watering of an orange grove was an indispensable flourish in any well-rounded defense of a reclamation bill. Federal statesmen referred often to the experience of the states in experiments with land disposal, and to the outcome of earlier federal policies— though they seldom agreed as to what the experiments proved. By the 1880's, the work of irrigation technicians and the research findings of the Department of Agriculture were being discussed, often in highly technical detail. Congressional specialists in land problems, who were passionate political arithmeticians, deluged the House and Senate with endless columns of figures culled at their command by the overworked clerks of the General Land Office.

But when it came to interpreting this information and applying it to the rationalization of policy, congressmen, whatever their interest or their platform, were largely combined together in a liberal consensus. The antitheses freedom and feudalism,

[79] The requirement that *land* in irrigation projects be sold in small units to actual settlers, whether by private or public developers of water, was generally held to mitigate the charge of monopoly. Dolph, (Rep., Ore.), *Cong. Record*, 52 Cong., 1 sess., 5145, June 8, 1892. Sen. Newlands (Dem., Nev.), *Cong. Record*, 58 Cong., 2 sess., 3668, March 25, 1904; Sen. Thomas H. Carter (Rep., Mont.), *ibid.*, 60 Cong., 1 sess., 4214–4218, April 1, 1908.   [80] See n. 2.

variously construed, supplied the polar dimensions which gave meaning and direction to their rhetorical images of the West.[81]

What I have tried to argue here is that the common ideology of the parties to the debate over land policy is better termed "liberal" than "agrarian." What is bad is not commerce and industry, but monarchy and feudalism. What is good is not merely agriculture; it is competitive individual proprietorship. There is much antiurban rhetoric, but often it is ambivalent. Congressmen idealize rural life in the West while simultaneously predicting that westward expansion will bring flourishing cities to the mountains and the plains.

The liberal image of the West is conveyed in a series of antitheses between what is American and what is European. In Europe since the fall of Rome, the monopoly of land by aristocrats has bred an economic subservience of the majority that is reflected alike in political tyranny and mass poverty. Under industrial conditions, land monopoly fosters monopoly of economic and political power in the industrial corporation as well as in the rural aristocracy and increases the misery of the proletariat, both rural and urban. It has done so in England and Ireland, and may do so in the United States. To escape Europeanization— which is equated with tyranny, poverty, and class warfare—the United States must above all avoid land monopoly. It must maintain a system opposite to that of Europe, and thus constitute itself a polity of freeholders who are economically independent and politically sovereign.

In its economic aspect, the liberal consensus entails the assumption that rapid devolution of public property into private hands is an essential condition of economic development and that all policies must be tested by their contribution to the growth of national wealth. These assumptions pose key questions for policy-makers: whose private hands? how much? and how fast? It

[81] For a recent elaboration and application of the notion that people think in antitheses, see George A. Kelley, *The Psychology of Personal Constructs* (2 vols.; N.Y., 1955).

is on these questions that the parties divide, for the rhetoric of "development" is so all-encompassing that almost anyone's interest may be construed by a clever political arithmetician as meaning almost everyone's "development."

It is on the questions of who, how much, and when that crucial differences over values—as opposed to differences over appropriate means of achieving agreed-on ends—appear. Prior to the late 1840's, most of these differences center about the issue of rapid, as opposed to controlled, settlement of the West by small farmers. Whigs generally assert that a controlled and gradual development of the West will create stable communities populated by industrious and thrifty people and achieve a natural balance between the development of agriculture and the development of industry. They, together with a few southern Democrats, equate uncontrolled development with a shiftless population and an anarchic social order. Democrats argue that more rapid, less constrained development will accelerate the growth of national wealth and social equality; they view squatters, not as shiftless or anarchic, but as enterprising and brave.

Beginning with the debates over railroad grants in the 1840's and accelerating with the emergence of problems centering about the disposal of nonagricultural lands, a second difference in values appears. If economic development is the *sine qua non*, may the rancher or the railroad corporation or the timber baron have in some cases a claim superior to that of the small proprietor? Their advocates thought so. And now the price of rapid development appears to be, not anarchy, but monopoly, inequality, Europeanization. Or so land reformers like Julian and Holman see it. It is in their impassioned attacks upon commercial feudalism that we find expressed the belief in the antithesis of stability and development which so tortured the Whigs of an earlier era. But we find also, explicitly realized, that antithesis between headlong economic growth and stable economic *equality* that Marvin Meyers finds implicit in the ideology of the Jacksonians of the 1830's. The reformers, not the exploiters, of the post Civil War era are the true nostalgics; and they are a minority.

Thus it was not just agrarianism that was threatened by geographic conditions across the wide Missouri and by the coming of an industrial age. It was American liberalism itself, that self-annihilating set of principles enshrining at once free contract, free competition, free land, and equality. The safety valve of the frontier was a safety valve of liberalism; so long as land was there for the taking, Americans hoped that liberty to take it might produce equality among the takers. Congressional debates on land policy provide an instructive illustration of the gradual and painful discovery that the hope was illusory. Perhaps this discovery was the more painful precisely because "liberal" values were construed so starkly, in antithesis to values deemed "feudal" and "European." The demise of liberalism threatened not only the small farmer or businessman; it challenged persistent and widely held conceptions of American national identity.

Maine and Its Public Domain: Land Disposal on the Northeastern Frontier

DAVID C. SMITH

Nearly all historians of land policy have directed their attention to the federal public domain and its disposal. A complete story of the transfer of public lands into private hands would also have to take into consideration the land holdings of the original thirteen states, as well as the lands under the control of Tennessee, Vermont, and Texas, all of which had lands not technically part of the federal domain.

Lands held by the original thirteen states passed, by and large, quite quickly into private ownership.[1] Indeed, the disposition of the land is part of the colonial history of these states. Only one of the original thirteen had land to dispose of during the greater part of the nineteenth century and thus was in more or less direct competition with the federal government's land-disposal plans. That state was Massachusetts. The history of the disposal of the Massachusetts public domain, however, is really a story of

---

[1] An exception was Georgia, and the disposition of the Georgia lands, as well as the formation of a land policy for this southern state, is discussed in Milton Sidney Heath, *Constructive Liberalism: The Role of the State in Economic Development in Georgia to 1860* (Cambridge, Mass., 1954), chs. iv, v, vi.

the Maine public domain, since Maine split off from Massachusetts in 1819 and 1820.

The story of the Maine lands offers an opportunity to study the movement of land into private hands at a time when lands were a drug on the market. Maine, faced with internal pressures and competition from outside, was forced to resort to many different methods to attract settlers to its lands.

Among the methods utilized by this northern state were the adopting of a type of homestead law, the granting of lands to academies and other institutions of learning, the attracting of European immigrants by grants and gifts of land, and even the granting of a large tract of land to railroad promoters. All these efforts were undertaken in direct competition with the federal government, and although they served to transfer the land in question from public to private ownership, they did relatively little to fatten the treasury of the state or to attract much population.

The failure was not entirely due to the competition. The location in northern latitudes, the thinness of the soil, the lumbering economy, and the attraction of industrial developments elsewhere after 1860 all contributed to the failure of Maine's policy. It is the policy itself, and not so much its failure, which directly concerns us here.

Some of the area presently enclosed within the boundaries of the state of Maine was granted to prospective speculators and settlers before the Revolution. A line drawn due west from Portland would indicate on the south most of this land. After 1783 the ungranted land beckoned the citizens of Massachusetts as a solution to the monetary problems created by the war. A land office was set up, and sales of the northern lands commenced. The lands moved slowly, and in 1786 a lottery was started to raise money by disposing of some fifty townships between the Penobscot River and Passamaquoddy Bay areas. The lottery was only partially successful, as only 165,280 acres were disposed of by this method.[2]

[2] Oscar and Mary Flug Handlin, *Commonwealth: A Study of the Role*

With the lottery promotion, interest in the Maine woodlands did begin to rise. This interest was increased at first by the advertising efforts of General Henry Knox, who owned land from one of the original grants, and later by the purchase of 2,000,000 acres, half on the Kennebec River and half on the Penobscot River, by William Bingham of Philadelphia.[3] As a result many institutions, such as projected banks, canals, roads, and bridges applied for grants of land to be sold to defray construction costs, to provide working capital, or to set up endowment funds.[4] By 1820, Massachusetts had disposed of 6,070,638 acres, which added to the land (3,785,488 acres) disposed of before 1783, made a total of 9,856,126 acres. When Maine took control of its own destiny, about half the land area of the state had already gone into private hands.

In 1820 much of the land had not yet been surveyed. Indeed, according to Greenleaf's map, most of the area north of a line drawn from Magalloway to Vanceboro was unknown.[5] Initially Massachusetts offered the unsold land to Maine at a price that would have worked out to about $.023 per acre, or $188,922 for the 8,000,000 or so acres. Maine refused the offer, so until 1853, when the then remaining lands were purchased by Maine, a dual land policy was pursued, in which the land agents of both states had to participate.[6] The 1820 independence agreement had pro-

---

of Government in the American Economy (New York, 1947), 86–92, 225, on Massachusetts' policy toward her Maine lands.

[3] Frederick S. Allis, Jr., ed., *William Bingham's Maine Lands, 1790–1820*, Publications of the Colonial Society of Massachusetts, Collections, XXXVI, XXXVII (Boston, 1954).

[4] For educational grants, see H. C. Marr, "Grants of Lands to Academies in Massachusetts and Maine," *Essex Institute Historical Collections*, LXXXVIII (Salem, Mass., 1952), 28–47.

[5] M. Greenleaf, *Map of the State of Maine* (Portland, 1820, 1829). The 1829 map is easily accessible in facsimile in [Lillian Tschamler], *Report on the Public Reserved Lots* (Augusta, Me., 1963), in a pocket at the back of the pamphlet.

[6] Much of the remainder of this article is based on the records of the Maine Land Office, which are quite complete and are presently maintained in the office of the State Archivist in Augusta. When I used

vided for separation of the lands. Initially, in the first five ranges (the so-called settling lands) each state took every other township.[7] As the rest of the land was surveyed, the agents divided it in a similar fashion. Much of the correspondence between the land agents of the two states was concerned with which lands to survey, the division of the lands, the cost of maintenance of men in the field, road building, the prosecution of trespassers, and other such day-to-day problems of the Land Office.

Trespassing was the big problem. Over and over again the Maine land agent, who seemed at first to take the lead in the land business, wrote to his Massachusetts counterpart.[8] Trips were taken to Moosehead Lake, to the St. John River, and up the Kennebec, both for surveying purposes and for obtaining evidence of trespassing. In 1831, for instance, men were sent to Moosehead, across the portage to the Penobscot and to Chesuncook Lake, thence to Umbazooksus Lake to the Allagash portage, and down the Allagash to the St. John. They were instructed to find out what settlements had been made and by whose authority, what improvements were being contemplated, and on whose lands they were to be located. In addition the instructions went on, "You will observe the lakes, ponds, rivers,

---

them, they were located in the vault of the Forest Commission in Augusta. They were not in the best order, and every time I have had occasion to use them, I have found new materials. Basically they include letter books (in letterpress) of the Maine land agent for the years 1829–1835, 1850–1860, 1864–1867, deed books, survey notes, field notes, maps, books of bills paid, money received, advertisements placed, and so on. They also include a letter book (copies) "Massachusetts Land Agent to Maine Land Agent [and others], 1835–1850." Letters referred to are in this collection. Other materials will be cited as to location. I am indebted to Lillian Tschamler and Austin Wilkins (the present Forest Commissioner) for guidance in the use of these materials as well as space to work on several occasions.

[7] Greenleaf's 1829 map shows the division of lands in the settling ranges very well.

[8] Letters of Daniel Rose (Maine land agent) to George W. Coffin (Massachusetts land agent), October 9, 1829, and February 14 and April 25, 1831, are examples. Most of this correspondence occurred because of a trip by Rose through the north country in the summer of 1829.

and streams of water, the falls and millsites on them, and their capacity for navigation and floating of logs and timber." The surveyers were instructed to observe the geology of the area, the soil, the products of the soil, and "especially the pine and other valuable timber." [9]

Roads were built into the wilderness to ease the difficulty of access for prospective settlers.[10] The land agent attempted to get private investors to improve the Penobscot for log driving.[11] Border difficulties with the British were always part of the land agent's life.[12] In addition to all these matters the agent was concerned with selling the land as he was directed and with obtaining the proper stumpage payments on the state-owned lands. The bulk of his correspondence was concerned with these twin problems.[13]

Prior to 1824 little activity took place. In 1823 a legislative resolution had called for the sale to actual settlers in five-hundred-acre lots. The next year an act was passed that set up a policy to be followed with respect to the state lands. The land surveyed was to be designated in hundred-acre lots, with the first forty contracts in each town to go at thirty cents an acre,

[9] Rose to John G. Deane and Edward Kavanaugh, July 11, 1831.

[10] Rose to Eben Heald, June 13, 1831, describes first beginnings of a road from the Mattawamkeag River to the Aroostook area.

[11] Rose to Nathaniel Towers, July 29, 1831: "I think that the river might be so improved as to generally insure the getting down the logs from Chesuncook Lake in one year."

[12] Dennis Fairbanks to Rose, June 10, 1831; Rose to Samuel E. Smith, July 22, 1831, to John Webber, Feb. 23, 1832, to Moses Burley, Aug. 24, 1832; Coffin to John Davis, United States Senate, April 6, 1836: "I consider it of great consequence to the States as well as to the Provinces that this dispute should be brought to a close speedily."

[13] See, on the early period, Rose to William Bragg, April 14, 1829, to Hasen Mitchell, Dec. 21, 1829; to J. Wyman, Jan. 8, 1830; to Capt. David Sturgis, March 31, 1831; to Frederick N. Blish, April 12, 1831; to Stephen Varney, April 18, 1831; to Peleg Sprague, Nov. 5, 1831; to Robert F. Dunlap, July 27, 1832; to Ansyl C. Clark, Aug. 6, 1832; on stumpage, to William R. Miller, Nov. 1, 1832; to Samuel Westen, April 25, 1833. See also advertisements for a timber auction placed July 12, 1831.

payable half in cash and half in road labor. Settlers were to clear fifteen acres, plant ten in grass, and construct a house within the first four years. The rest of the land on each township was to go for sixty cents an acre, and additional purchases were allowed up to five hundred acres, with the provision that for all purchases of over three hundred acres the buyer was responsible for settling two extra persons.

These lands were denominated as "settling lands." They were located in the first five ranges of townships west of the eastern line of the state and north of the earlier purchases and grants. A second general category were designated as "timber lands"; they were located on ungranted land and mostly west of the settling lands. They were available only in five-hundred acre lots, with half of the payment due in cash, and the remainder in three equal installments. In addition, two hundred acres and a millsite would go to the first person building a saw and grist mill within three years after the opening of a township for settlement. The law also provided for the setting aside of a thousand acres in each township for reserved lots to be used for educational purposes. It provided, furthermore, for the protection of squatters' rights on the public lands.[14]

This basic law was modified fairly often, but not in a wholesale fashion. In 1825 prices were increased, and the land agent was instructed to dispose of meadow, hay, and waste land in mile-square lots, either at public auction or private sale; he was also allowed to sell timber "where it was decaying." In 1826 payment was allowed in three annual equal amounts, after a third had been paid in cash. The state retained a lien on the land. In 1828 the law was overhauled, and the duties of the land agent were more closely defined. The new law provided that no more than eight townships a year could be sold from the timber lands.

---

[14] *Public Laws, Maine, 1824*, ch. cclxxx, 993–997. The thousand-acre provision on the public lands dated to provisions in the 1786 lottery. See Ava Chadbourne, *History of Education in Maine* (Lancaster, Pa., 1936), for some account of their usage. Also see [Tschamler], *Report,* for the modern period.

The agent was to fix an upset, or minimum, price and hold a public auction; sales were limited to one township per person per year. The settling lands could also go at public auction to stimulate sales, with payments to be made in eight years, and with the principal due in quarterly annual payments the last four years. In 1831 the minimum price was established at fifty cents an acre, with four years' credit allowable. Stumpage permits could be granted for three years, but under strict regulation.

In 1835 the law was again modified. Townships were to be sold only after survey and lotting. The maps, plans, and field notes were to be open for all to inspect. Settling lands were to go to actual settlers only, at a minimum price of fifty cents an acre. These lands, however, could be commuted by road labor, so that they became a homestead grant, in fact. This introduction of the homestead principle, that is, that bona fide settlers should receive lands so that they would be attracted to the state, marks a victory for those who felt that agriculture would be the salvation of Maine. Little opposition was expressed to the new law, probably because the large lumber operators and speculators were purchasing their lands west of the settling townships.

The other sale provisions of the 1824 law were restated. Other lands were to go at public auction, but if unsold, the price could be lowered at the discretion of the land agent. Payments were to be made with one-fourth in cash and the rest in annual payments. No more than five townships a year were to be disposed of in this way. The settling lands were to be advertised in Boston, Concord, and all Maine newspapers. In 1838 the mill provision was reinstated.[15] In later years, as Maine lumbermen began to exert pressure to keep the state timber from the market

---

[15] *Public Laws, Maine, 1825,* ch. cccxvi, 1058–1059; *1826,* ch. ccclxvi, 1094–1096; *1828,* ch. cccxciii, 1160–1165; *1830,* ch. cdxc, 1261–1262; *1831,* ch. dx, 1298–1303; *1835,* ch. cxcii, 295–300; *1838,* ch. cccliv, 511. For convenience, citations to these laws will be in roman numerals. For a typical advertisement of the land agent see Franklin (County) *Register,* Oct. 3, 1841. This offered settling lands on T4R5, 5R6, 6R5, 8R5, 9R4, 9R6, 10R5, 11R5, 11R6, 12R3, 12R5, 13R4, FR2, ½HR2, and DR1. The land went in four yearly payments, with the first three in

in order to preserve higher prices, new laws usually applied only to sales of timber or stumpage.[16]

In 1850 the duties of the land agent and the regulations concerning the settling lands were rewritten. The most important provisions stated that the prospective entryman must be an American citizen, that two hundred acres was the total to be granted, and that they were to be paid for in road labor, not cash, at the rate of fifty cents an acre, with one-third due each year. The older provisions for the construction of houses and the clearing of fields were continued.[17] In 1853, Maine purchased the remaining lands from Massachusetts,[18] and after this time little

road labor and the fourth in cash. The settler had to build a house within four years and clear the land. If twenty persons would within three years erect a saw and grist mill in a town without one, they would get one extra lot each, and the company would get one for the mill. No person could obtain more than four lots. The agent said that a road was available to the Aroostook River and some water transportation was possible on the river. Mills had been erected in FR2, 9R4, and 11R5, and new mills were scheduled for 1842 on 9R6, 11R6, and DR1. As the agent said, "This is the best season ever and the Army post recently established means that new roads will be coming, . . . mail routes established, new markets opened for produce, and the settler will feel additional security from any border difficulty." Finally he indicated that with the fertile soil and the roads and mills "young men can with industry and economy secure for themselves an honorable competency." This advertisement also appeared in Maine newspapers such as the Calais *Advertiser*, Waldo *Signal*, Piscataquis *Herald*, *People's Press* (Norridgewock?), Kennebec *Journal*, Portland *Advertiser*, Oxford *Democrat*, York County *Herald*, and Lincoln *Telegraph*, and also in the New Hampshire *Statesman* and the Boston *Atlas*.

[16] *Public Laws, Maine, 1838*, ch. ccclix, 520–521; *1843*, ch. xxxi, 69–71; *1844*, ch. cxxix, 131–132; *Private and Special Laws, Maine, 1846*, ch. cdvii, 528. No permits were to be granted on the St. John or its tributary waters except where large supplies had already been moved into the woods. Also see *Legislative Resolve, Maine*, March 9, 1832, and *H. Doc.* 51, 1843, on stumpage permits and timber sales.

[17] *Public Laws, Maine, 1850*, ch. cxcvi, 193–196; ch. ccvi, 202–203.

[18] The relevant documents are *H. Doc.* 39, 1852; "Legislative Resolves, Maine, 1852," ch. cdxiii, printed in *Public and Special Laws, Maine, 1852*, 399; *1853*, ch. vi, 5, ch. lvii, 30–31, ch. lxiv, 33; *Resolves, Extra Session, 1853*, chs. lxxx, lxxxiii; and *H. Doc.* 12, 1854.

change took place in the basic policy. One change did come in 1853, when the state limited the sale of timberlands to ten township annually, and required sealed bids to be proffered with a tender of 10 per cent of the original purchase price. The terms were one-third down and the remainder in three annual payments. Stumpage was due at the state's figures during the time the land was in the process of conveyance. Private sale was possible, however, at the discretion of the land agent.[19]

How much land went into private hands from each category is difficult to say. Some of the records of the land office were lost in a fire in 1835, and before that time reports are sketchy. Also, before 1838 little distinction was made in reporting between settling lands and timber lands. Tables 8[20] and 9[21] give some idea of the sales and other business in the period 1824–1853.

[19] *Public Laws, Maine, 1853,* ch. xlvi, 49–50.

[20] This table is derived from a study of the *Reports,* Maine Land Agent (Augusta, Me., in the years involved); *H. Doc.* 38, 1843; and *Sen. Doc.* 12, 1853. The figures for value received include both money and valuation placed on road labor. Sometimes the land agents commuted the labor time in the reports and did not specify the actual cash. From 1842–1852 the split was cash $15,461.98, and road labor $16,102.68, making a total of $31,564.66.

[21] "Report of Commissioners Authorized to Purchase the Lands of Massachusetts Lying in the State of Maine," *Public Documents, Maine, 1853–4* (Augusta, 1855). Undivided lands sold in this same time amounted to 956,003 acres. In addition 100,958 acres of public reserved lands were disposed of by county commissioners from 1845–1850 when these lands were taken from the land agents and placed under the county jurisdiction. The total land disposal in this period was as follows:

Settling lands	134,799 acres	$ 79,286.73
Land sales	2,800,029	1,652,659.19
Undivided lands	956,003	875,778.90
Reserved lots	100,958	35,015.91
Timber and grass stumpage		507,005.62
Totals	3,991,789	$3,147,746.35

These figures differ slightly from those sometimes put forward, but my figures include only Maine lands and Maine money, and are only for the period 1820–1852, as far as I can identify it.

The tables show that Maine had fallen into the same trap as the federal government. Although it sought to sell or grant its lands to actual settlers and small holders, the bulk of the lands went into the hands of the great lumbermen and speculators.[22] Maine attempted to control this by limiting the acreage available

Table 8. The disposition of settling lands in Maine, 1838–1855

Year	Acreage	Value received
1838	12,827	$ 9,428.27
1839	6,642	4,903.88
1840	15,869	12,259.83
1841	24,183	16,251.12
1842	1,530	1,019.48
1843		4,157.51
1844		6,575.43
1845	(Total sales,	8,941.83
1846	1843–1852, in	2,523.21
1847	acres:	1,734.22
1848	58,152)	1,579.92
1849		767.65
1850		1,356.02
1851		2,141.81
1852		1,064.90
1853	(Year of transfer—no sales)	
1854	5,050	1,431.00
1855	10,546	4,150.45
Totals	134,799	$79,286.73

in any year, but the incongruity of a land policy that promoted speculation and advanced the interests of the wealthy through credit arrangements and large holdings effectively limited the population growth to the areas specifically named as settling towns.

The state did not go beyond its homestead policy however. Immigration to its lands was aided by the expenditure of just under $170,000 for road building from 1825 to 1849.[23] Many thought these roads would solve the problem of immigration. As

[22] "Deed Books," I-II, from my study of deeds granted before 1853.
[23] *H. Doc.* 17, 1849.

122

Table 9. Land sales in Maine, 1825–1852

Year	Acreage	Average price
1825	1,448	$ .84
1826	36,711	.50
1827	12,092	.40
1828	101,909	.22
1829	263,676	.31
1830	129,483	.21
1831	162,282	.28
1832	21,621	.68
1833	92,393	.66
1834	70,989	.42
1835	230,146	1.45
1836	2,630	.99
1837	3,274	1.66
1838	12,837	.71
1839	33,558	1.48
1840	18,050	.88
1841	17,868	.43
1842	1,661	.28
1843	147,657	.45
1844	48,459	.60
1845	47,310	.86
1846	105,625	.77
1847	101,220	.46
1848	145,708	.495
1849	342,913	.31
1850	39,823	.47
1851	310,802	.50
1852	297,413	. . .
Total	2,800,029	

one observer noted in 1837 when commenting on the completion of the survey for the proposed Canada road (a road still not built, incidentally):

The ease and novelty of the route, together with the romantic scenery of the lake [Moosehead], would make this a favorite tour for parties of pleasure and draw a large amount of travel through the state. This, however, is but of secondary consideration. Villages would spring up at each end of the lake, serving a neuclii [*sic*] around which in every direction, new settlements would cluster.

Hamlets would soon be scattered along the Penobscot to the borders of Canada and the fertile shores of the Chesuncook would be covered with cultivated farms.[24]

This comment was made just after the wild speculation of 1834 and 1835, a boom concerned primarily with privately owned land, and one which did not much affect public-domain sales but which, when it failed, did create a depression in both timber and land sales, as well as in timber values, in the state.[25] In fact, it was not until 1843 that the land agent could remark that settlement was prospering, although he was still complaining about squatting and trespassing.[26]

In his correspondence he was less sanguine. The land was good; he wanted to accommodate everyone; actual settlers would get preference; but, alas, his efforts met with "ill success." [27] To those who would bring settlers special help would be given.[28] Even trespassing was to be dealt with indulgently.[29]

The officials of Maine and Massachusetts met several times to coordinate their business. The most important occasion was in January of 1832. The land was all reclassified, but the agreement did not amount to much. Settlement still lagged.[30]

In 1842 it was estimated that 6,400,000 acres still remained

[24] Land Agent, *Report*, 1837 (Augusta, 1838), 5–6.

[25] See Richard Wood, *A History of Lumbering in Maine, 1820–1861* (Orono, Me., 1935), 74–82.

[26] Land Agent, *Report*, 1842, 1843 (Augusta, 1843, 1844). In 1850 (Augusta, 1851), he wrote, "Better Days are dawning."

[27] "Letter Books, 1829–1833," generally, and see Rose to Peleg Sprague, Nov. 5, 1831, for the quotation.

[28] Rose to Zebulon Bradley, Feb. 25, 1833, regarding land in T4, O.I.P. (Old Indian Purchase).

[29] Series of letters concerning trespass on T10, N.B.P.P. (North of Bingham's Penobscot Purchase) (present Forest City) and in the Schoodic River area generally (present St. Croix), March and April, 1833, especially Rose's instructions to Moses Burley, March 9, 1833.

[30] Maine Legislative Resolve, March 28, 1831; Massachusetts Legislative Resolve, June 22, 1831; Agreement, Daniel Rose and George Coffin, Jan. 19, 1832; Rose to Coffin, May 21, 1832; to John Webber, May 21, 1832; to Webber and Rufus Gilmore, no date (summer of 1832); Rose

unsold.[31] Trespassing remained a problem. From 1825 to 1843 each state expended about $12,500 to thwart this nuisance.[32] Although some complained that land and stumpage were not available except for favored individuals, the evidence from the letter books is that both agents wanted to withhold a great amount of land from sale and not sell stumpage either, because much timber was stolen and receipts were low.[33] Proprietors were given slightly better treatment,[34] but the general word from the agent was, "I am very much afraid that so much land being sold, will cause a reaction, and bring another bursting up among the operators like 1846—which we should regret very much when too late to remedy." [35] Later the Massachusetts agent said, "Let us sell no more," at least until "the crooked times shall become straight." [36] The Maine agent encouraged actual settlers and prospective small holders. For such individuals ". . . our State has adopted a very liberal policy . . . which offers rare enducements to men of limited means." [37] In fact, he advertised, "Good roads lead directly from here to there." [38]

---

and Coffin to Reuben Whittier, April 18, 1833; Webber to Coffin and Rose, Nov. 18, 1833.

[31] Coffin, Levi Bradley (a former Maine land agent), and Elijah Hamlin (the then Maine land agent) to Daniel Webster, June 3, 1842.

[32] Abstracted in Coffin to Marcus Norton, Jan. 30, 1843. Also see "Notice to Trespassers," Bangor, 1834, copy in letter book; Coffin to [?] Hodgdon, Sept. 3, Oct. 14, 1834; trespass notices, Nov. 8, 1843, also in letter book; Coffin and Bradley to Webber, Sept. 20, 1843.

[33] Complaints are noted in Coffin to Samuel Cony (Maine land agent), Sept. 9, Dec. 8, 1848. On sale difficulties, see Cony to Zebulon Ingersoll, Dec. 20, 1848; Coffin to Samuel Cook, May 25, 28, 1849; to Ingersoll, June 26, 1849; to Cook, July 19, 1849; to John H. Clifford, Sept. 15, 1849; to Cook, Oct. 17, 1849.

[34] Coffin to Cony, Sept. 1, 1848; to Daniel Rockwood, Nov. 15, 1850.

[35] Coffin to Cony, Feb. 28, 1850, as well as March 12, 1850.

[36] Coffin to Cony, Jan. 11, 1849. See also Coffin to Cony, Sept. 29, 1848, March 6, 27, 1849, and Aug. 17, 1850.

[37] Lot M. Morrill (Maine land agent) to Pearson Cogswell, March 5, 1831, answering a request from some sort of joint settlement idea: "Send someone to examine and report. Every facility and information will be extended."

[38] Morrill to R. B. Richardson, March 5, 1851.

The pressures in Maine from lumbermen and farmers grew throughout the first thirty years of the state's separate existence. It was felt that the Massachusetts control of some of Maine's land was detrimental to the state's future. Gradually lobbies encouraged study of the possibility of purchasing the remaining equity from Massachusetts. In 1853 the purchase was completed,

Table 10. Land conveyances in Maine, 1854–1860

Year	Homestead lands *	Total of other lands
1854	5,050 acres	
1855	10,456	14,966
1856	10,394	33,832
1857	3,337	6,199
1858	34,279	42,865
1859	46,350	80,930
1860		39,712 (total of both)
Totals	109,866	218,504

* Extent of lands conveyed by payment with road labor

although few people knew the actual extent of the holdings of the state once the transaction was finished. In successive years official estimates differed by about 200,000 acres.[39]

Table 10 gives some idea of the transactions in land from the time of the completion of the purchase to the Civil War.[40]

During this time the land office continued its earlier policies. The agent answered questions from prospective settlers, dealt with the ever present problems of trespassing, sold his lands, and bargained with prospective purchasers over stumpage rates.[41]

[39] *H. Doc.* 14, 1856; *H. Doc.* 37, 1857. The purchase from Massachusetts covered 1,198,330 acres; see *H. Doc.* 12, 1854, for a listing of the locations. The total unsold amounted to probably 2,000,000 acres in 1854.

[40] Land Agent's *Reports, 1854–1860* (Augusta, 1855–1861); also cf. *H. Doc.* 26, 1858.

[41] Noah Barker (Maine land agent) to Ira B. Curtis (St. Albans, Vt.), Sept. 9, 1858: "Sir: I cannot think of any part of this country where our citizens can obtain homes so cheaply and safely for their families as they can of our state." On trespass, see Barker to Charles Perley

Although Maine was apparently stricter in its dealings with prospective settlers than the two states had been before,[42] still the lands seemed to drift into the hands of the great land owners—that is, all except those which had been designated as settling lands.[43]

The Civil War discouraged purchasers, and land sales fell off except for a burst of activity in 1863. Table 11 indicates the

Table 11. Land conveyances
in Maine, 1861–1868

Year	Acreage
1861	9,967
1862	21,857
1863	145,336
1864	55,930
1865	60,481
1866	119,634
1867	130,655
1868	23,872
Total	567,722

amount of land transferred to private ownership from 1861 to the time of the great disposal to the European and North American Railway,[44] of which more later.

(Woodstock, N.B.), April 7, 1858; to Spencer Arnold (Presque Isle, Me.), April 8, 1858; on stumpage, a series of deeds and contracts in "Deed Book," II, 91–97, all dated 1860 1861.

[42] Morrill to Sumner Whitney, Oct. 10, 1855: "My impression is that the state through her Legislature intend [*sic*] to be more exacting in the management and protecting the wild lands than heretofore." Also see "Annual Message," Gov. William G. Crosby, 1855, *Public Documents, Maine, 1856* (Augusta, 1857), 167–168.

[43] The first five ranges west from the eastern line of the state, and north of the Bingham Penobscot Purchase were originally so designated. Later two more ranges were added, 6 and 7 (*Legislative Resolves, Maine, 1855,* ch. cclxi, 249). In all, this amounted to about 125 townships, or close to 3,000,000 acres.

[44] Compiled from Land Agent, *Reports, 1860–1870* (Augusta, 1861–1871). The figures for road-labor lands are included in these totals.

Much of the business concerned stumpage sales on the public reserved lots (the thousand acres set aside for educational purposes in each township), and on the unsold state lands.[45] The state apparently did not care how the timber went as long as large amounts were cut and the money promptly received.[46] Trespassing continued to be a problem, especially on lands not conveyed because of noncompletion of the settling duties.[47] The state timber scalers were instructed to watch such timber thieves, as in the following letter:

Attend to the lines enclosing the state lands in that vicinity, scale all [down?] timber, and be particular to see that no operations shall be made upon state lands except as permitted above. After getting the van [?] of all the teams and scaling up the lumber you will take a tour to Fort Kent and post up the office about operations thereabouts *in* the state.[48]

Inquiries concerning the possibility of settlement on the vacant state lands continued to come in,[49] but few people followed as western land opportunities also beckoned. Some observers indicated the possibility of making good homes in the north country, as did the following letter writer just after the war.

I am eighteen years old, have a good set of teeth and believe in Andy Johnson, the star-spangled banner and the Fourth of July. I have

[45] See nearly all the letters preserved in "Letterbook, 1866."

[46] Isaac R. Clarke (Maine land agent) to Messrs. Dwinel Brothers (Caribou, Me.), Nov. 8, 1866; to W. H. Cunliffe (Fort Kent, Me.), Dec. 3, 1866; to Capt. D. Randall, Dec. 11, 1866; to John A. Rivers (Sherman Mills, Me.), Dec. 12, 1866; and to W. C. Creasay [Clancy?] (Seven Islands, N.B.), May 2, 1867, in particular.

[47] See, especially, Clarke to John R. Carpenter (Linneus, Me.) Dec. [?], 1867; to Enos Bishop (Presque Isle, Me.), Dec. 12, 1867; to Luther Gowen, Dec. 13, 1867.

[48] Clarke to R. H. Stuart, Dec. 17, 1867. Stuart was the state scaler on T8R18, T9R15, T9R16, and T9R18, all state-owned and permitted by Clarke.

[49] See I. R. Clarke to B. N. White (Chesterville, Me.), June 29, 1865; to J. C. Madigan (Houlton, Me.), July 1, 1865; to Dr. J. C. Graham (Castle Hill, Me.), Nov. 31, 1865.

taken up a state lot, cleared up eighteen acres of it last fall, and seeded ten of it down. My buckwheat looks first rate and the oats and potatoes are bully. I have got nine sheep, a two-year-old heifer and two bulls, besides a house and barn. I want to get married. I want to buy bread and butter, hoop skirts and waterfalls for some person of the female persuasion during life. That is what is the matter with me. But I don't know how to do it.[50]

Despite such plaintive appeals, people continued to go west,[51] and the newspapers were driven to editorialize, urging people to "Stay at Home!" and to "Stick by the State." As this last editorialist said, "Farmers! Be of good Courage. Study and Practice the economy of your fathers. Maine's blighted interests and industries shall yet bloom again. Her happy and prosperous homes of the past shall yet be prosperous and happy in the future."[52] Editorials were also written to attack the West as an area in which confidence men, sharpers, and others waited to gull the innocent eastern farmer.[53] Some writers claimed that in Maine, as well as in the West, large crops of great value could be raised. One needed only to practice thrift and hard work.[54] Still

[50] Printed in Portland, Me., *Daily Eastern Argus*, July 20, 1865, from "Aroostook County." The best description of life on this frontier in the years before the Civil War is in a novel, *Now-A-Days!* by Mrs. Laura J. C[urtis] Bullard, published in New York and Boston in 1854 by T. L. Magagnos.

[51] See Portland *Daily Eastern Argus*, July 25, 1876; April 26, 1877; Feb. 10, 1880, and March 30, 1883, for specific accounts of immigrant trains to the west.

[52] Bangor, Me., *Daily Commercial*, Jan. 8, Feb. 5, 1872.

[53] See Portland *Daily Eastern Argus*, Jan. 11, 1872 and July 24, 1886, for two virulent examples.

[54] For accounts of such crops taken from the entire geographic area of Maine see *ibid.*, Sept. 27, 1876, and Nov. 9, 1882; and Bangor *Daily Commercial*, Sept. 5, 1878; Oct. 19, 1878, quoting the Kennebec *Journal*; and Jan. 1, 1885. Also see Wilton *Record*, Aug. 25, 1886; and Oct. 27, 1886, quoting the Somerset *Reporter*; Phillips *Phonograph*, Jan. 15, April 16, May 7, and Dec. 3, 1886: "How is that contrasted with the twelve bushels of wheat to the acre with which Dakota farmers have to content themselves?" The article claimed that a farm in Phillips had raised thirty-two bushels of wheat to the acre. For the Aroostook

the people went westward, as the advertisements of the glories of the West far overshadowed the promise of the "Garden of the North," as the newspapers called the Aroostook Valley.[55]

The state still owned lands; what to do with them became a question for many officials to ponder. Two solutions were finally reached, one designed to attract settlers from Europe to Maine's vacant acres, the other to let someone else do the attracting by making him responsible for the land. As early as 1850, Governor John Hubbard had said that perhaps free gifts of land to actual settlers might solve some of the settlement problems,[56] and in 1858 it was proposed to the legislature that German immigrants might aid the state. It was suggested that a township be set aside for such immigrants, who would receive the land upon the completion of settling duties.[57] Nothing came of this idea until William Widgery Thomas, a Maine native who had served Lincoln at the 1860 convention and who had been awarded a minor post in Sweden, returned to the United States

Valley see Presque Isle *Sunrise*, Aug. 23, 30, Sept. 27, and Oct. 4, 1867, and for a very early comment, the Belfast *Workingman's Advocate*, Dec. 22, 1830: "These settlers on the upper river of the St. John are but the pioneers of a mighty army of emigrants who will ere long be seen to spread themselves over the valley of the St. John and Penobscot." For New Brunswick's attempts to keep her young men home, see *Report on the Agricultural Capabilities of the Province of New Brunswick*, by J. F. W. Johnston (Fredericton, N.B., 1850). After the Aroostook War the border between Maine and New Brunswick, though settled by the Webster-Ashburton Treaty, existed primarily as only a legal impediment to travel, and until the railroads came at the end of the century the two political areas were as one, geographically and economically.

[55] Newspapers from 1865 to 1873 are filled with such advertisements, with often as many as five or six different railroads or land companies calling for settlement or investment at the same time. When covered wagons passed through Bangor on their way to the Aroostook Valley, newspapers put the news on the front page. See Presque Isle *Sunrise*, Oct. 25, 1867, quoting from the Bangor *Whig*.

[56] Gov. John Hubbard, "Annual Message, 1850," *Public Documents, 1851* (Augusta, 1851).

[57] *Sen. Doc. 22*, 1857. This involved the construction of roads and houses and the clearing of lands as in the original settling-lands law.

to complete his education.[58] He proposed that his native state grant a township to prospective Swedish settlers, whom he promised to attract. The state appointed him immigration commissioner, set aside Township 15, Range 3 (the present New Sweden), built houses on the surveyed lots, provided cookstoves and utensils, and awaited its new citizens. After the first year a second town was set aside in the same way,[59] but it was soon found that most of the state's settling lands had already been alienated. Although many were later to advocate this solution to the state's problems of a shrinking population and vacant acres, it was not feasible.[60]

During this period the state continued its policy of grants to educational institutions—35,721 acres in 1862–1863, for instance.[61] All together, Maine and Massachusetts granted 945,214 acres in this way,[62] although as late as 1869 close to 60,000 acres set aside for this purpose were as yet undistributed. In the previous five years, however, close to 190,000 acres had either been granted or otherwise passed into the hands of private individuals with the monies going to the institutions.[63]

[58] The only biographical information is in *Dictionary of American Biography*, "William Widgery Thomas," XVIII, 147.

[59] The best accounts are in Land Agent, *Report, 1870* (Augusta, 1871), 11–12; Board of Immigration, *Report, 1870* (Augusta, 1871); W. W. Thomas, Jr., "Swedish Colonization in Maine and New England," in *The New England States* (New York, 1897), III, 1244–1248; and Michael U. Norberg *et al., The Story of New Sweden* (Portland, 1905). The other town was 115R4, present Stockholm.

[60] Editorials in Portland *Daily Eastern Argus*, Dec. 9, 1871, and Aug. 9, 1886. The paper sponsored a trip into the northern wilderness for prospective capitalists, but no land was available for sale. See also Bangor *Daily Commercial*, Aug. 1, 1883, an anonymous letter from Caribou, and Jan. 2, 1886, quoting Thomas, who had returned to New Sweden for a visit from his post as minister to Sweden. Also see for comment annual messages of Governor Nelson Dingley, 1874 and 1875.

[61] Land Agent, *Report, 1863* (Augusta, 1864).

[62] *H. Doc.* 100, 1879, "Lands Granted to Educational Institutions in Maine," and H. C. Marr, "Grants of Lands."

[63] *H. Doc.* 90, 1869, "Disposition of School Lands (for Fund) Set

The state of Maine and its officials did not know how much land was left. Perhaps close to a million acres remained. The slow disposal and the failure to attract many immigrants revived older attempts at obtaining a land grant for a railroad to connect Maine with the Maritime Provinces. "The short route to Europe," as it was called, might provide an answer to the question of land disposal. If the railroad were granted the land, it would take on the task of obtaining the settlers, and the headaches of land ownership could be passed to others.

Attempts at providing a land grant had first come during the fifties,[64] but it was not until 1864 that a grant of ten townships was made. This grant was apparently too small, since the railroad was not built, and in 1868 the grant was canceled. Then the next year the remainder of the state's public lands, 734,942 acres, was conveyed to the embryonic railroad.[65] The new road, named the European and North American Railway, was charged with

---

Aside April 13, 1857." The land agent usually advertised these lands (or their stumpage) for three months, and then held an auction for the institution involved. For instance he sold on Sept. 11, 1867, T8R17 and T10R17 (less the southeast quarter) for Bates College. I. and G. Stetson, noted lumber dealers, purchased the land for $23,000, or about $.45 an acre, after spirited bidding from an upset price of $.30. Terms were one-third cash, and the balance in one-third payments, due in one and two years. The dealers also sold stumpage for the Westbrook Female Seminary for a ten-year period at the same auction (Presque Isle *Sunrise*, Aug. 9, Sept. 20, 1867).

[64] *H. Doc.* 42, 1858, "Memorial of John Poor . . . ," and *H. Doc.* 32, 1859. The latter was an attempt to provide steamship service from Rockland to Calais for immigrants, to connect with a railroad scheduled to run from Portland to Rockland. Some attempts were made by the state to aid private road building with gifts of money. See Frederick J. Wood, *The Turnpikes of New England . . .* (Boston, 1919), 211–212, and Minnie Lee Atkinson, *Hinckley Township or Grand Lake Stream Plantation* (Newburyport, Mass., 1923), 29–30, about a road supposed to run from Princeton to Milford. It was surveyed and a few rods grubbed out, and then construction terminated. The money was refunded.

[65] *H. Doc.* 68, 1872, is a copy of the deed; also see, by counties, the listing in *Sen. Doc.* 57, 1869.

selling its lands to actual settlers under the terms of the state's law regarding the "settling lands." It was to encourage immigration by appointing an immigration agent and by advertising the lands for sale.[66] The railroad attempted to enlarge its grant by claiming lands set aside for other purposes. Trespass claims against the road and its agents, however, were upheld, and the lands remained in the hands of the state.[67] The road, running from Bangor to Vanceboro, via Winn and Mattawamkeag, was built during the next year. It connected with a sister road in New Brunswick extending from the border to Saint John, via Frederiction. A steamship line was supposed to provide the European connections.

The road did make some attempt at selling its lands,[68] but of its total holdings, less than one-third went into private hands before the road went bankrupt, and the remaining lands were eventually sold at auction to pay part of the debt. Purchases were made by the road's successor, the Maine Central Railroad, and also by prominent lumbermen. Before the auction sales occurred, the legislature made one or two attempts to force the road to live up to the terms of the grant, but none of these attempts amounted to much.[69] The depression of 1873, the cost of shifting to stand-

[66] *Public Laws, Maine, 1868*, ch. dciv; Land Agent, *Report, 1868* (Augusta, 1869).

[67] Land Agent, *Reports, 1872–1875* (Augusta, 1873–1876), and Bangor *Daily Commercial*, March 28, 1875. This last news story concerns the final disposition of the stumpage money. The company was allowed to retain it, while the state kept the lands.

[68] J. A. Purinton (Immigration Agent, European and North American Railway?), *Situation, Character, and Value of the Settling Lands in the State of Maine, Published for the Information of Immigrants* (Bangor, 1871). According to this pamphlet, residence in Aroostook County was a specific against tuberculosis and malaria. Copies of the pamphlet are extremely rare. I used one in the Bangor, Maine, Public Library. It has an excellent map of the settling ranges and of the territory held by the road.

[69] *Sen. Doc.* 21, 1879. This became law; see *Public Laws, Maine, 1879*, ch. cxxvi. The road was to survey "within a reasonable time." See also *H. Doc.* 168, 1881. If the road failed to comply, the land agent was to

ard gauge,[70] the attraction of western lands, and one suspects, the opportunity to alienate these lands to large holders were too great obstacles to overcome.[71]

Only a small amount of land business now remained. It consisted of the disposal of timber rights on ten townships of the railroad land grant that had been reserved for school-fund purposes and a few settling lands. There were all together 65,684 acres of timber lands, 126,844 acres of settling lands that had been contracted for but not proved up, 246,843 acres of settling lands that were unsold and uncontracted for, and 86,685 acres of school-fund lands. Lands with no incumbrances amounted to 399,270 acres.[72]

The timber lands were soon sold; the settling lands were then declared by the state legislature to be "unfit for settlement," and the land agent was instructed to dispose of them. An auction was held in Bangor, and some 140,000 acres changed hands, at an average price of just over a dollar per acre.[73] As usual the large landowners were the biggest purchasers. Instructions were issued to close down the state land office because it was wasteful, but after its closing it was discovered that lands were still held by the state. Sales were begun again, and in 1875 another auction

survey and sell at railroad expense. The measure was postponed indefinitely by the Senate on March 17, 1881 (*Senate Journal, 1881*, 425).

[70] This took place on Sept. 15, 1877, after six weeks' work. See Portland *Daily Eastern Argus*, Sept. 17, 1877.

[71] No history of the road has been written, other than an almost worthless master's paper at the University of Maine, and a diatribe for political purposes published at Portland in 1923 (State Chamber of Commerce and Agricultural League, *History of the Land Grant to the European and North American Railway*). Some account of it appears in my unpublished thesis, "A History of Maine Lumbering, 1860–1930," Cornell University, 1965. For the auction of the land see Bangor *Daily Commercial*, Sept. 21, 1882.

[72] Land Agent, *Report, 1868* (Augusta, 1869). The timberland townships were set aside March 4, 1868, by the legislature. For the location of undisposed lands, see *Sen. Doc.* 67, 1870, which lists them.

[73] About the auction see Bangor *Daily Commercial*, Sept. 23, 24, 1874; and Oxford (County) *Democrat*, Sept. 29, 1874.

was held.[74] All the lands were not sold, and the land agent held a private sale in his office a month later.[75] The last auction was held in 1878; it disposed of another 10,000 acres or so of scattered holdings.[76] By this time the land agent could report "that all the public lands of the state having been disposed of, no further favors are now within the power of the state to grant for homesteads to settlers." [77]

The business of the land office was now confined to rectifying mistakes,[78] selling stumpage,[79] protecting and caring for the public lots,[80] quieting Revolutionary War claims,[81] and winding up the business of transferring land for those who proved up their settling claims.[82] In 1890 the position of land agent was merged with the newly created post of Forest Commissioner, and since that time the business of the land agent has been

[74] Bangor *Daily Commercial*, Jan. 1, Feb. 24, Oct. 28, 1875. The land sales totaled 96,110 acres.

[75] *Ibid.*, Nov. 29, 1875. These lots amounted to 4,546 acres.

[76] *Ibid.*, Nov. 21, 1878.

[77] Land Agent, *Report, 1878* (Augusta, 1879). Little more can be said about these auctions than this, as the records of the land office are not extant from 1868 to 1888.

[78] W. H. McCrillis to Land Agent, June 19, 1878, asking for rectification of stumpage sales, attached to "Deed Book," II, 104.

[79] The records of the first sales after 1888 are preserved in Box 211 of the Forest Commission files.

[80] Much of the correspondence here is preserved in boxes labeled for the appropriate townships concerned, e.g., "Grand Lake Stream," "Eagle Lake," and so on, in the Forest Commissioner's files. The northern lands that were undivided were usually handled by the private proprietors, and the money distributed with an accounting to the state for the public lots. Both of these kinds of correspondence are nearly all extant after 1910, and occasionally some from the 1890–1910 period is available.

[81] These claims dated from a legislative warrant of March 17, 1835, authorizing a two-hundred-acre grant to each veteran or his widow. Most of these were disposed of in the thirties, but the last of them hung on until April 4, 1889. See Land Agent, *Report, 1889* (Augusta, 1890), for a recapitulation.

[82] Land Agents, *Reports, 1875–1890* (Augusta, 1876–1890), *passim*. This was a small business, as few claims remained this late.

carried on in the commissioner's office. Table 12 indicates the amount of acreage sold after the grant to the European and North American Railway.[83]

All together Maine disposed of close to 7,200,000 acres of land, of which about 1,750,000 acres were sold in conjunction with Massachusetts.[84] For the total the state received an average

Table 12. Land disposal in Maine, 1869–1881 (not auction or railroad lands)

Year	Acreage
1869	None
1870	None
1871	11,773
1872	1,334
1873	47,527
1874	79,239
1875	None
1876	None
1877	None
1878	1,029
1879	3,517
1880	410
1881	431
Total	145,260

of thirty-five cents an acre, as nearly as can be estimated. In addition it received money from stumpage before the lands were sold. The building of the European and North American Railway and the movement of people into the eastern half of Aroostook County (nearly its entire population presently is descended

[83] Land Agents, *Reports, 1870–1890* (Augusta, 1871–1890), abstracted. There are probably errors in these figures and in the other tables, but from the materials available, these are my best figures.

[84] The figures of [Lillian Tschamler], *Report,* 14, indicate 7,292,213 acres. My own estimate is 7,007,958 acres. The difference is due to the interpretation of dates to which land grants to schools should be credited, as nearly as I can tell.

from homesteaders on Maine lands) are additional benefits that cannot be included in ordinary ledgers.

It has frequently been fashionable to characterize the nine-teenth-century land policy as the "great land steal." [85] Looking back, however, it is difficult to see what else the state could have done, other than keep the lands for its own use. Few, if any, advocated this policy until after disposal had become a fact. The state was in competition with the federal government, with other states, and with private concerns. It was trying to dispose of lands that lay in an unhospitable climate and that generally had poor and thin soil. The only wealth was the timber cover, and lumbermen were not settlers. In attempting to move its lands, the state adopted a homestead policy of a sort nearly forty years before the federal government, sold its lands on credit terms, designated them for different types of prospective pur-chasers, attempted to attract settlers to its lands from abroad, and finally used the lands to aid the growth of a railroad in the wilderness area. If these policies were not entirely successful, it was not the fault of the state of Maine. Concern over its lands, however, was to be of some importance in the development of the forestry and conservation movements that have done so much to preserve the Maine woods. These movements are closely associated with the Forest Commission office in the years since 1890.

[85] This charge is brought up in times of political difficulty in Maine. For instance, it was an issue in 1895, and later in the period 1919–1928. For an analysis of these political battles see my "Lumbering in Maine."

PART II

PRIVATE INTERESTS
AND
LAND DEVELOPMENT

Frontier Attitudes
and Debt Collection
in Western New York

~⚬⁀⚬~

ROBERT W. SILSBY

When David Milner, the aged sexton of the village of Geneva,
New York, died, his epitaph was a proud reminder that he had
paid up his debts.

> David Milner here is laid
> His work's done—his debts are paid:
> He was a useful man in his station,
> Being *grave-digger* by occupation.
> But since he is dead, let's rejoice at his fall,
> For if he had lived, he'd have *buried us all*.[1]

This simple epitaph may also be an indication of the extent to
which debt influenced the thinking of the most humble in the
frontier community of western New York during the early
years of the nineteenth century. Travelers, many of whom made
their way across the area, often to visit the falls in the Niagara
River, frequently commented on the widespread use of credit
buying and the resulting burden of debt. Early historians of the
area often refer to the prevalence of debt among the settlers.

[1] Canandaigua *Ontario Repository*, March 20, 1821 (hereafter cited as
Ontario Repository).

More recent studies substantiate this picture and describe in a scholarly manner the land-selling operations and credit policies of such large landowners as the Holland Land Company and the Pulteney Associates. The later historians have examined the complex circumstances which, in the frontier community, led to liberal credit policies and complicated the problem of collecting debts.

Many settlers who migrated into western New York came with little cash with which to buy land or other necessities essential for farm-making on the frontier. For years, a difficult marketing situation complicated the problem of turning crops into cash so that debts could be paid off. Poor crop years, the depredations of wild animals, and frequent illness added further to the woes of the frontier farmer.[2] While there is little question that the problems of the debtor were indeed serious, perhaps the tendency of debtors to allow their obligations to run on for years was due as well to the settlers' attitudes toward their debts and to the creditors to whom they were due. The rather leisurely approach of some of those who were attempting to collect debts may also have been a factor in the widespread delinquency.

In the frontier community debts were contracted in a rather casual manner and often in excess of the ability to make prompt repayment. An early visitor commented on the way many spent their earnings on "unnecessary trifles." A family going to a shop to buy a bit of ribbon and tobacco often left with many articles it had no intention of buying. Usually the purchases were made on credit. The visitor believed that storekeepers often took advantage of their neighbors in this respect.[3] Another who traveled

[2] Three excellent studies deal with these problems: Paul Demund Evans, *The Holland Land Company* (Buffalo, 1924); Helen I. Cowan, *Charles Williamson, Genesee Promoter—Friend of Anglo-American Rapprochement*, in the Rochester Historical Society Publications, XIX (1941); and Neil Adams McNall, *An Agricultural History of the Genesee Valley, 1790–1860* (Philadelphia, 1952).

[3] Duke François de La Rochefoucault Liancourt, *Travels through the*

through the area noted that many farmers were in debt; he blamed their extravagance. Because payments were often made in produce, many, he felt, miscalculated their ability to liquidate their debts. The settler always expected to bring new land under cultivation in order to pay off his obligations, but when spring came, he was too busy to do it.[4] Adam Hodgson, the British observer, denounced the "habits of extravagance," which he felt were more extreme than in any European country. "Everything, even a horse, was often sold in credit; and few had fortitude to forego indulgences, however unsuitable, which those around them, with ampler means, were enjoying." [5]

Visitors were not the only ones who noticed the ease with which settlers contracted debts. Contributors to local newspapers were often critical of the rather careless way in which many became indebted. One condemned the tendency to buy unnecessary items on credit. "It is better to turn the old coat than run in debt for a new one. Old fashioned furniture is more comfortable in the end, than articles of taste unpaid for," he asserted.[6] In a similar manner, Poor Robert the Scribe, whose comments appeared frequently in the Geneva, New York, paper, was highly critical of the man who entered a store to buy a single article, saw twenty things that he liked, and bought them on credit. Often these foolish purchases were prompted by thoughtless wives and daughters, he argued. By urging and teasing, they frequently induced the man of the house to buy unnecessary articles that he could only purchase on credit. Hence, he would be dunned and sued and have "many an hour made wretched by their folly and imprudence." The writer urged the ladies to read

United States of America, the Country of the Iroquois, and Upper Canada, in the Years 1795, 1796, and 1797 (London, 1799), I, 292–293.

[4] John Howison, *Sketches of Upper Canada, Domestic, Local, and Characteristic, and Some Recollection of the United States of America* (Edinburgh, 1821), 277–278.

[5] Adam Hodgson, *Letters from North America, Written during a Tour in the United States and Canada.* (London, 1824), I, 341.

[6] Geneva *Gazette*, Oct. 24, 1810.

his section once a month until they knew it by heart.[7] Equally critical of female influence was one who declared, "When I see a man suffer a simple wife to run in debt, at the store, for whatever she fancies, I guess he will soon wish he had never been married."[8] Even worse, according to Poor Robert, was the habit of getting into debt at the tavern. "To grog—to toddy—to sling —to bitters! Oh horrid! What a bill!" he warned. His formula for happy living was summed up rather well in a few lines of poetry:

> How happy's the farmer who owes not a pound,
> He lays by his fifty each year that comes round;
> He fears neither constable, sheriff or dun;
> To bank or the justice has never to run.
> His cellar well fill'd, and his pantry well stor'd,
> He lives far more blest than a prince or a lord.
> Then take my advice, if a fortune you'd get:
> Pay off what you owe—and then keep out of debt.[9]

Although humor is sometimes a means of relieving tensions and frustrations that appear unresolvable, it may also be an indication that one does not view a problem very seriously. We can also learn something of the prejudices affecting the debtor-creditor relationship in the frontier community by examining the kind of humorous tale that must have appealed to many. That village newspaper publishers, many of whom were at-

[7] *Ibid.*, July 31, 1811, and Sept. 21, 1814.

[8] *Ontario Repository*, Feb. 6, 1816.

[9] Geneva *Gazette*, Sept. 21, 1814. No doubt these comments, coming from foreign travelers of some means and the more affluent members of the community, may be somewhat exaggerated. Their concept of "unnecessary trifles" and "extravagance" may well have differed from that of the settler in the pioneer community. Still, one is inclined to regard this as a fairly accurate picture of spending habits, not only for the community in western New York, but for many parts of the United States. See Marvin Meyers, *The Jacksonian Persuasion* (Stanford, Calif. 1957), 99-101.

tempting to collect long overdue debts, printed humorous jibes aimed at creditors and the lawyers who represented them is another indication of the rather indifferent attitudes of many toward these problems. One writer was concerned with the common idea that when a debt had run on for a number of years, there was little need to pay it. He cited the case of A, who had loaned a small sum to B with the understanding that it would be repaid in a week. After a year, A asked for his money and was told he would get it in a week. Finally, at the end of the third year, A threatened to sue if the debt was not paid at once. Amazed at such a threat, B exclaimed to a friend, "The trifling debt . . . is an old affair, an affair of several years standing, and yet he duns me as hard as if I had borrowed the money but a month ago!" [10]

The fate of the village printer, who was forced to sue one of his patrons when the latter refused to pay his bill, no doubt provided a chuckle for some. When served with a summons, the debtor exclaimed, "The d——d rascal, sue me, me who subscribed to his paper eight years ago, on purpose to encourage him. I'll be revenged on the rascal; I'll not take his paper any longer!" [11] Another writer related the story of the young man who sought lodging at a rooming house. He assured the landlady, "I am so much liked that I never left a lodging but my landlady shed tears." "Perhaps," she replied, "you always run off in her debt." [12] Fun was poked at the creditor in the tale of a debtor who was walking down the street with a very despondent look. When a friend inquired why he was so sad, he explained that he was insolvent. "Well," said his friend, "if that is the case, it is not you, but your creditors who ought to wear a woeful countenance." [13] A similar story was told of the person who was deep in debt and seemed very unconcerned. When a friend inquired how he could sleep quietly when he owed so

[10] Geneva *Gazette*, Oct. 2, 1816.
[11] Geneva *Expositor*, Nov. 19, 1808.
[12] Geneva *Gazette*, June 5, 1816. [13] *Ibid.*, July 22, 1818.

much, he replied, "I sleep very well—but I am astonished that my creditors can." [14]

Even though the debtor came out well in humorous stories, this was not true of the moneylender or the lawyer who helped him collect his debts. One wit gave a schoolmaster's definition of a money lender as one who "serves you in the *present tense;* he binds you in the *conditional mood;* keeps you in the *subjunctive,* and *ruins you in the future.*" [15] The legal profession was the target in the tale of a young lawyer who grew discouraged and decided to enter the tanning business. When a friend asked him why he had entered this business, he replied, "I have skinned long enough, and now think it time to be tanning." [16] The tendency, then, was to view the moneylender and the lawyer as the villains; the debtor, on the other hand, generally had the last laugh. No doubt this kind of thinking complicated the problems of collecting debts by influencing the behavior of creditors in their attempts to collect money.

A traveler who arrived in Rochester in the late summer of 1820 commented on the ease with which one could buy on credit in that frontier community. He had noticed "cash store" painted on stores in many parts of the United States, "to tell the customers that the shopkeepers sell only for cash, while they may almost be induced to sell even a thimble on credit." [17] The village merchant was not the only seller in the frontier community who offered generous credit terms. Land vendors, too, often offered to sell on liberal credit. When Charles Williamson began selling land for Sir William Pulteney and his associates during the 1790's, he offered land at a dollar per acre, allowing six years to pay. In most cases, the land was deeded to the buyer with the Pulteney agent taking a mortgage, usually for the full purchase price. The principal of the indenture was divided into two equal payments, with the first due three years from the date the purchase was made. Apparently many took advantage of this

---

[14] *Ibid.*, Oct. 6, 1819.   [15] Geneva *Gazette*, April 9, 1817.
[16] *Ibid.*, June 23, 1819.   [17] Hodgson, *Letters*, I, 360–361.

liberal offer, with no down payment required, and bought much larger tracts than they could possibly handle. George McClure, an early settler who helped clear land for Williamson's race track at Bath, told of a number of gentlemen who came in for the races each spring and fall and were tempted into land speculation by the land agent's easy terms. "Any respectable looking gentleman might purchase on a credit of six years, from one mile square to a township of land," he declared.[18] A traveler through the area in the fall of 1796 commented on the great number of speculators who were taking advantage of the Pulteney agent's credit system. He remarked that "every little town and village throughout the country abounded with them [speculators]."[19]

Even the settlers were lured into the game of speculation. It was easy to buy 500 or 1000 acres in the hope that the debt could be extinguished by reselling part of the tract at a higher price when land values had increased. When the chance to sell did not develop in time, the debtor was faced with interest charges on an excessively high debt, in view of the frontier situation and the difficulty of marketing crops. Even with the problem of converting crops into cash, the interest on a debt incurred to purchase 80 or 100 acres could no doubt have been kept up and the principal retired in a reasonable time. Of 195 mortgages taken by Williamson that ended in failure to pay, 135, or about 70 per cent, were on tracts of 200 acres or more. Since about 60 per cent of all the mortgages made to the Pulteney agent were on these larger tracts, this group resulted in a higher rate of failure.[20] Evidently the tendency to purchase excessively

[18] Guy H. McMaster, *History of the Settlement of Steuben County, N.Y.* (Bath, N.Y., 1853), 132.

[19] Isaac Weld, Jr., *Travels through the States of North America and the Provinces of Upper and Lower Canada during the Years 1795, 1796, and 1797* (London, 1799), 439–440.

[20] These statistics were compiled from data from the deed and mortgage records in the offices of the county clerk of Ontario County, Canandaigua, N.Y., and of Steuben County, Bath, N.Y.

large tracts was also characteristic of those who bought from the Holland Land Company.[21]

Operating in a situation where the position of the creditor was often regarded with humor, it is small wonder that land vendors had difficulty in collecting debts. The dismissal of Charles Williamson, the first agent of the Pulteney Estate, was due in large part to his failure to make any substantial collections on the huge debts that had accrued under his administration. It has already been suggested that many of his early sales to speculators may have contributed to his difficulties. But perhaps his benevolent attitude toward the settlers also accounted for his inability to make collections. In some cases, when a settler could not afford to build a house or make necessary improvements, Williamson either supplied the money or sent in his own workmen to do the job.[22] Families that settled at Caledonia were given a cow and a year's supply of wheat.[23] Three years after settlement had begun, many in the Bath area had to secure meat and grain from the agency to take them through the winter; the kindhearted Scotsman was forced to buy these supplies from the more prosperous settlements to the north.[24] No doubt Judge James Kent was right in commenting on the protective nature of Agent Williamson: "Williamson's demeanor toward them [the settlers] was benevolent after a lordly sort of fashion; it smacked indeed of such paternalism that it won him the title of 'Father of Steuben County.'" The judge compared Williamson's attitude toward the settlers with that of a Scottish chief of a clan, remarking that Williamson wanted to keep them "humble and dependent."[25] Apparently he was equally lenient with the settlers when it came to collecting debts due the agency. Foreclosure notices on mort-

---

[21] McNall, *An Agricultural History*, 33–34.

[22] Weld, *Travels*, 438–439.

[23] Henry O'Reilly, *Sketches of Rochester with Incidental Notices of Western New York* (Rochester, 1838), 155.

[24] Cowan, *Charles Williamson*, 108–109.

[25] John T. Horton, "The Western Eyres of Judge Kent," *New York History*, XXXV (April 1937), 161–162.

gage payments due in 1799 were inserted regularly in the Geneva paper, with the evident hope that they would pressure the mortgagor into paying. But action fell far short of the printed word. By the end of 1801, when Williamson was replaced as the Pulteney agent, only eight of these indentures had been terminated by foreclosure.[26] It was left to his successor, Robert Troup, to press the great number of delinquents for payment and finally to foreclose most of the mortgages that Williamson had taken.

While Agent Troup was successful in clearing up the obligations that Williamson had incurred, he approached the task of collecting debts due his own agency with an awareness of the public attitude toward creditors. He explained the situation thus:

In the administration of a government constructed like ours the people have an efficient & powerful agency. Thence results the obvious policy of managing the agency so as not to offend the people but on the contrary to engage their affections & if possible to secure their good will. . . . Where persons or things in republican governments are rendered disagreeable to the people no regular minded man living under a different form of government would imagine the various injuries which are somewhat wont to flow from what is called the public will! I have often deplored this vice of the republican system.[27]

Although Sir William Pulteney, the Englishman for whom Troup managed the agency, argued against any leniency in collecting from debtors, the Pulteney agent soon deviated from his instructions.[28] He explained his policy to Nathaniel W. Howell, a lawyer who desired to handle the agency's legal business:

[26] These statistics were compiled from data taken from the deed and mortgage records in the offices of the county clerk of Ontario County, and of Steuben County.

[27] Robert Troup to Sir William Pulteney, Nov. 1802, Pulteney Estate Letterbook no. 1, Collection of Regional History, Cornell University. I wish to thank Director Herbert Finch for permission to quote from this letter book.

[28] Instructions, Pulteney to Troup and others, Aug. 1801, *ibid.*

"I permit but few suits, to be brought for recovery of debts due the agency. My general custom is to receive payments large or Small, as the settlers can make them, and to endeavor to draw by the cards of kindness, rather than force them by the rigors of law to the completion of their contracts."[29] But it was still necessary to apply enough pressure to make sure that payments were made and in some cases to eject settlers. In a letter to one of the local agents, Troup explained his policy:

Whenever therefore the case may reasonably be presumed not to be absolutely desperate, and there is anything like a chance to get from the holder . . . the monies made payable by it [the land contract] we must faithfully endeavor by rigor or indulgence or such other means as circumstances shall render proper and expedient to get the monies and avoid forfeiting the contract. . . . But where on the contrary there is reasonable cause for presuming that the case is absolutely desperate and that we have no chance of getting the monies due and to become due on the contract . . . then it must be forfeited.[30]

Generally these were the procedures used by the Pulteney agents in attempting to collect debts.

To remind the settlers that they were indebted to the agency the agents were advised to make a tour through the settlements, either in the spring or fall, and make any collections that they could.[31] When payments fell behind, letters were sent requesting a settlement and threatening forfeiture of the contract or legal action.[32] In some cases, even more pressure was applied by serv-

---

[29] Troup to Nathaniel W. Howell, Nov. 22, 1808, Pulteney Estate Letterbook no. 4, Steuben County Clerk's Office.

[30] Troup to Robert Scott, Nov. 30, 1808, *ibid.*

[31] Troup to Samuel S. Haight, Oct. 17, 1809 and Troup to Joseph Fellows, Nov. 10, 1810, *ibid.*

[32] Troup to Daniel Dorsey, Walter Grieve, Isaac Mullenoer, Sanford Williams, and Amos Hall, Aug. 3, 1811, *ibid.;* Troup to William Atkinson, Azel Answorth, Moses P. Belknap, Jesse Moore, Henry Barber, Jacob Howe, Josiah Bissell, Jr., Roswell Hart, Abelard Reynolds, and Bradford King, Dec. 19, 1820, *ibid.*, no. 7.

ing notices on the debtors to quit the premises. Confronted with a long list of defaulting debtors from Steuben County, Troup ordered such notices sent, for he felt that they would create enough "alarm" to produce a considerable number of payments.[33] When pleas and threats failed to bring settlement, the final resort was either forfeiture of the contract or a suit to recover the debt. The latter was preferred, because it produced less hostility than a forfeiture of contract, which resulted in the settler's being ejected from his farm. But even in suing, a measure of discretion was used. Suits in large numbers would be costly, Troup explained to one of his agents, and furthermore, "the very idea of our litigating with the settlers, though we may have ever so much right on our side, cannot fail to fix a stigma on the reputation of our agency, which will have every unfavorable influence on the quiet and prosperity of the settlement, and our future sales."[34] Instead, he advised, if threats did not produce payments, "single out, two or three of the most noted delinquents, and have them sued for what they owe."[35] This, he felt, would induce others to make every effort to pay off their debts.

Although Troup occasionally canceled contracts and sued delinquent debtors, his policy toward them was generally lenient. During the early months of the War of 1812, he ordered his agents to delay evictions until the end of the war.[36] In a like manner, he refused to foreclose mortgages long overdue, because with the nation at war, foreclosure "would have the appearance of cruelty."[37] Apparently Troup was willing to listen and grant concessions when debtors faced unusual hardships. In the fall of 1811, he ordered his agents at Bath to discontinue a suit against Thomas Brownson, because he sympathized with his "story" and

[33] Troup to Dugald Cameron, March 13, 1823, *ibid.*, no. 7.

[34] Troup to Frederick Wolcott, Sept. 13, 1810, *ibid.*, no. 4.

[35] Troup to General Jacob Morris, March 6, 1811, and Troup to Samuel S. Haight, July 3, 1810, *ibid.*

[36] Troup to Andrew McNab and George Goundry, Dec. 18, 1812, *ibid.*   [37] Troup to Andrew McNab, Dec. 21, 1812, *ibid.*

had had it confirmed by a resident of the area.[38] Unfortunately, we do not know what misfortune had overtaken Brownson or another settler who applied to the Pulteney agent for relief. Troup wrote to the second debtor and granted his request: "I had no idea that your situation was so unfortunate as to put it out of your power to pay the small debt you have so long owed to the Pulteney Estate. I am truly sorry for your unfortunate situation; and I must be content to wait, sometime longer for the debt." [39]

Like the Pulteney agents, village merchants and businessmen offered to sell their goods or services on liberal credit terms. Newspaper advertisements testify to the fact that these vendors had impressive lists of store goods for sale, usually offering them on credit of from three months to one year. In the "Old Apothecary Store" one might buy, on approved notes at ninety days, a great variety of articles, including sweet-scented Itch Ointment, Aromatic Jaundice Bitters, peppermint and lemon lozenges, spices, and patent medicine.[40] Other merchants or craftsmen offered to sell livestock, household equipment, farm tools, and newspapers on credit. The frequency of such advertisements lead one to conclude that not only were credit purchases easily made, but that in fact purchasers were actually encouraged to buy on time.

The pious were sometimes even unable to seek salvation without going into debt. On one occasion, William Hortsen, the Geneva apothecary, advertised pew 42 in the Presbyterian Church for sale on twelve-months' credit, with interest.[41] Late in 1816, the pewholders of the church were called upon to settle their indebtedness to the trustees.[42] The Geneva Friendly Society, too, assumed an unfriendly attitude, threatening to exact

---

[38] Troup to Haight and Cameron, Oct. 3, 1811, *ibid.*
[39] Troup to J. Cochran, Sept. 18, 1819, *ibid.*
[40] Geneva *Expositor*, July 22, 1807.
[41] Geneva *Palladium*, Nov. 27, 1822.
[42] Geneva *Gazette*, Dec. 18, 1816.

penalties from those members who failed to pay their monthly dues.[43]

Liberal credit terms confronted the village merchant with the perpetual task of collecting the debts that were building up on his books. The most common procedure was to advertise in the local newspapers, urging those in debt to make payment or at least to come in and execute a note for the amount due. Many of the notices were routine, stating that debts were to be settled and giving the conditions. Some merchants, in an effort to increase the payment of obligations, offered to take various kinds of produce. The notices indicated that grain, pot and pearl ashes, pork, whiskey, hides, and skins would be accepted by various merchants in payment of debts. Others threatened legal action. One frustrated merchant warned that those who had not paid up by a given date would be called upon "in the *Name of the People*."[44] Joel Prescott and Robert Ashley of Phelps were more blunt, demanding that their debtors pay up on time in order to "avoid the trouble of seeing a constable."[45]

But in many cases the notices were hardly couched in a serious vein. William Tippetts of Geneva displayed some subtlety in calling on those who were in debt to pay up. If they did not pay him in time, he warned, they would have to pay his attorney, "with such additions as the ingenious profession of the Law may make."[46] Another "threat" was expressed in verse. Appearing in a New England newspaper, it urged prompt settlement.

> Man, woman, maid, in way of trade
> Who are to him indebted,
> Must call and pay—or their delay
> Will be by them regretted;
> And by him too; for he must sue,
> And that will cause him trouble;

[43] *Ibid.*, Dec. 16, 1812.

[44] Geneva *Gazette*, Aug. 12, 1812; Geneva *Expositor*, Dec. 3, 1806, July 27, 1808.   [45] Geneva *Expositor*, June 17, 1807.

[46] Geneva *Gazette*, Nov. 25, 1812.

> That unto them the cost and shame
> Shall make their debts quite double.

> With much delight he doth invite
> All those who have him trusted,
> To call with speed as was agreed,
> And have their claims adjusted.[47]

A Livonia merchant likewise used a blend of humor and directness: "The subscriber has a long time waited very patiently in order to see if his old friends would not take the hint to call and pay him the small demands he has against them." Since they had forgotten their debts, he was taking this opportunity to give them a "sly hint." If they did not take it, he warned, they could be sure that the "next *hint* [would] be a *Kick*." [48]

If one is to believe the notices that appeared in the newspapers throughout the area, one of the most neglected creditors was the postrider who delivered those papers. The notices were numerous and many were unusual, but the tone was such that one wonders how seriously they were regarded. One rider, for instance, requested those who owed for more than three months to look to Matthew 18:29. He suggested a sermon that might be written around this passage.

> Beloved brethren! Hearken unto me and attend to the words of my mouth! Pay the Postrider quickly, . . . lest at any time the Postrider deliver thy account to the attorney and the attorney bring thee before the judge and the judge deliver thee to the officer, and thou be cast into prison.
> Verily I say unto thee, thou shalt by no means come out thence, till thou has paid the utmost farthing!! [49]

Another, who imagined himself something of a poet, inserted a bit of poetry.

---

[47] *Ibid.*, Oct. 21, 1818.
[48] *Ontario Repository and Western Advertiser*, Oct. 13, 1812.
[49] Canandaigua *Western Repository*, Dec. 11, 1804.

Six months through many towns I've been,
And many friends I there have seen:
I brought you NEWS by night and day,
And now I humbly, ask for PAY.
Thro' storms of snow, hail, winds and rains,
To bring you News I've spar'd no pains.
O think on this, and truly say,
That Little O must have his pay.
Worn out myself, my horse, my clothes,
Three nights a week have no repose;
My money spent—the truth I tell;
O pity me, and pay me well.
To bring you News, next week I'll call,
With pleasure, hope to see you all;
Pray pay me well, and let me go—
Your humble servant Little O.[50]

Apparently the settlers were not easily convinced by his poetic efforts, for six months later Little Oliver inserted another notice. He reminded his subscribers that he had served them for a full year and would have to be paid at once. This time he managed to compose just a short rhyme:

Pray, pay me well, and let me say,
That faithful O has got his pay.[51]

Two months later the discouraged Oliver inserted his last notice, titled "My Last friendly Call." Apparently he had lost all heart for further rhyming. He explained that in four weeks he expected to discontinue his business and leave the state. He had made "every exertion" to be punctual with the papers but had received only one-fourth of the pay due him.[52]

Equally persistent, although probably no more effective, were the printers of the local newspapers. One, in wishing his subscribers a happy new year, commented that payment of money due "would be received and acknowledged with all the gratitude

[50] *Ibid.*, March 8, 1808.   [51] *Ibid.*, Sept. 13, 1808.
[52] *Ibid.*, Nov. 1, 1808.

excited by a *New-Year's gift*." [53] Another repeated the story of old Square Gable, who was performing a marriage ceremony. After rushing through the ceremony, the Square concluded by turning to the bridegroom and demanding, "Und now, vere ish mine dollar?" Like the Square, the printer explained, he must be paid at once for papers received from his office.[54] The printer of the Geneva paper used a notice that was no doubt more ingenious than successful in securing the payment of debts. It consisted of a diamond-shaped arrangement of letters that, he claimed, could be read in nearly two thousand different ways to produce the plea "Pay the Printer." [55]

Perhaps the leisurely approach of village creditors to the collection of debts resulted from the inadequacy of more drastic forms of seeking redress. The threat to sue for unpaid debts was not as powerful a weapon as it would have been in another place and time. Even if the creditor did secure a judgment against the debtor, it was frequently necessary to levy against his real estate or personal property. The sheriff was forced to sell the property at public auction. The shortage of cash on the frontier meant that a sale usually brought only a small percentage of the amount of the debt. A survey of fifty-three sales in Steuben County during the seventeen-year period 1799 through 1815 reveals that the creditor received enough to satisfy the full amount of the debt in only fourteen cases. Typical was the case of Mordecai Hale, who had a judgment against Solomon Bennett for $15,000. The sale of Bennett's property brought only $811.[56] In some instances the creditor or his agent appeared at the auction to bid on the land and save some of the debt. This was true in about 40 per cent of the cases mentioned above.[57] Therefore suits were

[53] *Ibid.*, Jan. 5, 1808.
[54] *Ontario Repository and Western Advertiser*, Nov. 12, 1811.
[55] Geneva *Gazette*, July 8, 1818.
[56] Steuben County Deeds, Liber 6, 328–330.
[57] This data was compiled from sheriff sales recorded in the Steuben County deed records.

used sparingly, and there can be little doubt that many debtors were well aware of this.

Debt collections were further complicated by the migratory nature of the frontier settlers. More than once the impoverished debtor chose to escape his obligation by fleeing from the area. George McClure, the Bath merchant, told of a group of settlers north of the village who were indebted to him for about four thousand dollars. The group moved into Canada without paying any of the money due him. Determined to secure his money, McClure followed them across the border and managed to collect about two hundred dollars from those who settled near Toronto. Traveling on to Detroit, he found the rest of them but was unable to collect any money. This was the extent of his collections on a rather sizable debt.[58]

The construction of the bridge across the Genesee River at Rochester offered harassed debtors a chance to escape the Ontario County sheriff, often to the amusement of onlookers. An early Rochester lawyer declared:

Many of our early residents, men who gave our city substance and fame, often owed their liberty temporarily, to their good luck in discovering this minion of the law, in time to beat him to the center of the bridge, by a neck. Then, from his point of vantage, he could wave salutation, not calculated to increase the composure of the officer, but quite satisfactory to the onlookers who are always with the winner.[59]

It is difficult to know how many debtors escaped their obligations by this means. That they were fairly numerous is evident in the action of the New York State legislature in passing a series of acts to regulate the sale of the property of mortgagors who had left the state and could not be located.[60]

[58] McMaster, *Steuben County*, 137–138.
[59] John D. Lynn, *The Life and Times of John Mastick*, VII, Rochester Historical Society Publications (1928), 125.
[60] *Laws of New York*, 8 sess., 55–57, 1784; 10 sess., 466, 1786; 24 sess., 262–264, 1800.

Perhaps fear of reprisal may have kept some creditors from pressing too vigorously for their pay. An early historian of Steuben County told of a merchant at Painted Post whose store burned the night after Christmas. When the merchant was missed, some felt that he had been murdered by his customers, "a disaster by no means unlikely to befall a merchant in a region where the position of debtor was much more pleasant and independent than that of creditor." [61] When the merchant appeared a few days later, suspicions were disproved, but the fact that they existed is an indication of the uncertain position of the creditor.

The collection of debts was further complicated because debtors were sometimes able to intimidate the law-enforcement officers. Levi Beardsley, who served as constable in Otsego County during the first decade of the nineteenth century, told of being struck on the head by a club when he attempted to serve a warrant on one burly fellow. In another case, while serving an execution, he was confronted with a man armed with a heavy stake, who threatened to knock him down if he approached. "He had a sinister look, that I did not like," Beardsley related. "I thought it would be ridiculous to have my head broken, and had no desire to make the experiment, so deeming 'discretion the better part of valor,' I rode off, and that was the last of it." [62] Occasionally it was the judge who became the object of intimidation, making it difficult to secure justice. Once, after an unpopular decision had been rendered, the bystanders, who had been well fortified at a nearby tavern, gathered around the judge and "commenced urinating on him, from every direction." [63]

Another form of pressure against creditors was used in the village of Rochester. In order to protect themselves in granting credit, a group of merchants formed a society to list those who were not good credit risks. It was soon branded the "Shylock Society" by the less fortunate members of the community.

[61] McMaster, *Steuben County*, 52.
[62] Levi Beardsley, *Reminiscences* (New York, 1852), 94–95.
[63] *Ibid.*, 153–154.

When the debtors of the village formed an organization that was pledged never to trade with a member of the "Shylocks," the creditors' society soon went out of existence.[64]

The land vendor in western New York faced problems in collecting his debts that were similar to those of the village merchant and businessman. When verbal threats failed to produce results, the next step was to begin foreclosure proceedings by inserting a notice in the local newspaper and posting the notice on the courthouse door. Often this was enough to convince the mortgagor either to pay off his debt or at least to keep up the interest payments. Of a total of 424 foreclosure notices listed in the local newspapers in the period 1789 through 1820, only 184, or 44 per cent, of the mortgages were actually foreclosed. In a number of cases, the mortgagee, after advertising the sale, agreed to a postponement, apparently to give the debtor another chance to pay. A mortgage given by Ebenezer Fitch of Bloomfield in March 1816 was advertised for foreclosure on June 9, 1819. The sale was postponed five times, and finally the mortgage was discharged in December 1820.[65] Thaddeus Chapin advertised the Canandaigua lots of Ezekiel Taylor to be sold at foreclosure February 21, 1816. Apparently he agreed to put off the foreclosure, because two years later another notice advertised that the lots would be sold on June 17, 1818. The sale was never held, however, because Taylor paid off his mortgage June 11.[66] In many cases, the threat of foreclosure, plus generous indulgence on the part of the mortgagee, made the sale of the land unnecessary.

Like the village merchant who sought redress through the sheriff's sale, the mortgagee found that foreclosure was often not a satisfactory way of collecting debts. When foreclosure sales

[64] Lynn, *The Life and Times of John Mastick*, 126.

[65] *Ontario Repository*, Dec. 8, 1818; Ontario County Mortgages, Liber 8, 239–240.

[66] *Ontario Repository*, Aug. 22, 1815, Dec. 16, 1817; Ontario County Mortgages, Liber 6, 356–357.

were held at the county courthouse or a convenient hotel or inn, the chances were that the land would sell for only a small portion of its value. At an auction held in Geneva in February 1824, for example, Guy Jackson bid $760 for two improved lots that had been mortgaged for $1550 in 1796. Because he was unable to pay cash, the land was struck off to an agent of the assignee for $100.[67] In another instance, a farm that had been mortgaged for $550.77 in 1820 was sold at public auction three years later to the only bidder, Andrew Young, for $75.[68] Even when contending bidders did appear, their efforts were often of little significance. When John Hedges' farm was sold in February 1815, Asa Perry bid $.50 and Samuel Anderson bid $1.00. Thus the mortgagee had little trouble in buying the land, which had been purchased in 1811 for $350, for a bid of $50.[69] Even though eleven bids were made for the farm of Simeon Brackett, land mortgaged for over $650 was sold for $205 at the inn of Timothy and Albert Hosmer at Avon.[70] These examples, typical of foreclosure proceedings in the frontier area, indicate the limitations of mortgage foreclosure as a means of collecting debts. More often than not, it was used only as a last resort—a means by which the mortgagee could get title to the land. One can only guess that debtors too were aware of these limitations and no doubt were less conscientious in making payments as a result.

The problem of debt in the frontier community was clearly the result of a variety of factors. But perhaps too much emphasis has been put on the difficulties of farm making and the problems of finding markets. Perhaps equally significant were the attitudes of the frontier community toward debts and debtors. Debts were contracted carelessly and often in excess of the debtor's ability to repay. Little or no stigma was attached to the debtor's position, but rather, when the debtor managed to outwit the

[67] Ontario County Mortgages, Liber 13, 83–84.
[68] Monroe County Mortgages, Liber 2, 364–366, office of county clerk, Rochester.   [69] Ontario County Mortgages, Liber 7, 276–277.
[70] *Ibid.*, Liber 11, 107–109.

creditor, it was regarded by many as a humorous incident. Thus many debtors were indifferent about paying their obligations and in many cases managed to avoid their debts altogether by some ruse or other. This, in turn, caused creditors to approach the problem of collecting debts with a good bit of caution. Some tried the humorous approach and, when it failed, used pleas and finally threats. But seldom were threats carried out, and only as a last resort.

The Mineral Lands of
the St. Mary's Falls
Ship Canal Company

~~◇~~

IRENE D. NEU

Land grants to the states as a form of federal aid were an old
story by 1852, the year in which Michigan received a donation
of three-quarters of a million acres of public land to subsidize the
building of a canal at Sault Ste Marie. The ordinances of 1785
and 1787 had set aside designated sections in the Old Northwest
for the support of schools. A law of 1822 embodied the first land
grant to a state for an internal improvement, giving Illinois a
right of way 180 feet wide for a canal from the Illinois River to
Lake Michigan. The following year Ohio was the beneficiary of
a grant that included not only the right of way of a projected
wagon road in the northern part of the state, but also a strip of
land one mile wide on either side, to aid in construction of the
road.[1]

Other grants for roads and waterways followed in rapid
order. By mid-century almost 3,000,000 acres had been given to
the states of the Old Northwest for the building of canals to join
the Great Lakes and the Ohio-Mississippi system. These grants,

[1] Matthias Nordberg Orfield, *Federal Land Grants to the States with
Special Reference to Minnesota* (Minneapolis, 1915), 37, 39, 91, 93;
Office of Federal Coordinator of Transportation, *Public Aids to Trans-
portation* (4 vols.; Washington, 1938–1940), II, 8.

one authority has observed, "were the true predecessors of the railroad grants, in that . . . the donations were in what became the standard pattern of alternate sections along the proposed route." In addition to grants for the building of specifically designated canals, a general grant of 500,000 acres for internal improvements had been made to each public-land state. In 1850, two years before the Sault canal grant, Illinois was the recipient of the first railroad land grant.[2]

The act "granting to the State of Michigan the right of way and a donation of public land for the construction of a ship canal around the Falls of St. Mary's" was signed by President Millard Fillmore on August 26, 1852.[3] The St. Marys River is the strait-like stream through which Lake Superior empties into Lake Huron. Opposite the city of Sault Ste. Marie is a series of rapids caused by a drop of some twenty feet in the level of the river. In the absence of a canal, the rapids prevented the passage of traffic from one lake to the other. The few small ships that plied the upper lake in the early 1850's had been hauled over greased tracks across the portage at the Sault—an operation requiring from one to three months' time. All freight had to be trans-shipped at the portage. The act of 1852 was a response by Congress to the Michigan legislature's decade-old, almost annually renewed, plea for aid in building the needed canal.[4]

As late as 1840, Senator Henry Clay of Kentucky could describe a proposed canal at Sault Ste Marie as "a work beyond the remotest settlement in the United States, if not the moon," but by 1845 the first major mining boom in the United States had erupted in the copper country of the Keweenaw Peninsula, "which reaches out like an index finger from the southern shore

[2] Orfield, *Federal Land Grants to the States*, 104; John Bell Rae, "Federal Land Grants in Aid of Canals," *Journal of Economic History*, IV (Nov. 1944), 168; U.S. Public Land Commission, *The Public Domain* (Washington, 1884), 258. The quotation is from Rae, p. 168.

[3] U.S., *Statutes at Large*, X, 35–36.

[4] Irene D. Neu, "The Building of the Sault Canal: 1852–1855," *Mississippi Valley Historical Review*, XL (June 1953), 28.

line of Lake Superior," some two hundred miles beyond the Sault. Fourteen companies were conducting mining operations in the vicinity of Copper Harbor, and thirty other corporations were being organized. The speculative bubble had burst by late 1847, but in 1850 some two thousand workers were to be found in the mining district. By that time, too, interest was being aroused in the iron deposits in Marquette County. Supplies for the miners piled up at the Sault, and ore from the mines lay on distant riverbanks or on the shores of Lake Superior awaiting transportation to the cities on the lower lakes. Small wonder that there was a general demand for a canal at Sault Ste Marie.[5]

By terms of the Sault canal grant, Michigan was to select 750,000 acres of any public land within the state that was subject to private entry, that is, that had not been pre-empted or reserved for other purposes. There were no restrictions as to the proximity of the land to the projected canal, the sections in which it might be located, or the character of the subsoil—important considerations in a state that was rich in both timber and minerals. Such generous terms might be attributed in part to a group of lobbyists from Michigan, including both Democrats and Whigs, who spent the winter and spring of 1851–1852 in Washington. The group was made up of men with financial interests in the Upper Peninsula. Some were doubtless hopeful of becoming canal contractors and therefore sharers in the land grant. All stood to profit from the free flow of traffic through a canal at the Sault. Working out of the hotel room of John A. Burt, one of their number, the pressure group followed the course of the canal bill and did all they could to determine its

[5] William Chandler, *History of the St. Mary's Falls Ship Canal*, III, Michigan Legislature, Joint Documents, no. 4, 1877 (Lansing, 1878), 4; William B. Gates, Jr., *Michigan Copper and Boston Dollars: An Economic History of the Michigan Copper Mining Industry* (Cambridge, Mass., 1951), 1, 3–6; Roy M. Robbins, *Our Landed Heritage: The Public Domain, 1776–1936* (Princeton, 1942), 142.

final form.[6] Perhaps they were responsible for an increase in the size of the proposed grant from 500,000 to 750,000 acres.[7] Clearly, however, in deciding upon the other conditions of the grant, Congress drew heavily upon precedent.

Since "the canal around the Falls of St. Mary's" was to be only a mile in length, the traditional designation of alternate sections along the proposed route could not be followed. It was only natural, then, that the framers of the canal bill should turn to the concept of the "floating grant"—that is, the grant that might be located anywhere on public land within the state to which the grant was made. Such a grant had been given to Ohio in 1828 to aid in the payment of debts that had been, or might be, contracted in the building of canals. Similar general grants for internal improvements were extended to the other public-land states by a law of 1841.[8]

Original restrictions on the federal government's disposing of

[6] "Material for Hon. John Burt's Biography" (MSS in John Burt's handwriting), Marquette County Historical Society, Marquette, Mich., 5–6; Chandler, *History of the St. Mary's Falls Ship Canal*, 5; John H. Goff, "St. Mary's Falls Canal," in Charles Moore, ed., *The Saint Marys Falls Canal* . . . (Detroit, 1907), 119; *History of the Upper Peninsula of Michigan* . . . (Chicago, 1883), 215. Three members of the lobby were J. Venon Brown, editor of the Sault Ste Marie *Lake Superior Journal* and Receiver of the United States Land Office in that place; Sheldon McKnight, a Great Lakes shipper with varied interests at Sault Ste Marie; and John Burt, a surveyor, "landlooker," and promoter in the Upper Peninsula. Brown was a Whig; McKnight and Burt were Democrats (Detroit *Free Press*, Dec. 4, 1852; Charles Lanham, *The Red Book of Michigan: A Civil, Military, and Biographical History* [Detroit, 1871], 467; "Material for Hon. John Burt's Biography," 12).

[7] The amendment that raised the amount of the proposed grant was actually introduced by Senator David R. Atchison of Missouri on August 17, 1852 (*Sen. Journal*, 32 Cong., 1 sess., 610).

[8] Orfield, *Federal Land Grants to the States*, 96, 101–102; Office of Federal Coordinator of Transportation, *Public Aids to Transportation*, II, 9; Harry N. Scheiber, "State Policy and the Public Domain: The Ohio Canal Lands," *Journal of Economic History*, XXV (March 1965), 88.

mineral lands had been eroding since 1829. A law of that year permitting the sale of the formerly leased lead mines in Missouri was the first of a number of statutes by the terms of which most of the nation's ore deposits were to pass into private hands. A system of permits and leases that had been applied to Michigan's copper country was abandoned in 1847 in favor of the outright sale of copper-bearing land at $2.50 to $5.00 an acre. In 1850, mineral lands in the Lake Superior district were ordered sold "in the same manner, at the same minimum," as other public lands, doubtless to encourage the opening of additional mines and thus to increase the nation's supply of domestic copper.[9] Since lands in the mineral district of Michigan could thereafter be purchased with military warrants that were at times selling in New York for as little as fifty cents an acre,[10] it would have been pointless for Congress to exclude such lands from the canal grant. Moreover, there seemed to be great concern, both in and out of Congress, that unless the *quid pro quo* were unusually attractive, contractors willing to build the canal, "in so remote a place," would not be found.[11]

[9] Gates, *Michigan Copper and Boston Dollars*, 6; U.S. Public Land Commission, *Public Domain*, 319–320.

[10] Dallas Lee Jones, "The Survey and Sale of the Public Land in Michigan, 1815–1862" (master's thesis, Cornell University, 1952), 92–93. Military bounty land warrants were a form of compensation to men who had served in the nation's wars. Such warrants could be used by the recipient to locate a specific number of acres anywhere in the surveyed area of the public domain that was still open to entry. An act of February 11, 1847, to provide land bounties for veterans of the Mexican War brought into existence almost 90,000 such warrants, good for more than 13,000,000 acres. Supplementary legislation in 1850 provided for 189,000 more warrants, embracing another 13,000,000 acres. Although military land warrants were not legally assignable until March 22, 1852, they were in the market before that date, for prices at which they were being sold were quoted in a New York newspaper as early as September, 1851 (*ibid.*, 91–93; U.S. Public Land Commission, *Public Domain*, 235, 237).

[11] A. N. Bliss, "Federal Land Grants for Internal Improvements in the State of Michigan," *Michigan Pioneer Society Collections*, VII (1886;

The concern was perhaps unwarranted. The Upper Peninsula was hardly as remote as those not familiar with it believed it to be. Except in the winter months, communication by water between Sault Ste Marie and Detroit was fairly regular, and the transporting of men and supplies to the canal site presented no problem. It was a generally accepted belief that the cost of the canal and locks would be under $500,000, a figure representing little more than half the value of the land appropriated by Congress, reckoning that value at the minimum government price of $1.25 an acre.[12] It was also anticipated that the state would remit taxes on canal lands for a period of years. That capitalists considered the canal contract "a good thing" may be inferred from the number of importunate would-be canal builders who presently appeared in Lansing, the state capital.[13]

In the spring of 1853 the state commissioners who had been charged by the legislature with the letting of the canal contract awarded it to a group of entrepreneurs that included Joseph T. Fairbanks of St. Johnsbury, Vermont; Erastus Corning of Albany, New York; and John Murray Forbes of Boston.[14] None of these men was a civil engineer; none had an interest in the building of the Sault canal merely for the sake of building a canal. All were speculators—risk-taking capitalists, if you will

---

reprint, 1904), 63; Chandler, *History of the St. Mary's Falls Ship Canal*, 4; *Cong. Globe*, 32 Cong., 1 sess. (1851–1852), XXIV, Pt. III, p. 1881. Later canal grants, all for the purpose of improving navigation between, or immediately adjacent to, the Great Lakes, and none for waterways exceeding two miles in length, were restricted to alternate, odd-numbered sections, as close as possible to the improvements. In these grants, mineral lands were entirely exempt from state entry (U.S., *Statutes at Large*, XIII, 520; XIV, 30, 80). See also Rae, "Federal Land Grants in Aid of Canals," 168, 175.

[12] Known estimates of the cost of constructing the canal and locks ranged from a low of $260,000 to a high of $403,500 (Neu, "The Building of the Sault Canal," 37–38).

[13] Charles T. Harvey to Erastus Corning, Jan. 6, 19, 1853, Corning Papers, Albany Institute of History and Art.

[14] Neu, "The Building of the Sault Canal," 33.

—who hoped to make money by advancing the capital needed for constructing the canal and by receiving the land grant in return, locating the land as advantageously as possible, and holding it for the rise in price that they thought must follow upon advancing settlement, improved transportation, and increased demand for timber, copper, and iron.

Some disappointed bidders for the canal contract and their friends alleged that the successful contractors had submitted the highest, not the lowest, bid, and implied that the commissioners had shown favoritism to "E. Corning and Associates." [15] Perhaps the charges were true (there is some contemporary evidence that seems to support them),[16] but there is no gainsaying the fact that the easterners had at least one honest advantage over their competitors: their reputation as "monied" men in a region that suffered from a chronic shortage of capital.

Corning and Forbes, especially, were well known in Michigan. The New Yorker had mercantile contacts and banking investments in Detroit that dated from the 1830's, if not earlier. Both men had for some years been prominently identified with the Michigan Central Railroad; both had recently shown an interest in a mineral-land speculation in Michigan's Upper Peninsula. Joseph T. Fairbanks and his brothers, Erastus and Thaddeus, also had land interests beyond the Sault. The family scale-manufacturing firm, E. & T. Fairbanks & Co., thanks to its ubiquitous agents, was a familiar name in every commercial center in America.[17]

It was a Fairbanks agent, young Charles T. Harvey, who called the attention of the eastern coterie to the Sault canal speculation. In November 1852, a spokesman for the Fairbanks

[15] Detroit *Free Press*, April 8, 11, 13, 18, 1853.

[16] *Ibid.*, April 13, 1853; James F. Joy to Corning, April 4, 1853, Corning Papers.

[17] John Murray Forbes to Corning, Nov. 22, 1852, Corning Papers; Detroit *Free Press*, April 5, 1853; Irene D. Neu, *Erastus Corning, Merchant and Financier, 1794–1872* (Ithaca, N.Y., 1960), 78, 105–108; Neu, "The Building of the Sault Canal," 26.

partnership explained to Erastus Corning that Harvey had been strongly solicited by businessmen in the Lake Superior region

to get us interested in taking the [Sault canal] contract, as they had confidence that if we undertook the operation, it would be done promptly substantially & in good faith; & much apprehension existed, that if the contract was obtained by Mich. people, the appropriation would be exhausted, & the work protracted & improperly done. He suggested that if you would become interested, we might also take hold of it.[18]

Through Corning, Forbes was enlisted in the venture. Later John F. Seymour of Utica, New York, joined Corning, Forbes, and the Fairbanks brothers in the speculation. This group, ably assisted by James F. Joy, John W. Brooks, and other Michigan residents, remained the moving spirits behind the endeavor.[19] On August 25, 1853, the canal contract was formally assigned to the St. Mary's Falls Ship Canal Company, a firm incorporated in New York. Corning was president of the new company. Joseph T. Fairbanks, Forbes, and Seymour served with him on the board of directors.[20]

The Canal Company, by the terms of the contract, was to build a canal and locks to the state's specifications in return for the 750,000 acres that Congress had appropriated for the purpose. The waterway was to be completed within two years— that is, by the spring of 1855—and the land was to be held by

[18] E. and T. Fairbanks and Co. to Corning, Nov. 16, 1852, Corning Papers. For the early career of Harvey, see Ernest H. Rankin, "Canalside Superintendent," *Inland Seas*, XXI (Summer 1965), 103–106. I am grateful to the Albany Institute of History and Art for permission to quote from the Corning Papers.

[19] Forbes to Corning, March 21, 1853, Corning Papers; Neu, "The Building of the Sault Canal," *passim*. Joy, a Detroit lawyer, served as counsel for the Michigan Central Railroad. John W. Brooks was superintendent of the road.

[20] Also on the board of directors were Joy, John W. Brooks, and John V. L. Pruyn, the latter an Albany lawyer and cohort of Corning (Neu, "The Building of the Sault Canal," 35–36).

the state until the work had been approved and accepted by the proper state officers. The entire acreage was to be tax-free for five years after it had passed into the possession of the contractors.[21]

State agents, nominated by the contractors and appointed by the governor, might begin the selection of acreages immediately. John Wilson, Acting Commissioner of the General Land Office in Washington, directed the Registers of the local land offices in Michigan to mark the canal agents' selections in pencil on the appropriate tract books and maps. After the Secretary of the Interior had given his approval of the selections, the Registers were to enter the canal lands in permanent form.[22]

To take care of its land business, the St. Mary's Falls Ship Canal Company in the summer of 1853 opened two land agencies, one at Detroit, the other at Sault Ste Marie. The Detroit office was placed in charge of George S. Frost, who, until his appointment by the Canal Company, had been chief clerk in the office of the United States Surveyor General at Detroit. Frost worked closely with John W. Brooks, superintendent of the Michigan Central Railroad and a member of the Canal Company's board of directors. Together the two men hired and directed the groups of "landlookers" and surveyors who in 1853 and 1854 located almost 500,000 acres, mostly of pine lands, in the Lower Peninsula and just over 76,000 acres of similar lands in the Upper Peninsula. The canal lands in the mineral districts of the Upper Peninsula, roughly 187,000 acres, were chosen in quite different fashion, under the direction of Charles T. Harvey, who, within a day or two of the canal contract's being awarded to his eastern principals, had been

[21] Detroit *Free Press*, April 5, 1853.

[22] John Wilson to the Register of the United States Land Office at Detroit, Sept. 14, 1852, General Land Office, Registers and Receivers Letter Record, XXXVI, 317–318, National Archives. Identical letters were sent to the registers of the other four land offices in Michigan—at Ionia, Genesee, Kalamazoo, and Sault Ste Marie.

appointed by Governor Andrew Parsons as a state agent to select canal lands.[23]

Harvey had more than a passing acquaintance with the Upper Peninsula. Indeed, if there was an authority on the many aspects of the Sault canal matter in 1852 and 1853, it was Harvey. Happening to be at Sault Ste Marie when the news of the passage of the canal bill reached that place in the late summer of 1852, he had immediately interested himself in the subject of a possible contract to build the canal. As we have seen, he called the venture to the attention of his employers, E. & T. Fairbanks & Co. Then he began to gather data on the proposed canal. During the season that he spent in the Upper Peninsula, he roamed the mineral districts, familiarizing himself with the area and listening to the gossip of explorers, miners, and promoters.[24] At some point he came to know J. Venon Brown, the receiver of the United States land office at Sault Ste Marie, which at that time served the entire Upper Peninsula.

The passage of the Sault canal bill was coincident with the opening of new and reportedly rich deposits on the copper range. Eager to forestall the speculators, who, as soon as navigation was open in the spring of 1853, would swarm into the land office at Sault Ste Marie, Harvey set out for that place at the first possible moment after the letting of the canal contract, bent upon claiming for the state, and consequently for the Canal Company, the tracts he had marked as especially desirable the

[23] Wilson to Charles Noble, surveyor general (Mich.), Jan. 15, 1853, General Land Office, Letters to Surveyors General, XV, 155, National Archives; Henry W. Walker to Corning, April 9, 1853, Corning Papers; John W. Brooks to Erastus Fairbanks, March 24, April 1, 20, 1854, Charles T. Harvey Papers, Marquette County Historical Society; *Report of the Directors of the St. Mary's Falls Ship Canal Co. to the Stockholders . . . , 1858* (Detroit, 1858), 4, 8.

[24] E. & T. Fairbanks & Co. to Corning, Nov. 16, 1852; C. T. Harvey, "Pioneer Sault Canal," in Sarah V. E. Harvey and A. E. H. Voorhis, comps., *Semi-Centennial Reminiscences of the Sault Canal* (Cleveland, 1905), 19; Rankin, "Canalside Superintendent," 105–106.

preceding autumn. By paying a premium fare, he obtained passage on the season's first steamer from Detroit to the Upper Peninsula. Some fifty miles short of Sault Ste Marie the ship was blocked by ice. From that point Harvey sent a messenger on snowshoes to the land office at the Sault. The messenger carried a letter to the receiver, J. Venon Brown, authorizing him to reserve for the state, and so to mark on the plat books, up to 300,000 acres in the Sault Ste Marie land district, including all unlocated lands in certain hastily described areas.[25]

Brown served Harvey and the Canal Company well. Guided, no doubt, by the surveyors' notes and by other records in the land office, he made lists of the available tracts that fitted Harvey's description and on April 27 submitted the lists to the Register for recording. Either Brown or Harvey filed a supplementary list on June 23, but most of the lands in the copper and iron districts that were subsequently conveyed by deed to the St. Mary's Falls Ship Canal Company were among Brown's original selections. In line with the instructions issued by the General Land Office, "most if not the whole of the tracts so selected were marked on the plats with the letter C," which meant that they were withdrawn from private entry, to await acceptance by the governor of Michigan and the Secretary of the Interior.[26]

"This mode of selecting the mineral lands was the only one which could be adopted," the directors of the St. Mary's Falls Ship Canal Company later explained to the company's stockholders, "for it would have been impracticable to examine the

[25] Wilson to Robert McClelland, Sept. 16, 1853, "Approved Lists & C, Sault Canal Land, Michigan, State Land Office," V, Lands Division, Department of Conservation, Lansing; C. T. Harvey, "Pioneer Sault Canal," in Harvey and Voorhis, comps., *Semi-Centennial Reminiscences of the Sault Canal,* 17–18. (Harvey's instructions to Brown are quoted in Wilson's letter.)

[26] Wilson to McClelland, Sept. 16, 1853, Department of Conservation, Lansing; George S. Frost to S. B. Treadwell, May 19, 1855, Records of the Michigan Department of Conservation, Lands Division, Michigan Historical Commission.

different tracts, leaving the same open for entry at the Land Office, by other parties or individuals, as the work of examination was going on." [27] But it was hardly to be expected that such an irregular procedure would go unchallenged.

The opening of navigation to the Sault brought the expected influx of miners and speculators. At the same time Brown, the receiver of the land office there, and Richard Butler, the Register, were relieved of their duties and replaced by William A. Pratt and Ebenezer Warner.[28] The rotation of land officers had nothing to do with the Canal Company's affairs, but rather reflected the change from a Whig to a Democratic administration in Washington. From the company's viewpoint the change was for the worse, because the new officers proved to be both incompetent and antagonistic to the canal contractors. Under the regime of Pratt and Warner, private entries in the tracts that had been reserved as canal lands by the action of Harvey and Brown were permitted to an estimated extent of from 25,000 to 50,000 acres. As a result, by September 1853, the legitimacy of the canal selections in the mineral districts was being contested in Washington.[29]

[27] *Report of the Directors of the St. Mary's Falls Ship Canal Co. to the Stockholders . . . , 1858*, 8.

[28] Wilson to Ebenezer Warner, June 6, 1853; Wilson to William A. Pratt, June 13, 1853, General Land Office, Registers and Receivers Letter Record, XXXVIII, 283, 311.

[29] John W. Brooks to George F. Porter, June 2, 1853, Joy Papers, Burton Historical Collection, Detroit Public Library; Wilson to Warner, June 14, 1853, General Land Office, Registers and Receivers Letter Record, XXXVIII, 320–321; Frost to Wilson, June 16, 1853, General Land Office Records, Letters Received (no. C5877), National Archives; Wilson to McClelland, Sept. 16, 1853, Department of Conservation, Lansing. In consequence of affidavits made by Butler, Brown, and Harvey relative to the confusing condition of the books and papers in the Register's office at Sault Ste Marie, the office was closed on orders from Washington dated June 28, 1853. Only after a special agent had been sent from the General Land Office to make a thorough examination of the office at Sault Ste Marie was that office permitted to reopen on August 10, 1853 (Wilson to Warner and Pratt, June 28, July 25, 1853,

The charges were essentially these: first, that under the Michigan law of April 5, 1853, the governor could appoint an agent to select lands only on the recommendation of the contractors, but that in Harvey's case the governor had acted without the formality of a recommendation; second, that even if Harvey's appointment was considered valid, he had no right to delegate his authority to Brown; and third, that since Brown, after depositing the lists of selections, had withdrawn them several times without leaving copies, his selections could not invalidate private entries that had been made before the final filing of his lists.[30]

John Wilson, by this time Commissioner of the General Land Office, in a letter to Robert McClelland, Secretary of the Interior, dated September 16, 1853, took the position that if the governor of Michigan had failed to comply with a law of the state, he was responsible to the state, not to the federal government. Wilson believed that Harvey's appointment was entirely legal and that his duties did not constitute a personal trust or confidence that he was implicitly prohibited from delegating. He could therefore perform them through the agency of another person, in this case Brown. Finally, if the Register at Sault Ste Marie permitted the lists that Brown had filed to be withdrawn from the office, the Register was guilty of dereliction of duty, but that could not affect the right of the state to any or all of the lands that were included in the lists. "The subsequent entries of these lands were on full notice of the previous [state]

General Land Office, Registers and Receivers Letter Record, XXXVIII, 401–402).

[30] Wilson to McClelland, Sept. 16, 1853, Department of Conservation, Lansing. On April 9, 1853, Henry W. Walker reported to Corning from Detroit: "Gov. P. appointed Mr. Harvey the agent to locate lands on the nomination of the contractors here" (Corning Papers). Since none of the contractors lived in Detroit, Walker doubtless referred to the men, all residents of that city, who had signed the contract as sureties —Joy, Franklin Moore, George F. Porter, John Owen, and Henry P. Baldwin. Perhaps this explains the charges of illegality surrounding Harvey's appointment.

selection," Wilson concluded, "and are clearly illegal and void." [31] McClelland concurred in the opinion, and this crisis in Canal Company affairs was safely weathered.[32]

Later attempts in both Washington and Michigan to prevent the selected lands, or parts of them, from passing into the possession of the company were likewise unavailing. Secretary McClelland consented to reconsider his decision of 1853, but he did not change it. A last-minute injunction granted in May 1855 by the district judge of the Upper Peninsula, restraining the state officers from delivering the lands to the Canal Company in payment for the canal, failed to reach Lansing in time to stop the formalities of transfer on May 25. According to the Democratic Detroit *Free Press* (which, upon occasion, seemed to speak for the Canal Company), the "fusion" state administration, or part of it, would have been glad to harass the company by withholding title to the lands, but the public wanted the canal and was not in a temper to permit delay in its being transferred to the state.[33] Nor were the representatives of the company in a mood to relinquish the canal until the lands were in their possession. "I drew up a written transfer of the Canal," reported John F. Seymour, who acted for the company on the occasion. "Mr. Brooks and I signed and *kept* it until half past seven when Mr. McKinney [the Secretary of State] handed me 40 patents and I delivered to him the transfer." [34]

Thus the St. Mary's Falls Ship Canal Company acquired a princely domain more than 1170 square miles in extent. Each of the forty patents that Seymour received listed the canal lands in a single county. The mineral lands lay entirely within three

[31] Wilson to McClelland, Sept. 16, 1853, Department of Conservation, Lansing.

[32] Wilson to Frost, Oct. 6, 1853, General Land Office, Miscellaneous Letters Sent, XXXVIII, 107–108, National Archives.

[33] John F. Seymour to Corning, Nov. 8, 1853, Corning Papers; Detroit *Free Press*, May 24, 27, 1855.

[34] Seymour to Corning, June 1, 1855, Corning Papers. Italics are in the original.

counties—Marquette, Houghton, and Ontonagon. In Marquette County, Harvey and Brown had entered 39,527 acres; in Houghton County, 90,157.58 acres; and in Ontonagon County, 57,221.26 acres—making a total of 186,905.84 acres.[35]

Marquette County was the scene of the "iron hills," ore deposits forming "regular mountains, from 50 to 250 feet high." The first mine was opened in the area in 1855, the year that the Canal Company received its land from the state. A second was opened in 1856, and a third in 1859. All three mines lay close together in Township 47 north, Range 27 west. In this township the Canal Company owned 9679 acres, while in the adjacent Township 47 north, Range 26 west, the company had title to 8819 acres. These two townships, it was reported as late as 1864, were thought to be unrivaled in the magnitude and purity of their ores. The remainder of the Canal Company lands in Marquette County were located in surrounding townships or between the iron hills and the village of Marquette or along the shore of Lake Superior.[36] "These lands are . . . valuable," the company's stockholders were told in 1858, "without reference to their mineral character, for the timber, which in that region is being rapidly consumed in making coal to supply the several iron manufacturing establishments already in operation near Marquette." [37]

The Canal Company's copper lands were in Houghton and Ontonagon counties, which at that time blanketed the Keweenaw Peninsula and the area at its base. "The rule which guided in the selection of the lands [in the copper country]," Harvey

[35] Patents, nos. 1–3, Record Book 375, "Miscellaneous Records and St. Mary's Falls Ship Canal Patents," Office of the Secretary of State, Lansing.

[36] *Ibid.*, Patent no. 3; St. Mary's Canal Mineral Land Company, *Reports upon the Value of the Company's Lands Located in the Iron Region of Lake Superior, County of Marquette, State of Michigan* (Boston, 1864), 5–7.

[37] *Report of the Directors of the St. Mary's Falls Ship Canal Co. to the Stockholders . . . , 1858*, 8.

later stated, "was to take all the lands on the Mineral Range of hills, not located at the time of the first entry [in April 1853], and beside these, two tracts of agricultural and timber lands, which from their locality it was thought would be valuable." [38] Harvey estimated that upwards of 85,000 acres of the company's approximately 147,000 acres in the two counties lay in the mineral-producing belt through the center of the peninsula. The remaining acres, some heavily timbered, were contiguous to the Minesota [*sic*] and other large working mines, or in the vicinity of Keweenaw Bay, Portage Lake, and the village of Ontonagon. [39]

The first concern of the Canal Company upon receiving its lands was to sell a portion of them and realize a return on the sum, just short of a million dollars, that had been paid out during the preceding two years for building the canal and locating the grant. [40] Harvey, with his usual zeal, prepared to place the lands in the mineral district on the market. In June 1855, he moved the company's northern land office from the Sault to the village of Marquette. Then a place of fewer than 1800 inhabitants, Marquette was nonetheless the principal urban area in Michigan west of the Sault and the business center of the iron and copper country. There Harvey commenced to take "an active part to promote railroads and other improvements," in an attempt to allay "the prejudices heretofore existing in the district . . . against the Canal Co. as a land Monopoly &c." [41]

[38] "Report of the Land Agent at Marquette," *ibid*, 32.

[39] *A Statement of the Plan of the St. Mary's Canal Mineral Land Company* . . . (New York, 1859), 11.

[40] Not only had the company's stockholders been called upon for the entire permissible capital of $1,000,000—an eventuality far beyond even the most pessimistic expectation—but because some failed to answer the repeated calls, the company had also sold bonds to the amount of $190,000, on which it was obliged to pay interest (E. and T. Fairbanks and Co. to Corning, Nov. 16, 1852; John W. Brooks to Corning, March 10, 1853, Corning Papers; *Report of the Directors of the St. Mary's Falls Ship Canal Co. to the Stockholders* . . . , *1858*, 16–17).

[41] Harvey to Seymour, Jan. 1, 1856, Seymour Family Papers, Collec-

Harvey also conceived plans "to employ advertising and printers ink generaly [*sic*] to bring the lands of the Company in the farming portions of . . . [the Upper] Peninsula into notice, in the same way which has been so successfully tried by the Illinois Central R.R.Co." So far as actual sales were concerned, however, he had little to report by the end of the year, having "bargained off" only six hundred to seven hundred acres in Marquette County. In Houghton and Ontonagon counties he had done nothing at all. Indeed, he complained, he had been restrained from making any but very limited sales by orders from the company's eastern headquarters. Negotiations were pending in Europe, Harvey had been told, for disposing of the lands in the mineral districts in a single unit.[42]

As early as April 1854, a group of American businessmen, including Henry W. Walker of Detroit and some unidentified New Yorkers, had offered to buy the St. Mary's Falls Ship Canal Company's mineral lands, when the company should receive them, for the government price of $1.25 an acre, plus one-half of the net proceeds that the purchasers might later derive from the sale of the lands. Nothing came of this, however. Whether the offer was withdrawn or was refused by the company is not known. The first intimation that a buyer was being sought in Europe is found in a letter of September 5, 1855, from John Murray Forbes to Erastus Corning. At that time the Canal Company's directors were discussing the advisability of sending agents abroad. In the spring of 1856, Corning, the company's president, was in Europe and there were rumors in Detroit that he had written of the imminent sale of "an undivided half" of the mineral lands to a group in Paris for $750,000. On April 7, 1856, Harvey was informed by John W. Brooks that "Mr. Corning under authority of the Board has lengthened out the

---

tion of Regional History, Cornell University. I wish to thank Director Herbert Finch for permission to quote from the Seymour Family Papers.   [42] *Ibid.*

time in which the sale [in Europe] can be made." Hope that the sale would go through extended into 1857, but the following year the Canal Company's directors had to report to the stockholders that the transaction had been "frustrated by unforseen [*sic*] circumstances, which prevented the principal parties in Europe from carrying out the purchase." [43]

By September 1858, 1,709.48 acres of the company's agricultural lands in the mineral districts had been sold—not an impressive showing to be sure—but the average price of $6.70 an acre was considered good. Harvey blamed his failure to sell additional acreage on the protracted negotiations with the European investors. Those negotiations had continued so late into 1857, he said, that the financial crisis of that year had already begun to affect land sales before he was free to promote the canal lands. Harvey also pointed out to the directors that the quality of the company's mineral lands was actually unknown, since little time, money, and effort had been spent on exploration during the long months that the European sale was pending. It was not until the season of 1858 that he had been given anything like an adequate amount of money for exploring. In that year he was permitted to spend $15,000 for the purpose. [44]

Meanwhile, toward the close of 1857, at the request of John V. L. Pruyn, the secretary-treasurer of the Canal Company, Harvey had prepared a report in which he suggested a plan "for the consideration of the Board of Directors, by which the Company's mineral lands could be more efficiently managed and disposed of." The plan called for the incorporation of a new company, "to be called the St. Mary's Canal Mineral Land Company, to which the whole mineral interest of the Canal

[43] Walker to Corning, April 1, 1854; Forbes to Corning, Sept. 5, 1855, Corning Papers; Harvey to Seymour, Jan. 1, 1856, Seymour Family Papers; Harvey to John W. Brooks, April 1, 1856; Brooks to Harvey, April 7, 1856, Harvey Papers; *Report of the Directors of the St. Mary's Falls Ship Canal Co. to the Stockholders . . . , 1858,* 9.

[44] *Report of the Directors of the St. Mary's Falls Ship Canal Co. to the Stockholders . . . , 1858,* 32–33, 37.

Company should be transferred." Harvey's plan was acted upon, with the directors of the Canal Company determining to incorporate the new company in the state of New York, since the parent company had been incorporated there five years before. At the request of the directors, Harvey went to Albany to see the necessary bill through the legislature.[45]

Well before the end of 1858 the St. Mary's Canal Mineral Land Company had been organized, with the head office in Boston and Erastus Fairbanks as president. On the first day of December of that year the directors of the company entered into an arrangement with the directors of the St. Mary's Falls Ship Canal Company for the transfer of the Sault canal lands in Marquette, Houghton, and Ontonagon counties to the new company. In return the Canal Company received 15,000 full-paid shares of Mineral Land Company stock, with a nominal value of $750,000. The remaining 5000 shares were to be sold and the proceeds used, essentially, for exploration of the company's lands.[46]

The Mineral Land Company was conducted as a land company only, not as a mining concern; the sole object of its directors was to dispose of its holdings to the best advantage. Agricultural and timber lands would be offered for sale at once and without reserve, at moderate prices and preferably to actual settlers. Mineral lands, after having been examined as thoroughly as might be necessary "to obtain a full knowledge of their character and value," would be sold, or leased "upon the English system of [the lessor's] receiving a percentage of the product of the mines." The proceeds from sales or leases, less the company's expenses, would be paid to the stockholders in the form of dividends.[47]

The property transferred to the Mineral Land Company in

[45] *Ibid.*, 36–37, 45.
[46] *A Statement of the Plan of the St. Mary's Canal Mineral Land Company*, 3–4.   [47] *Ibid.*, 4–5.

1859 amounted to 180,991.22 acres.[48] A comparison of this figure with the original patents reveals that in the four years that the Canal Company had held its lands, it had sold slightly less than 6000 acres in the mineral counties, an average of approximately 1500 acres a year. Such meager sales had failed to pay the costs of the land office at Marquette. That few persons with money to invest were sanguine about future land sales under the banner of the Mineral Land Company was apparent. As late as June 1863, the Canal Company still held 4627 shares of Mineral Land Company stock for which there was no market.[49]

The first recorded "sale" of land by the Mineral Land Company was in the form of an exchange of 1625 acres on the copper range for 10,000 shares in a newly formed organization, the Albany and Boston Mining Company. This transaction took place in the spring of 1860. "The arrangement," Erastus Corning wrote to Erastus Fairbanks, "is in my judgement a good one. I am anxious to get some mines in working condition to the end if they should prove favorable it would induce others to embark on the same operations." Corning himself took 250 shares of the new company's stock; Fairbanks subscribed to 200 shares. The 10,000 shares that had been paid to the Mineral Land Company were carried on the books of the Albany and Boston Mining

[48] Marquette County Deeds, Liber D, 57–66, Office of the County Clerk, Marquette, Mich.

[49] Cyrus Woodman to John V. L. Pruyn, June 11, 1863, Corning Papers. It is not clear if these shares were some of the 15,000 that had originally been transferred to the Canal Company, or if they were the bulk of the 5,000 shares that had been put into the market. It seems probable that at least 10,000 Mineral Land Company shares had been distributed by the Canal Company to its stockholders at the ratio of one share in the new company to one share in the older company. Corning, who on June 11, 1863, owned 1,080 shares of Canal Company stock, on August 3, 1865, held 1,825 Mineral Land Company shares. Some of the last-named he perhaps purchased in the summer of 1863, when he bid for 250 of the 4,627 shares then held by the Canal Company (*ibid.;* John N. Denison to Corning, Aug. 3, 5, 1865, Corning Papers).

Company as "$300,000 invested in land." About 1863 the Albany and Boston went through a reorganization. The number of shares held by the Mineral Land Company was reduced to 5,000, but those shares had a book value of $250,000. In the mid-1860's the 5000 shares were distributed to the stockholders of the Mineral Land Company "in proportion of one . . . share to four Mineral Land shares." Unfortunately for the promoters' hopes, during the first eight years of its existence the Albany and Boston Mining Company reported the production of only 393 short tons of copper ingots. After 1868 the company's mining operations apparently ceased.[50]

In the period from 1845 through 1865, ninety-four copper companies with holdings in Michigan had made capital calls on their stockholders for a total of more than $13,100,000. During the same period these companies paid only $5,600,000 in dividends, and most of them had no prospects for the future. A modern authority on the Michigan copper industry states that at the end of the Civil War the stock of only three or four Keweenaw enterprises represented a real asset for the companies' owners.[51] The reasons for this were the declining world price of copper and the problems encountered in opening the Michigan lodes.

The beginning of the downward movement in copper prices dated from the middle 1850's, the very time when the Canal Company came into possession of its holdings in Houghton and Ontonagon counties. By that period increased supplies of the metal from Chile, Spain, Australia, and the United States had easily offset the gradual decline in exports from the depleted copper mines of Devon and Cornwall in the United Kingdom.

[50] Corning to Erastus Fairbanks, March 28, 1860; circular signed by John N. Denison, treasurer, St. Mary's Canal Mineral Land Company, 1864 (?), Corning Papers; MSS reports of Albany and Boston Mining Company to the auditor general, state of Michigan, 1862–1872, Michigan Historical Commission.

[51] Gates, *Michigan Copper and Boston Dollars*, 10.

In 1865 world copper production was more than double that of 1845. Further, improved technology in iron manufacture brought fabricated iron into competition with copper utensils and equipment. In the early 1860's iron ships were coming into use; within a few years the market for copper sheathing to cover the hulls of wooden vessels weakened materially. "These developments not only tended to dampen the demand for copper but temporarily increased the amount of scrap flowing back into the supply stream." [52] A combination of higher duties on imported copper and military demands for the red metal temporarily increased the price during the Civil War, but after the war the prewar price decline was resumed. [53]

In addition to being the victims of a world copper glut, investors in Michigan's copper lands were at the mercy of a general ignorance concerning the mineral range itself. When the country was first opened to mining, one writer has stated, "the geology of the range was little understood, and the contents of veins were different in form from what had been seen in other countries." [54] The mass deposits that caused so much excitement in the 1840's another writer has described as "geological freaks." The really significant deposits, he continues, "were of finely disseminated metal in amygdaloid and conglomerate rock, running to great depths, and seldom outcropping in a fashion which would make proving of potentialities rapid or inexpensive." [55] To spend a few thousand dollars, or a few hundred thousand, for exploration and experimental mining was usually to throw money away.

What was true of Michigan's copper range was true, to a degree at least, of its iron district. Hardly had the Upper Penin-

[52] *Ibid.*, 7–8.

[53] *Ibid.*, 8; A. P. Swineford, *History and Review of the Copper, Iron, Silver, Slate and Other Material Interests of the South Shore of Lake Superior* (Marquette, Mich., 1876), 67–68.

[54] Swineford, *History and Review of the Copper, Iron, Silver, Slate and Other Material Interests*, 68.

[55] Gates, *Michigan Copper and Boston Dollars*, 10.

sula's transportation problem been alleviated by the opening of the Sault canal, when the depression of the late 1850's sharply reduced the market for iron ore. Wartime demands revived it, with the result that 1862 was remembered by at least one old-timer in the area as "the first year of dividends." A decade of prosperity followed. In 1873, it was claimed, more than a fourth of all the iron produced in the United States was made from Marquette County ore. But after that year the curtain of depression came down again.[56] Even in the decade of prosperity prior to 1873, investors in the iron district lost over a million dollars. One reason given for the losses, predictably enough, was the unfamiliarity of iron men from other regions with the quality of the Marquette ores. Even the inferior ores of the district were often superior in quality to the ores these experienced men had known in other places. Consequently, they gladly settled for the inferior, only to lose out in competition with the better ores in the area. T. B. Brooks, a reliable observer, attributed two-thirds of the failures of mining enterprises in the Marquette district to this cause. The other third he ascribed to the small quantity of ore in the seams that were opened, although the quality was satisfactory.[57]

After 1864 the St. Mary's Canal Mineral Land Company had no problems in the iron district, for in that year the company sold its remaining holdings in Marquette County (almost 34,000 acres), to the Iron Cliffs Company, a new corporation under the control of Chicago and Northwestern Railroad interests. The sale was for $500,000, a sum that averaged out to a little over $14 an acre. Payment was spread over two years; the last installment was met in February 1866.[58]

[56] S. P. Ely, "Historical Address, Delivered July Fourth, 1876," *Pioneer Collections, Report of the Pioneer Society of the State of Michigan*, VII (Lansing, 1886; reprint, 1904), 169.

[57] *Geological Survey of Michigan* (9 vols., New York, 1873–1903), I, 190–191. T. B. Brooks was largely responsible for the first volume of this work.

[58] Denison to Corning, Feb. 20, 1866, Corning Papers; Saul Benison,

The dividends that resulted from the sale to the Iron Cliffs Company were, happily, not the first that the directors of the St. Mary's Canal Mineral Land Company were able to distribute. A circular dated March 14, 1863, and signed by the company's treasurer had informed the stockholders that a dividend of 12 per cent, that is, of six dollars a share, had been declared. Six weeks later a further dividend of ten dollars a share was paid.[59] Clearly, the Mineral Land Company was feeling the effects of the wartime boom.

On April 20, 1863, John W. Brooks, who was then living in Boston and who was a member of the Mineral Land Company's board, wrote to Erastus Corning, reporting on the company's affairs:

Since January 1st we have sold about $334,000 worth of land, received about $184,000 cash and have due about $150,000 payable in from short periods up to an extreme of 13 months. . . . [The] dividend of $10 per share . . . nominally took 200,000$ but as we pay on only 15000 shares the other 5000 being not full paid we have money enough to pay that amount. The amount which would go to the credit of the assessable stock is set apart as a fund for exploration &c and to make this fund full up to the $10 per share the next 16000$ received will go to its credit. Then further receipts would be to the credit of [the] dividend fund.[60]

"Railroads, Land and Iron, a Phase in the Career of Lewis Henry Morgan" (doctoral dissertation, Columbia University, 1960), 225; Alexander Clarence Flick, *Samuel Jones Tilden, a Study in Political Sagacity* (New York, 1939), 163, 509; *Geological Survey of Michigan*, I, 24, 38. In May 1891 the Iron Cliffs Company was consolidated with the Cleveland Iron Company, another old Marquette County concern, to form the Cleveland-Cliffs Iron Company (Henry Raymond Mussey, *Combination in the Mining Industry: A Study of Concentration in Lake Superior Iron Ore Production* [New York, 1905], 98–99).

[59] Circular of St. Mary's Canal Mineral Land Company, March 14, 1863, signed by Denison; Brooks to Corning, April 20, 1863, Corning Papers.

[60] John W. Brooks to Corning, April 20, 1863, Corning Papers.

Before many months had passed, the Mineral Land Company announced yet another dividend—a large one of 38 per cent, or nineteen dollars a share, "holders of assessable stock to have fourteen dollars a share credited them on stock account, to make their shares full paid." By February 1866, the company had distributed at least forty-five dollars a share on the 15,000 shares that had originally been transferred to the St. Mary's Falls Ship Canal Company. In addition, an undetermined amount had been paid to the holders of the company's other 5000 shares, either in lieu of stock assessments or in the form of cash.[61] At last the canal contractors were beginning to enjoy the returns they had dreamed of a decade before. As yet, however, they had failed to recover their original investment, to say nothing of interest on that investment, and sadder still, they had let the biggest prize in their grasp—the Calumet and Hecla properties—slip through their fingers.

According to the historian of Michigan's copper industry, the most important development in American copper mining during the years 1867 to 1884 was "the opening up of an exceptionally rich and vast mineral body by the Calumet and Hecla Mining Company." By 1873 the company's share of Michigan copper production was more than 65 per cent, and this at a time when the state's copper industry was beginning to dominate the United States copper market.[62]

The discoverer of the Calumet conglomerate lode was Edwin J. Hulbert, a surveyor and civil engineer, who had helped run the township and section lines on the Keweenaw Peninsula.[63] In 1853 he was employed for some weeks at the United States land

[61] Circular of St. Mary's Falls Mineral Land Company, undated but probably issued in 1864; Denison to Corning, Aug. 3, 1865, Feb. 20, 1866, Corning Papers.

[62] Gates, *Michigan Copper and Boston Dollars*, 39, 43.

[63] C. Harry Benedict, *Red Metal: The Calumet and Hecla Story* (Ann Arbor, Mich., 1952), 28–29.

office in Sault Ste Marie, copying maps and manuscripts under the direction of the Register, Ebenezer Warner. According to Hulbert's own account, while making tracings from the plat books, he noticed that the "C" which was used to designate Sault canal lands *varied a little not only in form but in color.* Later he was to claim, "That letter 'C' through the various colors employed, gave me . . . *the Key for purchase of lands . . . , upon one tract of which was opened . . . the Calumet-Conglomerate.*" [64] If Hulbert indeed found the "key" to the location of the Calumet lode in that fashion, he profited from one of the most remarkable coincidences in mining history, for neither Charles T. Harvey nor J. Venon Brown could have known of the fantastically superior quality of the copper deposits in two of the hundreds of sections they chose en bloc. What is far more likely is that Hulbert became aware of the Calumet lode in 1855 while running the survey for a road from Copper Harbor to Ontonagon—a claim that he also makes in his rambling reminiscences.

About 1860, Hulbert bought a promising tract of public land on the copper range a few miles from Torch Lake, in Township 56 north, Range 33 west. The tract included part of section 13. Backed by a group of Boston capitalists who formed the Hulbert Mining Company, Hulbert continued his explorations, and in 1864 discovered the Calumet conglomerate on the company's property in that section. The conglomerate was copper-bearing at the point of discovery. According to J. D. Hague, who was at the time manager of the Albany and Boston mine and a confidant of Hulbert, had the exploratory pit been sunk 400 feet to the northeast, the conglomerate, if found at all, would have appeared almost barren. Immediately after Hulbert's discovery, the officers of the Hulbert Mining Company, acting upon his advice, purchased an additional 200 acres in section 13 that

[64] Edwin J. Hulbert, *"Calumet-Conglomerate": An Exploration and Discovery Made by Edwin J. Hulbert, 1854 to 1864* (Ontonagon, Mich., 1893), 74. The italics are in the original.

belonged to the St. Mary's Canal Mineral Land Company. The price they paid was thirty-five dollars an acre.[65]

Later in 1864, Hulbert excavated what appeared to be an ancient copper pit on the Mineral Land Company's property in section 14, to the west of the discovery pit. Here Calumet's Number 1 shaft was later opened. Section 23, adjacent to section 14 on the south, belonged to the Mineral Land Company in its entirety, and Hulbert was convinced of the continuation of the conglomerate into that section. Hulbert then obtained Hague's cooperation in an effort to buy from the Mineral Land Company part of section 14, the whole of section 23, and other tracts in the township. Hague managed to obtain an option on the land at the price of $100 an acre, but he and Hulbert were unable to raise the money for the purchase, since the "parties in Boston" whom Hague approached for financial backing considered the venture too speculative. Hulbert, however, borrowed $16,800 from Bostonian Quincy A. Shaw with which to buy the coveted part of section 14. In 1866, Shaw and his brother, Parkman, supplied an additional $60,000 for the purchase of section 23. In this section the Hecla mine was later opened.[66] The negotiation of the last purchase took place at the Mineral Land Company's office in Boston, Hulbert having hastened to that city to raise money when he feared others were about to buy the section. "Persons may wonder," he wrote in 1893, "why the rule of the St. Mary's Land Co., 'to refer all applications for land to the Agent at the Lake for approval and valuation,' was in my case suspended; it was in that I had a long and intimate acquaintance with most of the directors, who treated directly with me." [67]

Treating directly with Hulbert may well have been a mistake

[65] *Ibid.*, 49, 135; Benedict, *Red Metal*, 35–36.

[66] Benedict, *Red Metal*, 36–37; Hulbert, *"Calumet-Conglomerate,"* 135, 139–140. The Calumet and Hecla Mining Company was formed in May 1871 by the consolidation of the Calumet and Hecla properties and two minor concerns, the Portland and Scott mining companies (Gates, *Michigan Copper and Boston Dollars*, 42).

[67] Hulbert, *"Calumet-Conglomerate,"* 140.

on the part of the board, for the Mineral Land Company's agent in the Lake Superior district in 1866 was Henry D'Aligny, a successor to Charles T. Harvey, who had returned to the East. D'Aligny, a well-trained mining engineer, was a man whom Hulbert greatly respected, not only for his knowledge, but also for his probity and his devotion to his employers' interests. Hulbert claimed D'Aligny as a friend and may have been as indiscreet in his revelations to him concerning the Calumet conglomerate as he was to Hague and others.[68] The directors of the Mineral Land Company, in selling section 23 for what they doubtless considered a good price but without consulting their local agent, lost a potential fortune. By 1884 the Calumet and Hecla Mining Company, which succeeded the Hulbert Mining Company, had distributed over $25,000,000 in dividends on a paid-in capital of $1,200,000. The shares of the company in 1884 were worth another $25,000,000.[69]

The Civil War boom that created a demand for copper lands and generated dividends for the shareholders of the St. Mary's Canal Mineral Land Company gave way to a postwar depression that lasted from 1867 to 1871. Copper prices in the two years from 1871 to 1873, however, were at exceptionally high levels, and while the effect of the financial crisis of 1873 was sharp, it was not as long-lasting in the copper industry as in some other sectors of the economy. The second half of the 1870's witnessed a remarkable recovery in Michigan copper production. The opening of rich new mines in Houghton County in the middle of the 1880's and at the end of the 1890's insured the continuation of the prosperity of the Michigan industry into the twentieth century, despite increasing competition from the Far West copper fields.[70]

The stockholders of the St. Mary's Canal Mineral Land Company shared in the good years of the last quarter of the nine-

[68] *Ibid.*, 61, 139–140; Benedict, *Red Metal*, 35–37.
[69] Gates, *Michigan Copper and Boston Dollars*, 44–45.
[70] *Ibid.*, 39–40, 54–55, 65–66.

teenth century. At least three important new mines were opened on property that had belonged to the company, and the company became a shareholder in the new enterprises. Other mineral lands, as well as timber lands to a considerable extent, were also sold. The company paid cash dividends of $8.50 a share in 1898 and of $29 a share in 1899.[71]

Despite the late rally in the fortunes of the Mineral Land Company, by the beginning of the twentieth century the return on the roughly $225,000 invested in the mineral lands of the Sault canal grant had hardly been spectacular.[72] Total dividends to January 1, 1901, amounted to $2,200,000.[73] A quarter of a million dollars placed at 5-per-cent interest per annum, compounded, would have produced approximately the same return in the same length of time. The new century, however, was to

---

[71] *Ibid.*, 65–66, 245; Horace J. Stevens, comp., *The Copper Handbook: A Manual of the Copper Industry of the United States and Foreign Countries* (Houghton, Mich., 1902), II, 252.

[72] The investment figure was arrived at by prorating the cost of the canal ($910,925) to the company's acreage in the mineral districts (nearly 187,000 acres of a total 750,000 acres) and adding approximately $25,000 for estimated land-office and other expenses. The estimates are surely low. For the cost of the canal see *Report of the Directors of the St. Mary's Falls Ship Canal Co. to the Stockholders . . . , 1858*, 16.

[73] From time to time the Mineral Land Company distributed to its stockholders the mining company stocks that it received in part or full payment for land sold. By 1901 these distributions amounted to one share of Tamarack Mining Company, one and one-quarter shares of Baltic Mining Company, and one and one-half shares of Trimountain Mining Company for each share of Mineral Land Company. The Tamarack mine, which was opened in 1883, was on the Calumet lode. Rather less spectacularly productive than the Calumet and Hecla properties, Tamarack was nonetheless listed as late as 1904 as one of the six most important mines in Michigan. The Baltic and Trimountain mines were on the Baltic lode, which had been opened at the end of the 1890's and was to be the second most productive Michigan mining area in the early twentieth century. Another mine on the Baltic lode was that of the Champion Mining Company, of which the Mineral Land Company in 1901 owned half the stock (Gates, *Michigan Copper and Boston Dollars*, 65–66; Stevens, *Copper Handbook*, II, 252).

justify the early hopes of the Canal Company investors for greater profits.

In March 1901, the St. Mary's Canal Mineral Land Company was reorganized and emerged as the St. Mary's Mineral Land Company. One purpose of the change was to raise capital for the development of mines on the company's own account. The new company, chartered under the laws of New Jersey, had a capitalization of $5,000,000 divided into 200,000 shares, with a par value of $25 each. Six shares in the new company were exchanged for each $50 share in the old company, while 20,000 shares of the new stock were sold at par to old shareholders, "the rights to subscribe to this stock commanding a considerable premium." Some 60,000 shares went into the market. The company flourished. During its first twenty-eight years—that is, before the end of 1929—it paid over $223,000,000 in dividends, almost $112 on each $25 share, an average yearly return of approximately 16 per cent on the par value of the stock.[74] The return to old shareholders who had benefited from the reorganization of 1901 was three times as great. Thus, long after the speculators of 1852–1853 were in their graves, another generation enjoyed the profits from the Sault canal venture.

[74] Stevens, *Copper Handbook*, II, 252; Walter Harvey Weed, comp., *The Mines Handbook, Succeeding the Copper Handbook, Describing the Mining Companies of the Two American Continents* (Suffern, N.Y., 1931), XVIII, pt. I, 1201.

Vicissitudes of
an Absentee Landlord:
A Case Study

~⟨|⟩~

HENRY COHEN

In 1847 the Washington banker William Wilson Corcoran, aided by well-placed political friends, bought from the United States government about 100,000 acres of land in ten states. These tracts, with other acquisitions, made him a substantial absentee landlord and speculator. His most important holdings were in the Middle West, especially in richly endowed Illinois, where frontier was changing into granary. The absentee landlord has been a subject of some controversy, then and in retrospect. He has often been characterized as a parasite who made no substantive contribution to justify, morally or economically, his profits. On the other hand, the absentee landlord is sometimes described as an entrepreneur who took risks and helped to stimulate regional settlement and growth. Corcoran's correspondence, which survives in profusion (although the pertinent ledger books do not), furnishes an unusual opportunity to study in detail one of the breed. His experience will suggest some conclusions about the value of the vocation.[1]

[1] Distinctions may be made between the estate-building landlord and the speculator, although in practice these categories shade into each other. Cf. Allan G. Bogue, *From Prairie to Corn Belt: Farming on the Illinois and Iowa Prairies in the Nineteenth Century* (Chicago, 1963),

Vicissitudes of an Absentee Landlord

I

The tracts purchased from the government had been repossessed from defaulted debtors. Many had originally been entered by land-office or other officials, including William Linn in Illinois; the Boyds in Mississippi; the Rectors in Mississippi, Arkansas, and Missouri; Lucius Lyon and Henry R. Schoolcraft in Michigan; Samuel Milroy in Indiana; and Samuel Swartwout in Texas. These lands were sold by the Treasury in 1847, by the use of sealed bids and according to arrangements somewhat advantageous to Corcoran. The advertisements were published in the Washington *Union* from August through October, when many potential buyers were away from the capital on vacation. Immediate payment was required, and Corcoran had the cash. In some cases the Treasury rejected higher bids on individual tracts be-

---

45–46. See also Paul Wallace Gates, "The Role of the Land Speculator in Western Development," *Pennsylvania Magazine of History and Biography*, LXVI (July 1942), 314–333; Allan G. and Margaret Beattie Bogue, "'Profits' and the Frontier Land Speculator," *Journal of Economic History*, XVII (March 1957), 1–24; Margaret Beattie Bogue, *Patterns from the Sod. Land Use and Tenure in the Grand Prairie, 1850–1900* (Springfield, Ill., 1959); Thomas LeDuc, "Public Policy, Private Investment, and Land Use in American Agriculture, 1825–1875," *Agricultural History*, XXXVII (Jan. 1963); and Robert P. Swierenga, "The Western Land Business: The Story of Easley & Willingham, Speculators," *Business History Review*, XLI (Spring 1967). The focus of this essay will be on Corcoran's holdings in Illinois. I am indebted to the Social Science Research Council for supporting the research for this essay and to California State College, Long Beach, for secretarial services. The references for this essay are chiefly to the correspondence of Corcoran, his private secretary, agents, tenants, and buyers, in the letterpress copies of the Corcoran Papers, which are almost all bound and indexed; additional material is in the Riggs Family Papers. Both collections are in the Manuscript Division, Library of Congress, Washington, D.C. From considerations of space, I have omitted many redundant references. A fully documented, if primitive, version of this essay is in Henry Cohen, "Business and Politics from the Age of Jackson to the Civil War: A Study from the Career of W. W. Corcoran" (Ph.D. dissertation, Cornell University, 1964).

Table 13. Agricultural lands bought by Corcoran from the U.S. in August 1847

State	No. of tracts	No. of acres (rounded to nearest 10)	Price per acre (average)	Cost (rounded to nearest $10)
Mississippi	97	15,310	$ .38	$ 5,820
Indiana	7	460	.41	180
Illinois	157	22,810	.38	8,280
Missouri	15	2,400	.38	910
Arkansas	13	2,150	.41	880
Arkansas	17	1,550	.26	390
Michigan	27	2,800	.38	1,060
Virginia	1	40	1.25	50
Total	334	47,520	$ .38	$17,570

Table 14. Other lands bought by Corcoran from the U.S. in August 1847

State	Description	Amt. (acreage rounded to nearest 10)	Cost (rounded to nearest $10)
Texas	1 tract	48,440 acres	$1,000
Virginia	Coal lands in W. Va.	9,000 acres	350
New York	N.Y. City lots	44 lots @ $30	1,320
New Jersey	Miscellaneous town and suburban lands	770 acres and 40 lots	850
Illinois	2 townsites	39 lots	390
Michigan	5 villages, 1 townsite	31 lots	400
Arkansas	1 townsite	26 lots	260
Total			$4,570

cause his tender for all the land in a county or state yielded a greater total return. Corcoran obtained most of what he wanted. Tables 13 and 14 indicate the extent and cost of his acquisitions.[2] Corcoran's bids compare with the going price for public land of

[2] Corcoran to Solicitor of the Treasury (bids for land), Oct. 25, 1847, list of properties won by Corcoran, Nov. [?], Treasury Archives, National Archives; advertisement, Washington *Union*, Aug. 17 *et seq.*, 1847.

$1.25 per acre, less at least 10 per cent when payment was in scrip issued under various bounty-land acts.

These tables indicate most, but not all, of Corcoran's acquisitions. In the 1840's and 1850's he bought, in exchange for scrip, about 10,000 acres in Illinois at sheriffs' sales for nonpayment of taxes. He obtained about 3,000 acres and some village lots in Michigan through tax and ordinary sales. Other purchases included several thousand acres in Indiana bought jointly with Senator Jesse Bright of that state for approximately $2 an acre, and a one-third share of 3,500 acres of cotton lands in Lafayette County, Arkansas, for warrants costing $2,600. More than $10,000 was expended for at least a dozen quarter sections in the Delaware Indian Tract and other areas of Kansas, and for acreage near and in Leavenworth and the projected townsite of Quindaro.[3]

Corcoran also held some coal lands. He acquired a tract in Rock Island, Illinois, an area favored since the 1830's by speculating Washington politicians. Much more promising were 14,100 acres in Randolph and Kanawaha counties in what later became West Virginia. Most of the acreage Corcoran acquired from the Treasury in 1847, and in 1857 he invested another $5,000, as a member of a group of businessmen and politicians, in an ambitious Kanawaha County purchase.[4]

The last large venture grew out of the transcontinental drive

---

[3] In 1854, Corcoran declined to join speculator Solomon Sturgis in raising £10,000 to £20,000 in England to buy Illinois land. There may have been nonpecuniary motivations in some of the Kansas investments: Corcoran later wrote that his only purpose in many of them was to benefit Major Deas, his agent. Nevertheless Corcoran always required good prospects of profit.

[4] Corcoran (hereafter abbreviated C.) to Richard Fay, Feb. 10, 1857, Jan. 21, April 21, 1859, C. to W. S. Wetmore, April 21, 1859; C. to W. Rosecrans, March 18, copies of agreements of Feb. 4, 1857, Feb. 2–3, 1859, and Oct. 5, 1858, memos, Oct. 22–23, Feb. 4, 1857, Feb. 15–16, 1861, C. to John B. Seymour, Jan. 31, 1859, C. to Nicholl, Feb. 12, 1859, C. to Bright and others, Jan. 15, 1861, C. letter books; Allan Nevins, *Emergence of Lincoln* (2 vols.; New York, 1950), I, 312.

of the Northern Pacific Railroad. In 1870–1872 Corcoran furnished three-eighths of a joint account for purchases and entries along the railroad's projected route or near such infant towns as Portland and East Portland, Seattle, Walla Walla, Olympia, and Astoria. After various disputes were resolved the speculators held 379 acres in Oregon, and 8,433 in Washington Territory. A total of 7,253 acres had been entered at $1.25 and the rest entered or bought at from $2.50 to $100 per acre, for a total outlay of $36,700.

II

Corcoran hired purchasing agents through his Washington connections. Some agents were political acquaintances, like Orlando B. Ficklin, congressman from Illinois, and Thomas Ewing, Jr., son of the Ohio politician, who was employed in Kansas. A number of army men furnished services to Corcoran on the Kansas frontier (where much of the officer corps was apparently so occupied). Furthermore, James Tilton, an official on leave from the Northern Pacific Railroad, was well suited for carrying out Corcoran's northwestern plans: his subagents included employees of the railroad.[5]

Reliable resident agents were needed for handling sales, rentals, improvements, title disputes, protection against squatters and timber thieves, and some litigation. A typical contract for a local resident agent before the Civil War paid a hundred dollars a year for safeguarding property and 5 per cent for collections (perhaps 3 per cent when notes were taken instead of cash). Sometimes several representatives were used for the same tracts to check each other. Resident agents were usually politicians, for-

[5] Ficklin also served other important businessmen and politicians (C. to Deas, Dec. 26, 1856, C. letter books; John Slidell, E. Riggs, Jr., Ficklin agreement, March 19, 1857, and other papers, Riggs Papers). From the politicians' point of view these transactions represented anything from routine business and favors for constituents to patronage. All stripes and parties are represented in the correspondence.

mer politicians, or persons recommended by politicians. Ficklin and James C. Conkling, former congressmen, were employed in Illinois, and William Woodruff, a prominent editor-politico, in Arkansas. Sometimes government officials were hired after leaving office, for example, Ransom Gillett, Corcoran's attorney in New Jersey and New York and previously a Register and solicitor for the United States Treasury Department, and N. B. Walmsley, a county revenue commissioner in western Virginia. Where Corcoran lacked personal contacts, recommendations were obtained from the local congressman or senator. Legislators commonly served as intermediaries without pay for constituents, but sometimes they were themselves land agents or speculators.[6]

Agents were often unreliable: Ficklin was honest, "but he seem[ed] to carry most of his business in his head and breaches [*sic*] pocket"; representatives in Michigan and Missouri left correspondence unanswered and taxes unpaid, incurring penalties. One agent proved altogether too vigorous for comfort: A. N. Lancaster, a Wall Street-based speculator with a formidable reputation and subordinates throughout the West. In 1864 he applied to manage the Illinois lands, proposing to sell off tracts with imperfect titles and to keep half of the proceeds. He was refused on grounds of a potential conflict of interests and the exorbitant charge. Lancaster was hired as general agent—but to work only outside of Illinois, where lay by far the most lucrative and attractive properties. Resenting this restriction, he told one of his henchmen to "let Corcoran's land go to the Devil." Still he was retained, partly from fear that he was too dangerous to cross. His commission was 10 per cent of sales, double or more than that of other agents. When friction persisted, his services

[6] Woodruff had been agent for Romulus Riggs of Philadelphia, a wealthy merchant and uncle of Corcoran's partners (C. to Woodruff, March 25, May 23, 1848, C. to Gillett, May 7, June 7, 1851, C. to Walmsley, Dec. 1, 1853, C. to John L. Robinson, May 28, 1855, C. letter books; Woodruff to John Elliott, Riggs Papers).

were dispensed with.[7] Nevertheless an unreliable agent was better than none. Some, indeed, were able and trustworthy, for example the Arkansan Woodruff, his successors Shall and Miller, and two former high Texas officeholders, Starr and Amory.[8]

In view of the mixed results of hiring from a distance, Corcoran found it desirable to send his own men west. William Gouge, the old Jacksonian monetary publicist, drew up reports from Mississippi, where he also owned land, and from Arkansas and Texas. In 1865, Simon L. Sommers, an experienced surveyor and Corcoran's former troubleshooter, was hired as general overseer at $1,400 per year, which was raised in 1866 to $1,800, plus expenses.[9]

Corcoran always exercised strict control over policy, even when he was abroad during the Civil War. When he was in the country, he made all final decisions about the disposition of particular tracts. This irritated both Lancaster and Sommers. The latter, priding himself on his knowledge and experience, was offended by the restrictions and almost resigned in 1858. Afterward Sommers and Corcoran worked smoothly together: the landlord continued his close supervision, but Sommers proved his ability and integrity and his advice was usually followed. He remained general agent and resided in Illinois after Corcoran's death in 1887.

III

Land, once acquired, had to be vigorously defended. Some titles were clouded from the first; others later became so, espe-

---

[7] Lancaster was praised by Edward K. Collins, the erstwhile shipping magnate; Josiah Lombard, president of the Fifth National Bank of Chicago, was another reference. Lombard also represented a British merchant banker and in-law of the Riggs family, William C. Pickersgill.

[8] Some of Ficklin's leases, as late as 1872, were verbal.

[9] C. to Gouge, April 2, 1851, Aug. 27, Dec. 18, 1856, C. letter books; Gouge to Corcoran and Riggs, June 21, 1852, Riggs Papers.

cially before Sommers was hired to provide continuing oversight. He tabulated the situation as of October 1859:

	Acres, clear title	Estimated value	Acres, defective title	Estimated value
Illinois	8,952	$119,303	15,209	$274,423
Michigan	1,000	6,480	1,560	16,194
Indiana	2,240	13,360	378	15,560
Mississippi	5,420	14,163	10,120	83,665
Missouri	0	0	1,920	10,880
Texas	1,170	5,840	36,332	18,166
Totals	18,782	$159,146	65,519	$418,888

Four months later,[10] after the successful conclusion of a number of suits and some sales, a breakdown was made for Mississippi (with more realistic valuations).

	Acres	Estimated value
Occupied under adverse titles	3,380	$15,720
Claimed under adverse titles and not occupied	4,560	14,890
Clear titles	5,520	11,200

There were myriad causes of title disputes. The ineptitude of primitive bureaucracies was always a threat. Discrepancies in the spelling of names, omissions of seemingly unimportant words, and other errors had to be caught and corrected. Corcoran noted "the remarkable looseness with which land matters are handled in Mississippi"; 280 acres in Pope County, Arkansas, were endangered because land in Range 21 was listed in Range 20. Even if successfully defended, claims might cost, in lawyers' fees, one-third to one-half of the value of the land. The problems were apparently far more common in the South than the North.[11]

[10] Copy of table dated Oct. 18 and Oct. 31, 1859, and of list, Feb. 10, 1860, C. letter books.

[11] C. to Gouge, May 5, 1851, C. to Streeter, April 22, 30, 1857, C. to Woodruff, April 30, 1857, Oct. 4, 22, 1858, C. to Junius Hillyer, June 5, 1858, Hyde to C., June 13, Hyde to Woodruff, July 3, C. letter books.

Officials often helped set matters right, but sometimes they were mulish. A missing federal marshal's deed left a gap in the chain of conveyances of 6,000 acres in Mississippi. Sommers denounced the "stupidity and perverseness" of Treasury Solicitor Junius Hillyer, who refused to violate precedent by issuing a duplicate deed for a decade-old transaction. Sommers considered taking the matter to a "higher power," presumably Secretary of the Treasury Howell Cobb, "but there is a strong indisposition both to control a subordinate and to undo what a predecessor did." There were twenty-two occupants contending for the land involved. Fourteen were successfully sued, and the rest compromised, receiving a 25-per cent discount on purchases or rentals.[12]

Multiple ownership rights often lurked unseen. Dower rights might provide the basis for a claim of at least nuisance value. In Missouri, Corcoran learned that he had only one-third of a title, for want of a signature on an ancient conveyance; besides, a missing deed took eleven years to obtain. Meanwhile, fifty to sixty heirs had unknowingly sold parcels. For a time the title was so confused that even efforts to pay taxes failed. When litigation began, a change of venue was ordered: this sort of mess was so common in the area that practically all the lawyers had committed themselves on the legal issues and no impartial judge could be

[12] C. to Singleton and to James Drane, March 10, 1851, Oct. 8, 1860, C. to Butterfield, Commissioner, General Land Office, March 21, 1851, memos and lists, March 25, 1851, Nov. 17, 1856, Dec. 22, 1857, Aug. 17, 1860, Hyde to Gouge, June 23, 1851, C. to Gouge, July 11, 1851, C. to Terrence McGowan, Feb. 8, 1855, C. to Campbell, May 30, 1857, April 24, 1858, April 4, Sept. 8, 1859, Jan. 27, Feb. 10, March 28, May 1, 1860, C. to Jacob Thompson, Nov. 11, 1857, C. to William Clark, Nov. 11, C. to Sommers, Dec. 7, 1857, March 11, 1858, C. to Hendricks, Jan. 5, Oct. 15, 1858, Hyde to Hillyer, Sept. 23, 1858, Aug. 14, 17, 1860, Hyde to Pleasants, March 11, Aug. 14, 1858, C. to Hillyer, Feb. 11, 1859, Hyde to C., Nov. 30, 1859, Feb. 2, 1860, Hyde to Campbell, Feb. 18, Aug. 14, 1860, Hyde to Tilton, Jan. 12, 1871, Hyde to Drummond, March 16, C. letter books; Sommers to C., Dec. 11, 1857, Feb. 26, March 8, 1858, Sommers to Campbell, March 4, unbound letterpress copies, C. Papers.

found. It took nearly two decades for Corcoran to establish ownership.

In another instance, a railroad land grant interfered with land administration in the Northwest. The Northern Pacific claimed all odd-numbered sections along its route. The General Land Office prohibited conflicting entries made after mid-August 1870, but the order took two months to reach distant land offices. During this interval many entries were made, including 3,335 acres for Corcoran and his partners. The ensuing conflict was decided in favor of the speculators by Land Office Commissioner Willis Drummond, but Secretary of the Interior Columbus Delano suspended the judgment on advice of Attorney General George Williams, an Oregonian. Delano finally allowed the railroad 1,688 acres. Claims to 800 acres were suspended pending clarifying legislation, but none was forthcoming, and after nine years they were canceled. This left 847 acres, patents for which were finally issued under Secretary of the Interior Henry M. Teller. Corcoran's secretary, blaming political influence for the reverses, had hoped pressure by settlers similarly affected would benefit the speculators, but he was disappointed.[13]

By far the most numerous title defects stemmed from the often mixed causes of tax payments and adverse possession. Western statutes generally provided that possession plus tax payments for seven consecutive years gave title. Corcoran's first step after the 1847 purchase was to pay delinquent taxes before federal repossession, something U.S. agents had sometimes neglected to do. He either did not pay, or paid under protest, taxes for the years the federal government held title; the courts ultimately upheld his contention that the lands were not subject to

---

[13] Hyde to Tilton, March 2, June 15, Dec. 9, 1872, April 18, 26, May 23, June 14, 1873, Hyde to various commissioners and other officials, G.L.O., June 17, Nov. 4, 1872, April 17, 1873, Sept. 16, 1879, Feb. 13, March 4, 11, 1882 July 30, 1884, memos, Feb. 17, June 18, 1873, Hyde to Bright, May 15, 23, 1873, Hyde to Lawrason Riggs and to Smedberg, Aug. 29, Oct. 8, 1873, Sept. 4, 1879, Hyde to Mackall, Aug. 20, 1879, Dec. 7, 1883, Hyde to W. C. Riggs, March 20, 1882, C. letter books.

state or local levies. Corcoran hoped in vain that all tax titles would be invalidated; at the same time he himself made use of them.[14]

A kind of guerilla warfare against absentee landlords was endemic in the West. At first Corcoran was inclined to accept the advice of an Illinois agent to let taxes go unpaid until the sixth year; the rates and penalties in frontier days were so slight that delinquency was, in effect, a form of cheap credit. The influx of the land-hungry changed this casual attitude. Squatters occupied tracts and rushed to pay taxes, which conniving local officials sometimes refused to accept from the absentee landlord. In Texas, Sommers had to face down a mob of squatters bent on terrorizing him by a threat of lynching. Occupants might be intimidated by ejectment proceedings, but were first urged to become tenants, even though rents might be merely nominal, to establish recognition of title. It was better yet to install a tenant on almost any terms before squatters arrived or to hire an agent living in the vicinity to take physical possession.

A tenant having nothing to lose might neglect his responsibility for taxes. In troublesome Missouri, where Corcoran mailed payments to local sheriffs, some of these officials united with tenants or squatters by pocketing Corcoran's money, thus cheating him and forcing the land into tax sales. With duplicate payments, and with penalties and interest, redemption might cost double or triple the original purchase price. Yet, even when

[14] C. to O. Holmes, Aug. 9, 1848, C. to Starr & Amory, Sept. 20, 1848, May 4, 1852, C. to Solicitor of Public Accounts, Jackson, Miss., Aug. 10, 1848, C. to sheriff, Attala County, Miss., Aug. 28, memo, Nov. 27, C. to Woodruff, Jan. 20, 1849, C. to Gillett, March 2, May 19, 1849, extracts from Conkling to C., March 14, 1855, March 20, C. to Commissioner, G.L.O., Sept. 29, 1858, Hyde to Conkling, Sept. 2, 1863, Hyde to Sommers, Aug. 22, 1865, C. to Sommers, March 24, 1866, C. to Arrington & Dent, March 12, 1867, C. letter books; Sommers to C., May 31, June 29, July 3, 1858, unbound letterpress copies, C. papers; Wright v. Mattison, 18 Howard 50; Theodore Leonard Carlson, *The Illinois Military Tract: A Study of Land Occupation, Utilization and Tenure* (Urbana, Ill. 1951), 62.

taxes were paid and registered, without clear physical possession the property would be insecure, for it became established legal doctrine that possession defeated tax title. In 1864, 1,000 acres and two town lots in Illinois were listed as "lost by adverse payment"; two years later tax payments on 5,600 acres were discontinued and claim to them abandoned, chiefly because of the statute of limitations. (There had been seven years of adverse possession.)

When titles were clouded, compromise was preferred to the expense and uncertainty of legal proceedings, but suit was filed when the case was strong and an adversary's demands excessive or when action was necessary to forestall use of the statute of limitations. Where title was "worthless" or "bad," Corcoran was content to sell a quitclaim for $100 or more. In an instructive Illinois case he claimed that his tax title was worth one-third of the land's estimated value of $3,200 but offered to take $800. In response to an offer of half that amount, he followed the usually effective tactic of proposing to split the difference and threatening to sue if he was refused. In this case a tenacious opponent offered $450, which was accepted.[15]

Only the strongest cases were prosecuted. Care was taken to stay out of state courts or to convey title to an out-of-state friend so that appeals could be taken to the federal courts. (As a resident of the District of Columbia, Corcoran was legally barred from such appeals.) Consequently, despite occasional symptoms, favoritism toward residents of the state where the lands were located was not a significant courtroom problem. As might be expected, Corcoran had the benefit of the best counsel, from such men as Josiah A. P. Campbell, the future Chief Justice of Mississippi. Of all Corcoran's state and federal cases, includ-

---

[15] When Corcoran lost title, he recovered the cost of his improvements (C. to Conkling, May 20, 1867, Hyde to Fort and Craft, Nov. 22, 1867, Hyde to Sommers, Sept. 23, 1868, June 19, 1882, C. to Richard Lloyd, June 21, July 9, Aug. 29, Sept. 2, 1870, Hyde to Lloyd, Aug. 22, C. letter books).

ing several that were carried to the Supreme Court, he lost only one, and that perhaps through fraud.[16]

Corcoran was at last forced to adopt a socially constructive solution for title problems. Reluctant to incur expenses for development, he initially intended to keep at least some land virgin, renting only for pasture while the value rose with the increase in population. The short-sightedness of this policy was proved by thousands of acres of lost title. When Sommers became overseer, he urged that possession of worthwhile properties be tangibly evidenced by substantial improvements, especially fencing, at costs estimated at from two to ten dollars per acre. His employer hesitated, questioning whether the gains would equal the costs, but finally yielded. Thereafter there were no fresh difficulties worthy of note.[17]

IV

Apart from title considerations, there was ample reason to sell or lease. Taxes rose quickly with growing population and social investment. Increases were most rapid in fertile Illinois, slowest in the poorer, more backward South. In 1856, Corcoran was exasperated by rates which in some Illinois counties had multiplied two to five times in two years. In 1859 he was outraged by school taxes of 4 per cent of assessed valuation; he paid $315 on one section. Taxes were generally payable in coin. In the early

[16] Hyde to C., July 9, 1855, C. to Campbell, Aug. 18, 1858, July 8, 1860, C. to Clarke and Walker, Oct. 12, 1859, Hyde to D. W. Middleton, Oct. 21, Nov. 12, 1867, C. to Hill, April 9, 1870, C. to Dent and Black, April 11, C. to Sanford, May 5, C. to Sommers, Aug. 20, 1870, Feb. 5, April 21, 1873, June 23, 1879, C. to L. Riggs, Dec. 23, 1872, Hyde to clerk of the Supreme Court, April 6, 1883, C. to J. B. H. Smith, April 17, C. letter books; Hyde to C., Dec. 12, 1867, unbound letterpress copies, C. Papers; Riggs v. Boylan, 20 Federal Cases 774, 776; Riggs v. Collins, 20 Federal Cases 824, 14 Wallace (81 U.S.) 491; Dirst v. Morris, 14 Wallace (81 U.S.) 484.

[17] C. to Moore, Dec. 4, 1860, C. to Sommers, June 22, 1866, Aug. 20, 30, 1867, C. to Sommers, March 20, 31, May 18, 1869, Hyde to Sommers, Oct. 9, 30, 1867, C. letter books.

days of the Civil War, Treasury notes, acceptable elsewhere, were refused for taxes in the Illinois, while depreciated paper had to be accepted for rents. By 1860, Corcoran's Illinois taxes exceeded $2,000, twice the total on his other holdings. Still, the Illinois tax was only about 1 per cent of the estimated value, though a higher percentage of the assessed valuation. The maximum rate seems to have been reached in Kansas, where one tax of 6 per cent in 1859 tempted Corcoran to unload. Although he resented rising taxes, the old banker agreed to make small grants of up to one acre for schools when he was advised that such grants would be "wise as well as generous."

Discrimination against absentee owners was widespread in the administration of the law. In Illinois, however, it seems to have been somewhat less of a danger than elsewhere, and in the North less than in the South. A customary technique was to pad assessments. In an extreme instance, in Illinois in 1875 an $800 drainage assessment was cut to $320 when a case was brought before the justice of the peace, and to $200 on appeal to the county court; even then further appeal was considered. At each higher court level the judges tended to be less sensitive to local pressures and more attuned to property rights, absentee as well as resident. Farther south an earlier case had a different outcome. Discrimination was written into the law in Arkansas, where residents evaluated their own property but absentee holdings were appraised by local officials. In 1858 Gouge reported that an adverse claimant appraised twenty-six disputed lots plus twenty-seven clearly his own at $350; simultaneously the official appraisers, in assuming that Corcoran was the owner, evaluated the twenty-six lots alone at $8,000. Usually he could only grumble and submit; sometimes he refused to pay, on the chance that the land would not be bid in at the tax sale, in which case payment could be postponed indefinitely with slight penalty. High rates occasionally induced him to relax terms in order to stimulate sales.

Depredation was another problem. Timbered tracts were most vulnerable, especially if sawmills were nearby. When trespassers were known, they were taken into court only as a last resort. Not only was it expensive, but it was also prudent to accept even a modest settlement "rather than multiply suits and thereby increase the feeling against nonresident land owners." Large losses were sustained; on one tract they were estimated as two-thirds of the value.

Initially, in the 1850's, rentals were relatively modest, generally corresponding to the going rate of interest on the value—the sale price—of the property. They varied from slightly under ten cents to about a dollar per acre per year, with most between thirty-five and seventy-five cents. Leases ran for one to five years, with the landlord retaining the right to repossess for sale on "reasonable" notice. Corcoran preferred the longer lease: short-term tenants often minimized input, mined the soil, and pulled out, leaving depleted soil and disrepair. Similarly, nonresident tenants were not accepted. Some, perhaps many, of the smaller tracts were leased to adjacent landowners. Half the leases were for under a hundred acres, few for more than two hundred. In Coles County, Illinois, one-quarter of Corcoran's acreage was rented; elsewhere, less.

Terms included detailed provision for improvements and penalties for waste. Tenants were required to install permanent fencing. Specifications sometimes called for osage-orange hedges in whole or in part, but usually for wood: "Good and substantial post and plank fence consisting of five rails 6″ wide of the best usual material, around the whole line, to remain there permanently," read a contract for an unusually large tract of three quarter sections. At $1.50 credit per rod, the rent would be reduced by one-half over the five years of the lease. On expiration of the lease, a tenant might remove all improvements but the fences; meanwhile the improvements provided the only security for payment of rent. Corcoran refused to promise compensation for improvements unless he gave prior approval, since he wanted to maintain control of quality and cost and was afraid to trust the estimates of strangers.

By 1861, Corcoran was ready to experiment with large-scale permanent improvements in place of cash payment for rent. A rigorous four-year contract commencing March 1 for an unbroken quarter section of prairie required the cultivation of at least 60 acres by July 1 and the addition of at least 240 rods of outside fence, intermediate fencing, a stable, and a house costing at least $160. By July 1, 1864, the rest of the arable land was to be cultivated and a corncrib built. A cash rent of $350 per year was set if the stipulations were not carried out.

This type of contract was used increasingly, especially after Sommers became overseer in 1865. At times, he noted, the value added to the tract by improvements would be greater than the obtainable cash rent. Accordingly, the right to sell during the life of a lease was sometimes waived or a pro rata reimbursal guaranteed. The older and simpler contract continued to be used, and variations were developed, e.g., a less ambitious program of improvements with money rent beginning the third year of a five-year contract. Corcoran spent heavily to upgrade unoccupied tracts and to make advances to tenants for improvements, although he lamented the cost and periodically slowed or suspended outlays.

Debts were a perpetual problem. Even in good times perhaps one-fifth of the annual rents were at least a year overdue. During severe depressions, like those that began in 1857 and 1873, arrears mounted to well over half. Corcoran was firm in insisting on adherence to contracts after the depression of 1857, granting only brief extensions of notes and refusing to renew leases for tenants chronically overdue. He rejected a farmer's request for a cancellation of arrears for the yet uncultivated portion of his lease. When rents were small, Corcoran demanded advance payment. It was because of the difficulty of making collections at this time that he first sent Sommers west.

By mid-1860, Corcoran had learned to make concessions, especially to retain desirable tenants. He forgave rent on uncultivated holdings and took notes for arrears, charging the usual interest of 10 per cent. Often security was present in improvements and personal property, and sometimes in land owned by adjacent farmers, whose tenancy represented a step toward expansion. If notes were not paid at maturity, judgments could be obtained readily and the risks of suit minimized. However, the last legal recourse was seldom taken, since substantial recovery seemed unlikely when a debtor was hard up.

Corcoran reacted more reasonably to the depression of the 1870's. When tenants' resources were exhausted, arrears were forgiven and rates reduced about 25 per cent. Advances were made to finance harvests in exchange for liens against crops. The number of share-crop rentals, previously few, increased significantly. The policy was not purely generous: Corcoran was extremely reluctant to forgo money rents and accept payment in labor, materials, or improvements, but with many tenants in a position to move or to farm only their own holdings, concessions had to be made. In the end, losses from bankruptcy, absconding, unfulfilled obligations for improvements, and so forth, were not serious; if anything, their unimportance is surprising, in view of Sommers' bleak dispatches of 1878 under the heading "Hard Times in Illinois." [18]

At first Corcoran was inclined to hold his Illinois properties,

[18] C. to Sommers, Feb. 8, 1858, C. letter books; C. to McMillan, June 22, July 16, Aug. 25, Sept. 21, 1858, *ibid.* There was one attempt to operate a cotton plantation at long range. Before the Civil War, Senator Robert W. Johnson borrowed $20,000 from Corcoran and $10,000 from George Riggs against a mortgage on a 1,840-acre Arkansas plantation. The war left him bankrupt, and Corcoran and Riggs took over the property. The original loan accumulated interest, and purchase of a previously unsuspected prior mortgage raised the investment to more than $100,000. Although valued at $120,000, the land attracted no buyers and was rented for sublease to sharecroppers. The rent, paid in cotton, was worth about $6,000 in 1870 and would have been again in 1871 if 90 per cent of it had not disappeared en route to New Orleans. Informed that the land was being neglected, Corcoran set up his nephew and a partner as superintendents and financed their purchase of the Riggs interest. The total return on the 1872 crop was $7,200; on the next, under $6,700. In 1874, Corcoran leased his two-thirds of the plantation to his agents for three years at $4,500 per annum. They were to bear all

but he soon began to accept offers that were clearly above the current value. In other words, what were intended as investments became speculations. Corcoran declined an offer to enter the mortgage business, preferring to buy good land with clear title at a price "which will promise a fair profit in the course of two or three years." A partial exception to this policy was made in Illinois, where 4,600 acres were set aside as a permanent estate for his grandchildren. The only other real estate so treasured were urban sites in Washington, D.C., and Superior, Wisconsin.[19] In 1879, however, the severe depression indicated that the time of great gains was past, and the aging investor decided to sell all his agricultural land when prosperity revived prices. Prosperity returned but still he wavered. By the end of 1884 he decided against further improvements except where they were unavoidable to conserve existing values.

Almost all sales were on credit. The customary terms for the standard quarter section were one-third down and the rest in two equal annual installments at 6 per cent interest, but 10 per cent (as permitted by District of Columbia law) on overdue balances. In rare instances interest varied with prevailing local rates. For smaller tracts, half down and a year's credit for the balance, or even full cash payment, was the general rule; in larger transactions, one-quarter down plus three annual installments. Corcoran often insisted upon cash payment for wooded tracts; otherwise the timber might be stripped off, leaving the denuded land inadequate as security. In the 1880's, after the decision to liquidate, he liberalized his terms somewhat.

---

expenses, and share taxes and insurance. Poor crops and prices led to late payments and reductions to $3,100, then to $2,500 for 1878, and to $2,000 for the following year. The rent was raised to $2,500 when conditions improved, but by 1882 it was again six months in arrears. This investment—whose origins were partly political—was Corcoran's most unfortunate. In the end it was written off and the property given to his nephew.

[19] The Superior speculation is analyzed in chapter x of Cohen, "Business and Politics from the Age of Jackson to the Civil War."

Corcoran did not sell to speculators. Their willingness to pay a certain price was prima-facie evidence that more could be obtained directly from cultivators. In fairness to them, he gave tenants the opportunity to match acceptable offers. During depressions payment delays were allowed, sometimes without penalty, but never reductions of price. Bothered a few times by defaulted agreements, Corcoran reserved the right to sell at better terms before the first payment was received. The over-all growth of Illinois's prosperity could be seen in his records: repudiations and foreclosures grew steadily rarer and many buyers saved on interest by completing payment before maturity.

There remain for consideration the prices and profits realized. Corcoran began selling Illinois land early in the 1850's at $2.00 to $10.00 per acre. Prices increased within that range, then reached $12.50 early in 1855. Within a year $20 was the usual asking price, sometimes more, and as high as $60 for eighty timbered acres in Cook County. By mid-1857 at least four thousand acres were sold, one-fifth of his possessions in the state. After a trip west Corcoran decided his prices had been much too low. (He came to the same conclusion on a visit to Mississippi in 1860.) By then only the most wretched and isolated land would bring much under $10 per acre.[20]

The depression of 1857 deflated values by up to 25 per cent, and sales slowed considerably. The war brought renewed price advances; prices reached $30 per acre and at least partly compensated for currency inflation. Sales and prices sagged briefly in 1865, when agents reported that rising taxes made many anxious to sell. Illinois money, one advised, was flowing into the new issue of federal bonds instead of into land. Prices soon recovered,

---

[20] The spread of the railroad network sharply increased values. There were also sales of right of ways to railroads, generally a hundred feet wide, for which a stiff price was exacted: in one case $1,000, plus the erection and maintenance of a substantial fence. Payment was sometimes taken in stock, before company bankruptcies in the late fifties brought an insistence on cash.

with sales generally at $30 to $45 an acre, but sometimes at as high as $53.[21]

The trend was interrupted briefly by the depression of 1873; in 1875 prices climbed to $50 per acre. Corcoran was never to receive much more than that, and there were setbacks in the late seventies and at intervals thereafter, although real prices were firm over the long term when account is taken of the deflationary trends of the next two decades. Demand also increased for cutover and brush land as the more desirable areas were settled, and rents kept pace with rising expenditures for improvements. It appears that when costs of improvements, taxes, interest, and so forth, are set off against income and monetary changes, the best time for sales was the period immediately following the Civil War.

Except for Illinois, results were less satisfactory before the war. Corcoran liquidated almost all his original Mississippi holdings. The average sale was at $3.00, with some as high as $7.00, and the profit was large. Elsewhere sales were slow, probably covering expenses and interest but yielding a modest profit only in Michigan. There 800 acres out of 3,100 were sold at about $5.00. The dislocations and sectional impoverishment brought by the war slashed the values of remaining southern land. Corcoran was informed in 1870 that he would be lucky to get $2.00 per acre in Mississippi, where taxes were described as heavy and increasing. He was unable to find a permanent agent there. The Arkansas lands brought little gain, some of them having disappeared under floods and stream-bed changes of the Mississippi. (In 1856 Corcoran had refused to share the $4,000 cost of a levee.)[22]

[21] In 1868 an offer of $75,000 cash for Corcoran's 7,560 remaining acres in the Military Tract by a bargain-hunting speculator, James T. Erskine, was refused.

[22] Finally, in 1873, Corcoran decided to rid himself of his troublesome and profitless Mississippi and Texas properties by donating them to the Episcopal dioceses there. Mississippi law forbade gifts of land to churches, but this obstacle was surmounted, apparently by special legis-

In Kansas, where Corcoran sold in the late seventies and early eighties at prices up to $10, the gains were fairly sizable; in Indiana and Missouri they were slight. Enough of the Michigan lands were sold before the war to assure a profit. Over a thousand acres were later traded for a thirty-three-acre property in Mt. Vernon, New York, at no great gain on either side; to judge from other offers the practice of swapping was common. Corcoran and his fellow speculators were glad to be rid of their Pacific Northwest holdings in 1887 for $52,000, covering initial costs of $36,700, and $13,000 for expenses and a small commission. No account was taken of the interest for sixteen years, although this was partly offset by the appreciation of the dollar. The townsite lots fared poorly. Some of the towns that were conceived were never born, while others remained mere villages. A few grew too slowly to repay expenses. In these, the losses may have been heaviest, as taxes drained resources without commensurate appreciation. In Leavenworth, Kansas, for example, the burden reached 7 per cent of assessed valuation, five times the rate in Washington, D.C.

Hopes for the coal lands also went unfulfilled. Sommers estimated that royalties at a half cent per bushel (about thirteen cents per ton) would ultimately yield $87,000 from the mines at Rock Island, Illinois. The land was leased for one cent per bushel, or an income of about $1,500 annually in 1856 and 1857. The depression of 1857 ended the harvest. Thereafter competition intensified while the easily mined surface coal was being stripped away. Royalties dwindled, and exploitation ceased permanently during the Civil War. The West Virginia coal lands

---

lative enactment. In Texas, where Sommers had run the risk of being lynched, the church was dismayed to learn of the legal and political embroilment in which the gift involved it. Dubious remarks in the diocesan newspaper brought a $500 donation from Corcoran for legal expenses and the doubtful explanation that the church would stand a better chance of gaining title than would an absentee landlord. Corcoran valued the tract at $19,000; the original cost, taxes, other expenses, and interest totaled almost $10,000, of which none had been recovered.

proved even more disappointing and in 1873 the partners exchanged their land for stock in two mining companies, which promptly went bankrupt. Corcoran donated his 14,000-acre tract at the fork of the Little and Big Kanawaha rivers to the Episcopal Diocese of Virginia.

Thus, of Corcoran's nonurban land speculations, only those in Illinois brought large profits; on the others he at best broke even. Only in Illinois did rentals furnish enough revenue to repay most, if not all, of the expenses. In 1857 ten leases there brought in $500; in 1860, sixteen yielded $1,100. A decade later, in 1870, the rentals were $2,300; the next year, $3,000; and by 1874, over $6,000. In the course of the 1870's much more of the previously vacant land was leased, and annual rents climbed above $10,000, except when depressions caused reductions. In addition, as tenants occupied the land, they assumed the tax burden. After 1880 the rent rolls declined as sales continued, but as late as the year following Corcoran's death—March 1888 through February 1889—fifteen remaining properties returned $3,700.

At least three-fourths of all dues for rents and purchases fell more than a year behind after the depression of 1857, some as many as three or four years; perhaps one-quarter had to be written off. However, the proportion overdue and uncollectable was sharply reduced as unreliable tenants were weeded out and prosperity slowly increased. Although it was common in difficult times for half the rent to be more than a year late, collectable arrears earned interest. The total of overdue notes, from sales —chiefly—and rentals as of 1885 was $15,000, of which less than $3,300 seemed collectable. Some went back as far as 1850; many, if not most, originated in the difficult years of the late seventies. (Several were from outside Illinois.)

In the absence of ledgers an exact reckoning of the returns is impossible, but the correspondence yields evidence for a rough estimate. There is available a full summary of Illinois sales for the five years 1863–1867: the annual average was more than $10,000, at from $8 to $45 per acre. This average was approximated or surpassed in many years; there were few in which proceeds were under $5,000. As late as 1888–1889, the last year of available records, there were two sales for $5,700. Receipts from Illinois sales ultimately exceeded $200,000 by a considerable margin.[23]

The only reasonably full and unified account of expenses is for August 1, 1865, to March 4, 1867, during the period of heaviest outlays for improvements. Sommers' account, including payments for improvements, redemption fees, and so forth, totaled almost $15,000, a rate equaling or exceeding the proceeds of sales in those years but never again approached. (It is not clear whether his salary is included. A negligible part of these expenses was incurred outside Illinois.) Outlays were sharply reduced thereafter, or rather, passed on to the increasing number of tenants and buyers.

Rents probably totaled around $150,000, after allowance for bad debts. This amount almost certainly reimbursed for original investments and for capital and administrative expenditures, and probably returned interest as well. The receipts from sales, more than $200,000, were free and clear. It was a long time before profits materialized, but from about 1870 they were substantial: a reasonable guess would be at least a 10-per-cent annual average on net investment. The results of dealings elsewhere were inconclusive, but they had only negligible effect on the Illinois returns. The latter were clearly greater than Corcoran could have achieved by investing at random in securities, though perhaps exceeded by the fruits of his Washington real estate.[24] Through

[23] The account of receipts for 1888–1889 is from the auditor's reports accompanying William W. Corcoran, Will no. 3001, probated Feb. 29, 1888, Register of Wills, District of Columbia. The payments itemized are not explained, other than as receipts from Sommers. It is reasonable to assume that the two entries in four figures represent sales, while those in two or three figures are rents.

[24] For yields (and conversely, prices) of various classes of bonds, see U.S. Dept. of Commerce, Bureau of the Census, *Historical Statistics of the United States: Colonial Times to 1957* (Washington, 1960), 656;

special circumstances more than half the Illinois land (and much land elsewhere) had been bought at less than 40 per cent of the regular government price of $1.25 per acre, but the Illinois profits would have been impressive even had the going rate been paid.[25]

V

Absentee landlords, it is claimed, contributed to developing regions through investments, loans, tax payments, advertising, and community leadership.[26] Corcoran's case does not support these contentions. True, he made some improvements, but the cost of these, together with taxes and payments to agents living in the West, did not approach in amount the outflow of revenues. Little or no advertising was necessary, and there is little indication of constructive participation in community affairs by

---

and Frederick R. Macaulay, *Some Theoretical Problems Suggested by the Movements of Interest Rates, Bond Yields and Stock Prices in the United States Since 1856* (New York, 1938), A 108, A 142ff., A 172. Corcoran had erratic experiences with bonds until after the Civil War, when security improved and yields declined (i.e., existing portfolios showed capital gains). Changes in value roughly coincide with those of Corcoran's Illinois properties, with the latter perhaps relatively more secure.

[25] The Johnson plantation was the sole major loss. The origins of the loss of the Johnson plantation and certain other losses were as much political as financial (Cohen, "Business and Politics," 250–253). For highly exaggerated notions that land was a major source of Corcoran's wealth, see the New York *World* obituary, misc. Corcoran material, Manuscript Division, New York Public Library; and David Cole, *The Development of Banking in the District of Columbia* (New York, 1959), 270–271, which uncritically draws on an older writer, who in turn simply conveyed the earlier gossip. The returns were large compared to the investment, but on a negligible scale compared to the fortune Corcoran had acquired in banking.

[26] Paul Wallace Gates, "Frontier Estate Builders and Farm Laborers," in Walker D. Wyman and C. B. Kroeber, *The Frontier in Perspective* (Madison, 1957), 143–164, and his introduction to the *John Tipton Papers*, ed. Nellie A. Robertson and Dorothy Riker (Indianapolis, 1942), I, 49. See also A. Bogue, *From Prairie to Corn Belt*, 45–46.

Corcoran or his agents. In microcosm, his career as an absentee landlord could be taken to represent to some degree a colonial relationship between regions or an exploitative relationship between economic classes as they carry out their social functions. The West's loss was the East's gain: the profits of Corcoran's operations in the Illinois country added to his benefactions in the city of Washington.

Absentee ownership, however, brought losses that were no one's gain. It bred irresponsibility, fostering the plunder of land by neighbors and tenants. It diverted energies and talents into socially wasteful intrigues and litigation and needlessly complicated administration. But as time went on, improved administration and the increasing demand for good land diminished these problems, compelling tenants to act constructively in order to hold their places and making the landlord's position more secure. Perhaps the authoritarian or paternalistic oversight of an able resident administrator weeded out the incompetent and disciplined the irresponsible more rapidly than would have ownership by settlers responsible solely to themselves. What chiefly mitigated the perniciousness of absentee holdings was the fact that the inhabitants were not defenseless. Partly in consequence, landlords were usually flexible and sometimes considerate enough to try to please tenants.

The Scott Farms in a New Agriculture, 1900-1919

MARGARET BEATTIE BOGUE

The history of American agricultural land tenure abounds in unexplored problems and unanswered questions. Farm tenancy, one neglected facet of the rural scene that is as old as the colonial period, deserves further historical study. At times in various parts of the United States tenants have constituted the majority of farm operators. More often they have been a significant minority. Agricultural economists and rural sociologists, aware of the importance of the tenant-landlord relationship in the total tenure picture, turned their thoughts to analyzing the social and economic significance of tenancy long before historians took interest. Not until the 1930's, when New Deal farm policies focused on the problems of tenant farmers, did a handful of students face squarely the task of placing tenancy in historical perspective. Now, three decades later, we have made a start, but only a start. Twentieth-century tenancy, especially, remains neglected.[1]

In the Collection of Regional History at Cornell University are the personal and business papers of a midwestern landowning family, the Matthew T. Scotts, which shed considerable light

[1] For an illuminating study of foreclosure tenancy in the twentieth century based upon the business records of Rockwell Sayre, see Allan G. Bogue, "Foreclosure Tenancy on the Northern Plains," *Agricultural History*, XXXIX (Jan. 1965), 3–16.

upon tenancy in the corn belt in the "golden age" of American agriculture and during World War I, roughly from 1900 to 1919. The quality of the remaining business records makes it possible to test some accepted judgments about absentee landlords and absentee land ownership, to catch an intimate glimpse of tenant-agent-landlord relationships, to study the increase in farm rents and land values in a period of unprecedented prosperity, and to see how these increases influenced land use. On the Scott holdings one sees competition among tenants for good farms, the efforts of owner and tenant to maximize income, the problems landlords faced in trying to find suitable agents, and the influence of time and continuous cropping upon rich prairie land. Here we find renter and owner trying to solve problems of "tenant right," or compensation for unexhausted tenant improvements. Also here we find a good example of the agricultural college at work among tenants to help them improve their farming methods.

In the early twentieth century the Scott farms totaled about eleven thousand acres, lying principally in the rich black grand prairie of Illinois and partly in the rolling grass lands and fertile Missouri tributary bottoms of western Iowa.[2] These farms had long been in the possession of the Matthew T. Scott family of Bloomington, Illinois. Scott acquired most of them, along with thousands of acres of prairie land, in the mid-nineteenth century and developed them with tenant labor. The details of their nineteenth-century history are related elsewhere and need not detain us.[3] In 1891 he died, leaving the farms to his widow, Julia.

Born in Danville, Kentucky, in 1840, Julia Green was the daughter of a minister and college president. After formal

[2] The Scott farms were located in Champaign, Ford, Livingston, McLean, and Piatt counties, Illinois, and in Mills, Monona, and Calhoun counties, Iowa.

[3] Margaret Beattie Bogue, *Patterns from the Sod: Land Use and Tenure in the Grand Prairie, 1850–1900*, Collections of the Illinois State Historical Library, XXXIV, Land Series, I (Springfield, 1959), 85–112.

schooling in Kentucky and New York, she married in 1859 and moved to Chenoa, Illinois, as the wife of a pioneer landlord, Matthew T. Scott. There in the little village that was the family's projected townsite, located in the midst of the Scott tenant farms, she set up housekeeping in elegant style, by frontier standards. The Scotts made Chenoa their home during the critical years of the land and farming business. At Chenoa some of their children were born, and there in 1866 Julia Scott's sister, Letitia Green, married Adlai Stevenson, grandfather of the late Adlai E. Stevenson. In the Scott house in 1868 was born the first of the Stevenson children, Lewis Green Stevenson, who later played a prominent role in managing the Scott lands. In 1870 the Scotts moved to Springfield, and two years later to Bloomington, some twenty five miles south of Chenoa, eventually making a spacious old red-brick house on East Taylor Street their home.[4]

During Matthew Scott's years of experience as a landlord, Julia learned much about the business of managing the farms. She regarded the Illinois and Iowa lands as the choice assets among Matthew's growing and varied business interests. In the 1870's, when he became involved in various speculative ventures, he deeded, probably at her suggestion, 4,000 acres of the best of the farms to her as financial security.[5] When in 1891 he died of pneumonia, contracted after inspecting his farms in a cold spring rain, Julia stepped into the landlord's role, well schooled for the task. She began a new chapter in her life in settling her husband's million dollar estate.

For some years business matters connected with the estate took much of her time. In addition she became deeply interested in the Daughters of the American Revolution, serving as Illinois

[4] Georgia L. Osborne, comp., *Brief Biographies of the Figurines on Display in the Illinois State Historical Library* (Springfield, 1932), 139.

[5] U.S. Treasury Department, Office of Commissioner of Internal Revenue, "Estate of Julia G. Scott (died April 29, 1923), Protest against Assessment of Deficiency Estate Tax" (n.p., n.d.), 162, in the possession of Mrs. Carl S. Vrooman, Bloomington, Ill. Hereafter I shall cite this as "Estate of Julia G. Scott."

state vice president from 1901 to 1905, and as president of the national society from 1909 to 1913. She gave much time to charitable causes, among them a relief committee to help World War I orphans.[6]

Julia Scott retained throughout her lifetime her high regard for the farms as an investment. In settling the estate, she chose to sacrifice other properties and to keep the farms. She wanted the lands to remain in the family and for all members to learn the farm business.[7] When, in 1919, she decided to divide the land formally between her daughters and herself, she stipulated that their farms should be held by them during their lifetimes and that thereafter they should become the property of their issue.[8]

By any definition of "absentee," the Scott farms must be classed as absentee-owned. Julia's many interests made close personal supervision of the property impossible for her. Her main management problem was recruiting and maintaining a group of agents to administer her plans. For almost two decades after the death of Matthew Scott, Julia retained the system of management that had been in effect for years. James Colter, a reliable Scott tenant, toured the lands in Illinois and Iowa, selecting tenants, signing leases, collecting rents, supervising improvements, and at times doing some of the maintenance work himself. As Julia's agent, he sold rent grain and advised her concerning tenant selection, improvements, rental terms, and tenant disputes.[9] He was an able, experienced farmer and Jack-of-all-trades, with great loyalty to the Scott family.

The farms in western Iowa required closer supervision than

[6] Osborne, *Brief Biographies*, 139.

[7] "Estate of Julia G. Scott," 145–146, 149.

[8] Deeds, Jan. 27, 1919, Julia G. Scott to Letitia Bromwell, and to Julia Vrooman, "Estate of Julia G. Scott," 104–105, 111–115.

[9] Affidavit, Jan. 1, 1898, Matthew T. Scott Collection. Unless otherwise indicated, cited documents are in this collection. I wish to thank Dr. Herbert Finch, Director of the Collection of Regional History and University Archives, for permission to quote from the Scott and Stevenson papers.

Colter could give them from Chenoa. For a number of years the owner tried to maintain a local agent in each of the Iowa counties. At the turn of the century, bankers at Malvern, Gilmore, and Whiting, Iowa, handled all types of agent's duties between Colter's visits at intervals of four to six months.[10] A few years later, two of the bankers dropped out of the picture and their place was taken by farmers in Strahan and Lohrville, Iowa, both of whom had qualifications similar to Colter's, including long years of practical farming experience. Both worked under his direction. Probably they were hired in an effort to give the tenants closer supervision. Between 1906 and 1913, Julia Scott put the management of the Mills County and Calhoun County farms under one agent, thus reducing the number of local agents in Iowa to two—one banker and one farmer. She changed personnel in 1913 and in 1914. Finally, in 1915 she placed Hiram Vrooman, her daughter's brother-in-law, in charge of her Iowa lands.[11]

A significant change in the management system occurred in 1909, when Julia Scott became convinced that the farm program needed revision. She turned over the supervision of the McLean County lands to Lewis G. Stevenson. Shortly afterward she designated him as agent for all her lands in Illinois and Iowa,[12] a job he continued to hold until her death in 1923. He did not replace the other agents; they came under his direction.

The Scott family paid their agents in a number of ways. Some received commissions ranging from 5 to 10 per cent of the gross rental receipts.[13] Occasionally an agent worked for a fixed fee. These arrangements were quite usual ones in the corn belt. More unusual was the arrangement Julia Scott made with Lewis G.

---

[10] Estate account, 1904.　　[11] From a study of the Scott Collection.

[12] Agreement, Aug., 1909, L. B. Thomas and Son to Messrs. Fred S. James and Co., Jan. 31, 1910.

[13] Cashier, Gilmore Exchange Bank, to James Colter, March 7, 1898; W. B. Whiting to Julia G. Scott, July 6, 1903; George W. Strohl to Julia G. Scott, Sept. 29, 1910.

Stevenson in 1919, when by formal deed she changed his salary from 7 per cent of gross rents to a life estate of 700 acres of Monona County, Iowa, land.[14]

The Scott agents represented the types of agents usually employed in the late nineteenth and early twentieth centuries in the Midwest. They came from the ranks of local real estate dealers, loan agents, bankers, and retired farmers. Also we see harbingers of the present, when university-trained farm managers offer their services to landlords. Early in the century Julia Scott assigned the business responsibility for certain of the farms to her daughters. By 1910, both Julia Vrooman and Letitia Bromwell had begun to employ "experts." [15] The records do not yield a complete list of these "new-style" farm managers, but their qualifications are clear. They had both practical farming experience and some agricultural-college training. They were more systematic and businesslike in keeping farm records and accounts than their older counterparts. They furnished the owner with statements of acreages planted in different crops, yields, and, on request, plats of the fields.[16] Julia Scott seems to have preferred yet a different type of agent from any of these. She felt most secure in her farm business when she had a member of her family acting as her representative.

Julia's experience with the farms falls into two well-defined periods. In the first, from 1891 to 1909, management methods and policies initiated by Matthew Scott were continued. He had designed his system to suit the economic realities of the decades from the 1850's through the 1890's, when the big tasks of prairie farming in east-central Illinois and western Iowa were breaking the prairie, constructing initial improvements, discovering what crops best suited the land and climate, and solving major land-use problems like the drainage of wet lands and the enclosure of

[14] Contract, J. G. Scott with Lewis G. Stevenson, Jan. 27, 1919, "Estate of Julia G. Scott," 115–119. Hereafter these two persons will be referred to as Scott and Stevenson.   [15] Stevenson to Scott, Sept. 23, 1910.
[16] See, for example, the Jan. 7, 1914, report of the Calhoun County agent.

crop. Low but ever rising land values, long periods of relatively low prices for midwestern farm produce, and modest but slowly rising rents characterized the major part of Matthew Scott's years as a prairie landlord. Under such circumstances he tried to keep capital outlay for improvements low and encouraged tenant development of the lands, often renting in return for sod-breaking or the construction of certain specific improvements. Sometimes he leased land with the understanding that the tenant furnish the buildings and remove them at the end of the lease. The closing years of Scott's life were marked by a more rapid rise in land values and rents in central Illinois. Beginning in 1885 he initiated a tiling program, for tile drainage of wet prairie soils had already proved profitable. Scott passed to his heirs a modest legacy of farm improvements.[17]

When Julia Scott fell heir to the farms, the currents of economic change had already made themselves felt. The pioneer days were gone. Illinois and Iowa had assumed a special role in the national agricultural economy as producers of corn, oats, hogs, and fattened cattle.[18] Commercial corn-belt farming in 1900 justified larger investments in capital improvements by the landowner than ever before, a more intensive use of the land, and ever increasing investments in machinery, equipment, and skill by the farmer.

Just how aware Julia Scott was of these changes we do not know. She had been schooled in the practice of spending modestly for farm improvements and this may have influenced her thinking. The financial pressures both of settling Matthew Scott's estate and of family needs discouraged a large outlay for the farms. Also, low prices for corn and oats held share rents at a modest level throughout the 1890's.[19] As a result Julia Scott kept

[17] M. B. Bogue, *Patterns from the Sod*, 107–109.
[18] Allan G. Bogue, *From Prairie to Corn Belt* (Chicago, 1963), 280–287; M. B. Bogue, *Patterns from the Sod*, 138–155.
[19] L. J. Norton and B. B. Wilson, *Prices of Illinois Farm Products from 1866 to 1929*, Bulletin no. 351, University of Illinois Agricultural Experiment Station (Urbana, 1930), 494–495, 500.

expenditures for repairs and improvements low. During the first period of her management such outlays ran to a few thousand dollars annually and only now and then to as much as four to five thousand dollars when she spent more to advance the tiling program.[20]

The years between 1900 and 1914 are still regarded as a kind of ideal, a golden age, for the American farmer. The demand both at home and abroad for farm commodities was brisk, and prices in general were high. Farmers benefited particularly, because the prices they received for crops were relatively high in comparison to what they paid for those items they had to buy. Also, they gained from an increase in their capital investments. On a nationwide basis the average value of farm lands and buildings increased by about twenty dollars per acre between 1900 and 1910, compared to an average rise of only about three dollars per acre in the whole forty-year period between 1860 and 1900.[21] The corn belt benefited to a greater degree than did many other agricultural areas.

During the first decade of the twentieth century the value of part of the Scott Illinois farm acreage more than doubled.[22] Land values climbed in Iowa too. One Scott agent noted in 1908, "I expect to see Iowa lands sell as high as Illinois lands in a very short time after it is fairly well drained." [23]

As the owner saw the value of her holdings increase and as she compared her rental income with that of other landowners, she realized that her lands were not earning as much as they should. The problem was many-sided. Some of the farms had been under cultivation for as long as sixty years with little thought given to conserving their natural fertility. In the first decade of the twentieth century, these farms generally produced yields of

[20] Statements of farm expenditures, James G. Colter to Scott, 1892–1909.

[21] Allan G. Bogue, "The History of American Agriculture," *Encyclopedia Americana*, 1963 rev.   [22] Stevenson to Scott, May 6, 1911.

[23] Strohl to Scott, Sept. 26, 1908.

corn and oats that fell below the county averages reported in the federal census.[24] While variations in classification techniques in published soil reports prevent a summarizing of soil types on the Scott lands, they had superior prairie soils capable, under proper management, of producing greater-than-average yields. All the cultivated lands showed signs of abuse and deteriorating productivity.[25] Considerable tiling remained to be done. Many of the buildings had fallen into disrepair. Some farms were without barns and sheds other than those furnished and owned by the tenants.[26] An Iowa agent reported in 1909 that he was having trouble renting Calhoun County land because of dilapidated buildings.[27] On some of the Illinois farms no improvements had been made for twenty-five years.[28] One tenant's wife wrote in 1908, "Our porches are both getting to be very bad. The floors are all rotten and the roof leaks so that they are no good at all, in fact the whole house needs shingling."[29] Lewis Stevenson reported that the properties were "run down fearfully" and "sadly neglected."[30] From Iowa, George W. Strohl advised the owner, "The time has come if you wish the best class of tenants that the farms must be put in good tillable condition and buildings in good repair."[31] The existing evidence suggests that many of the Scott tenants were indifferent farmers.

From the ranks of her family came two very able men to help Julia Scott design and initiate a new management policy. One was her nephew, Lewis G. Stevenson, schooled as an educator and experienced in the national and state politics of the Democratic party. His qualifications as a farm manager stemmed from

[24] *United States Census, 1900,* VI: *Agriculture,* Pt. II, *Crops and Irrigation; United States Census, 1910,* VI: *Agriculture 1909 and 1910.* The yield figures for the Scott farms are derived from post cards, 1901–1910, in the Scott Collection.   [25] Stevenson to Scott, Oct. 7, Nov. 16, 1910.

[26] *Ibid.,* Sept. 26, 1910.   [27] G. W. Strohl to Scott, Aug. 8, 1909.

[28] John Strohl to Carl Vrooman, Jan. 8, 1909.

[29] Mrs. T. T. Cornell to Scott, Aug. 25, 1908.

[30] Stevenson to Scott, Oct. 15, 1910.

[31] G. W. Strohl to Scott, June 10, 1910.

business experience, from his lifelong association with prairie farming, and from his reading and thinking about farm problems.[32] The other was Carl Schurz Vrooman, Mrs. Scott's Harvard-educated son-in-law, a social critic of liberal persuasion, a thinker, a writer, and an active participant in the Populist cause, who in 1896 had married the younger Julia G. Scott.[33]

At the time of his marriage Carl Vrooman possessed a greater grasp of the problems of farmers in politics, particularly of the Populists of the plains states, than of their practical problems in running farming businesses. However, he quickly became interested in corn-belt agriculture and spent much time studying the scientific publications of the United States Department of Agriculture and the agricultural experiment stations, and much time observing and thinking about every-day farm problems in the corn belt. When Julia G. Scott made part of the lands the business responsibility of the Vroomans and the Bromwells, Carl Vrooman tried to use his growing knowledge to improve farm productivity. Letitia Green Scott, the sister of Julia Scott Vrooman, married Charles Bromwell.

In 1916 while serving as Assistant Secretary of Agriculture, Vrooman spelled out his views in a Department of Agriculture farmers' bulletin designed as a practical guide for corn-belt farmers and landowners. Drawing upon his experience with the Scott farms, he wrote in an effort to help all corn-belt farmers, "especially the farmer whose soil has been run down by continuous grain farming."[34] "To make a money-maker of a farm" so abused, Vrooman advised farmers to grow legumes, raise live-

[32] J. L. Hasbrouck, *History of McLean County, Illinois* (Indianapolis, 1924), II, 928–929.

[33] Ross E. Paulson has skillfully portrayed Carl Vrooman's career in public life, along with the careers of his brothers, in *Radicalism and Reform: The Vrooman Family and American Social Thought, 1837–1937* (Lexington, Ky., 1968).

[34] Carl S. Vrooman, *Grain Farming in the Corn Belt with Live Stock as a Side Line*, U.S. Department of Agriculture Farmers' Bulletin, no. 704 (Washington, 1916), 1.

stock as a side line, keep farm accounts, use "horse sense," try to secure adequate capital to "farm right," utilize the services of county agents, and to study the bulletins of the federal Department of Agriculture and the state agricultural colleges.[35] "Most landlords," he wrote, "would make larger profits on their fixed investment in land and buildings if they would invest enough additional capital to provide first-class improvements."[36] Tenants also would earn more, he believed, if they could make larger investments in pure-bred livestock, fertilizer, and hired help. Although the Scott papers do not reveal just how much time and effort Carl Vrooman devoted to the farms, they show clearly that his study and ideas impressed Mrs. Scott and influenced her thinking.[37]

Whether Lewis G. Stevenson or Carl Vrooman exerted the greater influence upon her farm-management policies remains a puzzle. Both men were interested in achieving the same result, the introduction of more modern farming methods that would bring the Scott lands up to their productive potential and at the same time conserve their value for future use. The major difference in the thinking of the two men about the Scott farms arose over management personnel. Stevenson favored using men without formal training who had a practical knowledge of farming, whereas Vrooman preferred "experts," men with agricultural-college training.[38]

When in 1909 the ideas of these two men began to be translated into action, the second period of Julia Scott's management of the farms began. It continued until her death in 1923. During this second period, Mrs. Scott authorized a campaign of improvements that enabled her to receive top rents. She encouraged her tenants to attend short courses for farmers offered at Ames and Urbana and endorsed a farming program designed to

[35] *Ibid.*, 2–3.   [36] *Ibid.*, 3.

[37] Stevenson to Scott, March 25, May 19, 1911, March 21, 1915; G. W. Strohl to Scott, Sept. 18, 1911; Scott to Stevenson, Feb. 24, 1913.

[38] Stevenson to Scott, Sept. 23, 1910; Scott to Stevenson, July 27, 1911.

restore and conserve soil fertility. Her rental income and the value of her property rose sharply.

To Lewis G. Stevenson, who had already chalked up some years of experience as a farm manager, fell the task of administration during the new regime.[39] He proposed to build up soil productivity, to renovate old improvements and supply new buildings and tile drainage as needed, to bring wasted land into production, and above all, to teach tenants more modern methods of farming. As the farms improved, better tenants would automatically gravitate to them.

Significantly, the renovation program began with the Chenoa farms, the lands which had been under cultivation longest. Stevenson entered into a seven-year contract with Julia Scott whereby he leased 2,000 acres of her Chenoa farms, guaranteeing her a rent of $5.50 per acre for four years and $6.00 per acre for the next three years and promising to spread twelve tons of manure per acre on the lands during the term of the lease.[40] In the following year Julia Scott gave him the responsibility for the general management of all her Illinois and Iowa farms.

Lewis Stevenson began the job with a personal survey of the lands, conducted in a new automobile purchased for him by Mrs. Scott. He wished to evaluate the abilities of the tenants, to determine the needs of each farm, to inventory the possibilities for bringing wasted land into production, and to convince the tenants that learning new farming techniques was good for business.

Stevenson colorfully described his mission in a letter to Julia Scott in September of 1910:

You would either laugh (or cry) to see me tonight while waiting here in this little store for a train. I am mud from head to foot, a little battle scarred but still carrying the banner. For the last five

[39] See Stevenson Papers, Collection of Regional History and University Archives, Cornell University.

[40] Agreement, Aug. 19, 1909; L. B. Thomas and Sons to Messrs. Fred S. James and Co., Jan. 31, 1910.

days I've been visiting the farms—going over them and planning the work with new tenants and arranging with old. I've rigged up a tent & cooking outfit & have been sleeping in the farm yards. . . . We got caught in the rain here and have had to leave the car for a day or two till it dries up & the roads get better. I am well pleased with the new tenants, also pleased with the attitude of the old ones. I've made some rather radical changes which they at first opposed but have now accepted.

[As for raising the general level of the farming business], first must come barns, sheds & fences—good tenants will follow with the land being properly cared for & built up in the mean time. I am not entirely satisfied with the tenants I am getting but they are an improvement on those I have let go & have been secured after a lot of investigation & hard work. They are absolutely the best that could be secured with present improvements and conditions of farms. I'll soon set a different standard & gradually change the methods.[41]

The shift from the old policy to the new caused some friction. The owner understood how necessary changes were and that improvements and tenant education cost money. But, understandably, she had second thoughts as the bills poured in. By the fall of 1910, with her Iowa agent suggesting that his commission should be increased, with estimated costs for essential buildings and tiling at hand, and with bills stacked up before her, Julia Scott decided she had had enough. In worried indignation she wrote to Stevenson:

Of course the tenants understand that you & Strohl and Colter have started a campaign of improvements that I am to pay for—and no one can tell where this campaign will stop—Only I am not going to permit myself to be embarrassed financially by attempting more than I can afford—this or any year. So far I believe the plans have been thought out and matured carefully and just so far as I can respond to calls for money, without embarrassing myself financially & conflicting with other plans of my own—I will do so—but I will

[41] Stevenson to Scott, Sept. 23, 1910.

be the judge of the limit myself—Everything I have promised this
year I will most assuredly do.[42]

By mid-November the discussions about improvements, short
courses, and the like had grown so spirited that Julia Scott
decided her agents needed a vacation. She asked Stevenson and
the Iowa agent "to go to French Lick Springs and tonic up. . . .
There is no call for you to kill yourself or wear yourself out." [43]
Despite the fact that sparks flew intermittently over the years in
this agent-owner business relationship, Julia Scott and Lewis
Stevenson maintained a firm friendship and a real respect for each
other.

One of the ways in which Stevenson tried to get more income
from the Scott farms was to bring all partially used or wasted
acreage into more intensive use. In some cases this meant investing further thousands of dollars in tiling. In others, it meant
diking, removing timber and stumps, or mastering overgrown
hedge fences that shaded and sapped valuable land. In an effort
to control hedges, Stevenson occasionally brought legal action
against tenants who failed to trim fences as specified in their
leases. He believed that such action set a good precedent.[44]

Central in the plan of renovating the farms and bringing
larger rents to the owner was the program of tenant education.
He brought his pedagogical training to bear on the Scott tenants,
with telling effects. By January of 1910 he had talked some of
them into going with him to Champaign to attend short
courses.[45] Eight months later he had convinced most of the
Illinois tenants, old and new, that time at Champaign was time
well spent and would guarantee a larger income. He commented
to Julia Scott, "I have talked my head off getting them to agree
to go down. They are all willing. Money could not be invested
better." [46]

[42] Scott to Stevenson, Dec. 8, 1910.　　[43] *Ibid.*, Nov. 12, 1910.
[44] Stevenson to Scott, May 6, July 12, 1911, March 4, 1912.
[45] Julius F. Funk to Stevenson, Jan. 24, 1910.
[46] Stevenson to Scott, Sept. 26, 1910.

Meanwhile, in Iowa, on Stevenson's insistence George W. Strohl was trying to get the Scott tenants to attend short courses at Ames. His first efforts bore meager fruit. Strohl reported in February 1911 that he had been able to talk only two into going. Optimistically he remarked, "They were well pleased and are desirous to go again. If we can only get them started they wont feel so bad about going." [47] By midsummer all the Mills County tenants had attended short courses.[48]

Stevenson tried to encourage them to apply quickly the lessons they had learned. On March 1, 1911, he addressed a letter to all the Illinois tenants urging them to test their seed corn immediately. He followed up the letter with visits to the farms at planting time to see what quality of seed was going into the ground, to make sure that each farmer had prepared the land well, and to insist on replanting if the quality of work did not meet his standards.[49] By midsummer the tenants reportedly had come to appreciate fully the necessity of carefully selecting seed corn, properly curing it, and testing it. Stevenson informed Julia Scott, "It will be worth several thousand dollars—many—to you this year." Meanwhile some of the old tenants who had been balking at the short-course idea for eighteen months began to see the advantage of a little learning. Stevenson reported about one stubborn case that he "woke up after 40 years asleep." [50]

Having driven home the lesson on seed corn, Stevenson early in the summer of 1911 turned his energies to another phase of the revised farming system, raising livestock. Most of the Scott tenants prior to 1910 had kept very few, if any, livestock. As an integral part of a much needed soil-building program, Stevenson wanted them to diversify their farming to include feeder cattle, sheep, or dairy cows. At first he talked to the tenants about the advantages of keeping livestock. Then he had some attend dairy lectures. Most of the Illinois tenants, by June of 1911, had signed

[47] G. W. Strohl to Stevenson, Feb. 20, 1911.
[48] Stevenson to Scott, July 12, 1911.   [49] *Ibid.*, May 6, 1911.
[50] *Ibid.*, July 12, 1911.

agreements to feed cattle. The next step was to begin supplying the farms with buildings that would make dairying possible. He explained to the owner the advantages of dairy cattle over feeders: "This change [from feeder to dairy] will produce at least 3 times the amount of manure but will cost a little more for sheds. It is very desirable even at that." The limited resources of the tenants provided the major obstacle to the program. Good milk cows cost from eighty to a hundred dollars apiece. For a start with ten cows a tenant needed about a thousand dollars. Stevenson proposed that Julia Scott help tenants buy cows.[51] She rejected the idea as too risky for her, but wanted to support the program by building sheds for all of the renters who wished to start dairies.[52] During the next few years dairying made slow, steady progress.

The livestock program in general made notable advances. High beef and lamb prices must have helped to persuade tenants that raising livestock made business sense. By 1915 cash-grain farming on the Scott lands had given way to a more balanced system. The twenty-nine Illinois farms boasted an average of 35 cattle and sheep. The three Mills County, Iowa, farms claimed a total of nearly 600 sheep, steers, and cows. The 370 work horses on the Illinois farms and the 47 in Mills County also produced considerable manure for the lands.[53]

Along with the promotion of livestock enterprises went other steps to rebuild the tilth and fertility of the soil. Where it was practical to purchase and haul manure to the farms, the owner agreed to pay one-half of the cost. Locational factors placed severe limitations on this program.[54] Raising livestock on the farms often proved a much better solution. Early in his management experience, Stevenson tried to persuade tenants to buy

[51] *Ibid.*, June 18, 1911.
[52] Scott to Stevenson, June 23, 28, July 1, 1911.
[53] Statement, 1915, Scott Collection.
[54] Stevenson to Scott, Oct. 7, 1910.

manure spreaders. By the spring of 1911 all but two of the Illinois group had done so.[55] In addition to manure, much of the land received phosphate, with owner and tenant sharing the costs equally.[56] On Stevenson's insistence, the tenants introduced nitrogen-fixing plants into the usual cropping regime. Some planted clover; others tried alfalfa.[57] The manager began the alfalfa experiment cautiously in 1911, sending seed and planting directions to a dozen of the best tenants.[58] By 1915 alfalfa ranked as an important money-maker on the farms.[59] Remaining records do not show that Stevenson tried regular crop rotation as a means of soil improvement.

By many yardsticks, the Stevenson years of management were good, progressive ones. Charged with the task of making Julia Scott's farming business well paying, Stevenson proceeded with a program that improved the economic position of both the tenant and the owner and at the same time took into account the long range value of productive farm soil. He managed tenant personnel realistically and reasonably. He relied on frequent visits during the crop season, on rewards in the form of generous improvements to encourage the good farmers, on the withholding of such benefits until slow, balky, or hostile tenants followed his directions, on the termination of the leases of those who absolutely refused to cooperate, and on the occasional court suit as an example of what those who failed to live up to the terms of their leases might expect. He was friendly in his dealings with tenants and praised them generously whenever they showed that they were trying, learning, and improving their farming methods. In general the educational ventures succeeded well. But Stevenson could not always triumph over ignorance and prejudice against education. Some tenants, wedded to their ways,

[55] *Ibid.*, May 19, 1911.   [56] *Ibid.*, Sept. 23, 1910.
[57] *Ibid.*, March 25, May 6, 1911.
[58] Stevenson to tenants, July 15, 1911.
[59] Reports, income and expenditures, Scott Farms, 1916.

forfeited their leases rather than comply with short-course requirements. About really good farmers Stevenson became enthusiastic. He wrote to Julia Scott in October 1911:

I am camped in Emil Carlson's yard & I am so pleased with his first year that I can't refrain from telling you. . . . He is perfectly splendid, has as good a crop as I've seen any place this year. Has lived up to his every obligation & even more. This place is now a *stock farm* & will in time be one of the best in the state. Carlson has *30 horses, 34 cattle, 20 sheep* & *12 milk cows.* He has finished his plowing & has all his seed corn picked—has one room full of shelves all full of fine seed corn. He will spend (pay ½) for a car of phosphate. . . . This Carlson farm is a joy to me & I always feel thoroughly happy on it.[60]

Finally, in the relationship between agent and owner Lewis Stevenson proved himself much more than satisfactory. Family ties, lifelong friendship, education, ability, and experience combined to make the business association of owner and agent successful. Even if at times there were differences of opinion, Julia Scott endorsed enough changes to salvage the farms from what had been a shabby, rundown, exploitive business. As she gratefully acknowledged in 1919, Lewis Stevenson had "greatly enhanced" the earning power of her farms.[61]

Although under Stevenson's management the owner-agent-tenant business relationship worked quite well, the experience of one of Julia Scott's local agents in Iowa shows the relationship in a less favorable light. Let us consider why the Iowa business developed problems. First of all, the distance between the owner and the farmers, and between individual farms prevented smooth administration. The three groups of farms were far apart, seventy-five to a hundred miles as the crow flies. Travel by a combination of railroad, muddy roads, horse and buggy, and horse and saddle made them expensive to supervise. Mrs. Scott

[60] Stevenson to Scott, Oct. 13, 1911.
[61] Contract, Jan. 27, 1919, "Estate of Julia G. Scott," 115–117.

seldom visited the Iowa lands and knew most of her local agents and tenants only slightly. She relied on correspondence and on the reports of her general managers to keep her informed. The system of agents and subagents became so unwieldy that sometimes confusion arose about which agent was responsible for what. Once the owner wrote about the sale of Monona County rent grain: "I would like to know how many people I have to pay commissions for selling that stuff. I certainly do not propose to pay you and Strohl and Mr. Whiting all." [62]

The owner's desire to have her family understand the land business led to further complications. By informal agreement Julia Scott designated certain of the Iowa farms as the business responsibility of the Vroomans and the Bromwells. The agents reportedly found the arrangement confusing. One wrote, "I would like to know where I am at before long and under whose directions I am to work. Too many cooks usually spoil the broth." [63]

Correspondence relating to the Iowa farms suggests that neither agent nor owner nor tenant was very well satisfied. It abounds in references to alleged tenant chicanery, dishonest merchants, swindling agents, nepotism, misunderstood farmers, ingratitude, and almost every complaint imaginable. Read uncritically, these letters paint a dismal picture of human relations, but one must remember that agents and owners wrote primarily about their troubles. For every troublesome tenant who made the correspondence sizzle, there were a dozen or more whom the owner and agent considered good, honest, serious, and hard working. For every legal action the owner found necessary, dozens of problems were settled amicably. For every tenant who despised his landlord's representative, there were many who got on well with him.

The experience of George W. Strohl, an able and conscientious Iowa agent, reveals precisely what troubled each party

[62] Scott to Stevenson, Sept. 7, 1911.
[63] G. W. Strohl to Scott, Sept. 29, 1910, Sept. 18, 1911.

to the arrangement. Strohl's strongest qualifications as agent came from a lifetime of farming experience. A prime example of the rural American success story, from humble beginnings as a laborer, he climbed the agricultural ladder to become a tenant, then a farm owner, and finally a farm manager.

In early 1906 Julia Scott, concerned about the quality of supervision her Calhoun County lands were receiving, requested Strohl, who was then agent for her in Mills County, to inspect the Calhoun County farms and report to her.[64] Shortly after he completed this assignment, she hired him to manage these farms also. He lived at Malvern, southeast of Council Bluffs, and consequently had to travel well over a hundred miles to tend to Calhoun County matters. According to his own testimony, Strohl's management of the lands, from 1906 to 1913 was fraught with difficulties. His letters reveal that the problems causing friction were the improvement program, agent compensation, purchasing procedures, and tenant personnel.

In Strohl's judgment, Julia Scott needed to spend a liberal amount on her farms to repair existing buildings, to build new sheds and fences, and to tile the lands. Basically the owner agreed with him, but because she did not have a firsthand knowledge of the farms and of her farm personnel, she tended to be conservative in authorizing improvements. The problem dominated the correspondence between agent and owner during Strohl's years as agent. It assumed the largest proportions in 1909 and 1910, when it was concerned with the tiling of the Calhoun County farms.[65] Julia Scott felt that the cost of both tile and labor ran far too high, out of all proportion to Illinois prices. Finally she ordered the work stopped. Strohl defended his position, referring to the local wage rate: "There is such a great amount of tiling in Calhoun Co. at the present time that the

[64] A. J. McDermott to Strohl, Feb. 13, March 6, 1906; G. W. Strohl to Scott, Feb. 2, March 8, 1906.

[65] G. W. Strohl to Scott, March 26, 1909, June 10, 24, 1910; G. W. Strohl to C. S. Bromwell, April 6, June 5, 1910.

demand for men of that profession are at a premium. Taking in
consideration all the tile work in Calhoun County you are not
paying any more than other ditchers are getting for the same
sort of work." [66] In a letter written a few months later, as owner
and agent continued to debate the tiling question, he stated his
views on the importance of the work: "Those lands are too
valuable to lose the use of for one season and every year that you
fail to have this land drained means considerable loss to you." [67]
Ultimately the work was resumed.

Closely associated with the improvement program were purchasing procedures. Because tenants were inclined at times to
buy materials in the owner's name for repairs or improvements
without first securing her consent or that of her agent, Julia
Scott needed to control such purchasing. The practice at times
got out of hand and resulted in expenditures she would not have
authorized. On several occasions Iowa tenants presented the
owner with bills for unauthorized purchases, suggesting that
they would not pay their cash rents until the owner had settled
with them. [68] Such cases were most unpleasant to handle. Usually,
if small amounts were involved, it was simpler to pay than to
take the case to court. Strohl tried to avoid these problems by
informing all tenants that they should have either his or the
owner's permission before buying and charging anything. Also,
he notified the local merchants of this requirement. The problem
was a recurrent one, never completely solved. [69] It loomed large
in the Illinois correspondence in 1915. [70]

Strohl's compensation was also a source of friction. For a time
he received 5 per cent of the rental proceeds and now and then a

---

[66] G. W. Strohl to Scott, March 26, 1909.   [67] *Ibid.*, June 10, 1910.

[68] G. W. Strohl to Scott, Jan. 26, 1907, Jan. 30, Oct. 7, 1911, March 4,
1912.

[69] G. W. Strohl to Scott, March 31, 1907, June 15, 1910, Oct. 7, 1911,
March 4, Nov. 10, 1912.

[70] Scott to Stevenson, Jan. 4, 5, Feb. 1, 13, March 4, 1915; Stevenson to
Scott, Feb. 2, 3, 7, 25, 1915; George Fasking to Scott, Feb. 11, 1915.

generous bonus for his services.[71] In 1910 the salary matter
erupted into a controversy as the direct result of the transferring
of the business responsibility for part of the Iowa farms to the
Vroomans and the Bromwells. The central issue was whether or
not in certain cases Strohl should receive, in addition to the
established 5 per cent, a payment of 5 per cent of the cost of
improvements made on some of the farms. He contended that
this work took a considerable amount of his time. The correspondence does not show how the matter was finally settled.[72]

Disputes over the improvement program and salary must have
seemed insignificant to Strohl in comparison to some of his
occasional difficulties with tenants. One example reveals the most
unpleasant side of this agent's work. Strohl had genuine problems in dealing with a Mr. Johnson, tenant on 720 acres in
Calhoun County which he operated as a grain and livestock
enterprise. In the summer of 1910 the tenant and agent argued
about repair work and improvements that the owner had agreed
to have done. Johnson complained directly to the owner about
the way the work was being done and about her agent's business
manners. In reply Strohl claimed that Johnson wanted to "run
bills" for which the owner would be responsible, that he
was abusive, dishonest, and a "raskel." [73] The correspondence
warmed up together with the corn-belt summer. The tenant
complained that promised improvements materialized slowly and
that Strohl neglected to visit the job and push the work along;
meanwhile, the tenant was hard at work in the fields trying to
raise a good crop. In reply Strohl fulminated that Johnson had
failed to carry out his part of the agreement for hauling materials, that he talked abusively to carpenters and masons on the job
so that it was very hard to get anyone to work on it, and that he
bragged about town that he would have Strohl discharged and
take his job. "Now in regard to his being busy in the crops he

[71] G. W. Strohl to Scott, Jan. 5, 1908.
[72] *Ibid.*, Sept. 29, 1910, Sept. 18, 1911.   [73] *Ibid.*, June 15, 1910.

himself dont do anything but run to town [in a buggy] and play pool." [74]

To make matters worse Johnson's well ran dry in mid-July and he put the problem into a lawyer's hands for settlement.[75] Prompt repair of the well solved this difficulty, but the discord between agent and tenant continued. Strohl reported happily to the owner in September that he had found new tenants for the farm "who will not want a modern home built and who will care for what they have." [76] In a similar case earlier, Julia Scott had intervened, sympathized with the tenant, and settled the argument to his satisfaction and Strohl's extreme annoyance. In the later case she wrote to Johnson supporting her agent's position and sent the letter to Strohl for approval before it was posted. Strohl took no chances in closing his business dealings with Johnson. He placed the lease in the hands of an attorney in case legal action should be necessary to collect the rents.[77]

Strohl's association with the Scott farms came to an abrupt end in February 1913. Ironically, on the same day that he took pen in hand and outlined his proposals for upgrading the quality of farming on the Mills County and Calhoun County lands, the owner decided that she would take Carl Vrooman's advice and assign to him the Calhoun County farms.[78] When Strohl learned that he had been relieved of responsibility for Calhoun County, he resigned his Mills County job too. Both Mrs. Scott and Stevenson deeply regretted losing Strohl, on whom they had depended so often for help in administering the Iowa farms. Strohl resigned without realizing why he had been relieved of the Calhoun County farms.[79] Once more, distance, lack of rapport, and a clumsy administrative system complicated the Iowa farm business.

[74] *Ibid.*, July 5, 1910.   [75] *Ibid.*, July 19, 1910.
[76] *Ibid.*, Sept. 28, 1910.
[77] G. W. Strohl to Scott, Jan. 30, March 4, 1911.
[78] Telegram, Feb. 23, 1913, Vrooman to Scott; Scott to Stevenson, Feb. 24, 1913.   [79] Stevenson to Scott, March 14, 1913.

Turning from the owner-manager, capital-supplying aspect of the business, let us consider the tenants, who also furnished some of the needed capital but whose major contribution was labor to plow the prairie soil, feed the cattle and hogs, milk the cows, and cultivate the corn. Judging from their names, the Scott tenants could trace their family origin to German, Scandinavian, and British stock. Most of them were nonlandowners with limited capital. A few had their own farms and rented Scott land as a means of enlarging their businesses. Some of the Scott tenants successfully climbed the agricultural ladder in the first two decades of the twentieth century, stepping up from the tenant to the landowner class. As for their abilities as farmers, they were a mixed lot, ranging all the way from very good to very poor. In terms of farming ability, the quality of tenant personnel steadily improved between 1891 and 1919. The farmers were generally cautious and occasionally hostile toward the owner's educational program. After experiencing its benefits, most of them willingly cooperated.

The Scott leases were in most respects orthodox documents, standard printed forms widely used throughout the corn belt that specified farming procedures, safeguarded the owner's property and equity in growing crops, and called for rents that squared with local rates for comparable land.[80] These leases became unorthodox after 1910, when they required tenants to study farming and apply what they learned or, in the language of the lease, "to co-operate with said Lessor in employing and finding out the latest and most effective methods of scientific farming." [81]

These interrelated problems in the business relationship bothered the Scott tenants. First was the matter of improvements: To what extent should the tenant be expected to contribute time, effort, and even materials to improve the landlord's property? If he did make improvements, should he be compensated? Legally

[80] Leases, Scott to Martin Henke, Feb. 21, 1903; to Gust Pearson, March 1, 1904. [81] Lease, Aug. 22, 1919.

any tenant improvement belonged to the landlord. Under short-term leases, this fact made it folly for a tenant to spend much time, labor, or money on a farm he might be compelled to leave shortly. Most corn-belt leases were written for short terms, usually one year. The duration of a lease, therefore, was a second major issue between owner and tenant. These problems were compounded by a third, that of rent increases, which were both frequent and substantial in the first two decades of the twentieth century.

The agricultural press recognized the seriousness of these problems in the economic and social life of the Midwest. In an editorial entitled "The Necessity for Longer Farm Leases," the *Breeder's Gazette* deplored the tendency to blame tenants for not participating fully in school, church, and farmers'-club activities. The tenant "would not be restless if given real encouragement to persist in one spot for a term of years and to put something into the soil in return for what he gets from it." Landlords should help tenants to learn about soil conservation, encourage them to keep livestock, and write leases to foster long-term tenure.[82]

In 1915, *Wallace's Farmer* called public attention to the twin problems of short-term leases and tenant rights. With 40 per cent of corn-belt farms tenant-operated, argued the editorial, it was high time for state legislatures to enact laws that would "give the tenant his rights" and at the same time protect landlords. Tenants needed longer leases and laws to protect their investments in improvements on rented land. Landlords needed legislation to protect them from tenants who wasted soil fertility.[83]

The editorial had little impact either on midwestern legislators, who strongly represented landowning and landlord groups, or on farmers, whether they were owners or tenants, partly because the times were prosperous. But prosperity is only part of

[82] LIX (March 8, 1911), 634. [83] XL (Jan. 22, 1915), 108.

the explanation. For a half-century critics had discussed the undesirable consequences of tenancy.[84] They had, however, attracted scant attention to the issues of length of lease and compensation for improvements, because many tenants and landlords, aware of these problems, found their solutions individually.

Throughout the history of the Scott farms, owner and tenant settled tenure problems by unwritten agreement. Both Matthew and Julia Scott wanted tenants to remain on their lands as long as they fulfilled their leases. Scott tenants did not fear that they would have to give up their farms at the end of the stated one-year period until the years of great agricultural prosperity in the early twentieth century. Then, with farm earnings high, with competition for rented land keen, and with the owner insisting on ever higher standards of farming as she made larger investments in improvements and adjusted rents upward, the tenants became worry. When they learned that rent increases closely followed campaigns of owner-financed improvements, some sought -year rather than one-year leases, with guarantees against rent increases during the lease term. Some simply left the land. To all tenants Julia Scott and her agents gave assurance that they could expect to rent their farms year after year as they had in the past if they accepted the changes, lived up to the terms of their leases, and farmed well. One year continued to be the usual length of tenure in Scott rental contracts. This, the owner believed, protected her from irresponsible tenants.

As for compensating the tenant for improvements, again the Scott farmily and its tenants generally settled matters by mutual agreement. Sometimes the tenants sold their unexhausted improvements to the owner, and sometimes to the incoming tenant.[85] Since the farms were not in very good condition, the

[84] M. B. Bogue, *Patterns from the Sod*, 176–184.
[85] G. W. Strohl to Scott, Jan. 5, 1908, Oct. 7, 1911, March 4, Oct. 27, Nov. 10, 1912; John Strohl to Vrooman, Jan. 8, 1909; Vrooman to J. Colter, Feb. 19, 1909; Stevenson to Scott, Sept. 26, 1910, Dec. 4, 1911; Scott to Stevenson, Aug. 14, 1911.

improvement problem loomed large in the tenant-landlord relationship during the second period of Julia Scott's ownership, when the renovation program got into full swing. The major contribution of the tenants to the improvement campaign was labor. They often agreed in their leases to haul materials and to fill ditches for tilers. Frequently such arrangements worked smoothly, but not always.[86]

During the first two decades of the twentieth century, Julia Scott increased the rents for the Illinois and Iowa farms in a number of ways. The most obvious was to ask a larger share of crops and a higher cash payment for pasture land. In Illinois the owner wished to improve all the farms to the point where they could be leased for one-half of the crops, the share for which the best farms were rented. Until 1910 many of the Scott lands brought two-fifths of all grain; some, one-half of the corn and two-fifths of the small grain; and a few, one half of all crops. By 1912 the goal of half shares had been attained. Cash rents for pasture land did not increase greatly. Most of the Illinois farms brought $4.00 to $5.00 per acre for pasture in 1900.[87] Common rents for pasture in 1918 were $4.00, $5.50, and $6.00 per acre.[88]

As for the Iowa farms, at the turn of the century some share rents were as low as one-third of all crops. Others stood at two-fifths of the corn and one-third of the small grain. Cash rents for pasture were generally $2.50 and $3.00 per acre. By 1910, George W. Strohl had succeeded in raising rent levels on the Mills and Calhoun County farms to two-fifths of all grain and $3.50 per acre for grassland. Other lease changes increased rents. Tenants began paying according to "Government survey" rather than according to enclosed acreage. They were required to deliver their rent grain to market rather than to store it on the farm. They also began making a greater labor contribution to

[86] John Strohl to Vrooman, Jan. 8, 1909; G. W. Strohl to Scott, Feb. 2, Dec. 7, 1906, March 31, 1907, Jan. 5, Sept. 26, Dec. 9, 1908, Jan. 7, Aug. 30, 1909.

[87] Leases and correspondence, 1900–1910, *passim*.

[88] Stevenson, "Report of Scott Farms," Jan.–Dec., 1918.

the improvement program.[89] In 1911 some of the Iowa tenants paid one-half of the corn and two-fifths of the small grain, plus $4.00 per acre for pasture.[90] In 1919 the owner asked for, and her Iowa tenants agreed to pay, one-half of the corn and small grain, plus a straight $10.00 per acre for both hay and pasture land. Another lease change meant larger rent: tenants agreed to furnish the seed for small grain, an item the owner had supplied in the past.[91] Finally, after more than sixty years of landowning, the Scott family leased its Iowa farms at a rent equivalent to that received from the Illinois lands.

Because a detailed consideration of the rental income from the Scott farms taking into account its relationship to the price index, to land values, and other factors has been reserved for treatment elsewhere, at this time I shall present a general summary of income during the first two decades of the twentieth century. The lands commonly yielded *gross* cash and share rents of $5.00 to $8.00 per acre prior to World War I. Once the global conflict had made its impact on prices of farm commodities,[92] rental income increased sharply. Translating $1.39 to $1.50 per bushel for corn, $.80 for oats, $2.00 for wheat, and $11.00 per ton for alfalfa into rental income,[93] the Scott lands returned a *net* rent ranging from $9.00 to $15.00 per acre from 1917 to 1919. Such income induced Julia Scott to divide the lands by deed among the members of her family so that the recipients of income shared the burdens of management and taxes directly.[94]

[89] G. W. Strohl to Scott, Aug. 30, 1909, Sept. 29, 1910.

[90] *Ibid.*, Aug. 31, 1911.

[91] Hiram Vrooman to Scott, Sept. 20, 1918, July 5, Aug. 19, 1919.

[92] A. B. Genung, "Agriculture in the World War Period," *Farmers in a Changing World, Yearbook of Agriculture, 1940* (Washington, 1940), 277–296. The rental figures cited in this paragraph were compiled from estate accounts and reports of Scott Farms by Stevenson, and correspondence in the Scott Collection, also from "Estate of Julia G. Scott," 145.   [93] Reports of Scott Farms by Stevenson, 1916, 1918.

[94] "Estate of Julia G. Scott," 145–149, 183.

Although rental income was large, it is just part of the story of the benefits of two decades of agricultural prosperity. The tremendous rise in land values in Illinois and Iowa between 1900 and 1920 increased the worth of the Scott farms from less than half a million dollars in 1900 to more than two and a half million in 1920.[95]

Finally, where did the Scott farms stand in relation to the agricultural community? Prior to 1910 they came close in some respects to fitting the resident farmer's evaluation of absentee-owned, tenant-operated land. According to this hostile and unsophisticated view, absentee landlords were parasites. They were fond of cash rents, showed more interest in income than in conserving their land, owned carelessly cultivated and run-down property, and failed to support such local necessities as schools and roads.[96] The critics might have claimed that the Scott lands fitted at least the run-down, carelessly cultivated, and soil-wasting characterization of their indictment. By 1919 the picture had changed greatly. The Scott farms had assumed an entirely different role in the community. The owner and her advisers were pioneering in the field of tenant education. They tried to discover and to apply the best advice agricultural science had to offer. They supported local farm-improvement organizations. They stood in the front ranks of the advocates of a new agriculture.

[95] This estimate is based upon figures from the published U.S. Census reports of 1910 and 1920. County average values were derived first by adding the value of land and buildings and then by dividing the total by the total acres in farms. This was done for each Illinois and Iowa county. These county averages were then used to estimate the value of Scott holdings in each county. Finally the estimated county values were added to find the grand total estimated value for all the Scott farms (*United States Census, 1910*, VI: *Agriculture; United States Census, 1920*, VI: *Agriculture*, Pt. I).

[96] Paul W. Gates, *Frontier Landlords and Pioneer Tenants* (Ithaca, N.Y., 1945), 53.

PART III

ECONOMIC DEVELOPMENT
OF THE WEST

Barrier to Settlement:
British Indian Policy in the
Old Northwest, 1783-1794

‿⚬‿

ROBERT F. BERKHOFER, JR.

Despite three generations of scholars who have provided new
perspectives on the complicated history of relations between
the British and the American Indians on the Old Northwestern
frontier after the Revolution, an important element of the story
still remains to be assessed. The role of the so-called Indian
Confederacy is not unknown, but its significance in post-Revo-
lutionary diplomacy has not received sufficient attention. From a
focus upon this diplomatic intermediary as it was used by the
British to consolidate the Indians and frustrate American plans, a
whole new perspective emerges to clarify British and American
Indian diplomacy in the decade after the Revolution.

Authorities differ about the goals of British policy at the end
of the Revolution, although no one doubts that British influence
over the Indians depended upon the retention of the forts occupied by English soldiers at the close of the war but situated in
territory that had been ceded to the United States by the peace
treaty. Samuel Flagg Bemis maintains that the British kept the
posts because most of the pelts in the Canadian fur trade came
from south of the new boundary stipulated in the treaty.[1] A. L.

[1] Samuel F. Bemis, *Jay's Treaty: A Study in Commerce and Diplomacy* (rev. ed.; New Haven, 1962), 6–23.

Burt argues that the fur trade was secondary to the fear of Indian reprisal for the ceding of the territory to the hated Yankees.[2] The results of research in the documents would seem to support Burt, but more important, such an investigation quickly reveals that both reasons were short-lived and subordinate to the overriding concern of the Canadian officials to retrieve the territory given away by the diplomats.

Indian defection from the King's cause worried the British officials in Quebec and the posts as early as the so-called defensive policy inaugurated in 1782. With the overthrow of the war ministry by the peace proponents in Parliament, Governor Haldimand at Quebec was instructed to withdraw the "savages" from the frontier.[3] This seeming retreat by the British in the midst of victory so dampened Indian enthusiasm for their British allies that the commanders of the upper posts feared surprise attacks. Haldimand therefore ordered Sir John Johnson, son of Sir William Johnson and newly appointed Superintendent General and Inspector General of Indian Affairs, on a tour of these posts to "reconcile the Indians to the change of system which has given them offence." Johnson was to assure the red allies that the suspension of hostilities did not mean peace and that the King's favor extended to them as much in peacetime as in wartime.[4]

[2] Alfred L. Burt, *The United States, Great Britain, and British North America from the Revolution to the Establishment of Peace after the War of 1812* (New Haven, 1940), 82–105.

[3] Frederick Haldimand to Lord Townshend, Oct. 23, 1782, Colonial Office Records, ser. 42, vol. 15, 115–116 (transcripts in Public Archives of Canada, Ottawa). For the general background of the defensive policy, see Samuel F. Bemis, *The Diplomacy of the American Revolution* (rev. ed.; Bloomington, Ind., 1957), 189–205.

[4] Haldimand to John Powell, May 28, 1782, Haldimand Papers, Manuscript Group (MG) 21, G2, vol. 104, 315–317, Public Archives of Canada; Haldimand to Henry Dundas, Sept. 9, 1782, *ibid.*, vol. 96–2, 184–186; Robert Mathews to Major Ross, Sept. 9, 1782, *ibid.*, vol. 125, 62–64. Although much of Haldimand's correspondence is published in the *Michigan Pioneer and Historical Collections* (40 vols.; Lansing, Mich. 1877–1929), I have preferred citing the corrected transcripts in the Public Archives.

Governor Haldimand feared that the Americans would take advantage of the defensive policy and the Indian discontent to capture the forts. Thus he argued with the London officials that the rebels had to be prevented from possessing the Ohio territory, which he believed belonged to the Indians anyway, as a result of prior treaties with the King. Otherwise the Americans would find little difficulty in dispersing the Indian allies of the crown and marching on the posts. He felt that the Indians must be kept favorable to the English cause:

Knowing that by their allegiance, we have hitherto, with a handfull of troops, kept possession of the Upper Posts, and that without their cordial assistance, it will be impossible to maintain that Country—therefore, Policy; as well as gratitude, demands of us an attention to the Sufferings and future Situation of these Unhappy People involved on our account, in the miseries of War with an implacable Enemy.[5]

Therefore he believed that the Indian Department should cultivate Indian friendship as assiduously as before the inauguration of the new policy.[6]

Into this tense situation were injected rumors of the proposed peace treaty between England and her former colonies, including a stipulation for the cession of the Ohio country to the Americans. When Haldimand received the preliminary articles of peace in April 1783, he thought the proposed cession of territory so prejudicial to relations between the British and the Indians that he kept them secret and immediately ordered the upper-post commanders to redouble their watch on their red allies in order to prevent surprise attacks.[7] The news could not be long concealed from the Indians, because it was in the American interest to inform the various tribes friendly to the crown of their new status and their new sovereign. British commanders

[5] Haldimand to Lord Townshend, Feb. 14, 1783, Haldimand Papers, vol. 56, 50–52.

[6] Lord North to Haldimand, April 10, 1783, *ibid.*, vol. 45, 76–77.

[7] Haldimand to Ross, April 26, 1783, *ibid.*, vol. 125, 107.

and Indian Department agents did everything in their power to prevent, or at least forestall, such disclosures. They refused to let the messengers sent by the Americans talk to the Indians, imprisoning at least one of them, and got the Indian delegations bearing such news drunk, if necessary.[8]

The news soon leaked out, and those Iroquois, or Six Nations, tribes that had sided with the English during the war sent two men to visit Haldimand to learn the truth about their lands under the peace treaty. The Governor replied evasively that he had received no information about the final treaty and knew only the gossip they themselves had heard. He requested the Indians to remain "quiet" until he had received official orders.[9] Immediately upon the conclusion of this conference, Haldimand stated his future policy to his superiors in London. He would attempt to persuade the Iroquois to relocate in Canada and would attempt to reconcile all the allied Indians with the Yankees. He would urge the upper-post commanders to be on guard against surprise attacks by friendly Indians, and at the same time he would give "every satisfaction" to the Indians, in order to show them that England still valued their friendship.[10]

[8] Allan Maclean to Haldimand, May——, 1783, Indian Affairs Papers, Record Group (RG) 10, A9, vol. 15, 84–85, Public Archives of Canada; Maclean to Haldimand, May 9, 1783, Haldimand Papers, vol. 103, 147–148; John Butler to R. Mathews, May 3, 1783, in E. A. Cruikshank, ed., "Records of Niagara," *Niagara Historical Society Publications*, XXXVIII (1927), 51–52; Maclean to Haldimand, June 17, 1783, Haldimand Papers, vol. 103, 203–204; Maclean to Haldimand, June 28, 1783, *ibid.*, 232–234; R. Hays to R. Mathews, Dec. 2, 1783, *ibid.*, 409. For the American side of this story, see Ebenezer Allen's report to Congress, Aug. 12, 1783, Papers of the Continental Congress, item 78, vol. 1, 433–435, National Archives; and Frank Severance, "The Niagara Peace Mission of Ephraim Douglass in 1783," *Buffalo Historical Society Publications*, XVIII (1914), 115–142.

[9] Conference, May 27, 1783, State Papers, ser. Q, vol. 21, 236–243 Public Archives of Canada. (Another copy, dated May 21, is in *ibid.*, vol. 26–1, 5–12.) Also see report in Claus Papers, MG 19, ser. F, vol. 3, 243–244, Public Archives of Canada.

[10] Haldimand to Lord North, June 2, 1783, State Papers, vol. 21, 229–234.

In line with his aims, Haldimand again dispatched Sir John Johnson to Niagara. The commander there, like his fellow officers elsewhere, feared Indian reprisal for the treaty cession. He was certain that "Sir Johns not appearing, will make them Conceive matters to be worse than they really are." [11] Sir John assured the Six Nations Indians and some Huron deputies that despite the

peace which seems to give you great uneasiness on account of the boundary line agreed upon between His Majesty's Commissioners, and those of the United States, yet you are not to believe or even think that by the line which has been described it was meant to deprive you of an extent of country of which the right of soil belongs to, & is in yourselves as sole proprietaries as far as the boundary line agreed upon, and established . . . in the year 1768 at Fort Stanwix, neither can I harbor an Idea that the United States will act so unjustly, or impolitically as to endeavor to deprive you of any part of your Country under the pretence of having conquered it.—The King still considers you his faithful Allies, as his children, and will continue to promote your happiness by his protection, and encouragement of your usual intercourse with traders with all other benefits in his power to afford you.

After urging his listeners to surrender their prisoners and promising them a large cargo of gifts, Sir John concluded, "I must recommend to you to be unanimous among yourselves and not to separate, or scatter about your country, and thereby weaken yourselves, and lessen your consequence and to advise your young men to desist from all acts of hostility," lest Yankee resentment lead to war again. An Indian chief replied that the Indians would heed his advice and, significantly for our story later, transmit this information westward. [12] On the last day of

[11] Maclean to Haldimand, May 2, 1783, Haldimand Papers, vol. 103, 118–120. An Indian agent believed likewise (John Butler to R. Mathews, May 3, 1783, in *Niagara Historical Society Publications*, XXXVIII [1927], 51–52).

[12] "Proceedings with the Indians of the Six Nation Confederacy and Sir John Johnson Held at Niagara in July 1783," Haldimand Papers, vol. 119, 195–207.

July 1783, after both public and private meetings, Sir John reported, and the Niagara commander concurred, that he had left the Indians in the best of humor and hopeful for the future.[13]

This council had two results of importance for relations between Americans and Indians: the first real reply (by the Six Nations) of any Indian tribe to a United States invitation for a peace treaty and the revival of the Western Confederacy of Indians. These results mark, in my opinion, the shift from a "defensive" policy by the Canadian officials with regard to the forts and the Indians to an offensive policy of trying to undo the territorial cession. While fear of Indian attack led to the initial decision to retain the upper posts in order to assure the Indians of continued British protection, the very success of that plan prompted Haldimand and his subordinates to use the Indians' allegiance to keep the Americans from occupying and settling the territory they possessed by treaty but could not dominate militarily because of those Indians.

The officials at Quebec had hit upon the essentials of an idea of a neutral Indian barrier state as a device to thwart American plans of occupation and settlement. Samuel Flagg Bemis maintains that the creation of the barrier state only became official British policy in the early 1790's, after the defeat of two American expeditions sent against the Indians, but Haldimand's actions and words indicate that he conceived basically the same idea as early as the beginning of negotiations for the signing of the definitive treaty between Great Britain and the United States, and long before he learned of the actual signing itself.[14] Although Bemis is correct in maintaining that the neutral Indian barrier state only became official policy during the winter of 1791–1792, Haldimand proposed the basic idea to his superiors in late 1783, and his policy was tacitly accepted by the home government. In a letter dated November 27, 1783, he reveals the

[13] John Johnson to Haldimand, Aug. 7, 1783, Haldimand Papers, vol. 115, 137; Maclean to Haldimand, July 31, 1783, *ibid.*, vol. 103, 293–295.
[14] Bemis, *Jay's Treaty*, 155–168.

connection he sees between the retention of the posts, the Indian Confederacy, and the nature of the barrier these created to American occupation and settlement:

They [the Indians] entertain no idea (though the Americans have not been wanting to insinuate it) that the King either had ceded or had the right to cede their territories or hunting grounds to the United States of North America. These people, my Lord, have as enlightened ideas of the nature and obligations of treaties as the most civilized nations have, and know no infringement of the treaty of 1768 which fixed the limits between their country and that of the different provinces in North America can be binding upon them without their express concurrence and consent. Your Lordship will observe that the object of their general confederacy is to defend their country against all invaders. In case things should proceed to extremities, the event no doubt will be the destruction of the Indians, but during the contest not only the Americans but perhaps many of His Majesty's subjects will be exposed to great distresses. To prevent such a disastrous event as an Indian war is a consideration worthy the attention of both nations, and cannot be prevented so effectively as by allowing the posts in the upper country to remain as they are for some time. . . . It would certainly be better for both nations and the most likely means to prevent jealousies and quarrels that the intermediate country between the limits assigned to Canada by the provisional treaty and those established as formerly mentioned by that in the year 1768 should be considered entirely as belonging to the Indians, and that the subjects neither of Great Britain nor of the American States should be allowed to settle within them, but that the subjects of each should have liberty to trade where they please.[15]

Here, but for the addition of an offer of British mediation, is the essence of the concept of the neutral Indian barrier state advanced nine years later by the London officials in their instructions to the British minister to the Washington administration.

Unlike Burt, I see the major purpose for retaining the posts to

[15] Quoted in Burt, *United States, Great Britain, and British North America*, 93.

be the establishment of a barrier to American settlement, and not
the prevention of either an Indian uprising against the British or
savage warfare against the Americans. The manipulation of the
Indians and the success of the confederacy idea depended upon
the retention of the posts and the domination of the lands and
Indians around them. From these bases of power and influence,
the Canadian officials hoped to undo the diplomatic blunder of
the cession. While Canadian and English officials appeared to
urge the Indians to be at peace with the Americans, they at the
same time tried to frustrate any American attempt to occupy the
lands ceded in the peace treaty. Thus Haldimand, his successor,
and their subordinates were willing to allow the Americans to
make peace with the Indians after the war only at the price of
the barrier state. This price was, of course, totally unacceptable
to the United States government, because of both national honor
and financial need. Land-hungry speculators and frontiersmen
and eager creditors demanded the only major resource possessed
by the Continental Congress and, later, the new federal government. Since the United States government during most of the
decade after the Revolution could not dominate the Indians
militarily, it could only use threats of expropriation or offers of
payment.[16] Under these circumstances the British could use the
Indian Confederacy as long as the fundamental conditions remained unchanged.

The confederacy originated in an attempt of the British to
strengthen their allegiances with various Indian tribes. In late
March and early April of 1780, Guy Johnson, the nephew of Sir
William, and his successor as Superintendent of Indian Affairs
for the Northern Department, met with three thousand Iroquois
tribesmen to sharpen their axes for war and to urge them to send

[16] United States policy is the subject of an article and a book by
Reginald Horsman: "American Indian Policy in the Old Northwest,
1783–1812," *William and Mary Quarterly*, 3d ser., XVIII (Jan. 1961),
35–53; *Expansion and American Indian Policy, 1783–1812* (East Lansing, Mich., 1967).

a delegation of chiefs westward to the Shawnees, the Delawares, and "Hurons and their Confederacy" to get those tribes to act in conjunction with the English against the rebels. He then gave Kayashota, a pro-British Seneca spokesman, and twenty-five other chiefs a wampum belt and a message for the western Indians.[17] In the middle of June the delegation returned and reported that all of the western tribes except the Hurons had united and formally agreed to fight the Yankees.[18] These conferences were well attended and manipulated by British Indian Department agents, as was the one held the next spring at Detroit. There the Shawnees requested the aid of the Six Nations and the other tribes in defending their country against the Americans. The commander at Detroit told the assembled tribes:

I now give you my opinion that it would tend for the general good, did you all gather together and form yourselves in one great body, by which means you will be able to frustrate any designs the enemy may have ere they penetrate in your Countries. I am happy that my opinion coincides with that of my children.

Kayashota immediately concurred with the idea: "We brownskins are but one, and that we the Six Nations are come here to open your ears, to attend to what is good, or what we our father [the British ruler] may recommend." Joseph Brant, the well-known Mohawk friend of Sir William Johnson and himself a captain in the British Army, approved this sentiment, and then Kayashota led the war songs.[19] A year later, at another Detroit

---

[17] Conference, March 31, April 4, 5, 7, 1780, Indian Affairs Papers, RG 10, A9, vol. 12, 242, 248, 253; Guy Johnson to Alexander McKee, April 6, 1780, Claus Papers, vol. 2, 201–202; G. Johnson to McKee, Aug. 12, 1780, *ibid.*, vol. 35, 195–196.

[18] "Proceedings of a Meeting with the Deputies of the Six Nations on Their Return from the Southward," June 17, 1780, Haldimand Papers, vol. 119, 143–151; Henry Bird to A. S. DePeyster, June 3, 1780, *ibid.*, vol. 100, 425–427; Haldimand to G. Johnson, July 24, 1780, *ibid.*, vol. 107, 127–129.

[19] Council, April 26, 1781, Indian Affairs Papers, RG 10, A4, vol. 13, 1–8.

council, one Cherokee chief said that his tribe had joined the "General Alliance," and another addressed the Six Nations: "It's you that formed this plan of uniting us with your elder Brethren the English and we readyly took it." [20]

The confederacy used by the British as a diplomatic device between the Indians and the Americans after the Revolution was a revival of the idea of a general alliance with the Six Nations serving as the leader and communications link between the Quebec officials and the tribes of the West. The Niagara commander reported to Haldimand on the re-initiation of the confederacy at Sir John Johnson's conference with the Iroquois in July 1783 at the Niagara post:

Some of the principal Indian Chiefs of the Six Nations, have made a proposall to Sir John Johnson that a few of them are to go to Sandusky to have a meeting with the Western Nations [tribes], and to form a General Confederacy of Union and Friendship amongst themselves[;] the Six Nations are to be at the head of the Confederacy, consisting of thirty-five Nations, and the chiefs here are to get their younger brethren [western tribes] to avoid every act of Hostility whatever, without their Consent and aprobation—Sir John Johnson will give your Excellency the particulars.[21]

According to the minutes of the Sandusky Council, Joseph Brant and Alexander McKee, the Pennsylvania loyalist who headed the Indian Department at Detroit, pushed vigorously for the formation of a confederacy. McKee read Sir John's Niagara speeches and later urged unity upon the various tribes. Brant told the assembled Indians about the wrongs perpetrated by the Yankees upon his tribe, repeated Sir John's statement about the

[20] Council, July 6, 1782, *ibid.*, 138–145.

[21] Maclean to Haldimand, July 31, 1783, Haldimand Papers, vol. 103, 293–295. This portion of the letter was not thought of sufficient importance to copy and transmit to Lord North. For more "particulars," see Maclean to Haldimand, Aug. 8, 1783, *ibid.*, 318–321; and J. Johnson to Haldimand, Aug. 11, 1783, *ibid.*, vol. 115, 138.

validity of the 1768 boundary line, and requested the tribes to lay down their hatchets except in case of attack. Finally, he exhorted the assembled Huron, Delaware, Shawnee, Mingo, Ottawa, Chippewa, Pottawatomie, Creek, and Cherokee:

We the Six Nations with this belt bind your hearts and minds with ours that they may be never hereafter a Separation between us, let there be Peace or War, it shall never disunite us, for our Interests are alike, nor shou'd anything ever be done but by the Voice of the Whole, as we make but one with you.

The southern tribes appeared interested in this proposal, but the western Indians showed little interest in such a union during the council, but at its conclusion Brant requested that a few western chiefs return with the Six Nations delegates to Niagara in order to assist the Iroquois tribes in conducting negotiations with the Americans.[22] Despite apparent Indian apathy toward the idea of confederation, Brant maintained in later years that the tribes had agreed at this meeting to make peace only as a united group,[23] and the Niagara commander interpreted the activities at Sandusky as establishing "a League offensive and defensive with the Southern and Western Nations and have agreed, Except in their own defence if attacked; or their country invaded; they are ready and willing to be at Peace and friendship with the Americans, provided the frontier men makes no Encroachment on their Lands &c."[24]

Upon the return of the Six Nations delegation from Sandusky with thirty-six "confederates," a council with the British Indian

[22] "Minutes of Transactions with Indians at Sandusky," Aug. 26–Sept. 8, 1783, *ibid.*, vol. 103, 349–350.

[23] Council, Oct. 1786, Indian Affairs Papers, RG 10, A9, vol. 16, 166–179.

[24] Maclean to Haldimand, Sept. 27, 1783, Haldimand Papers, vol. 103, 370–374. Here as elsewhere I stress the British aegis for the organization of the confederacy, unlike Randolph C. Downes, in *Council Fires on the Upper Ohio: A Narrative of Indian Affairs in the Upper Ohio Valley until 1795* (Pittsburgh, 1940), 151, 181, 191, 282–284.

Department officers and the Niagara commander was called immediately. Again the Niagara commander assured the Iroquois and other Indians that their lands had not been ceded to the Americans in the peace treaty, because the King could not give away what was not his by the 1768 treaty. At this council, a Cayuga chief indicated very explicitly the ideal chain of communications in the confederacy when he told the other Indians that the Iroquois would "continue to follow the advice [of] our Brother the English . . . , [and] Therefore wish you to encourage your young men to follow the same path, and look to us for advice, as we do to our Brethren the English for thiers [*sic*]."[25]

From this narrative of the origins of the confederacy, we see how the idea could be used by the British to counter American plans. The basis of the confederacy was said to be unanimity, and political scientists have long noted the difficulty of achieving this unanimity. Attaining consensus within a single tribe was difficult enough, let alone in an organization of thirty-five tribes. Thus the Americans were frustrated in their demands for cessions because positive action was impossible given the organizational framework of the confederacy. The British, often unsuccessful in keeping the Indians united, had nothing to lose from a lack of action and everything to gain from the *status quo*. For the Americans to gain their ends in relation to the Indians, they had to deny the validity of the Confederacy and disunite the tribes; the British had only to exhort the tribes to stay united and to hold to the line of 1768. Finally, the Six Nations, more directly under British control than any other tribe, acted as a communications link between the officials in Quebec and the western Indians. British official opinion at this time was that "the conduct of the western Indians, (the infinitely more numerous people) will always be governed by that of the Six Nations, so nice a management of them may not, therefore, be necessary—some presents and marks of Friendship are due them for their

[25] Meeting, Oct. 2, 1783, Haldimand Papers, vol. 119, 240–245.

Services, and should from time to time be dispensed among them." [26]

That the councils regarding the confederacy and peace negotiations in general were rigged in favor of British aims can scarcely be doubted after reading one rather long sentence from the "Instructions for the Good Government of the Indian Department." According to these instructions, the manipulation of a council was rather simple:

As Indians are in general curious, and wish to carry News to their villages, the [British Indian Department] Officers should be cautious not to relate any [thing] to them, but what they know to be facts, and these should be distinctly told, for the mistaking, or not properly understanding a piece of News, has been known to alarm and estrange whole Nations [tribes] from a Post, for which and other reasons, the Agents at the Posts should endeavor to make one or two sober and intelligent Chiefs of the Indian Nations living at or near their Posts their friends and Confidents [*sic*], and on any occasion of calling together a Council to have them present, and make one of them their speaker, having him prepared before the meeting, and when met they should be further directed to have the interpreter to prompt him in what the officer intends to say, which is the custom among themselves, their speakers having commonly prompters, and speeches so delivered will always have more influence than coming from an Interpreter being delivered their own way.[27]

The most famous of these spokesmen was Joseph Brant, but the frequent repetition of other names, such as Kayashota, in the British minutes of these councils indicates that the meetings were conducted by Indians who spoke with British tongues. Such Indian Department agents as Alexander McKee at Detroit and

[26] "Memorandum Respecting Public Matters in the Province of Quebec Submitted to the Consideration of the Right Honble Lord Sydney, by General Haldimand—16 Mar. 1785—," State Papers, vol. 295, 7.

[27] March 27, 1787, Simcoe Transcripts, ser. 2, vol. 2, 144–156, Public Archives of Canada.

John Butler at Niagara were assumed to have complete influence over the tribes in their locality through these spokesmen and their interpreters.[28]

How the confederacy was used to hinder American aims and further British goals may be seen concretely in the events surrounding the first American attempt to make a peace treaty with the Six Nations. The initial letters from General Philip Schuyler of the Northern Indian Department were carried to Niagara by the Indians. The commander or the chief Indian officer forwarded them to Sir John Johnson, who in turn transmitted them to Haldimand. The substance of the reply trickled down through the bureaucratic channel to the Indian agents and thence to the Indians.[29] The Indians' reply to Schuyler therefore stressed that the Six Nations could make peace only as part of the confederacy and inquired about American encroachments beyond the 1768 boundary. It also stated that the Indians could not—implying would not—attend any council until the next year.[30] Schuyler's speech in answer to this message was sent westward with an Iroquois deputation for the consideration of the entire confederacy, because as John Butler explained to Sir John, the Six Nations, before making any treaty with the Continental Congress, desired a general council with the confederates at which they hoped "mutually to Consult, and fix upon some measures that may lead to their interest, and safety; they think by calling all the principle men of their brethren together, and acting in conjunction with your good advise, which they hope

[28] For example, Haldimand was assured by the commander at Niagara "that the Six Nations will do nothing but by the advice of Colonel Butler [their agent]" (Maclean to Haldimand, Sept. 14, 1783, Haldimand Papers, vol. 103, 355).

[29] Such a chain of command may be followed in J. Johnson to Haldimand, Sept. 8, 1783, *ibid.*, vol. 115, 144–145; and Haldimand to J. Johnson, Sept. 11, 1783, *ibid.*, 147.

[30] Answer to Schuyler's speech, Oct. 22, 1783, *ibid.*, vol. 119, 246–248; Joseph Brant to Philip Schuyler, Oct. 23, 1783, Schuyler Papers, Box 14, New York Public Library.

to receive on the occasion, will be of great use to them on the day of the General Treaty."[31]

In line with unofficial British policy, events moved as slowly as the Indian agents could delay them toward the first Six Nations treaty with the Americans. First, the agents attempted to dissuade any Indians from going to any councils with either the commissioners from New York State or the United States. When the messenger from the Continental Congress' commissioners arrived at Niagara, for example, an Indian officer proudly related how he got the Six Nations to view the "message in its proper light—in consequence of which they burried [*sic*] it," by pointing to the ideal of the confederacy.[32] When this stratagem failed with the New York council, the agents tried to get the meeting place moved to a location that was near Niagara and under British surveillance rather than near Albany and under American influence.[33] When this effort also failed, the agents gave the departing delegation liberal amounts of advice beneficial to the English as well as to the Iroquois cause, as one man saw them.[34] Finally, the Indian Department officers sought to allow only Indians of unquestioned loyalty to be delegates, but without complete success.[35] They furthermore supplied Brant with a letter stating that the delegation possessed no power to conclude a treaty but was only to settle preliminaries for a future conference with the entire Indian Confederacy.[36] The

[31] J. Butler to J. Johnson, March 17, 1784, Indian Affairs Papers, RG 10, A9, vol. 15, 109–112.

[32] John Dease to J. Johnson, Sept. 18, 1784, Haldimand Papers, vol. 103, 458–461.

[33] Mathews to Brant, June 15, 1784, *ibid.*, vol. 65, 38–41; Mathews to J. Johnson, June 17, 1784, *ibid.*, vol. 64, 49–50; J. Johnson to Mathews, July 12, 1784, *ibid.*, vol. 115, 274–275.

[34] See, for example, Alexander Fraser to ———, Sept. 27, 1784, *ibid.*, vol. 112, 208–209.

[35] J. Butler to J. Johnson, Aug. 30, 1784, *Niagara Historical Society Publications*, XLI (1930), 69–73.

[36] Fraser to ———, Sept. 27, 1784, Haldimand Papers, vol. 112, 208–209; the letters of Brant to H. Glen, Aug. 11, 1784, in Franklin B. Hough, ed.,

New York commissioners failed to get any land cessions at all,[37] and Brant and many other delegates left before the United States commissioners arrived in October 1784 to dictate a treaty to the few remaining Indians, who ceded all Iroquois claims west of the Pennsylvania boundary.[38]

This treaty was subsequently repudiated in councils with the British and in messages to the Americans.[39] At the advice of the deputy Indian agent, the Indians dispatched messengers to request Congress to send representatives to a meeting at Niagara to reconsider the whole matter.[40] The western deputies immediately spread the invitation to a council at Niagara for the whole confederacy to study the treaty.[41] Before this council met, the Six Nations sent a delegation to get Sir John's advice. He understood their exasperation at the Yankees and again repeated British offers of protection and relief short of military action. He advised the Indians to tell Congress that the treaty was invalid.[42] No record seems to survive of the council itself, but accounts of

---

Proceedings of the Commissioners of Indian Affairs, Appointed by Law for the Extinguishment of Indian Titles in the State of New York, I (Albany, 1861), 26–27.

[37] The council's proceedings are in Hough, *Proceedings,* 35–58.

[38] The proceedings of this council are in Neville B. Craig, ed., *The Olden Time* (2 vols.; Pittsburgh, 1848; reprinted Cincinatti, 1876), II, 406–428. A biased account of both the state and federal treaties is in Henry S. Manley, *The Treaty of Fort Stanwix, 1784* (Rome, N.Y., 1932).

[39] Council at Loyal Village, Aug. 2–3, 1785, State Papers, ser. Q, vol. 25, 136–144.

[40] Dease to Henry Hamilton, Sept. 16, 1785, *ibid.,* 183–184; Brant to Scanandoa, Aug. 26, 1785, Samuel Kirkland Papers, Hamilton College Library, Clinton, N.Y.; James Deane to [Congress], Sept. 15, 1785, *ibid.;* Brant to Congress, [Aug. 26, 1785], Papers of the Continental Congress, item 30, 471.

[41] Alexander McKee to Dease, Sept. 5, 1785, State Papers, ser. Q, vol. 25, 86–87.

[42] Speech to Sir John Johnson, Nov. 11, 1785, Indian Affairs Papers, RG 10, A9, vol. 15, 179–181; Sir John's speech to the Six Nations, Nov. 18, 1785, State Affairs Papers, ser. Q, vol. 26–2, 378–381.

it allow us to reconstruct the proceedings. The Six Nations relayed Sir John's message to the confederates, and then all the tribes agreed to hold another conference to the west. The British Indian agent, as always, urged the confederacy to remain united and to discountenance any meetings with the Americans not attended by all. He even asserted that many of the American messages must be counterfeit, because they stated that the King had ceded Indian lands to the Yankees.[43]

From this example of treaty-making emerges quite clearly the cycle of activities associated with each attempt of the American government to negotiate a treaty with the various tribes in the decade after the Revolution. Before a meeting, British agents held a council to prepare the delegates with thoughts and words for the coming conference with the Americans. They exhorted the Indians to stand by the confederacy and to claim the 1768 boundary. No delegation, said the agents, had any power except from the confederacy, and no treaty was valid unless signed by all the tribes. The agents even tried to select the delegates, especially the chief spokesmen. To keep even these trusted allies from American influence and perhaps bribes, they preferred the "fireplace" for all meetings to be located in territory dominated by the posts retained by the British. When the British agents were successful, no treaty of cession issued from a conference with the Americans. When they were not successful, councils were called under British auspices to repudiate the cessions adverse to British interests by claiming that the treaties were in violation of the unanimity principle of the confederacy. Such treaties were said to be "partial treaties" signed by a "few young men" not authorized by the general Indian alliance.

[43] Six Nations Council at Niagara, June 25, 1786, State Papers, ser. Q, vol. 2, 527 ff. For the version for American ears, see Captain Sam's speech, Papers of Continental Congress, item 150, vol. 1, pt. 2, 511–512; Major North to Josiah Harmar, July 29, 1786, Harmar Papers, Draper Collection, 1W 146–147, Wisconsin State Historical Society; William Butler to Richard Butler, Sept. 11, 1786, Papers of Continental Congress, item 150, vol. 2, pp. 9–13.

With the basic pattern in mind, we need only to provide a hasty sketch of how it worked out in the sequence of treaty-making and Indian diplomacy until 1795. Essentially the sequence consists of the basic pattern repeated at three different times: when the Americans tried to obtain cessions in the peace treaties at the end of the Revolution, when they sought to ratify the previous treaties in 1788, and again when they attempted in 1793 to make peace before Wayne's triumphant expedition into the western territory.[44]

The treaty of Fort Stanwix with the Six Nations was but one of three treaties sought by the American commissioners at the end of the Revolution. After the Iroquois treaty, the commissioners moved to Fort McIntosh at the mouth of the Beaver River, where some Wyandot and Delaware and a few Ottawa and Chippewa had gathered in response to the commissioners' invitation. Again the Americans informed the Indians of their status as a conquered people and of the necessity for a land cession as compensation for the losses inflicted by the savages on the Americans during the war. The four tribes, in a treaty dated January 1785, ceded all their lands, except for a reservation, to the United States. Then the commissioners arranged for a meeting at Vincennes with the Shawnee, Miami, Wea, Piankashaw, Pottawatomie, Kickapoo, and other Lake tribes in order to ratify the McIntosh Treaty line.

At the moment of the invitation, those tribes were gathered at Detroit to consider the Stanwix and McIntosh treaties. The skillful McKee watched over the conference, and the Indians repudiated both treaties as partial ones made without confederate consent. In fact, the reaction to the United States commissioners' invitation was so hostile that the commissioners decided to move the proposed conference from Vincennes farther east to a hastily

---

[44] The story of these years may be followed in outline in the books by Bemis, Burt, Horsman, and Downes already cited. Each presents at best only a partial view of the history and needs to be supplemented by reference to the original sources.

built Fort Finney at the mouth of the Great Miami. Only some Shawnee signed a treaty on January 28, 1786, ceding all their lands east of the Great Miami.

Several councils were held at Niagara by the Six Nations and the other tribes in the area dominated by Detroit as a prelude to a meeting of the confederacy at one of the Shawnee towns. When the American forces invaded that town, the conference was moved to Detroit, where a grand council was held in December 1786. Before that meeting, Brant and other Iroquois spokesmen harangued those tribes most likely to accede to American designs to support the confederacy and the 1768 boundary. Brant, according to one Indian agent, had to "prepare their minds for this meeting, and allways urges unanimity to the whole in their intended deliberations, and tells them not to lose sight for a moment, of that noble idea . . . *they were Lords of Soil, and that all the White People are intruders or Invaders.*" [45] So it is not surprising that the message from the council to Congress repudiated the three treaties of Stanwix, McIntosh, and Finney and insisted that lasting peace could be obtained by the United States only by treating with the whole confederacy. If Congress wanted peace, it should send representatives to a council with the whole alliance the next spring, and in the meantime it should stop all surveys and settlement north of the Ohio River. Because Brant was not successful in gaining complete agreement to the 1768 line, the Ohio River boundary was not stipulated as was usual, and Congress could and did take advantage of this omission. [46]

From this council also went a request to the British officials to specify just what aid they would give the Indians in their struggle. [47] The replies, from the new governor, Guy Carleton—now

[45] P. Langan to Daniel Claus, Dec. 14, 1786, Claus Papers, MG 19, F1, vol. 4, 131–136, Public Archives of Canada (his italics).

[46] "Speech of United Indian Nations at Their Confederate Council . . . ," Nov. 28–Dec. 18, 1786, State Papers, scr. Q, vol. 27–1, 69–75.

[47] Langan to Claus, March 17, 1787, Claus Papers, vol. 4, 149–155.

Lord Dorchester—down to the agents, were cautious. They urged peace with the Americans but implied that if war broke out and the retained posts were threatened, the Indians could expect active military intervention. As a result of such cautious answers, some British officers worried once again about keeping the allegiance of some of the more bellicose tribes.[48] The underlying aim of Indian policy continued to be the establishment of the barrier state, as was clear from Sir John's instructions to McKee. He was glad that the Indians realized so fully what their future would be if they permitted the Americans to settle in their country:

Our Situation in that case would be very little better—for which reasons I think it best to encourage them all in our Power to draw a certain line between them and the Americans, allowing as large a scope as they can with Safety to themselves and attention to their hunting ground, beyond which they ought not to be permitted to Settle. . . . I therefore see nothing left for . . . [the Indians] but Unanimity in their Councils, and a Steady and firm Opposition to their encroachment, this line of conduct once determined on would secure peace to them for a few years.[49]

Since Congress delayed answering the confederates' message from Detroit, two major British-Indian councils were held to prepare for the conference with the Americans. In December 1787, people at a meeting in the Miami country to consider treaty terms with Congress fell to bickering about boundaries, in spite of Brant's efforts to maintain unity.[50] Only in the middle of 1788 did Arthur St. Clair, the newly appointed governor of the

[48] Guy Carleton to J. Johnson, Nov. 27, 1786, State Papers, ser. Q, vol. 27-1, 82–84; Carleton to J. Johnson, Dec. 14, 1786, *ibid.*, 86–88; Mathews to Brant, May 29, 1787, quoted in Walter H. Mohr, *Federal Indian Relations, 1774–1788* (Philadelphia, 1933), 120–121.

[49] J. Johnson to McKee, Sept. 2, 1787, Indian Affairs Papers, RG 10, A9, vol. 16, 181–5.

[50] William Wilson, Information from the Indian Country, Feb. o, 1788, Papers of the Continental Congress, item 150, vol. 3, 133–137, 141–142; Arthur St. Clair to Henry Knox, Jan. 27, 1788, *ibid.*, 23–26.

newly organized Northwest Territory, receive instructions to call a council to secure at least the reconfirmation of the three previous treaties.[51] Another preliminary council was then called at Detroit to consider for a second time the forthcoming American conference at Fort Harmar. Perhaps to conceal cleavages within the confederacy, negotiations between the Indians and St. Clair began by correspondence carried by messengers. The confederates demanded one meeting place and a treaty with the entire membership; St. Clair wanted another meeting place and refused to recognize any confederacy. Both sides disagreed over the placement of the boundary line between red and white men. With so little agreement, many of the confederates left for home, to the satisfaction of the British.[52] Brant and the agents were not able to maintain unity, however, so some tribesmen went to Fort Harmar, where they signed two treaties confirming the preceding treaties. To St. Clair and the Americans, the signing and the rift separating the tribes looked like the end of the confederacy.[53] With the denunciation of these treaties as contrary to the principles of the confederacy, another cycle of conferences was completed.

The lack of results from this round of negotiations prompted

[51] *Journals of the Continental Congress*, ed. W. C. Ford and G. Hunt (Washington, 1904–1930), May 2, July 2, Aug. 12, 1788, XXXIV, 124–126, 285–286, 411–441.

[52] Dorchester to Sydney, June 9, 1788, State Papers, ser. Q, vol. 36 1, 251–254; Dorchester to Sydney, Oct. 14, 1788, *Niagara Historical Society Publications*, XL (1929), 48–50; copies of the correspondence between the Indians and St. Clair, manuscript treaties, 1778–1795, G. Appendix to the Minutes of the Treaty of Fort Harmar, 1789, in the Anthony Wayne Papers, Historical Society of Pennsylvania, Philadelphia. I owe the latter reference to Mr. Donald H. Kent, Director of the Bureau of Archives and History, Pennsylvania Historical and Museum Commission, Harrisburg, Pa.

[53] Proceedings of council, Dec. 13, 1788–Jan. 11, 1789, Indian Affairs Papers, RG 10, A9, vol. 16, 214–283; St. Clair to Knox, Jan. 18, 1789, in William H. Smith, ed., *The Life and Public Services of Arthur St. Clair . . . with His Correspondence and Other Papers* (2 vols.; Cincinnati, 1882), II, 108–109.

preparations for war by both the Indians and the Americans. Brant went among the tribes once again urging them to unite behind the confederacy, but most tribes seemed more interested in going to battle. In fact, some tribes would have given the "war pipe" to the Detroit commander but for the vigilance of McKee.[54] Henry Knox, Secretary of War in President Washington's new government, decided upon the double policy of placating the Iroquois by remedying their complaints in an attempt to split them from the confederacy and of putting down the other Indians by force.[55] The British for their part attempted to thwart his Iroquois plans,[56] and the Indians defeated the American expedition led by General Harmar in 1790 in two skirmishes.

Knox again, in 1791, attempted to keep some Indians neutral while the Americans warred on other tribes. To wheedle the Iroquois from the English and the confederates, Knox sent Timothy Pickering to distribute presents and offer aid in becoming civilized to those Iroquois still residing in the United States.[57] He also ordered Colonel Thomas Proctor on a mission of peace to the Indians on the Maumee and Wabash rivers. Since some Seneca and other Iroquois chiefs agreed to accompany such a mission, Proctor stopped at Niagara. There the commander and the Indian agents thwarted his plans at every turn, even refusing him a vessel on which to travel westward.[58] Dorchester approved of the commander's acts but deplored his openness in performing them, since official policy was to encourage peace between the

[54] Dorchester to Sydney, June 25, 1789, State Papers, ser. Q, vol. 42, 58–60; Dorchester to Sydney, July 15, 1789, *ibid.*, 62.

[55] An account of the council held by Timothy Pickering to placate the Senecas may be found in his journal, Pickering Papers, vol. 16, 65–107, Massachusetts Historical Society.

[56] *Ibid.*, 46.   [57] *Ibid.*, vol. 60, 78–103.

[58] Proctor's journal is published in *Pennsylvania Archives*, 2d ser. (Harrisburg, 1876), IV, 553–622. The British actions may be seen in State Papers, ser. Q, vol. 50–1, 167–171, 202–214, and vol. 51–2, 754–760.

Indians and the Americans.[59] Thus once again is revealed the difference between the core and the façade of British policy.

By this time Dorchester had struck upon the idea of urging the Indians to request the mediation of Britain between them and the Americans as the capstone to the formation of the whole barrier state. To this end he directed Sir John to have his agents secure from the confederated tribes a statement of their terms for peace with the Americans. Sir John thereupon ordered the faithful McKee to organize a conference to produce such a statement. In immediate response to these orders, McKee went to the Miami rapids and began gathering the Indians together. He also instructed Brant on what he was to do to produce such terms as Dorchester desired.[60] Brant and the Indian agents were again unsuccessful in producing agreement on a boundary line; nevertheless deputies were selected to journey to Quebec to state to Dorchester the peace terms he desired to hear.[61] The problem of confederate disunity never really bothered the British, for a few months later the second American expedition led by St. Clair was so ignominiously defeated that the Governor even lost the personal papers he carried.

After this second defeat, in 1791, the neutral Indian barrier state emerges as a subject of formal instructions from the officials in London to George Hammond, their minister to the new federal government in Philadelphia. Because Hammond knew that the proposal of formal British mediation between the United States and the Indians was too repugnant to American officials, he himself never broached it formally but, rather, fell back upon the Dorchester suggestion that the Indians formally

[59] Dorchester to Gordon, June 2, 1791, State Papers, ser. Q, vol. 50–1, 219–20; cf. Dorchester to J. Johnson, June 2, 1791, *ibid.*, 218.

[60] McKee to J. Johnson, April 1, 1791, *ibid.*, 150–152; Dorchester to J. Johnson, Aug. 1, 1791, *ibid.*, vol. 52, 254–255.

[61] On disunity, see Brant to J. Johnson, June 23, 1791, *ibid.*, 251. For the meeting with Dorchester, see *ibid.*, Aug. 14, 1791.

request the intervention.[62] Coinciding with the latest step in the development of the barrier state was the arrival of John Graves Simcoe as lieutenant governor of newly created Upper Canada. Simcoe hated the rebellious Americans and always suspected them of designs upon the upper posts, so he readily fell in with the new policy as outlined to him by Hammond. The Lieutenant Governor was to engineer, without the appearance of collusion, a "spontaneous" demand by all the Indian tribes for British mediation in their conflict with the Americans. All aid short of active armed intervention was to be given the tribesmen. Forthwith Simcoe ordered McKee, in words echoing his own instructions from Hammond, to hold a council.

It is to endeavor to impress the Indians, now meeting from the farthest Parts of Canada, of *themselves* to solicit the Kings good offices. It is to be extremely desired that, *that* Solicitation should be the Result of their own spontaneous Reflections. In all cases it will be adviseable, after the repeated assurances of our Neutrality, which we have given to Congress, that there should appear nothing like Collusion, or any active Interference to inspire them, with such a Sentiment; a suspicion of that tendency would infallibly tend to defeat the Accomplishment of our Object; It will also be essential that all the Indian Tribes bordering on the British Possessions, should concur in the Solicitation; not only as so numerous a Confederacy, would present to the Americans the Appearance of an increased accumulation of Hostile Force, but also, as a consolidation of the Indian Territorial Claims, and Rights, which is requisite to the Formation of so extensive a Barrier, as we have in Contemplation, you no doubt will be persuaded, as well as myself, that it is neither the Interest, nor the Inclination of His Majesty's Government, to commence *offensive* Hostilities, against the United States; it will be highly proper, to guard the Indian against any Expectations of that Sort; In the event of Congress's refusing to admit our mediation upon this Ground.[63]

[62] Both Bemis, in *Jay's Treaty*, 156–169, and Burt, in *United States, Great Britain, and British North America*, 117–123, tell this story well.
[63] John G. Simcoe to McKee, Aug. 3, 1792, Simcoe Transcripts, ser. 4,

The ostensible reason for the request for British mediation was that the British would supply the documents necessary for proof of the Indian boundary of 1768.

In spite of the Indian victories in battle, the British agents still had to work hard to achieve confederate unity, because the American policy of enticing the Iroquois away was succeeding. Thus, according to the documents, the council near the Maumee rapids in early October 1792, was mainly an exchange between the western Indians, who scolded the Six Nations for their treachery to the confederacy in dealing with the Americans, and the Six Nations, who in their own defense asserted the essential honesty of the American negotiations with them. Finally, the Iroquois delegates submitted to the general will of the council. The united Indian tribes demanded the 1768 boundary once again, the destruction of all American forts beyond this line, and a council of confederates with the Americans the next spring at Sandusky, where the British were to be present with the documentary proof of the Indian boundary claims.[64] McKee and Simcoe both thought that the council resulted in exactly what was needed to carry out Hammond's plan.[65]

The usual cycle of conferences began before the council with the Americans. The western tribes and the Iroquois both held separate meetings about what to do at the general council. Because of disagreement between and within these two groups over a boundary line, another council preliminary to the general meeting was held. There the disunity continued, with the Six Nations and some other tribes holding out for a recession back to the Muskingum River, while the rest stoutly insisted on the Ohio River as the boundary. As a result the Six Nations delegates were

vol. Dd, 8–15, Public Archives of Canada, reproduced in E. A. Cruikshank, ed., *The Correspondence of Lieut. Governor John Graves Simcoe*, I (Toronto, 1923), 207–209, but dated incorrectly.

[64] Council at Au Glaize, Sept. 30–Oct. 9, 1892, *ibid.*, 218–231.

[65] McKee to Simcoe, Sept. 11, 1792, Simcoe Transcripts, ser. 4, vol. Ee, 6–8; Simcoe to A. Clarke, Nov. 3, 1792, *ibid.*, vol. A3, draft (the stricken words in the manuscript have been omitted).

excluded from many of the secret sessions of the confederates. Although Butler, McKee, and the interpreters all urged unity as they had been ordered to and supposedly did not care whether the Muskingum or the Ohio was stipulated, it seems likely that McKee held out, in the secret sessions, for the Ohio. Probably because of the disunity, McKee suggested that the confederates confer with the American commissioners through a delegation rather than in an entire council. These negotiations through intermediaries soon ended in stalemate over the boundary line, and the commissioners left for home.[66]

In line with the expected failure of this treaty attempt, Secretary Knox continued to implement his two-pronged policy of peacemaking with the Iroquois and warmaking on the western tribes. Even during the Sandusky council, General Anthony Wayne was organizing another expedition against the hostile tribes. Since the abortive council broke up so late in the season, he postponed his march until the next year in order to avoid repeating the disaster of St. Clair. The threatened advance of Wayne frightened Simcoe and Dorchester into erecting a new fort on American soil, at the Maumee rapids—Fort Miami. Shortly before ordering this further violation of American territory, Dorchester gave an inflammatory address to the Indian messengers who had related to him the results of the Sandusky council. He implied that the United States and England would soon be at war again and that the Indians could choose their own boundary line. Simcoe read this speech to the Indians as he prepared to build Fort Miami. No wonder the Indians assumed that the British would not only supply them, as always, but would also fight on their side in the coming battle with the hated

[66] The most recent account of this council is in Reginald Horsman, "The British Indian Department and the Abortive Treaty of Lower Sandusky, 1793," *Ohio Historical Quarterly*, LXXX (July 1961), 189–213, but also see Burt, *United States, Great Britain, and British North America*, 127–131, and Downes, *Council Fires on the Upper Ohio*, 322–324. More complete information on the preliminary councils can be found in the correspondence in the Public Archives of Canada.

Yankees. They were disappointed in this expectation. Wayne defeated the Indians directly beneath the guns of Fort Miami, but the garrison never marched out to help the Indians. Wayne's victory at Fallen Timbers in August 1794 was not so important in demoralizing the confederates as was this failure of the British to intervene actively on the side of their red allies. No Iroquois warriors helped in this battle either, for American policy had lured them away.[67]

Despite British efforts to regain the Indians' confidence by provisioning them through the hard winter and despite exhortations by Simcoe and the Indian agents, the demoralized tribes came in one by one to make peace with Wayne. In the middle of the summer of 1795, Wayne called a council of the western tribes to confirm the treaties of Stanwix, McIntosh, and Finney and to hand over sixteen strategic spots for forts. By the Treaty of Greenville, the United States finally obtained the eastern and southern portion of present-day Ohio and part of Indiana. Though the British Indian Department may have been ready to call a confederate council to repudiate this treaty as the agents had arranged so often before, the failure to march to the aid of the Indians the previous year meant the defeat of any such plan.[68]

Thus finally the series of councils preceding and succeeding an American treaty with the Indians came to an end. The British withdrawal from the posts in 1796, as provided for by the Jay Treaty, only confirmed what the Indians already knew. The British had abandoned them to the Americans. While broader policy made expedient the utilization of Indian allegiance to foster the creation of the barrier state, the officials in London

---

[67] The modern account of the subject indicated by the title is Reginald Horsman's "The British Indian Department and the Resistance to General Anthony Wayne, 1793–1795," *Mississippi Valley Historical Review*, XLIX (Sept. 1962), 269–290, but additional material may be found in the unpublished correspondence in the Public Archives.

[68] *Ibid.*, 283–289.

allowed the governor at Quebec and his subordinates to manipulate the confederacy and play their diplomatic games. With the outbreak of the war with France, circumstances changed so that the London officials would sign Jay's Treaty and abandon the Indians. Therefore it was not American force but British misfortune that ended the cycles of councils that produced the pattern of British and American diplomacy in dealing with the Indians in the decade after the Revolution.

As always, relations between whites and Indians depended, not upon friendship, but on other interests. In this case, relationships among European powers affected both the Indians and the Americans. To say that the British exploited their Indian allies does not mean that manipulations by the Indian agents in council were not to the real interest of the Indians. According to many historians, they probably were, but about this we can only guess, basing our conclusions on our hypotheses about Indian behavior and desires.[69]

---

[69] Such a hypothetical approach to the Indian side of history is the basis of Downes, *Council Fires on the Upper Ohio*.

The Ohio-Mississippi Flatboat Trade: Some Reconsiderations

HARRY N. SCHEIBER

The historian's standard portrayal of the 1815–1860 "transportation revolution" naturally emphasizes the major technological innovations of the period—the paved highway, the steamboat, the canal, and the railroad—which changed the character of interregional trade in America. Ordinarily given far less attention is the remarkably persistent western flatboat trade of that era. No dramatic technological change marked the trade, unless we count navigational improvements on the rivers. No superficially precise records of clearances and arrivals, nor of ton-miles hauled, survive from the flatboat trade, comparable with what we have for the railroads and canals. Contemporary newspaper reporters gave no systematic attention to the prosaic little craft that braved river waters to carry the Northwest's farm produce down to southern plantation wharves and the docks at New Orleans. Yet the flatboat trade was as important because of its continuing economic role, down to 1860, as it was because of the colorful rivermen and folklore for which it is best remembered. It now appears appropriate to inventory what data we do have on the flatboat trade and to reconsider the trade in the larger context of ante-bellum economic change in the West.[1]

I

Prior to the advent of the steamboat on western waters, the agricultural surplus of the Old Northwest reached outside markets mainly by way of flatboat shipments to New Orleans. To be sure, some of the higher-priced products—notably meat, whiskey, and some flour—commonly were shipped eastward by wagon, through the mountains. But this overland flow of produce was attributable mainly to the economies involved in returning loaded wagons. By 1820–1825, the National Road was carrying 10,000 tons of merchandise westward to Wheeling each year, while another 30,000 tons were brought annually over the Pennsylvania Turnpike to Pittsburgh; rather than return with empty vehicles, the wagoners could afford to carry even relatively bulky produce at low prices.[2]

Even in the early 1820's, when these two east-west wagon roads were open, probably most of the western exports, figured in terms of value, and no doubt most, in terms of weight, were being sent to outside markets by flatboat. Popularly termed "arks," "Kentucky flats," or "broad-beams," the boats were oblong, about 18 to 25 feet wide, and commonly 50 to 100 feet long. Relatively simple to build, they were constructed of heavy beams, and they cost perhaps one dollar per foot for flats 25 feet

[1] Paul W. Gates, *The Farmer's Age* (New York, 1960), 174–178; Thomas Senior Berry, *Western Prices before 1861* (Cambridge, Mass., 1943), especially ch. iv; and Charles Ambler, *A History of Transportation in the Ohio Valley* (Glendale, Calif., 1942), all treat economic aspects of the flatboat trade. Leland D. Baldwin, *The Keelboat Age on Western Waters* (Pittsburgh, 1941) is a social history.

[2] Arthur L. Kohlmeier, *The Old Northwest as the Keystone of the Arch of Federal Union* (Bloomington, Ind., 1938), 7; also, R. C. Downes, "Trade in Frontier Ohio," *Mississippi Valley Historical Review*, XVI (March 1930), and Isaac Lippincott, *Internal Trade of the United States, 1790–1860*, Washington University Studies, IV, no. 1 (St. Louis, 1916), 98.

wide.[3] They held 25 to 100 tons of cargo, according to their size, in the period before 1850. During the 1850's, when the average size of flats was larger than in earlier years, the average load probably ran from 120 to 140 tons. The heaviest load ever carried to New Orleans by flatboat before 1850 was about 180 tons; but in the fifties, 150-by-24-foot boats carried loads weighing up to 300 tons.[4]

Specific physical characteristics of the flat cannot easily be given, since embellishments and variations were subject to the whims of the thousands of farmers, merchants, and adventurers who built boats for their individual purposes. But the basic design is well enough known. Planks and beams were crafted into a "floating box," with sides high enough to protect the cargo. At the center or in the stern there was a wooden cabin, or else wooden sidings on which a cloth roofing could be hung. Fittings were included for one or more pairs of large oars, and often for a rudder.[5] Construction probably required about six weeks when the boat was built by an individual with some help from his family. But there were specialized firms which built flatboats in the 1850's, no doubt in a much shorter time. One of

[3] Baldwin, *Keelboat Age*, 54, states that $1.00 to $1.50 per foot can be taken as the price in the early nineteenth century. Even allowing for dollar value changes over a period of time, other evidence corroborates this view.

[4] Frank H. Dixon, *A Traffic History of the Mississippi River System*, National Waterways Commission, doc. no. 11 (Washington, 1909), 14, gives the 300-ton estimate; Gates, *Farmer's Age*, 175, cites the New Orleans *Picayune*, 1850, that 180 tons was the largest load received there up to that time. A petition of residents of Washington County, Ohio, Aug. 4, 1838 (MS, Ohio Canal Commission Papers, Ohio State Archives), cites 110-foot boats as carrying maximum cargoes of 130 tons. This tends to support Gates's contention, as the 110-foot boats were among the largest in use. R. L. Jones gives 140 tons as the upper limit of flatboat loads after 1865, in "Flatboating down the Ohio and Mississippi, 1867–1873," *Ohio Historical Quarterly*, LIX (July 1950), 287–288.

[5] William T. Utter, *The Frontier State*, History of the State of Ohio, ed. Carl Wittke, II (Columbus, 1942), 176 ff.; Baldwin, *Keelboat Age*, 47 ff.

the major advantages of an investment in flatboat construction was the possibility of recouping some of the original cost by selling the lumber after the breaking-up of the boat at the downriver destination.[6]

Even before the Louisiana Purchase assured the free transit of American goods on the Mississippi, the lure of the New Orleans trade dazzled men of the West. The flatboat was the means by which settlers sought to reach the New Orleans market, with its prospects for cash sale of the products of a country formidably separated from the Atlantic seaboard by mountains. One recent Pennsylvania emigrant wrote in 1804 from Lancaster, Ohio: "Flower whe sell at 3 Doller a 100. We heart that Flower Sels at new Orleans at 10 Dollers a Barrel. If that is so whe shill have a fine marget hear for wheat groos Right whell heer."[7] The simple vision of this man underestimated—indeed poignantly so— the difficulties that would be involved in getting his ten dollars a barrel at New Orleans. For the flatboat trade imposed grave personal dangers on the men who guided boats downriver by oar

---

[6] Costs of timber for construction were operating costs; moreover, they comprised a variable dependent upon differentials in lumber prices between the point of construction and the point of destination. Cases are recorded of full-sized boats selling for as little as $11 in 1835, but such appear aberrational. With intensified settlement and urbanization in the South, the price of lumber at New Orleans and on the river probably rose, in the long run. In the late 1830's, it was said that flats about 60 to 80 feet long sold for half to three-fourths of their cost. The large boats of 100–110 feet sold for their whole cost. For data on the recouping of timber investment, cf. Berry, *Western Prices*, 24–25; John G. Clark, "The Antebellum Grain Trade of New Orleans," *Agricultural History*, XXVIII (July 1964), 134 *et passim*; H. E. White, "An Economic Study of Wholesale Prices at Cincinnati," mimeo. (Cornell University Library, 1935), 34; and G. R. Taylor, "Agrarian Discontent in the Mississippi Valley," *Journal of Political Economy*, XXXIX (Aug. 1931), 476 (on 1800–1810 average costs) *et passim*.

[7] David Carpenter to family, March 17, 1804, Carpenter Papers, Ohio Historical Society, Columbus (hereafter abbreviated OHS). I wish to thank the Society for permission to quote from the Carpenter and other papers.

and by pole. The vicissitudes of river trade have been romanticized well enough in the travelers' accounts and in the folk tales of Mike Fink and other men of western waters. But an even more vivid sense of what marketing by flatboat involved may be captured from the surviving records of the farmers and merchants who navigated the Ohio and Mississippi rivers in the day of the flat.

II

In every farming village on the Ohio and its tributaries, most of the young men probably went down to New Orleans at one time or another, either to take their family farms' surplus to market or to serve as hired hands. A letter from a Hillsboro, Ohio, man to his friend John Trimble, a storekeeper who had gone downriver, was doubtless typical of many sent to neighbors absent on the river for the four months or more necessary to reach New Orleans and return. Trimble's correspondent complained that the town seemed deserted, with all its young men on the river. Concerned for his friend's safety, he wrote, "I am anxious to witness [your] return, and hope that you will not engage any longer in trading to Orleans, but to New York, when our canal is completed." [8]

The perils of the trade did not bear upon personal safety alone: there were also serious economic risks. Consider the fate of grain purchased by Amasa Delano of Chillicothe, then the commercial center of the Scioto Valley in south-central Ohio. In late 1816, news of favorable grain prices in New York reached eastern Ohio. Several Chillicothe merchants had ridden out on horseback to meet the postal express; by learning of the price changes first, they gained a crucial advantage over Delano, who had remained at home. His competitors brought up the wheat in the locality before he understood what was happening, so he was

[8] Joseph McDowell to John Trimble, March 24, 1826, Trimble Family Papers, OHS; also, Richard L. Power, *Planting Corn Belt Culture* (Indianapolis, 1953), 146–147.

forced to travel "by night and day, through fen, bog, quagmire, morass, and deep swamp" to purchase wheat from farmers in the countryside. Only a few weeks earlier, wheat had fetched twenty-five cents per bushel, but now Delano was forced to pay seventy-five cents to farmers upon delivery of their grain to the gristmills on the Scioto. He bought nearly five thousand bushels in this way.[9] Amasa shrewdly sold out his stock of grain locally —and in good time, for those who bought his wheat did not fare so well. One buyer lost two flatboats in a flood on the Scioto, never even reaching the Ohio River in his effort to make New Orleans. A third boat, "with a full cargo, has never been heard of since she left Natches," Delano's brother wrote, "and it is thought that the steersman has sold her and 'cleared out' with the proceeds." Two other boats did reach New Orleans, where they found the market glutted—a problem that continually plagued western flatboat men, since so many went downstream at once on freshets after periods of low water. With prices unfavorable, the merchant had shipped his grain on to Baltimore, only to find prices even lower there than at New Orleans. Besides, he sustained "a loss of considerable wheat damaged on the passage."[10]

Two other merchants who bought from Delano also encountered well-known problems at New Orleans: a glutted market, spoilage, and a lack of sufficient ocean-ship cargo space in which produce might be sent out quickly from New Orleans to eastern or European markets. One merchant "brought up the rear with the last flotilla, and is now in . . . N. Orleans; he states that there was about 30,000 barrels of flour in market, that arrived previous to that time—besides a large quantity of sour flour, and that daily increasing—prices 7 dollars per barrel, declining and no

[9] Amasa Delano to Jabez Delano, Nov. 18, 1816, Delano Family Papers, Baker Library Archives, Dartmouth College. I wish to thank Dr. Edward C. Lathem for permission to quote from the Delano Papers.

[10] Ira Delano to Jabez Delano, Sept. 6, 1817, *ibid.* Dixon, *Traffic History,* 14, asserts that two-thirds of the annual flatboat arrivals at New Orleans came in January and February.

sales effected—all ships and vessels in port engaged for freight, and no probability of vessels enough arriving shortly to enable the owners of flour to ship. His flour cost him from 10 to 11 dollars." [11]

Others in the Scioto Valley who tried to market livestock by flatboat met similar difficulties. One of the region's leading cattlemen wrote in 1823 that early spring freshets had flooded the Scioto and that the river was "literally covered with crafts conveying off produce, property, and articles of every kind and denomination that you could possibly think of, and many that you, nor no other person except a Yankey, would not think of taking to market." He estimated that boats were departing from the Scioto for the South at a rate of thirty a day, with some three hundred expected to leave during the year. Usually he and his neighboring cattle raisers drove their herds to Philadelphia or Baltimore, or else they sold locally to eastern drovers. But prices in the East were so poor that some of the cattlemen instead tried shipping livestock by boat to New Orleans. Like the grain merchants who had dealt with Delano, however, they found a badly glutted market. The New Orleans wharf authorities refused to permit stock boats to land at the city, so they had tied up at landings above New Orleans; according to one deckhand, "he could have travelled a mile at least on Stock boats, by stepping from one to another, that lay along the shore." Needless to add, news from the Gulf port did not give the Scioto stockmen much hope for profits that year. [12]

The western farmer or merchant might well want to avoid bearing personally all the risks of marketing in so hazardous a situation. But when he could not exchange his produce on a quasi-barter or cash basis with nearby wholesalers at cities like Cincinnati or Wheeling, he became a flatboat man despite him-

[11] Ira to Jabez Delano, Sept. 6, 1817, Delano Papers.
[12] Felix Renick to William McNeill, March 15, 1823, McNeill Papers, West Virginia University Library. I wish to thank West Virginia University Library for permission to quote from the McNeill Papers.

self. Typical of men in this position was James Trimble, brother of the Hillsboro man mentioned earlier. In late 1822, Trimble hauled a load of produce, obtained from farmers who traded at his country store, to a nearby town on the Ohio River. Discovering "no opportunity of selling to advantage" there, he decided to take the cargo downriver. By offering fifty dollars each to some neighbors for the trip, he engaged deckhands for three or four flatboats. Embarking in December, Trimble safely passed the falls at Louisville (a major hazard, unnavigable in low water), but upon reaching the Mississippi, he encountered ice floes.[13] Once the ice had cleared, Trimble attempted to sell to plantations and towns along the way, above New Orleans. Some of the produce he sold at retail, but at Natchez he left pork and beef on consignment with a commission firm. In April, he reached one of the bayous of Louisiana, where he tied up to sell his pork, beef, and tallow. Despite favorable prices, sales were slow; heavy rains had flooded local creeks, making it impossible for farmers to reach the site with their teams. In the meantime he was joined by scores of other flatboats, which competed with him for sales.[14]

Trimble's dealings with his neighbors and customers indicate the far-flung network of barter relationships on which the western trade rested. He purchased flour from a Hillsboro farmer, agreeing to pay a hundred dollars in cash and an additional fifty in promissory notes to one of the farmer's local creditors, one E. Collins. As part of his own settlement with Collins, Trimble then exchanged bulk pork for barreled pork, taking the barreled meat downriver with him. Only upon his arrival in Louisiana did Trimble learn that Collins had deviously marked as pork several barrels of beef, worth $2.50 per barrel less than pork. But the complexities had only begun to unfold. At his bayou stopover, Trimble reported a $300 sale to "a very good man" on credit

[13] James Trimble to John Trimble, Nov. 7, Dec. 28, 1822, Trimble Papers. [14] *Ibid.*, April 25, 1823.

(at 20-per-cent interest) secured by another's countersignature; Trimble then purchased six bales of cotton "at from six to ten cents in Barter. I will sell a part of it in New Orleans if I can, if not take it home [by steamboat]." Not least of his pleasures was a chance meeting with an old debtor, now "married and living in indianna on the wabash," which enabled Trimble to collect his three-dollar debt.[15]

Collecting small debts from recently married Hoosiers was small compensation, however, for the time and risks involved in the flatboat trade. So long as prices held up at unusual levels, as they had during the prolonged Anglo-French wars after 1793 and the War of 1812, the profits offset the well-known perils. But in normal times, the shortcomings of New Orleans all militated against the trade: the port was distant from European markets, its harbor was too shallow for heavy-draft ocean vessels and was dangerous to navigate for all ships, the city lacked adequate storage facilities and its climate damaged perishable produce, and the city government levied high wharfage charges and other fees. The governor of Indiana thus expressed a western commonplace when he declared in 1828: "The celebrated New Orleans is annually bringing our enterprizing population to bankruptcy and ruin." Rather than rely forever upon "the fluctuating and perishable market" at that city, he asserted, westerners would do better to build a canal or railway over the Rocky Mountains, "with a view to a more profitable trade with the Kingdoms of Asia." In a more laconic vein, a scientist visiting the Scioto Valley in 1832 wrote that in earlier years corn regularly had been taken to New Orleans in flatboats. But "the uncertainty and great fluctuation of prices in that market and the unavoidable dangers of this kind of navigation, has caused this trade to be now almost entirely abandoned. Farmers . . . make a greater profit and a surer one by staying at home."[16]

[15] *Ibid.*
[16] Governor James Ray to Allen Trimble, Jan. 30, 1828, Official Governors' Papers, OHS; MS diary of Increase Lapham, OHS.

No doubt the farmers of the Scioto and of Indiana were still too preoccupied with other ambitions to think of a rich China trade, but the perils of New Orleans were among the principal motives for their state canal-construction projects, embarked upon in the 1820's and 1830's with a view toward opening direct routes to the East via the Great Lakes.[17]

III

Given the force of complaints against New Orleans and the river trade, it appears curious at first that the flatboat commerce on the rivers should have persisted with vigor well into the 1870's. An important reason was low transfer cost as compared with steamboat rates: as a rule, costs for flatboat shipment were about one-fourth to one-third lower than steamer charges on downriver freight.[18] But what must be explained further is why the river trade remained great enough to support both steamboat and flatboat. First, the canal routes between the eastern seaboard and the West were opened slowly: the transportation revolution occurred in stages, beginning with the completion of the Erie Canal in 1825; from 1833 until 1845 only the Ohio Canal and its branch lines offered a through water route between the Ohio River and Lake Erie. The other great western canals that linked the Ohio Valley with the Lakes were completed in 1845 (the Miami and Erie) and 1848 (the Illinois and Michigan, and Indiana's Wabash and Erie Canal). Moreover, the canal-lake routes —the Erie route, and also the Ohio River-Pittsburgh-Philadelphia outlet via the Pennsylvania Mainline System—were closed to traffic for up to three months each winter. This was the pork-packing season, with spoilage so great a hazard that southward shipment of pork was practically imperative. Further, the structure of freight charges on the only canal (the Ohio and Erie)

[17] H. Scheiber, "The Ohio Canal Movement, 1820–1825," *Ohio Historical Quarterly*, LXIX (July 1960), 231 ff.

[18] Berry, *Western Prices*, 45 ff.; R. Buchanan to J. Trimble, Jan. 5, 1826, Trimble Papers. See also Louis C. Hunter, *Steamboats on the Western Waters* (Cambridgde, Mass., 1949), 25 ff.

which *did* link lake and river regions prior to 1845 discouraged through shipment. Therefore, the southern half of the Old Northwest—roughly speaking, the region south of the National Road—continued to rely upon the New Orleans outlet and the southern market, which was expanding quickly as cotton moved westward, for its exports.[19]

Also contributing to the persistence of the flatboat trade was the ease with which flats could navigate the shallow tributary rivers or the Ohio River itself in periods of low water, when steamboat traffic was impeded. On the river steamers, there were also occasional shortages of cargo space and marked seasonal fluctuations in rates. The very individualism of local farmers who, whether from good business sense or plain stubborness, insisted on taking goods downriver themselves if local prices did not suit them, was itself an impetus to continued flatboat traffic. Moreover, the decline in upriver steamer charges for passenger travel made it safer and less expensive for flatboat men to return home from New Orleans. Also, urban markets along the Ohio River and on the Mississippi above New Orleans offered expanding opportunities for flatboat traders. And in the region lying west of the Mississippi, distance dictated that it was more economical in any event to ship goods downriver to St. Louis or New Orleans than on the longer route to cash markets in the East, especially prior to the advent of railroads in the trans-Mississippi country.[20]

IV

Precise measurement of the flatboat trade by either the number of boats or the volume carried is difficult, especially since

[19] Kohlmeier, *Old Northwest, passim;* John G. Clark, *The Grain Trade in the Old Northwest* (Urbana, Ill., 1966), *passim;* Ohio Canal Commission, *Fourteenth Annual Report* (Columbus, 1836), 4.

[20] H. Scheiber, *Ohio Canal Era* (Athens, Ohio, 1968). William Switzler, in *Commerce of the Mississippi and Ohio Rivers,* 50 Cong., 1 sess., H. Ex. Doc. 6, Pt. II, serial 2552 (Washington, 1888), 222, overemphasizes the decline in flatboat trade in the 1850's; cf. Hunter, *Steamboats,* 56–57.

many of the boats terminated their voyages at small way ports that kept no commercial statistics. The records of the commerce at New Orleans are available, however, and as late as 1840 an estimated 20 per cent of the freight on the lower Mississippi was carried by flats. Arrivals reported at New Orleans numbered nearly 3,000 in both 1845–1846 and 1846–1847, dropping to between 1,000 and 1,500 a year during the period 1848–1853. In 1854 arrivals were 701; they stayed at about that level until 1856, then declined to 541 in 1857. Because "the craft was so informal in its movements that its arrivals and departures could not readily be registered," presumably these data were underestimates; besides, probably about half the flats that traversed the Mississippi south of its junction with the Ohio terminated at way ports above New Orleans.[21]

On the Ohio and its tributary streams, flatboats were important for the transport of both bulk freight and high-priced produce such as vegetables, fruit, and even manufactured goods, throughout the steamboat era. One estimate of the number of flatboats passing Louisville during the long period 1849–1870 indicates some seven hundred boats annually. But above Louisville on the Ohio, Cincinnati—the leading distribution and wholesale center of the region, with a large urban population—was the terminal destination for most of the flats that poured downriver each year from the Muskingum and from towns and farms along the upper Ohio River itself. Thus in 1848 flatboat arrivals at Cincinnati numbered 1,500; in 1849 and 1850, nearly 3,000; in 1853, nearly 6,000; and in 1854, about 5,000. The proportion that, in the late 1840's, left their cargoes and were broken up at Cincinnati may perhaps be estimated in light of the traffic data for 1847: in that year, 3,336 flats arrived at Cincinnati, and 700 departed for destinations downriver, carrying an average cargo of about 75 tons.[22] As late as 1853, despite sharp

[21] Dixon, *Traffic History*, 14.
[22] R. L. Jones, "Flatboating," 287, on Louisville; Hunter, *Steamboats*, 55, and James Hall, *The West, Its Commerce and Navigation* (Cincinnati, 1848), 223, on Cincinnati.

annual increases in steamboat tonnage on the rivers, flatboats carried one-fourth of Cincinnati's downriver flour exports, one-seventh of the whiskey, and two-thirds of the bulk pork and bacon. In 1853, Cincinnati obtained direct railroad connections with the East; all her trade with the South consequently declined in volume—and afterward her flatboat commerce with southern ports fell radically. The only exception was the city's trade in bulk pork products; of these, flats still carried more than one-third of Cincinnati's down-river exports as late as 1858.[23] Until late in the decade, however, the city depended exclusively upon flatboats for her imports of coal—vital to the growing manufacturing industries located there and increasingly used for domestic heating.[24]

At Pittsburgh, Cincinnati's principal rival among the river cities for commercial and industrial hegemony, the reliance on flatboat commerce was no less impressive. Arrivals via the Ohio River were 100 in 1826, an annual average of 655 during the period 1839–1841, and an average of 674 in the years 1845–1857. But from the Monongahela and Allegheny rivers as well, flatboats came downstream to terminate at the city itself or at nearby towns. Total arrivals of flats in the urban region from all points were nearly 2,400 in 1847, when they brought a total of 118,410 tons of coal, manufactured goods, produce, stone, and other commodities.[25]

Aggregate estimates of the flatboat trade were of interest to Congress, the Army Engineers, local chambers of commerce, and commercial journalists; so there were occasional attempts to measure the over-all importance of the trade. In 1832, one such effort concluded that some 4,000 flats, with an average capacity of 40 tons each, annually descended the Mississippi. An estimated 2,000 men were engaged in building flats that year, with another 4,000 occupied in navigating the vessels. Flatboats were

[23] Computed from export statistics in William Smith, ed., *Annual Statement of the Trade and Commerce of Cincinnati,* 1851–1857 (annual vols.; Cincinnati, 1852–1858).

[24] *Ibid.,* 1857, 10.   [25] Hall, *The West,* 220; Hunter, *Steamboats,* 58.

said to carry some 600,000 tons of produce in 1846 (compared to 1,300,000 tons transported by steamer) on the western rivers. And in 1852, a knowledgeable western statistician estimated that 4,000 flats descended the Ohio and Mississippi rathers annually, carrying 100,000 tons of produce, "perhaps much more." [26]

During the 1850's the average size and capacity of the flats increased.[27] But in periods of low water, and on tributary streams where either snags and bars posed dangers to steamers or population was too sparse to sustain a steamboat trade, the smaller flats remained vital to maintaining exports to the South. It was as part of the more comprehensive shift in trade flow from the Old Northwest, caused by the advent of railroads that took much of the old river trade and rerouted it directly to the eastern port cities, that the importance of flatboats on the Ohio and Mississippi declined.[28]

v

The marketing organization of the flatboat trade did not conform to the stereotyped view that every boat carried cash crops to New Orleans and was manned by a Mike Fink or a simple farmer and a few of his neighbors. In the first place, as noted

[26] Hall, *The West*, 143; *De Bow's Commercial Review*, V (April 1, 1848), 377; Edward Mansfield in *Railroad Record* (Cincinnati), I (Feb. 2, 1854), 770. In 1816 a steamer captain reported 2,000 flats on the river between Louisville and Natchez; the following year, 500 flats were said to pass Cincinnati annually (F. P. Goodwin, "Building a Commercial System," *Ohio Archaeological and Historical Quarterly*, XVI [April 1907], 336–337). In 1843, a commercial journal reported tonnage on the Mississippi and Ohio rivers in 1842 as follows: 450 steamers, aggregating 90,000 tons, and 4,000 flatboats, manned by 20,000 men all together (*Hunt's Merchants' Magazine*, IX [July 1843], 99). The Wabash River, in Indiana, carried an astonishingly heavy flatboat trade: in 1828, some 1,200 to 1,500 flats descended the stream, and the volume was said to have increased by one-third annually up to 1834 (E. A. Cammack, "Notes on Wabash River Steamboating," *Indiana Magazine of History*, L [March 1954], 38).

[27] See n. 4, *supra*.   [28] See n. 19, *supra*.

earlier, there was an active trade on the upper Ohio's tributaries, much of it terminating at Cincinnati. Moreover, below Cincinnati, both urban markets and plantation wharves took much of the downriver produce carried on flats before they reached New Orleans.

In the second place, the internal structure of the marketing system—more specifically the typology of entrepreneurs and other operators engaged in the trade—was far from simple. The rise of the steamboat trade in the 1820's opened new options to shippers and farmers seeking transport downriver for their goods. The adjustments within the flatboat trade were conditioned by (1) technological limitations of the steamboat—limitations such as those barring steamers effectively from trade on the tributaries (sometimes on the main river itself) at low water; (2) the changing condition of navigation on the Ohio and its tributaries—for example, successive improvements by the Army Engineers (which helped reduce the hazards, and thus insurance charges as well, of steamboat travel), or the improvement of the Muskingum River for steamer navigation (which meant more effective steamer competition for the valley's trade); and (3) general economic conditions—the volume of tonnage, regional price differentials, the size of the harvest, the demand for cargo space, and so on—which governed steamer rates and which shifted, both seasonally and over the long term, the relative advantages of steamers and flats. In response to such changes, the marketing organization of the flatboat trade took on its distinctive configuration.

From the pre-steamer era, there survived the "dealer-boatman." He was the farmer, small merchant, miller, or general entrepreneur who bought and sold produce on his own account, carrying it to market himself by flatboat. As in the case of Trimble, noted earlier, a farmer or storekeeper probably seldom confined his cargo to produce he already owned. Rather, he would fill his boat's hold with whatever produce he could buy locally or on the way down the Ohio. Some boats went down with "straight loads" of hay, flour, or meat—cash products destined for sale in wholesale lots to commission houses at Cincinnati, St. Louis, or New Orleans. But the typical dealer-boatman loaded a "mixed" cargo worth, say, from $3,000 to $10,000, depending on the proportion in the load of such high-priced commodities as pork and cheese.[29] Miles Stacey of Marietta, a farmer and merchant who fits this category of boatmen well, described in his memoirs a typical cargo of the 1850's:

Say about 100 barrels of apples placed near the bottom where it was coolest. . . . About 600 barrels of potatoes in next. On top of [the] load 100 barrels of flour. The boats carried five tier of barrels all through and six in the center. In the bow of the boat we left a place to pack the pork (I usually butchered 60 or 70 hogs). We'd take about 20 barrels of beans, 25 of sauerkraut, 10 or 15 of onions, 3 or 4 barrels of buckwheat flour, 15 or 20 dozen brooms. I'd get 8 or 10 dozen buckets over at the bucket factory in Harmar.[30]

Like James Trimble thirty years earlier, Stacey did his best to sell at way points along the river, and he took consignments for delivery to commission houses downriver.

The inclusion of brooms and buckets in Stacey's list suggests that the dealer-boatman merged with a second type of tradesman: the "peddler-boatman." Like their counterparts who carried their stores in wagons that traversed the countryside, the peddlers made retail trading their full-time occupation. They sold at river towns, but more often at the little hamlets, plantations, and farms on the banks of the Ohio and Mississippi. Thus Levi Woodbury wrote in 1833: "At every village [on the lower Mississippi] we find from ten to twenty flat bottomed boats which besides corn in the ear, pork, bacon, flour, whiskey, cattle

[29] Report of Engineers, 24 Cong., 2 sess., *H. Doc.* 52 (Washington, 1836), 43; and Jones, "Flatboating," 287–288.
[30] "Flatboating on the Great Thoroughfare," ed. J. E. Phillips, *Bulletin of the Historical and Philosophical Society of Ohio*, V (June 1947), 21–23.

and fowls [31] have an assortment of notions from Cincinnati and other places, corn brooms, cabinet furniture, cider, apples, plows, cordage, etc. They remain at one place till all is sold out, if the demand be brisk; if not, they move farther down." [32] The business in 1850 of one such peddler-boatman, Jared Warner, who lived near Steubenville, Ohio, suggests something more of the rich variety that filled the holds of peddlers' boats. On one voyage, Warner purchased a used flatboat at Pittsburgh for thirty-six dollars and spent another fifty dollars to outfit it with cable and to caulk it and replace oars and rotted planks. He then set off downriver, purchasing at Wheeling saddles and commercial cigars from an auctioneer, in addition to shoes, boots, and powder from wholesalers. Later, he put in tobacco, tin reflectors, candles, percussion caps, salt, medicines, lace, sugar, guns, women's veils, and "one wolf Trap." At farms along the river, he bought pilot bread, apples and peaches, brandy, lard, and hides, all on his own account. He also accepted orders for articles wanted downriver: on this voyage, for example, he recorded the request of a Colonel Rowell for *Paradise Lost* and several other books. But along with his retail peddling, Warner undertook some trading in bulk farm produce, buying more than four thousand pounds of cheese at a cost of $227, and also butter costing $350. When he arrived at New Orleans, as his account books reveal, Warner had already sold much of this produce; and he appears to have made a gross profit of about 50 per cent. In addition, he acted as a commission merchant and forwarder for one farmer, from whom he took 14,000 pounds of cheese on consignment. [33] Risks of a personal kind, encountered daily by Warner and men like him on the treacherous waters of the river

[31] Cincinnati trade reports cited no exports of livestock by flatboat. Yet numerous memoirs and other descriptive accounts examined do mention fowl, cattle, and hogs loaded on boats. See n. 12, *supra*.

[32] Levi P. Woodbury, *Writings* (3 vols.; Boston, 1852), III, 430.

[33] Jared Warner, "Flatboat Book C," MS, Wisconsin Historical Society.

and in the southern swamps, are revealed in two terse logbook entries by Warner at Bayou Sara: "Young Allen died about 8 o'clock. . . . An old man on deck died same day about 12 o'clock sick two days." [34]

In contrast to the merchant-boatman and the peddler, both of whom carried goods mainly on their own account, there was a third type plying the rivers in flatboats: the "agent-boatman." He was a transportation agent only, a professional forwarder who assumed the title of captain and managed the descent down-river of one boat, or a fleet of boats, carrying goods owned by those who engaged him. It was the captains of the western rivers who employed the Mike Finks, the "sturdy race of men, of splended physique, indomitable energy and courage, some-what wild, and ready for a spree"—those skilled polemen and laborers who made up the crews of these fragile river craft.[35] In a petition for state-financed improvement of the Muskingum River, residents of the valley spoke affectionately of this "set of Hardy, Interprizing young men who, by a few voyages, become Masters of the down River Trade, & return with avails of their cargoes—in Money, which is the Life & main spring of our Aggriculture and Commerce." [36]

Like their counterparts the steamboat captains, the agent-boatmen sometimes traded in goods on their own account as a side venture; but unlike the steamer captains, they usually owned their own vessels and were not regularly employed by merchants who had invested heavily to build a boat. The impor-tance of agent-boatmen in the river trade is well illustrated by the operations of Davis and Smith, warehouse and commission merchants at Portsmouth, Ohio. Located at the southern termi-nus of the Ohio Canal, Davis and Smith regularly received shipments on consignment from farmers in the interior, with most of their cash trade in flour, corn, and pork. The firm

[34] *Ibid.* On disease, see also Baldwin, *Keelboat Age*, 89–90.
[35] Switzler, *Commerce*, 186.   [36] Petition of 1838 cited n. 4, *supra*.

shipped to Cincinnati and the southern markets both by flatboat and by steamboat, depending upon the availability of cargo space at any given moment, the prevailing insurance and transport charges, and the preference expressed in instructions given them by the merchants, millers, and farmers who supplied them.[37] Davis and Smith obtained flatboat transportation in two ways: by building boats themselves and engaging captains who were paid according to the weight of the cargo and the distance of the voyage; and by hiring captains who owned boats, again paying an agreed transport charge. At no time was title to the cargo given to the captain, and his instructions were usually to sell at a fixed minimum price along the river or to deliver to a correspondent merchant at Cincinnati or New Orleans, who received orders directly as to terms of sale.[38]

The increasing importance of agent-boatmen in the 1840's probably helped to bring down the insurance rates on flatboat shipments. For these professionals not only navigated the "new larger flatboats," 100 to 130 feet in length, but did so more capably than the small dealer-boatmen, who were no doubt better at the plow than the rudder. In the mid-forties, insurance rates on flatboat cargoes, like those on steamer freight, were down perhaps 50 per cent from the rates of the 1820's. But there was still a significant differential: published insurance data for 1849 show Cincinnati–New Orleans rates on freight by steamboat as 0.5 to 0.8 per cent of value, and by flatboat as 1 to 1.5 per cent on "tight casks," 2 to 3 per cent on "other property," and 5 to 7 per cent on grain and hay, which were much more subject to spoilage than the other staples of the trade. Thus, the rate

[37] Correspondence of Lancaster Lateral Canal Company with Davis and Smith, and with Potts, Young, and Davis, 1844–1853, Brasee Papers, OHS.

[38] For example, J. T. Brasee to Davis and Smith, Oct. 21, 1843, and to Shropshire and Ellmaker, Nov. 21, 1843, *ibid*. See also Berry, *Western Prices*, 24–25.

differentials between flats and steamers were partly offset by the cost of insuring cargoes.[39]

The specialized operation of the agent-boatmen lent itself well to still another economy in flatboating. More likely than dealer-boatmen or peddlers to build large boats in the newer designs, and to build them sturdily, the flatboat captains were less likely to sacrifice their investment in a boat for the sake of getting home more quickly. Thus in the late 1840's they began to use the towing services of steamboat operators when local market conditions made it unprofitable to break up their boats for sale as lumber; and at Cincinnati, no less than at New Orleans, the sight of flats being towed upriver for another trip down was commonly reported in the press.[40]

VI

The fact that agent-boatmen brought greater organization and a higher degree of marketing sophistication to the flatboat trade is indisputable. But it should not obscure a more important characteristic of the trade: that it was inviting to interlopers and, by its very nature, militated against the development of systemic marketing economies on the Ohio-Mississippi route.

This was a paradoxical effect. For on the one hand, the ready availability of flatboats, the ease with which such vessels could be built, and the low operating cost, all contributed initially to the strength of the southern trade route under canal competition. Even in the 1840's, when the western-canal phase of the transportation revolution was nearly completed, shippers located roughly midway between the Lakes and the Ohio (that is, in a position to ship either directly east via the western canals and the Erie, or else south to Cincinnati, the southern river markets, or New Orleans) often chose to ship southward. Aside from the

[39] Berry, *Western Prices*, 69. For a 10-per-cent-deductible insurance policy on flour sent down river to New Orleans by flatboat, one merchant paid a 1.75 per cent premium in 1846 (MS in Brasee Papers).

[40] White, *Wholesale Prices*, 34; Berry, *Western Prices*, 25.

natural advantage of being able to navigate earlier in the season
on the rivers than on the Great Lakes route, they were reacting
to the additional inducement of a highly elastic supply of shipping craft—flatboats that could be built quickly in response to
demand. In years when annual exports of western produce
reached peaks, as during the 1846–1847 period of crop failures
and famines in Europe, the river route therefore took a large
part of the total western-grain exports to New Orleans. In such
periods, grain that might otherwise have been shipped directly
eastward could not find cargo space on canal boats or lake
steamers, or could not stand the higher freight rates that canal
and lake vessels charged once the demand began to push against
the limits of available capacity.[41]

On the other hand, the ease of entry, the low cost of construction, simple technological requirements, and the other factors that
gave the trade its flexibility, in the long run militated against the
Ohio-Mississippi route in its competition with canal, and later
with railroad, routes to the East. For in the Great Lakes cities
and along the canals, merchants and forwarding companies did
not need to fear interlopers who might skim the profits of
commerce in the best years. They were willing, therefore, to
make heavy investments in warehouse facilities and to introduce
bulk-loading equipment. Merchants in the river towns could not
bear the risks of investment on the same scale.[42]

[41] In 1846, a boom year for wheat in the Old Northwest, the Ohio
Canal Commission reported that late in the shipping season "every
available means of transportation was in a short time brought into
requisition, without being able to accommodate a moiety of the business" on the canals and Lake Erie. Charges rose sharply as a result. In
1847, the entire American transport network was clogged by the heavy
flow of grain to the seaports (Ohio Board of Public Works, *Tenth
Annual Report*, Ohio Executive Documents, 1847, no. 31, 390–391).

[42] The Great Lakes trade is treated fully in Thomas D. Odle, "The
American Grain Trade of the Great Lakes, 1825–1857," *Inland Seas*, VII
(Winter 1951), 237–245, and VIII (Spring 1952), 23–28 (Summer 1952),
99–104 (Fall 1952), 177–192, and (Winter 1952), 248–254; and in Clark,
Grain Trade, ch. x. But see also the full account of New Orleans

Thus any reassessment of the flatboat trade must take account of its positive contributions: the service that flats provided in periods of low water; their important role on tributary streams where settlements were distant from canal facilities or where even small-draft steamers could not operate; the availability that made it possible to expand cargo capacity rapidly on the river route; and their continuing importance, even in the 1850's, in serving on the Upper Ohio and carrying produce to intermediate points between Cincinnati and the lower Mississippi. But a reassessment must also recognize the long-term effects of this essentially chaotic transportation system in vitiating the strength of the river route in its competition with the more direct eastern trade routes. Finally, a reappraisal must take account of the complexities within the flatboat trade itself, especially the various types of businessmen who engaged in it, and their diverse roles in the trade during the ante bellum period.

----

failures in James P. Cairns, "The Response of New Orleans to the Diversion of the Trade of the Mississippi River" (M. A. thesis, Columbia University, 1950); and in H. A. Mitchell, "The Development of New Orleans as a Wholesale Trading Center," *Louisiana Historical Quarterly*, XXVII (Oct. 1944), 933–963.

The Impact of Traders' Claims on the American Fur Trade

JAMES L. CLAYTON

The extinction of the Indian's rights to lands is an important and well-known chapter in American history. The extent to which land policy was turned to private gain through the payment of fur traders' claims for unpaid individual Indian debts out of tribal land-cession funds, and the extent to which the American fur trade for a time depended upon these claims are unknown but significant sidelights in that history.

I

The background of the legal philosophy of Indian land cessions and the long history of getting the Indian to relinquish title on his lands to the United States government have been well recounted elsewhere and need not detain us here. What is more important for our purposes is the fact that as early as 1793 the United States began unilaterally to assume the financial obligations of wardship in addition to paying for ceded lands. In that year Congress made provision for the President to furnish the Indians with "useful domestic animals, and the implements of husbandry." This practice continued until the early 1820's, and included the buying of spinning wheels, looms, and all kinds of agricultural implements.[1] Farming and blacksmith tools, grist-

---

[1] The most thorough study of Indian relations during this period is Francis Prucha, *American Indian Policy in the Formative Years* (Cambridge, Mass., 1962), 216 ff.

mills, and other implements for improving the agricultural skills of the Indian were commonly provided during the early decades of the nineteenth century. Little by little, to these simple agrarian items were added rations, clothing, and means of transportation; schools, churches, and houses were also provided.[2]

Nor were unusual financial commitments uncommon. For example, Congress once agreed to make payments to enable the Choctaws to organize and equip a "tribal corps of light horse."[3] Another time, federal officials consented to provide a Catholic priest for the Kaskaskias.[4] By the time the American fur trade began to be important, therefore, the federal government had already established a close, varied, and quasi-guardian relationship with the semi-independent tribesmen, and was accustomed to granting a variety of tribal requests which the government believed would promote the civilizing of the Indians.

On the other hand, the government of the United States was much slower to assert the rights of its own citizens *against* Indian tribes. The first recorded instance in which the federal government agreed to assume any claims against an Indian tribe was in the 1808 treaty with the Osages.[5] In order to quiet settler animosity against the Osages, up to five thousand dollars was set aside in that treaty to pay depredation claims submitted by white settlers for property stolen or destroyed by the Osages during the preceding five years. Thirteen years later Congress agreed to pay to Georgia a debt of $250,000 owed that state by the Creeks for property taken or destroyed before 1802.[6] These are the only instances of the payment of claims against the Indians out of treaty monies before the 1820's, and they were clearly motivated

---

[2] See Felix Cohen, ed., *Handbook of Federal Indian Law* (Washington, D.C., 1942), beginning at page 44, for an excellent study (including citations) of the various financial obligations assumed by the government from the earliest times.

[3] See Charles J. Kappler, ed., *Indian Affairs: Laws and Treaties* (5 vols.; Washington, D.C., 1904), II: *Treaties*, 193.

[4] Kappler, II, 68.   [5] *Ibid.*, 95.   [6] *Ibid.*, 196.

more by politics and expediency than by commercial or contractual considerations.

Therefore, when the federal government began to allow fur traders' claims against individual Indians for unpaid debts to be paid out of tribal funds, it departed completely from established policy. This apparently harmless innovation in collective responsibility for debt had an innocuous beginning with the signing of the Osage Treaty of 1825. Article 13 of that treaty states:

Whereas the Great and Little Osage tribes or nations are indebted to August P. Chouteau, Paul Balio, and Williams S. Williams, to a large amount, for credits given them, which they are unable to pay, and have particularly requested to be paid, or provided for, in the present negotiation; it is, therefore, agreed . . . that the United States shall pay to August P. Chouteau, one thousand dollars; to Paul Balio, two hundred and fifty dollars, and to Williams S. Williams two hundred and fifty dollars, toward the liquidation of their respective debts due from the said tribes or nation.[7]

These three claims represented barely 1 per cent of the money the Indians received from the government by that treaty and could not possibly have covered more than a fraction of the private debts owed to traders by Osage tribesmen at that time.

Although we cannot be sure, this provision for the payment of private debts out of tribal funds appears to have been an unsolicited and entirely gratuitous gesture by the Osage toward certain favorite traders. August Chouteau, the largest creditor, was a reputable trader who had been doing business with the Osages for years, but little is known about the other two creditors. William Clark, the former partner of Meriwether Lewis, a negotiator of this treaty, was superintendent of Indian affairs at St. Louis and not unmindful of the red man's welfare. He was personally acquainted with August Chouteau and probably knew the others. Clark raised no objection to this treaty innovation, nor did anyone else for that matter. Because the amount

[7] *Ibid.*, 220.

granted was a mere pittance compared to the amount owed, and because the character of at least the largest beneficiary is unimpeachable, we may assume from the scanty record that the policy of paying traders' claims had an innocent beginning.

This conclusion is buttressed by other, more general, considerations. First, traders were of inestimable value to the tribesmen as a source of economic necessities. Since early times the Indians had traded their peltry to white traders and had become dependent on the goods supplied in exchange. Second, the trader was often the Indian's counselor, especially in dealings with the government. Being slow to understand the full meaning of land ownership, title relinquishment, tribal promises binding on individual members, and a host of other concepts, he turned to the trader for advice. Sometimes this advice was in the Indian's interest, sometimes not. The point is that it was the trader to whom he turned. It seems only natural therefore to expect the better tribal-trader relationships to be close, friendly, and at times magnanimous.

The practice of paying debt claims sporadically but gradually expanded until it had become a fixed policy at Indian treaty negotiations by 1831.[8] Thereafter, considerably larger sums began to be paid to claimants. (See Table 15.) At first the amounts set aside for debt claims was small, and the few individual claimants were specified. Typical traders' claims inserted in treaties during the late 1820's read simply: "Thomas Robb $200, for goods heretofore sold to the Indians," or "McGeorge $300, for provisions sold to the Indians." [9]

Beginning with the Ottawa treaty of 1831, however, the number of claimants and the value of their claims had so increased

---

[8] The most complete and accurate data on Indian claims are in the Bureau of Indian Affairs, Special Files (particularly numbers 147, 181, 200, 206, and 208), National Archives. These are a series of small, classified folders containing unsorted miscellaneous data, such as commissioners' reports, claimants' affidavits, and Indian speeches.

[9] See schedule of claims, Kappler, II, 297.

Table 15. Fur traders' debt claims provided for
by treaty funds, 1825–1842

Year	Tribe	Amount
1825	Osage	$ 1,500
	Kansas	500
1826	Pottawatomie	9,573
	Miami	7,727
1828	Pottawatomie	10,000
1829	Chippewa	3,000
	Winnebago	11,601
1831	Ottawa	20,000
1832	Sac and Fox	40,000
	Pottawatomie	28,700
	Pottawatomie	62,400
	Shawnee	12,000
	Pottawatomie	20,700
1833	Quapaw	4,100
	Chippewa	175,000
1836	Ottawa	300,000
	Menominee	90,000
1837	Chippewa	70,000
	Sioux	90,000
	Sac and Fox	100,000
	Winnebago	200,000
1838	Miami	150,000
1840	Miami	250,000
1842	Wyandot	23,800
	Chippewa	75,000
	Sac and Fox	250,000
Total		$2,013,601

Note: The Senate prohibited the inclusion of debt
claims in treaty negotiations in early 1843.

Source: Compiled from Charles J. Kappler, ed.,
Indian Affairs: Laws and Treaties (Washington, D.C., 1903–1904).

that provision was made by the Secretary of War and the accounting offices of the Treasury Department for the "strictest scrutiny and examination." Although tacitly recognizing the "duty" of the tribe to pay debts owed by individuals, only "just and true" claims were thereafter to be allowed.[10]

In order to insure strict accountability, prompt settlement, and justice to the Indians (who might be taken advantage of by unscrupulous traders), the War Department, under the direction of Lewis Cass, established a series of regulations and policies pertaining to the payment of all debt claims.[11] These regulations required payment in specie to the Indians by a military officer except where the Indians would take bank notes. Payment had to be public, in the presence of at least two witnesses, and receipts had to be made in triplicate. Moreover, a record of all negotiations was kept and a transcript of the proceedings forwarded to Washington. In addition, Indians were allowed to make claims of their own against whites and could select goods in lieu of money if they desired.

In order to speed up payment, which sometimes involved thousands of Indians as well as scores of claimants, rations were issued to the Indians at the treaty grounds only if necessary, and then only for a period of three or four days. The mode of payment, whether to the chiefs or to the heads of families, was determined by the Indians themselves. Each claim was submitted by the Indian agent to the paymaster, who asked the appropriate chiefs if the claim was just. If the chiefs recognized a claim and agreed to its amount, it was paid to the trader, normally out of tribal annuities. If not, the claim was forwarded to the Commissioner of Indian Affairs who, after weighing the evidence, informed the tribe of his decision. A careful examination of the

[10] *Ibid.*, 338.

[11] See *Sen. Doc.* 72, "Revised System Laws for Indian Affairs," 20 Cong., 2 sess., 75–82, 1828. For a later but fuller explanation, see *H. Ex. Doc.* 229, "Execution of the Treaty with the Winnebagoes," 25 Cong., 3 sess., 5 ff., 1838.

Commissioner's files (see note 8, above) reveals that most of the Commissioner's decisions were against the trader.

The philosophy behind the payment of traders' claims was quite simple. The government was interested primarily in land cessions to provide room for a burgeoning population, and if paying a few traders' claims would speed up the process of negotiation, the War Department in the beginning saw no evil in the practice.[12] Furthermore, the good will of the traders was always valuable, and at times crucial, to the successful completion of important treaties. Claims by traders for unpaid credits were not, therefore, considered gratuitous donations by the government but were looked upon as "set-asides" and of no direct concern to the government.[13]

During the early 1830's, the War Department's policies on claim payments became much more exacting, because of growing belief that the Indian was incapable of adjusting to the civilization of the white man and a stiffening public opposition to payments of all kinds to Indians.[14] John Tipton, Indian agent on the Maumee, expressed a typical attitude when he said: "We have been reconciled to the expensiveness of our Indian Relations from the supposition that the money thus expended benefited that unfortunate people. This has been a delusion." He maintained that even though 2,300 Sac and Fox Indians in Iowa were receiving annually $47,000, they were still a miserable people.[15]

Others saw more specific evils. Many missionaries, such as the Pond brothers in Minnesota, believed that annuities had made

[12] See *H.R.* 474, "Regulating the Indian Department," 23 Cong., 1 sess., 95–128, 1834; and *H.R.* 489, "Ewing Investigation," 31 Cong., 1 sess., 63–65, 1850.

[13] See "Execution of the Treaty with the Winnebagoes," 41 ff.

[14] For a general discussion of this problem see *Sen. Exec. Doc.* 246, "Report with Senate Bill No. 159," 24 Cong., 1 sess., 1835. See also *H.R.* 474, "Regulating the Indian Department: 1834," 23 Cong., 1 sess., 1834.

[15] Robert Lucas, "Indian Affairs of Iowa in 1840," *Annals of Iowa*, 3d ser., XV (April 1926), 264.

the Indian less inclined to work.[16] A few thoughtful traders, such as the American Fur Company's Henry Sibley, openly admitted that annuities were the bane of the race.[17] Some, such as Indian Agent Lawrence Taliaferro, at Fort Snelling, believed that *any* payment of traders' claims by the government was immoral. Many more were coming to believe that most of the treaty payments went directly into the traders' pockets. Even some of the minor Indian chiefs began to oppose the system, because they felt that their share was taken by the main chiefs.[18] But most of all, it was the inevitable gross debauch engaged in by the tribesmen following these payments that turned public opinion against the practice.[19] Coinciding with the rising temperance movement, these drunken orgies provided numerous lurid examples for temperance advocates.

As a consequence of increasing public concern, reports from the War Department to Congress were becoming sharply critical of the annuity system by 1834. At the same time criticism of fur traders' claims was also intensified.[20] On this score the main objection to the payment of debt claims was a belief that Indians were charged exorbitant prices to cover unpaid credits; hence, traders were often indicted for taking a double profit.[21]

This charge is difficult to prove one way or the other. Credit had been granted Indians since the very beginning of the fur trade, and by the 1830's the average Indian was receiving fifty dollars annually in credits from his trader, according to one

[16] See Samuel Pond's statement in *"The Dakotas or Sioux in Minnesota as They Were in 1834,"* in *Collections of the Minnesota Historical Society* (17 vols.; St. Paul, 1872–1920), XII, 347.

[17] Henry H. Sibley, "Reminiscenses Historical and Personal," *ibid.*, I, 462.

[18] For a bitter struggle by subchiefs against Keokuk, see William Hagen, *Sac and Fox Indians* (Norman, Okla., 1958), 218.

[19] For a good description—one of many—see Edward Neill, "Occurrences in and around Ft. Snelling, from 1819 to 1840," *Collections of the Minnesota Historical Society*, II, 129.

[20] See "Regulating the Indian Department," *passim.*   [21] *Ibid.*, 37–41.

noted historian.[22] It was the accepted custom of the trade, however, to view the debts as tenuous at best after the first year. Certainly most Indians felt that they were absolved from their debts after one season, but the individual debtor was often willing to concede a tribal obligation for an indefinite period.[23] Even so, the exact amount of the credit after the first year was often at issue. According to Commissioner William Mitchell, who negotiated claims cases for several Great Lakes tribes, this was largely because the Indian believed he should not be required to pay debts to traders who, he believed, were growing rich, unless the Indian also grew rich in the trade.[24] Only rarely, therefore, did Indians pay debts after the first year.[25]

Despite general agreement that Indian debts, on the whole, were valid obligations that were seldom paid, it is still not clear whether these debts were generally based upon exorbitant prices. The prices charged by the American Fur Company in the Great Lakes region, for example, were not unfair.[26] Prices charged by many trading companies in the Rocky Mountains, however, tended to be exorbitant, often rising as high as 2,000 per cent over the initial cost of the goods.[27] Moreover, prices charged and debts paid varied from tribe to tribe, but this subject has not been studied sufficiently to fasten any unilateral responsibility on the fur traders as a group. Nevertheless a large, articulate, and diversified segment of the American public believed during the 1830's that the red man was being exploited and abused by white traders.

[22] Frederick Jackson Turner, *The Character and Influence of the Indian Trade in Wisconsin . . .* (Baltimore, 1891), 62.

[23] See *Sen. Doc.* 90, "Message from the President of the United States . . . concerning the Fur Trade . . . ," 22 Cong., 1 sess., *passim*, 1832.

[24] See Bureau of Indian Affairs, Special File 208, National Archives.

[25] *Ibid.*; see Special Files 137, 147, 181, 200, and 208.

[26] See James L. Clayton "The American Fur Company: The Final Years," (Ph.D. dissertation, Cornell University, 1964), ch. iv.

[27] One of the best studies on this area is Osborne Russell, *Journal of a Trapper* (Portland, Ore., 1955), 60 ff.

With such an attitude prevailing among important elements of the population, the War Department (now under Joel R. Poinsett) began in 1837 to issue more precise instructions to its claim commissioners. They were told:

Require the respective creditors to deposit . . . transcripts of their claims, exhibiting names, dates, articles, prices, and the original consideration in each claim. . . . If original books or entries cannot be produced, that loss or destruction must be proved. If the debt be against an individual Indian, he should be called before you, and each item in the account be explained to him and his assent or dissent to it be required.[28]

Once the claim was established, however, the "moral duty" of paying every just claim was pressed upon the Indians.[29] The War Department was interested in efficiency, not a new policy.

The Department's instructions were carried out with a vengeance by its appointed commissioners. For example, the commissioners for the largest claim settlement ever made, the Chippewa treaty of 1836, adopted the policy of reducing all traders' claims by one-half, in order, they said, to exclude claims based on the illegal sale of liquor or on debts of Indians outside the treaty area.[30] This decision penalized all legitimate claims and tended to place both good and bad claims on the same basis, thus encouraging trappers to present fraudulent claims or at least pad their accounts.

The debts for liquor, in most cases, did not amount to one-half the amount of the claim, and when the books were available for verification, these could easily have been stricken off. One-third of the value of the claim was deducted if it was based on testimony rather than records, and only a 50-per-cent advance on cost was allowed on any set of books. Few, if any, traders could have made expenses on an advance of only 50 per cent.

[28] "Execution of the Treaty with the Winnebagoes," 16.
[29] *Ibid.*, 6.
[30] See commissioners' reports on the Chippewa treaty of 1836, in Bureau of Indian Affairs, Special File 147.

No interest was allowed on accounts in the Chippewa treaty, nor any debts based on charity given, both wise provisions. The commissioners, moreover, were not always impartial toward the various traders. They were particularly hostile toward the American Fur Company's claims, because, they reported, the Company had "amassed wealth while its subordinate agents, clerks, and interpreters and the entire circle of Indian tribes whose hunts furnished the basis of trade had become impoverished." [31] Such discrimination was of course highly objectionable to the Company, but it was powerless to do anything about it.

In the Sioux treaty of September 1837, the commissioners reduced most claims, because they were based, in their opinion, on "exorbitant charges." [32] In addition, the commissioners reduced all claims by either 40 or 50 per cent rather than consider them individually, because they were in a hurry to catch the last steamboat back to civilization. [33] This of course meant that traders with valid, well-documented claims received only 10 per cent more than poorly documented, questionable claims. Whether the claimant received 50 per cent or only 40 per cent was determined by whether the commissioners believed he was a "sober" individual. It also helped if the claimant did not engage in undercutting his competitors. Ironically, the commissioners did not recognize the benefit to the Indian in instances of undercutting.

The claims commissioners at the negotiations for signing of the Pottawatamie, Ottawa, and Chippewa treaty of 1840 believed they had the legal duty to be the Indians' guardians. Traders' claims were allowed to bear interest, but no interest was allowed the traders on debts due them. [34] Moreover, Indian depredation claims were allowed only if they were admitted by the guilty parties. Sometimes the commissioners' biases led them

[31] *Ibid.;* see claim 51, "American Fur Company."
[32] *Ibid.;* see also the commissioners' reports in Special File 200.
[33] *Ibid.*   [34] See commissioners' reports, Special File 208.

to disallow debts based on the sale of playing cards or, in one instance, a debt for "turning the faucet on a brandy barrel— $120." [35]

Under these circumstances it was not long before many traders lost patience with their commissioners from Washington, whom they haughtily regarded as a sailor regards a landlubber. A meeting of claimants was called at Prairie du Chien in November 1837, in order to "enlighten" the commissioners who were coming to settle the Winnebago claims. [36]

What ensued was to become the most controversial of all claims settlements. First, the traders elected a five-man committee. They then agreed among themselves that the Winnebagoes, for the purpose of this settlement, were generally honest; hence, no account books would be necessary after one or two years. Next, in determining the existence of debts, the capital of the trading concern was to be the guide, not the accounts. The percentage of sales based on credit was arbitrarily fixed at 50 per cent, and the value of the individual trapper's claim was arrived at by again arbitrarily assuming that all trappers made sales amounting to 50 per cent of their capital. Thereafter, it was further assumed that one-third of these sales were never paid for; hence, each trader was to be paid 8⅓ per cent of his total capital investment, regardless of any other considerations. This arrangement would be easy for the carpetbaggers to understand, the traders felt, and the commissioners would certainly be able to catch their boat in time.

When the commissioners arrived at Prairie du Chien, the traders presented them with claims amounting to $528,219 and their committee's criteria for settlement. Lacking documentary evidence for most of the claims and strongly desiring to make prompt payment, the commissioners acquiesced to the traders'

---

[35] *Ibid.*

[36] See "Execution of the Treaty with the Winnebagoes," Commissioner James Murray and Simon Cameron's report beginning at p. 16, and Bureau of Indian Affairs, Special File 208.

method of adjustment. After hearing only verbal testimony for most of the claims, they awarded the claimants $168,168 on the basis of the traders' suggestions. This sum was then prorated at ninety-three cents on the dollar, so that the total would fall within the treaty limitation of $150,000 for Indian debts.

What was to have been a great barbecue for the traders, however, turned out to be cold porridge. The Commissioner of Indian Affairs, T. Hartley Crawford, refused to accept the findings of his appointed agents, who, he felt, had exceeded their authority by allowing claims unsupported by ledgers, vouchers, or account books. Crawford thereafter appointed an entirely new commission to begin proceedings afresh and sent it off to Prairie du Chien.

When these new commissioners arrived, they completely disregarded the traders' committee and concluded that poor bookkeeping practices had been deliberately followed in anticipation of government largess. Needless to say, the traders' version of the amount of their claims was not recognized. The traders thereupon charged that the new commissioners had not followed War Department instructions; countercharges were made by Crawford of trader duplicity and of naïveté on the part of the first commissioners. The whole sordid affair continued on after the meeting until the final result seems to be lost in obscurity. Needless to say, such inconclusive settlements did not occur thereafter.

II

It is helpful in understanding the impact of traders' claims on the American fur trade to examine how this innovation in government policy actually affected company operations. Since the American Fur Company was the largest and most important trading concern at that time and largely controlled the fur trade in localities where claims settlements were initiated, its reaction to this federal windfall is of more than passing interest.

The American Fur Company naturally looked with great

favor upon the War Department's policy of recognizing traders' debts. This unexpected windfall allowed the Company to make a double profit—in theory—on its merchandise, because the Company's profit margin was openly calculated to cover all unpaid Indian debts. The question was never discussed of whether it was ethical to take a profit at the time of sale and then again at the time the tribe was removed. The Company simply embraced the existing opportunity for enrichment, without any observable moral compunctions. Moreover, no stone was left unturned to get a favorable judgment on its outstanding claims.

Immediately after the War Department began to recognize traders' claims, the American Fur Company went to some lengths to get claims commissioners and interpreters appointed who were friendly to the Company.[37] Interpreters as often as not interjected their own ideas into official negotiations, and their good will was therefore indispensable. Usually the Company was successful in securing interpreters favorable to its interests, but a large number of claims commissioners were hostile—some unusually so.

Having so far as possible accomplished this basic aim, the Company next decided to submit only those claims which were "well documented" or "fair."[38] This meant simply that the Company did not deliberately pad its accounts. Such a policy was adopted because from the very beginning the Company officials believed the claims commissioners would be inclined to

[37] See Suydam, Jackson, and Company to G. W. and W. G. Ewing, Feb. 14, 1835, Ewing Papers, Indiana Historical Society, Indianapolis; Gabriel Franchere to Ramsay Crooks (president of the American Fur Company), July 17, 1837, American Fur Company Papers, New York-Historical Society, New York City, (hereafter referred to as AFCP); Crooks to John Whetten, Feb. 27, 1838, AFCP; Hercules Dousman to Henry Sibley, July 12, 1838, Henry Sibley Papers, Minnesota Historical Society, St. Paul; and Crooks to William Brewster, March 21, 1836, Aug. 29, 1837, and Brewster to Crooks, Feb. 23, March 10, April 11, 1836, AFCP.

[38] Crooks to Brewster, March 21, 1836, AFCP.

favor the Indian and leave the Company "in a mighty sorry position." There was some justification for this feeling, because during the two-year period 1836–1838, the Company presented well-documented claims valued at over $225,000, of which only $162,000, or 70 per cent, was approved.[39] Still, this was a far higher rate of approval than most traders received and may be largely attributed to good bookkeeping and friendly interpreters.

After presenting its claims, the Company took the stand that any attempts to influence the negotiations directly would be futile and might jeopardize the Company's position before the commissioners. Ramsay Crooks, president of the American Fur Company, advised his agents to cooperate with the commissioners and even offered to provide free transportation to a government paymaster in order to get a convenient place for a settlement meeting.[40] Crooks advised his traders not to compromise and not to accept a lesser amount once a claim was submitted, as this would suggest that the claim had been padded.

As usual, the American Fur Company urged its lobbyists in Washington to seek recognition of its claims and to have them paid as early as possible. James Duane Doty, Charles J. Nourse, and Charles Gratiot were the Company's regular lobbyists. John F. A. Sanford was the Company's special representative to the War Department. He was particularly active in reporting on the status of the Company's claims and apparently had some influence with the Secretary of War, Joel Poinsett. Doty was Wisconsin's territorial delegate from 1838 to 1841, and governor of Wisconsin and Superintendent of Indian Affairs from 1841 to 1843. Obviously, he was a good man to know. Doty worked closely with Sanford, giving him advice from time to time on claim problems. He also visited the Secretary of War when

[39] Compiled from records of the treaties of those years in the Special Files of the Bureau of Indian Affairs.

[40] Crooks to George Jones, Jan. 7, 1838, AFCP.

hostile reports on the Company were received by the Secretary.[41]

All of these agents took the position in their numerous contacts with Washington officials that the American Fur Company's claims should be recognized fully, because, they alleged, the Company was a powerful factor in getting the Indians to accept treaty provisions. This was largely true, but irrelevant with respect to the amount of the claims. The officials generally admitted the positive role of the Company in securing treaty acceptance whenever Company claims were recognized. Where the Company's claims were not recognized, however, the commissioners asserted, traders often opposed the government. Unquestionably, the bureaucrats were right in this belief, but there is no evidence that it affected their judgment one way or the other.

On the whole, Crooks believed that the War Department and its appointed commissioners were fair and thorough in their adjudication of the Company's claims. To be sure, payment was often late, and this caused considerable inconvenience to the Indians; but the fault lay with Congress, not the commissioners. With respect to the debts of half-breeds, which the treaties did not allow, Crooks was much less satisfied. "There is hardly a halfbreed in the country who does not owe us," Crooks exclaimed in 1838.[42] Here again, however, the Congress, not the commissioners, was held responsible.

The attitude of the American Fur Company's factors and independent traders was quite different from Crooks's. On occasion they composed and sent to Crooks threatening letters to be

[41] For background information on these agents, see Alice Smith, *James Duane Doty* (Madison, Wis., 1954) and Calendar Index, AFCP. For the extent of Crooks's efforts, see especially Crooks to Joseph Rolette, June 9, 1837, AFCP.

[42] Crooks to Pierre Chouteau, Oct. 17, 1838, Chouteau Collections, Missouri Historical Society, Saint Louis. I wish to thank the Missouri Historical Society for permission to quote from this letter.

forwarded to the Secretary of War.[43] These usually warned of Indian uprisings or "wars of extermination" if the traders' claims were not recognized. Crooks wisely refused to forward any of these missives, but did inform his lobbyists of their content.

The traders' pique did not confine itself to letter writing. Some of the Company's factors attempted to bribe their Indians into recognizing outfit claims, that is, claims of regional or district representatives of the Company. Such efforts were generally unsuccessful. Joseph Rolette, for example, paid over a thousand dollars for this purpose in 1839.[44] More important, some company factors acted in collusion with certain commissioners. One instance occurred in March 1838, when Hercules Dousman wrote William Aitken (both were Company factors) the following revealing letter:

Sibley writes to me that the Commissioner of Indian Affairs told him that he would get the Senate to alter the clause making allowance to Warren, yourself, and me, and that all the claims must come in on the same footing and be settled by the commissioners. I have remonstrated and done all I could to have the treaty ratified as made but can't say yet what will be done—in the meantime keep quiet and say not a word pro or con—it will be time to act when the Indians assemble next Summer.[45]

Sometimes Company traders conspired together in an effort to thwart the government's purposes by advising the Indians against signing treaties that did not provide for traders' claims. Solomon Juneau, Company factor at Milwaukee, for example, suggested in 1846 that all traders band together and place an article in the treaty recognizing their claims, which if rejected,

[43] For a typical letter, one of many, see Joseph Rolette to T. H. Crawford, March 7, 1839, AFCP.

[44] See Rolette to Crooks, Jan. 26, 1840, AFCP.

[45] Hercules Dousman to William Aitken, March 4, 1838, Henry Sibley Papers. I wish to thank the Minnesota Historical Society for permission to quote from this letter.

would nullify the whole agreement.[46] Juneau had evidently either forgotten that government agents and not traders drew up Indian treaties, or he was being realistic beyond the demands of prudence. With all their intrigues, however, the American Fur Company traders were far more anxious to see the successful adjustment of claims in accord with the commissioners' purposes —even if it meant only partial recognition of their debts—than to hinder the settlement process and receive nothing.

It is impossible to calculate with accuracy how much money the American Fur Company received from claim payments. Over $2,000,000 was paid to all traders in accordance with specific treaty stipulations, but information about the amounts paid to the various companies is not available. In addition, large but unstipulated sums were paid for authorized claims from annuity payments. These could easily have amounted to $500,000 or more. The American Fur Company probably received the lion's share of these specified and unspecified funds, because it largely controlled the trade of the tribes which allowed the most extensive traders' claims. (See Table 15.) The Company evidently received between $200,000 and $400,000, possibly more, from 1825 to 1842, but the records are inadequate to support anything more than an educated guess.

The funds provided the Company and its traders by the negotiation of its claims could not have come at a better time however. Much of this money was paid out during the severe depression of 1837–1843 and was the major domestic factor in helping the American Fur Company weather that financial crisis. Indeed, claim payments probably prevented a crisis among the Company's creditors at this critical juncture and may have prevented the collapse of the Company in 1842 had not an Ohio Valley fur war taken place shortly before.

Nor is it entirely coincidental that the Company was able to pay extraordinary dividends to its stockholders during these years but ceased doing so thereafter. From 1835 to 1838, inclu-

[46] See Solomon Juneau to Samuel Abbott, Dec. 10, 1846, AFCP.

sive, the American Fur Company paid out dividends amounting to 50 per cent.[47] Claims payments alone enabled the Company to pay such high dividends because several of the Company's outfits lost money during this period.[48] Moreover, the highest dividend (25 per cent) came in 1838, the worst year of the entire decade for the number of furs harvested.[49] The Company had been awarded over $130,000 in claims the previous year.[50] Presumably most of these were paid sometime in 1838. The only possible source for such a high dividend was claim payments.

Individual traders in the Company's employ were also given a new lease on life by the payment of their debt claims. Rix Robinson, in Michigan, was $22,989 richer after the Chippewa-Ottawa treaty of 1836. Joseph Rolette received over $8,000 as a result of the Sioux treaty of 1837. Small traders benefited proportionately. Philander Prescott, whose capital usually averaged only $2,500 per year, received over $1,000; and John Lawe of Green Bay, who maintained that he was in perpetual financial misery, received as much as $6,000 in a single year and could have obtained more if he had not been so backward in asserting his rights.[51] Such good fortune undoubtedly kept many old hands in the fur trade much longer than if they had been without this windfall.

III

By the end of 1842, practically all of the traders' debt claims had been submitted, and most of the Great Lakes tribes had

---

[47] Dividends were as follows: 1835, 10 per cent; 1836, no dividend; 1837, 15 per cent; and 1838, 25 per cent. See Crooks to Wildes and Co., July 30, 1836; John Whetten to William Brewster, Feb. 20, 1837; and Crooks to Brewster, May 18, 1839, AFCP.

[48] The Western Outfit lost money in 1836 and 1837, the Sioux Outfit lost money in 1837, and the Northern Outfit probably lost a modest amount during these years owing to the mismanagement of its factor.

[49] See Clayton, "The American Fur Company," 54.

[50] See Bureau of Indian Affairs, Special Files for 1837.

[51] Crooks to John Lawe, April 4, 1839, John Lawe Papers, Chicago Historical Society.

ceded their lands to the government. At the same time, agents of the government were becoming more alarmed at the conse-quences of requiring by treaty the payment of specific private Indian debts out of tribal funds. By then it was generally agreed that even adherence to the strictest practices of claims adjust-ment had failed to protect the Indian from designing men. The Senate therefore resolved on March 3, 1843, "that in the future negotiations of Indian treaties, no reservation of land should be made in favor of any person, nor the payment of any debt provided for." We do not know the precise reasons for the Senate's action, as reporters were excluded for several hours of that day's session, and there is no record of a resolution or debate on this subject in the *Congressional Globe*.[52] It is quite probable, however, that the senators were acting under public pressure and believed by this time that private claims did not have sufficient color of legality to be incorporated in binding treaty provisions. Furthermore, since annuity payments in general were being widely criticized, the senators probably felt that the Indians should pay their own debts without government assistance. After March 1843, therefore, treaty provisions for the payment of private debts were scrupulously avoided; but as is common with reform measures, this resolution closed the door after the horse was stolen.

Despite the Senate's resolution, the tribesmen continued on their own volition to pay traders' claims from annuity funds for the next four years without government interference. There is no record of how much was paid, but the amount must have been substantial, because the Indians remained willing to assume these debts and the traders simply had them sign promissory notes which were paid "more or less punctually." [53]

In 1847 another blow was dealt the practice of paying debt

[52] The Senate resolution is quoted in "Ewing Investigation," 273.
[53] See "Petition of Pierre Chouteau & Company, W. G. and G. W. Ewing & Company, and S. Philips to William L. Marcy, Secretary of War," in "Ewing Investigation," 65.

claims. At that time the government began to pay annuities to heads of families rather than to the tribal chiefs, as had been the practice since 1834. It was assumed that this change would undermine the chiefs' authority and hasten the civilization of the Indian by making it easier for him to acquire private property. In addition, Congress provided that "All executory contracts made and entered into by any Indian for the payment of money or goods shall be deemed and held to be null and void, and of no binding effect whatsoever." [54] This provision was enacted to end the practice of paying any *unratified* private debt claims from annuity payments even if the Indians desired to pay and the claims were valid. Pierre Chouteau and George Ewing became alarmed at the possible implications of the new law and petitioned the War Department not to construe the act in a manner which would prohibit valid claims *already ratified*, i.e., agreed to by treaty but not yet paid. The War Department acceded to the request.[55]

The practice of paying private debt claims already recognized by treaty was finally brought to an end in 1854. Credit for ending this practice, by now grown iniquitous through long abuse, is due one man: George Manypenny, Commissioner of Indian Affairs and a champion of the Indian, Manypenny was boiling with indignation. In his annual report of that year to the Secretary of the Interior, Robert McClelland, he declared:

I deem it my duty to call attention to a recent transaction of a character clearly illustrating the propriety and duty of strictly adhering to the policy of exercising, as far as possible, such a supervision and control over the moneys payable to the Indians as will secure to them their full benefits thereof, and prevent their being fleeced by designing men, under corrupt and unequitious [*sic*] contracts or obligation, which in their ignorance they have been

[54] U.S., *Statutes at Large*, IV, 203.
[55] See William Medde's reply for the Secretary of War to Pierre Chouteau, May 19, 1847, "Ewing Investigation," 69.

induced to sign; *or by the recognition or allowance of claims and demands against them having no foundation in right or justice.*[56]

Manypenny asserted that no traders' claim, even if already ratified by treaty, was founded on "right or justice," because, he believed, Indians were not legally competent to contract and would sign any paper put before them. Certain state courts would have disagreed with him, as promissory notes signed by Indians were sometimes upheld, but this did not deter the Commissioner. Manypenny also asked McClelland to declare all executory contracts "of every kind and description" null and void and to request legislation from Congress that would fine any individual attempting to secure annuity money for the payment of debt claims.[57]

In order to emphasize the need for ending the payment of traders' claims, Manypenny next made public a scandal which had been building up for years. The scandal concerned the Menominee Indians, who had become dissatisfied with the treaty of 1848 ceding all of their lands in Wisconsin.[58] The compensation of $350,000 was less than just, they believed, and their new home west of the Mississippi unsuitable. When these feelings became known, the tribe was approached by one Richard W. Thompson, who encouraged the Menominees to place a claim for additional compensation before the government. Thompson asserted that he had sufficient influence in Washington to get the desired additional compensation by means of a new treaty, and asked the Menominees in return to allow him a percentage of the total amount secured. The Menominees took Thompson at his word and appointed him their legal representative, later agreeing to pay him one-third of the total amount received.[59]

At this time, without the knowledge of the Menominees or the government, a large number of old and often questionable trad-

[56] See *Sen. Ex. Doc.* 1, "Report of the Commissioner of Indian Affairs," 33 Cong., 2 sess., 211, 1854.
[57] *Ibid.*, 227.　　[58] See Kappler, II, 572.
[59] See "Report of the Commissioner of Indian Affairs," 211 ff.

ers' claims began to be gathered by George and William Ewing of Indiana, to be prosecuted against the tribe in the event the Menominees received additional compensation. These Ewing claims were to be paid out of the remaining two-thirds of the money requested by the Menominees, for no provision for the payment of debt claims had been made in the original treaty of 1848.

It soon became evident, however, that Thompson and the Ewings were acting in collusion to defraud the Menominees.[60] For example, the Ewings made a contract in 1851 with William H. Bruce, the Menominee Indian agent immediately prior to this period and a man of considerable influence with the tribe, to "aid and assist" the Ewings in getting the largest possible remuneration from their claims.[61] Bruce was to receive $10,000 for this service. During the next three years, claims against the Menominee tribe were worked up to $500,000 and made ready for presentation once the Senate agreed to grant additional compensation.

Having been satisfied during this interim that the affairs of the Menominees did justify additional compensation (the size of the 1848 Menominee cession had been considerably underestimated), the government consented to treat with them again. Negotiations were successful, and on May 12, 1854, the Senate agreed to allow the Menominees to remain in Wisconsin on a reservation and to pay them an additional $242,686.[62] In accordance with the resolution of 1843, the Senate made no provision for the payment of debt claims. Shortly thereafter the Ewings secured notes from the Menominees for debt claims totaling $168,332. Almost half of this figure was based on Thompson's claim for services in securing the additional money granted voluntarily by the Senate. To what extent, if any, Thompson influenced this legislation is unknown.

It was at this point that Manypenny brought the whole affair

[60] *Ibid.;* see App., Exhibits A to O.   [61] See *ibid.,* Exhibit H.
[62] Kappler, II, 626.

to light. After learning of the scandalous activities of Thompson and the Ewings, as well as the questionable contract with Bruce, the Senate undertook an investigation of the Ewings and placed the following provision in the very next treaty to come before that body: "The debts of Indians contracted in their private dealings as individuals, whether to traders or otherwise, shall not be paid out of the general fund." [63] This provision was inserted in every relevant treaty thereafter for a number of years.[64] Consequently no payment of any kind could be made to traders for Indian debts, either ratified or unratified. This treaty provision was written into the statutes in 1817,[65] at the same time that formal treaty making with the Indians was abandoned.

Thus ended one of the most controversial chapters in the history of the American fur trade. The practice of paying traders' claims had at least two positive consequences during the twenty-nine years it was carried on. First, the largest claim payments were made to the traders precisely during the years of gravest financial crisis, 1837–1843. These payments probably saved the American Fur Company from bankruptcy and certainly made an otherwise sluggish business profitable indeed. Second, the timing of these payments was doubly significant, since the beaver, the symbol of the fur trade, was beginning to decline in value and marketability. The payments were undoubtedly very helpful to the trader in his transition to dealing in other furs. Whether these two positive factors outweigh the unsavory reputation this practice eventually gave to the American fur trade is problematical. One suspects, however, that fur traders did not trouble themselves much about their historical image.

[63] Kappler, II, 633.
[64] See Kappler, II, 633, 635, 638, 645, 650, 656, 659, 663, 667, 675, 683, and 692.   [65] U.S., *Statutes at Large*, XVI, 570.

British Immigrants in the
Old Northwest, 1815-1860[*]

CHARLOTTE ERICKSON

By no means the largest group among the Europeans who migrated to the United States in the nineteenth century, English immigrants nevertheless made a modest impact upon the composition of the American population. During the decades between 1850 and 1890, while the United States remained the principal destination of passengers departing from England for overseas places, the English-born constituted about 10 per cent of the foreign-born population recorded in each census and a little less than 1.5 per cent of the entire population. The English were not sufficiently concentrated in any single state to exercise a great impact upon the size of a state's population or of its labor force. Only in the Mormon territory of Utah, where they comprised 18.5 per cent of the population in 1870, were the English statistically significant. The highest concentration of English-born inhabitants in any other state or territory was recorded in 1850 in Wisconsin, where the English formed 6.2 per cent of the population.

This mid-century concentration of English immigrants in Wisconsin is noteworthy. At that time commercial agriculture was still in its infancy in the state. According to census estimates,

[*] I am indebted to Professor Arthur John, as well as to the editorial committee for the volume, for reading and commenting on an earlier draft of this article.

the share of the male labor force engaged in agricultural occupations actually increased from 52 per cent, in 1850, to 86 per cent, in 1860. In mid-century a mere 8 per cent of Wisconsin's people lived in towns of more than 8,000 inhabitants, and the density of its population was 5.6 persons per square mile. In England, on the other hand, the census of 1851 reported that only about a fifth of the labor force was engaged in agricultural work and half of the people were living in towns and cities of more than 8,000 inhabitants.

In such contrasts lies the peculiar interest of the study of English overseas migration. Although the incidence of emigration was never so high as in certain other European countries, thousands of English emigrants were leaving a country with a rapidly developing economy in which agriculture was highly commercialized and opportunities for industrial work were expanding vigorously. The English migration to America provides an outstanding case of economic growth acting as an inducement to emigration, of heightened economic ambitions or social dissatisfaction rather than extremely low or depressed living standards.[1] In fact, emigration from England was higher in relation to total population during some of the years of confidence and rising real wages after 1846 than it had been during the troubled years of social unrest in the first part of the century.[2]

English emigrants have not proved easy for the historian to study, because no authorities collected information at the time about the parts of England from which people were emigrating and because the English as a distinctive group tended to disap-

[1] This emphasis on growth as a background to migration is to be found in United Nations, Department of Social Studies, Population Division, *The Determinants and Consequences of Population Trends* (Population Studies, no. 17), 1953, 111–114.

[2] N. H. Carrier and J. R. Jeffery, *External Migration: A Study of the Available Statistics, 1815–1950* (London, 1953), 14; Brinley Thomas, *Wales and the Atlantic Economy* (Cardiff, 1962), 7; *United Kingdom Census, 1841: Abstracts of the Answers and Returns, England and Wales* (London, 1843), 399, 458.

pear in the United States. Nevertheless, scholars have examined some aspects of English emigration. The standard works, based on official documents, probably place undue emphasis on assisted emigration, the plan under which the government subsidized persons going to the dominions or colonies.[3] More recently, scholars have turned their attention to the contributions that skilled British immigrants made to American industrial technology.[4] English agricultural colonies in America, which almost invariably failed to achieve their goals, have also received attention.[5] In contrast, the English and Scottish immigrants who entered American agriculture as individuals and in families have nearly escaped the historian's notice. Yet up until the panic of 1857, the prospect of engaging in agriculture was probably the strongest single force attracting English men and women to the United States. Even after that date a substantial minority continued to seek out the newer agricultural states as places of settlement.

Some indication of the strength of agriculture as an attractive force can be obtained indirectly from the distribution of English immigrants in the United States. The five states of the Old

[3] W. A. Carrothers, *Emigration from the British Isles* (London, 1929); Stanley C. Johnson, *A History of Emigration from the United Kingdom to North America, 1763–1912* (London, 1913).

[4] Rowland T. Berthoff, *British Immigrants in Industrial America, 1790–1950* (Cambridge, Mass., 1953); Frank Thistlethwaite, "The Atlantic Migration of the Pottery Industry," *Economic History Review*, 2d ser., IX (Dec. 1958), 264–278.

[5] Wilbur S. Shepperson, *British Emigration to North America: Projects and Opinions in the Early Victorian Period* (Oxford, 1957); Grant Foreman, "English Settlers in Illinois," *Journal of the Illinois State Historical Society*, XXXIV (Sept. 1941), 303–333, "The Settlement of English Potters in Wisconsin," *Wisconsin Magazine of History*, XXI (June 1938), 374–396, "English Emigrants in Iowa," *Iowa Journal of History and Politics*, XLIII (Oct. 1946), 385–420; Harcourt Horn, *An English Colony in Iowa* (Boston, 1931); John E. Inglehart, "The Coming of the English to Indiana," *Indiana Magazine of History*, XV (June 1919), 90–177; Jacob Van der Zee, *The British in Iowa* (Iowa City, 1922).

Northwest, all of which were still predominantly rural and agricultural in 1850, the first year for which we have any figures, contained two and two-thirds times as many English immigrants as the New England states. Compared with England, the Old Northwest was still economically underdeveloped in 1850. The English who settled there between 1817 and 1850 found themselves in a region of lower per capita incomes, a poorer standard of housing than most parts of Britain, more expensive manufactured consumer goods, inferior public facilities like roads and water supplies, as well as inferior churches, schools, and banks.

From 1850 onward it is possible to trace very roughly the destinations of newly arrived immigrants in each decade by looking at net changes in the number of English-born people in each state and territory. The movement of English migrants into the midwestern states continued unabated during the expansive fifties. Illinois made the greatest net gain in English settlers between 1850 and 1860, and Michigan, Wisconsin, Ohio, and even Iowa were among the ten leading destinations of English immigrants.

The decade of the sixties brought a decided shift in the distribution of English immigrants. After 1860 the Old Northwest lost ground as a destination. In contrast, southern New England, Pennsylvania, New Jersey, and the mining territories of the mountain region began to increase their share of the total number of English-born inhabitants of the United States. Even after 1860, however, a subsidiary stream of English immigrants continued to push into new agricultural areas. The plains states also increased their share of the English-born population between 1860 and 1890. (See Table 16.)

The 1870 census was the first to classify the foreign-born by occupation. It combined the English with the small number of Welsh immigrants in these statistics. As can be seen from Table 17, the English and Welsh who had settled recently in Iowa, Minnesota, and Kansas were strongly represented in agriculture

Table 16. Percentage distribution of English immigrants,
by region, 1850–1890

Region	1850	1860	1870	1880	1890
Mid-Atlantic	48.4	39.0	37.5	34.3	34.4
East north-central	28.5	32.4	29.7	26.7	23.3
New England	11.2	10.6	11.7	12.8	14.7
South and Southwest	7.0	6.6	5.0	5.3	5.1
West north-central	3.3	6.5	8.5	10.8	11.1
Mountain and Pacific	1.6	4.9	7.6	10.1	11.4
Total	100.0	100.0	100.0	100.0	100.0
Total English enumerated	278,675	431,692	550,924	662,676	908,741

Source: Calculated from figures for English-born inhabitants in *The Seventh Census of the United States, 1850* (Washington, 1853), xxxvi–xxxvii; *Population of the United States in 1860 . . . from the . . . 8th Census* (Washington, 1864), 620–621; *Ninth Census: The Statistics of the Population of the U.S., 1870* (Washington, 1872), 340–341; *Statistics of the Population of the U.S. at the 10th Census, 1880* (Washington, 1883), 493; *Compendium of the Eleventh Census: 1890, Pt. II; Misc. Doc., 52 Cong., 1 sess.* (Washington, 1894), 493.

in 1870. They were farmers in about the same proportion as the total employed population of these states. Even in Wisconsin and Michigan, which had received their largest increase in the number of English-born in the fifties, the concentration of these immigrants in agriculture was still pronounced as late as 1870. The representation of the English in agriculture was lower in states which had attracted potential farmers from England before 1850. Many of these farmers had settled in New York State and in the river counties of Ohio, Indiana, Illinois, and Missouri and had left their farms before 1870. Further evidence that destination and intended occupation were closely linked is the very low concentration in agriculture of the new English and Welsh immigrants in the industrial states of the East in 1870.

A study of the private letters of English and Scottish immigrants in the United States to friends and relatives in Britain stimulated my interest in these migrants who appeared to be moving counter to the main stream of overseas migration in the

Table 17. Shifts in direction of English immigration to the United States, 1850–1870, with proportion of English and Welsh labor force engaged in agriculture

States	No. of English (ooo's) 1850 (1)	Net increase of English (ooo's) 1850– 1860 (2)	Net increase of English (ooo's) 1860– 1870 (3)	% English and Welsh in agr. 1870 (4)	% Total population in agr. 1870 (5)	Index of representation 4 ÷ 5 (6)
1. States of English agricultural settlement, 1815–1850						
New York	84.4	21.2	4.1	21.1	25.0	85
Ohio	25.7	7.0	3.9	26.7	47.0	57
Illinois	18.7	23.1	12.1	40.0	51.0	79
Indiana	5.6	3.8	.6	37.5	58.2	54
Missouri	5.4	4.6	4.3	28.0	52.0	54
2. Agricultural states and territories with large immigration of English, 1850–1860						
Wisconsin	19.0	11.6	−2.3	62.0	54.5	114
Michigan	10.6	15.1	9.3	45.1	46.5	97
Iowa	3.8	7.7	5.1	46.9	48.3	97
Utah	1.0	6.0	9.0	60.2	61.8	98
Minn.	.1	3.4	2.2	62.8	56.5	109
Kansas	. . .	1.4	4.8	50.5	59.4	85
3. Industrial states with large immigration of English, 1860–1870						
Penn.	38.0	8.5	23.1	6.9	25.5	27
Mass.	16.7	7.2	10.3	3.5	12.4	25
New Jersey	11.4	4.5	10.8	6.5	21.3	31
Conn.	5.1	3.8	4.1	12.2	22.5	54

Source: See Table 16. Figures for the proportion of the labor force in agriculture (column 5) are drawn from Harvey S. Perloff and others, *Regions, Resources and Economic Growth* (Baltimore, 1960), 62 (material derived from estimates made by C. P. Brainerd and A. R. Miller).

nineteenth century, insofar as they were leaving a developed, industrialized country and industrial occupations to enter primary production in new regions. Letters from immigrant farmers have survived in far greater numbers than those from industrial workers.[6] It would, of course, be dangerous to regard

[6] Note the high proportion of letters from agriculturists in Alan Conway, ed., *The Welsh in America* (Cardiff, 1961).

the immigrants whose letters have survived as representative of the migration movement. Moreover, letter writers were probably a select group. One element of selection may have been that farmers in relatively isolated areas felt a particular loneliness which encouraged them to retain contacts with home more than did immigrants who settled in cities.

The letters enable us to examine in some depth the experience of thirty-four English and Scottish families who settled in Ohio, Michigan, Wisconsin, and Illinois between 1820 and 1850. The purpose of this essay is to consider the economic adjustment of these few families, whose stories have been reconstructed from their letters and from local records in Britain and America. In certain respects, the method is inferior to the study of agricultural populations in entire counties which has been undertaken by Curti and Bogue.[7] These writers have not distinguished the English and Scots from other English-speaking foreign-born, except to give examples of outstandingly successful immigrants. The sample of cases used here, infinitely smaller and drawn from the period before English emigration reached its peak, has the one important advantage that it permits us to examine the economic adjustment of a few families in the light of their origins and background in Britain.

It is sometimes assumed that, because they could understand the language of their adopted country, immigrants from England made an easy adjustment. They did not, however, escape the difficulties faced by other migrant groups. The vicissitudes of the English immigrant in American agriculture frequently arose from a divergence between his motives for emigration and the realities of farming in America. The letters suggest that he was fortified in his economic and social adaptation, not so much by the common language and legal institutions or his occasional familiarity with advanced farming techniques, as by attitudes of

[7] Merle Curti *et al., The Making of An American Community* (Stanford, Calif., 1959); Allan Bogue, *From Prairie to Corn Belt* (Chicago, 1963).

family loyalty and religious faith. His new situation required adaptability and responsiveness to a changed and changing environment. Yet many of these people emigrated precisely to avoid change, to escape from the uncertainties they associated with industrialization at home.

The greatest challenge was faced by the large number of immigrants who came from industrial occupations or urban regions. Such people often thought of farming as a way of life, rather than a commercial undertaking. They hoped to escape from price fluctuations and from taxes, to gain independence from employers, to live a more leisurely life, and to keep their families from dispersing.[8] Some agricultural laborers also shared these hopes. In contrast to assisted emigrants from agricultural counties in southern England with high poor rates, the laborers who used only their own savings and credit to emigrate probably came largely from the hinterland of developing industrial areas where opportunities for alternative employment were expanding and agricultural wages higher than in the less industrialized parts of the country. In emigrating, they were attempting, like the industrial workers, to recapture an older way of life, to escape from the changes they saw as inevitable in England. The more venturesome and commercially minded of the immigrants whose letters we have came from farming families in outlying regions some distance from the new industrial centers—from parishes in Hereford, Westmorland, and Dorset, for example, which were losing population.

Letters have survived from both farmers and industrial workers who were settling in the Ohio River Valley and along its tributaries between 1817 and 1837. The settlements near the Wabash in Edwards Country, Illinois, and in Vanderburgh County, Indiana, made before 1820 are well known. Through the immigrant letters one can follow the story of other families

[8] Charlotte Erickson, "The Agrarian Myths of English Immigrants," in O. F. Ander, ed., *In the Trek of the Immigrants* (Rock Island, Ill., 1965), 59–80.

who purchased uncleared woodlands on the ridges beyond the river valleys: in Athens County, Ohio, in 1818; in Columbiana County, farther up the Ohio River, in 1821; in Hamilton, Gallia, Washington, Adams, and Jefferson counties—all Ohio River counties—later in the twenties and during the thirties. One Scottish immigrant in 1830 took the canal and lake route to Cleveland, but then turned southeast to join relatives near the great bend in the upper reaches of the Ohio River. The letters also tell us about immigrants who settled near the Illinois River, in Tazewell, Peoria, and Pike counties, between 1826 and 1831, and on the Ohio River in Gallatin County, Illinois, in 1829. The latest examples of such settlers in wooded upcountry near the great river valleys were immigrants of the early forties who began farming in Hancock and Monroe counties in Illinois.

Before the forties, the canal and lake transport system was carrying pioneers into northern Ohio and Michigan. Families of emigrants from the Isle of Man began settling in Cuyahoga County, near the village of Cleveland, as early as 1826. We also have a case of a bachelor immigrant from a Norfolk farming family who followed his uncle's trail from Palmyra, New York, to Lenawee County, in southern Michigan, as early as 1830.

By the forties, Wisconsin is the source of most of the surviving letters. Immigrants who arrived in 1842 and 1843 settled in Racine County, near Lake Michigan, and also farther inland in Rock County, as well as in the lead-mining region of Grant County, on the Mississippi River in the western part of the state. By the late forties the letter writers were settling nearer the interior of the state, in Jefferson and Dane counties, and also farther north, in Manitowac. We also have letters from Scottish farmers on the prairies of northern Illinois, in Kane County.

Most of the immigrant letters and memoirs were written by people who settled on uncleared, unbroken land and who were engaged in farm making. Even those who had to purchase prior claims, or tracts previously settled, were not "fillers-in" in the sense of taking over farms ready for commercial exploitation.

For example, the improvements on the claim which Edwin Bottomley purchased consisted of some lumber prepared for building a cabin. Only two collections of letters have been found from immigrants who bought farms already cleared and cultivated.[9]

The search for cheap land led Englishmen into the Old Northwest in the early decades of its settlement. Morris Birkbeck and George Courtauld, men who had substantial amounts of capital, went west to acquire large estates. Farmers who brought more modest savings with them or who left money in a bank in England until they decided where to settle also found that they had to go beyond the mountains to bring their savings and the amount of land they hoped to acquire into line. Even more urgently, industrial craftsmen and farm servants who hoped to buy a farm for the three hundred or five hundred dollars they had saved were tempted to regions where government land was still available in large quantities. Before they migrated to one of the states where they hoped to get cheap land, many lived, worked, and saved for several years in the East. New York State was the principal staging point for would-be farmers, though many stopped also in states of the Old Northwest before they finally bought land.[10]

[9] In a survey of the biographies of 421 English and Scottish farmers whose careers were described in county histories of Lenawee County, Michigan, Washington County, Ohio, Hancock, Monroe, and Tazewell counties in Illinois, and Lafayette, Dane, Rock, Green, and Jefferson counties in Wisconsin, 105 subjects were specifically described as having cleared "wild" prairie or timbered land for a farm and only 17 as having bought improved farms. Many bought partially improved farms which still required much clearing, breaking, fencing, and farm and house building.

[10] In the above sample of English and Scottish farmers from county histories, 369 biographies gave details about the early careers of the subjects. Just over a third of them had lived in at least one other state before they came to the state in the Old Northwest in which they finally settled. Of the stopping points, New York State was by far the most important, but many also stopped for a time in another midwest-

Among the migrants stopping for a time in the East were industrial workers who wanted to become farmers but lacked funds. Handloom weavers, who had left England rather than change occupations, worked on power looms and even as spinners in the United States, using the jobs as steppingstones to farming. The members of the Morris family, from Chorley, Lancashire, are particularly interesting. Sending one brother to an uncle in western Virginia who helped him buy land in Ohio, the others settled in the Philadelphia region, following their trades—two as weavers and one as a blacksmith. In 1837 they all decided to take what savings they had accumulated and follow their brother Thomas to Ohio, not because they were unable to find employment, but because they saw other workers put on short time and wage rates weakening. They thought savings of three hundred dollars enough to start farming. Their sojourn in Philadelphia had merely been a stop at a way station on the road to their ultimate goal of acquiring subsistence farms.[11]

Occasionally immigrants advised relatives to emigrate precisely at times when land prices were low, because savings would go farther in land purchasing.[12] The low price of land attracted these potential farmers more than the low price of crops deterred them, because they regarded land as a basis for subsistence, not because they hoped to make capital gains from rising land prices.

Few instances have been found of Englishmen who worked on the transport projects or in the lumber camps of the Great

---

ern state. A survey of the birthplaces of children of British immigrants in seven census townships in 1850 and 1860 shows the same pattern of westward migration.

[11] Morris Letters, Houghton Muniments, DDHt 12, Lancashire Record Office, Preston, Eng.

[12] See, for example, a letter from Charles Rose, Scotch Settlement, near Lisbon, Ohio, Oct. 15, 1822, to John Rose, his nephew in Inverness. The Rose Letters are in private possession. See also John Birket, Mt. Pleasant, Ill., Dec. 25, 1841, to his brother in Lancashire, Birket Letters, DP/265–278, Lancashire Record Office.

Lakes region to get capital for purchasing land. Some of the immigrants from the Isle of Man who settled in northern Ohio in the late twenties worked on the canal that was to connect Cleveland with the Ohio. A Scots immigrant who arrived late in the season in 1830 was disappointed that canal work had already stopped.[13] One of the tenants on the Courtauld lands, near Athens, Ohio, considered canal employment but rejected it on the grounds of dangers to health and the uncertainty of obtaining cash wages.[14]

Most English immigrants who had neither capital nor industrial skills tried to get work on a farm, since a newcomer could learn to farm according to American methods while he saved for land purchasing.[15] About a sixth of a sample of 421

[13] H. Rose, Scotch Settlement, Ohio, Feb. 2, 1830, to his brother in Inverness, Rose Letters; W. T. Corlett, *The People of Orrisdale and Others* (Cleveland, 1918), 52. More references to canal work were made by immigrants in New York State around 1820 (Benjamin Smith ed., *Twenty-four Letters from Labourers in America to Their Friends in England* [London, 1829], 18, 24; Conway, *The Welsh in America*, 60, 61). In the survey of 421 English and Scots farmers who settled in the Old Northwest only 33 (8 per cent) men were found who later bought farms after having begun their careers in America in nonfarm laboring occupations. Of these only 9 individuals worked on transport projects and 2 in the Wisconsin pineries. In contrast 81 (20 per cent) had begun in skilled industrial occupations, including mining.

[14] *Courtauld Family Papers* (8 vols., printed privately; Cambridge, Eng., 1916), III, 1482. This work is available in National Central Library, London. For cases of Scots immigrants working in lumber camps in order to buy farms, see Curti, *The Making of an American Community*, 21; Archibald McKellar, Taylors Falls, Minn., Aug. 11, 1852, to his father in Iowa, McKellar Letters, Minnesota Historical Society, St. Paul. The sample drawn from county histories indicates that at least the more successful English and Scottish farmers rarely selected work in lumber camps or in canal or railway construction as means to achieve farm ownership.

[15] *Courtauld Family Papers*, V, 2047; John Knight, *Important Extracts from Original and Recent Letters Written by Emigrants in the United States of America* (Manchester, Eng., 1818), 25; Richard Hails, Lincoln, Mass., July 31, 1849, to his brother in Northumberland, Hails Letters, 865, Collection of Regional History and University Archives, Cornell

immigrants farmers whose biographies were analyzed worked as farm laborers before they bought land. One catches glimpses of these immigrant farm laborers in the letters, as well as in census manuscripts. At least two who worked for John Fisher in Michigan during the thirties bought land for farms from their savings. Immigrant farmers who could afford help were eager to hire their own countrymen on longer contracts or at lower wages than were customary where they had settled. They tried to persuade relatives to send out their young sons to work for board and lodging or to hire a "hind" for the immigrant farmer at one of the surviving agricultural fairs in England.[16] The inability or unwillingness of other immigrants to pay prevailing wages may also have encouraged newcomers to seek jobs on American-owned farms.[17] If the immigrant had worked in an

---

University. The same advice was often given to emigrants to the plains at a later period. See, for example, Percy G. Ebbutt, *Emigrant Life in Kansas* (London, 1886), 231–232.

[16] John Fisher, Franklin, Mich., Oct. 7, 1835, and Nov. 30, 1836, to his brother in Norfolk, Fisher Collection, 2815/104, Ipswich and East Suffolk Record Office, Ipswich, Eng. (a version of these letters edited by Louis Leonard Tucker appeared in *Michigan History*, XLV [Sept. 1961], 219–236); John Birket, Mount Pleasant, Ill., May 19, 1843, to his brother, Birket Letters; Robert Pollock, Cambridge, Wis., April 16, 1858, to his niece in Ayrshire, Pollock Letters, 805, Collection of Regional History; Milo M. Quaife, *An English Settler in Pioneer Wisconsin: The Letters of Edwin Bottomley* (Madison, 1918), 59.

[17] Though the numbers are small, these are the results of a count of British immigrant employees in four of the Wisconsin townships in which these letter writers settled:

	Employers		
Employees	Natives	Foreign-born	% working for natives
English	36	17	68
Scots	5	7	42
Irish	24	21	53
Total	65	45	59

The townships examined in the population schedules of the census of 1850 and 1860 were Porter and Union, in Rock County; Lake Mills, Jefferson County; and Christiana, Dane County. Immigrants obviously working for relatives were not counted.

English factory, he was likely to find farm labor both unremunerative and exhausting, whoever his employer might be. This was the reaction of a Huddersfield-born cloth finisher who came to Wisconsin in 1855 hoping to get land through farm labor:

I think I shall have to come back to Philadelphia and work right steady for about three years and then get a steady Wife and come west again any body with three Hundred dollars out here may live independent of any body helping them been a Farmer's Man out here is as bad as Been a Slave they wont hire any one if they can help it for no less than Six Months and more than Eight wages for good men 15 to 18 Dollars a Month and to pay it to you at fall I have had the offer of 12 Dollars a Month You must bear in mind they work all the Daylight God sends and a little more sometimes.[18]

Partly because of their attitudes, including their cherished independence, English immigrants sometimes immediately rented land. Employers who could not pay cash were willing to rent out land in exchange for labor.[19] In particular, workers with industrial skills found they they could rent a bit of land in return for work they did for the owner. A brickmaker might undertake to deliver a certain quantity of bricks, or a carpenter to provide rails cut for fencing or a specified amount of work on a house.[20] John Birket went so far as to give a man some land as payment for plastering his house.[21] Sharecropping was also a means open to immigrants without capital. In return for half the produce of the land, the immigrant might be provided with land, livestock, a team, and farm implements. One finds sharecropping mentioned

[18] Titus Crawshaw, Porter, Rock County, Wis., April 16, 1855, to his family, Crawshaw Letters, British Library of Economic and Political Science (hereafter cited as L.S.E). I wish to thank the Library for permission to quote from the Crawshaw and other letters.

[19] Quaife, *English Settler*, 110; *Courtauld Family Papers*, III, 1365; Thomas Morris, Aurelius Township, Ohio, Feb. 7, 1832, to his father in Lancashire, Morris Letters.

[20] *Courtauld Family Papers*, III, 1310; V, 2331–2332.

[21] *Portrait and Biographical Album of Peoria County, Illinois* (Chicago, 1890), III, 278.

in connection with English and Welsh immigrants in New York before 1830 and in parts of Ohio, Indiana, Illinois, and Wisconsin through the period 1820 to 1860.[22]

The private letters do not afford any examples of immigrants who acquired land from the profits of sharecropping. Through the letters one learns more about the supply aspect of share tenancy than about the demand aspect. The Courtauld family became absentee landlords after they returned to England in 1825, renting their American lands through an immigrant storekeeper. This agent arranged tenants for them on the basis of one-half shares, one-third shares, and sometimes fixed shares, but he complained constantly about the carelessness of tenants. A tenant to whom the Courtaulds rented land they had themselves cleared expected to be given the farm after five years' cultivation and decided to give up farming when the Courtaulds refused to deed it to him.[23] Other immigrant landlords were near enough to keep an eye on their tenants themselves. John Birket leased his Peoria land on shares during the midthirties because poor health (he was only thirty-five) made it difficult for him to continue to cultivate it.[24] A former silk manufacturer in southwestern Ohio, finding farming too onerous, decided to let his land for shares of corn which he planned to convert into whiskey.[25]

Many immigrants came to the United States with the idea that as landowners they would soon gain an independent income that

[22] See, for example, *Flint's Letters from America, 1818–1820*, in Reuben Thwaites, ed., *Early Western Travels* (Cleveland, 1904), IX, 39, 293; Conway, *The Welsh in America*, 59, 101, 123; Smith, *Twenty-four Letters*, 7, 11, 12, 23, 38; W. and R. Chambers, *Information for the People* (Edinburgh, 1842), 383; Elizabeth Cawley, ed., *The American Diaries of Richard Cobden* (Princeton, 1952), 187; Paul W. Gates, *The Farmers' Age* (New York, 1960), 44. In the survey of 421 farmers' biographies, 26 (6 per cent) rented land before purchasing farms.

[23] *Courtauld Family Papers*, III, 1315; V, 2042–2044, 2336–2337.

[24] John Birket, Peoria, Ill., May 7, 1835, to his brother, Birket Letters.

[25] Robert Bowles, Harrison, Hamilton County, Ohio, Aug. 10, 1823, to his brothers, John and Richard Bowles, Bowles Manuscripts, Ohio Historical Society, Columbus.

would free them from work. Most were clearly disappointed in this aim, but a few took a step in this direction by leasing out their land on shares and occasionally for cash rents.[26] The only share tenants among our immigrant letter writers were men who added to their original land purchase a bit of cleared land, rented on shares, which they could cultivate while they worked at improving their own land.[27]

In fact nearly all the immigrant letter writers brought capital with them for land purchasing, either directly from Britain or from the East. Some of them were also able to obtain funds from Britain in addition to their own savings. We have, however, no cases in which immigrants were as regularly provided with funds as the remittance men who flocked to northwestern Iowa in the early eighties.[28] Nor did they have access to capital from banks and other financial institutions, which was being invested in American farming and livestock raising at that time. The flow of funds in the early period was in the form of loans, gifts, and subsidies, obtained almost exclusively through the immigrants' own families. Earnings from industry, from investments in government bonds, and from rents were sent to midwestern farmers. For example, Edwin Bottomley's father, the manager of a woolen factory in Huddersfield, persistently subsidized his son's Wisconsin farming enterprise in the 1840's, partly with the idea that it might one day provide the father with a comfortable home.[29] For the few years during which they struggled to make

[26] Milo M. Quaife, ed., *A True Picture of Emigration* (Chicago, 1936), 152; Thomas Corlett, Granville, Ohio, Dec. 7, 1853, to his uncle in the Isle of Man, Corlett Letters, Manx Museum, Douglas, Eng.

[27] Quaife, *English Settler*, 48. See also Bogue, *From Prairie to Corn Belt*, 266–267.

[28] See for example, Van der Zee, *British in Iowa*, 75; Cowan Letters, microfilm, L.S.E., *passim*.

[29] Quaife, *English Settler*, 67, 73, 111, 133, 145, 149, 155, 163, 189. For the same reason, James Steel, a Scottish-born excise officer living in London in the 1840's, subsidized the farming operations and land purchases of his son Thomas, a frontier doctor, in Wisconsin (Steel Letters, Wisconsin State Historical Society Library, Madison).

farms in the wilderness of southeastern Ohio, the members of the Courtauld family expected and received gifts of money from Samuel Courtauld's income as a silk manufacturer in Essex.[30] Other immigrants tried to borrow from their families at a lower rate of interest than they had to pay locally or asked for gifts outright to meet a particular need.[31] Legacies were claimed vigorously.[32]

The ability of some immigrants to obtain money from England was not an unmixed blessing. They used such aid from their families for living expenses as often as for investment. A few neglected to make their farm enterprises self-sufficient at the earliest possible date, and others purchased more land than they could profitably farm or manage. One of the more successful immigrant farmers confessed that he was able to make money borrowed at 30 per cent in Michigan in the early thirties "answer my purpose."[33] Low-interest loans from England might act as a disincentive to profitable farm management, while high-interest loans obtained in the West could stimulate effective management.

A few immigrants tried to extend the base for the flow of capital beyond their immediate families. One means of doing this was to stress the returns to be made on industrial investments in a region. John Birket tried to raise capital for a sawmill, and the

[30] *Courtauld Family Papers*, II, 850; III, 1049.

[31] John Fisher, Tecumseh, Mich., July 12, 1831, to his mother; Robert Smith, Franklin, Mich., July 12, 1851, to Francis Fisher, Fisher Collection; Reuben Carpenter, Jefferson County, Ohio, Feb. 16, 1842, to his father in Gloucestershire, L.S.E.; *Courtauld Family Papers*, III, 1369, IV, 1899.

[32] Robert Smith, Franklin, Mich., July 12, 1851, Oct. 18, 1858, Oct. 22, 1860, Fisher Letters; Alfred Jones, Mo., July 30, 1864, Sept. 7, 1864, Jan. 17, 1880, to a Shropshire solicitor, L.S.E.; Edward Phillips, Greenville, Ill., Dec. 10, 1842, Vandalia, Ill., May 7, 1845, to his father, Phillips Letters, Salop Record Office, Shrewsbury, Eng.

[33] John Fisher, Franklin, Mich., 18 July 1832, to his mother, Fisher Letters.

Courtaulds for a silk factory, but little came of these attempts.[34] Appeals to England for charitable aid for schools and churches met with more response. Kenyon College, in Gambier, Ohio, may be the only survivor among these schools started with money raised in England. Jubilee College, in Peoria, is today only a historical monument. Edwin Bottomley did manage to get some money for a chapel and John Birket for a school, but they did not earmark the money for special purposes.[35]

Most of our immigrants could not hope to get financial assistance from Britain. They were able instead to borrow locally, even in remote areas. The local immigrant network, wider than that of the family, provided one source of loans. When the Burlends were in great difficulty, they appealed to a neighbor from Yorkshire, who at first refused to lend to them but changed his mind because he could not sleep after his refusal.[36] Fourteen years after he arrived in America, Andrew Morris finally repaid a loan from another immigrant from his neighborhood in Lancashire, who had settled eighty miles away from him.[37] Some immigrants with capital chose to put money out at interest at the high western rates rather than reinvest all their earnings in farm improvement or land.[38] One Scottish immigrant named William

[34] John Birket, Mount Pleasant, Ill., Dec. 25, 1841, to his brother, Birket Letters; Quaife, ed., *English Settler*, 58, 62; *Courtauld Family Papers*, I, 639.

[35] F. P. Weisenburger, *The Passing of the Frontier, 1825–1850*, in Carl Wittke, ed., *History of Ohio* (Columbus, 1941), III, 175–176; Thomas Ford, *A History of Illinois* (Chicago, 1854), 228–229; Quaife, *English Settler*, 108, 111, 125, 230; John Birket, Peoria, Ill., Dec. 7, 1834; Mount Pleasant, Ill., Dec. 27, 1841, Nov. 28, 1842, Dec. 14, 1842, to his brother, Birket Letters.

[36] Quaife, *True Picture*, 118–119. See also *Courtauld Family Papers*, III, 1245–1246.

[37] Andrew Morris, Aurelius, Ohio, Feb. 21, 1846, to his brother, Morris Letters.

[38] John Birket, Mount Pleasant, Ill., Dec. 25, 1841, to his brother, Birket Letters; Robert Pollock, Cambridge, Wis., April 16, 1858, to his niece, Pollock Letters; Quaife, *True Picture*, 148.

Richardson, who had been in Wisconsin for nineteen years, by
1860 owned four hundred acres of land, with only thirty improved and only ten dollars' worth of farm implements.
Though, in 1860, he called himself a farmer, in a later census he
simply referred to himself as a moneylender.[39]

The English and Scots immigrants in this capital-hungry region did not send money home. Before he had to purchase his
pre-emption claims, John Birket did, however, offer to pay the
rent on his father's Lancashire farm in a roundabout way. He
proposed to give the amount of the rent to another immigrant
from Lancashire, whose relatives would pay Birket's father.[40]
Another immigrant farmer in Wisconsin offered the proceeds of
the sale of his house in Scotland to his brother who had not
emigrated.[41] But these were exceptional cases, and in neither one
did any cash actually flow out of the region in which the
immigrants were living. While they were often willing to receive relatives on their farms and to give them a living while
they established themselves, the farmers did not offer to pay
passage. They were willing to offer young male relatives plenty
of work and abundant food and also to take in aged parents or
orphaned nieces, but they would not consider parting with cash.

Their farm enterprises required that profits be continuously
plowed back. Even these immigrants who bought so-called improved farms found that clearing and breaking the soil were a
major part of farm work in this region before the Civil War. If
the immigrant did not have enough capital to contract it out (the
Burlends once had a field broken in return for a watch), clearing
was a skill which he had to learn. It was a formidable task for the

[39] U.S. Census Manuscripts, Population Schedules, Cambridge, Dane
County, Wis., 1860, 14; 1880, 274; Agriculture Schedules, Cambridge,
Dane County, 1860, 171a.

[40] John Birket, Peoria, Ill., Dec. 7, 1834, May 7, 1835, to his father,
Birket Letters.

[41] John and Mary Thompson, Wingville, Grant County, Wis., 24 Jan.
1850, to his brother in Fifeshire, Wisconsin State Historical Society
Library, Madison.

inexperienced. Indeed, one Welsh immigrant in Utica, New York, commented in 1818, "The land is desolate wilderness of uncleared timber so that it is not worth the Welsh buying it." [42] Yet probably thousands of English and Scots immigrants tried clearing land. The Courtauld family, in the neighborhood of Athens, Ohio, in the early 1820's worked, became discouraged, set to work again, but finally gave up a desperate attempt to get a farm going. The clearing of ten acres a year was never more than an elusive goal to immigrants in wooded regions.[43] Few approached the five acres a year recently suggested as a more realistic norm for a family in timbered country before 1850.[44] It took Andrew Morris, a weaver from Lancashire, three years to clear thirteen acres. Another English immigrant, in Stark County, Ohio, boasted that he had cleared twenty acres of woodland in five years. The Burlends managed to clear between three and four acres their first year in Pike County, but found that this acreage was not a measure of the land they could add to production, because it still had to be fenced and plowed. One former handloom weaver in Iowa broke, cleared, and fenced forty acres between 1845 and 1858.[45]

Immigrants who had enough capital to hire labor for clearing

[42] Conway, *The Welsh in America*, 61.

[43] This was the average used for calculations of farm output by Wayne Rasmussen and Marvin Towne in National Bureau of Economic Research, *Trends in the American Economy in the Nineteenth Century, Studies in Income and Wealth*, XXIV (Princeton, 1960), 270. For statements of this as a goal, see Quaife, *English Settler*, 66; *Extracts from Various Writers on Emigration* (Norwich, Eng., 1834), 12, photostat, L.S.E.

[44] Martin Primack, "Land Clearing under Nineteenth-Century Techniques," *Journal of Economic History*, XXII (Dec. 1962), 484.

[45] Petition of Richard Stephenson, March 28, 1858, Fairfield, Iowa, Stephenson Papers, in private possession; John Knight, *Important Extracts*, 21; Quaife, *True Picture*, 86; William Morris, Aurelius, Ohio, Dec. 30, 1838, Barnsville, Ohio, July 14, 1841, to his brother, Morris Letters.

were often disappointed to find the supply inelastic.[46] Some English settlers in the river counties of Ohio and Illinois in the late twenties and early thirties complained of the indolence of the native-born. As James Knight put it, "Few work from principle . . . , not enough from necessity." [47] Immigrant farmers also found the plows they had bought or brought with them unsuitable for breaking new land, though travelers continued to laud the Scottish plows.[48] Another impediment to rapid clearing for some farmers from England was the high standard of clearing they visualized. "George and I have grubbed up stubbs out of numbers," wrote Robert Bowles, "and I intend to continue clearing for I hate to see them, and I wish my farm to look like an English one." [49]

Hopes of reducing farm-making costs and heavy-labor requirements induced many English immigrants who could not pay the price of an improved farm to purchase prairie land and oak openings. George Flower maintained that he and Birkbeck had bought prairie land for these reasons, so that every individual who came to their colony would be saved "a generation of hard and unprofitable labour." [50] Two years after he arrived in

[46] William Faux, *Journal of a Tour to the United States* (London, 1823), 232; Morris Birkbeck, *Letters from Illinois* (Philadelphia, 1818), 83–87.

[47] *Courtauld Family Papers*, II, 910, V, 2227, 2332; Quaife, *True Picture*, 131.

[48] Quaife, *English Settler*, 96; Robert Shedden, Kane County, Ill., 1842, to Andrew Foulds, photostats, L.S.E.; William Oliver, *Eight Months in Illinois* (Newcastle-on-Tyne, Eng., 1843), 97–98.

[49] Harrison, Hamilton County, Ohio, April 20, 1823, Bowles Manuscripts. I wish to thank the Ohio Historical Society for permission to quote from the Bowles Manuscripts. See also Smith, *Twenty-four Letters*, 17–18; Gladys Thomson, *A Pioneer Family: The Birkbecks of Illinois* (London, 1953), 70.

[50] George Flower, *History of the English Settlement in Edwards County, Illinois*, Chicago Historical Society Collections, I (Chicago, 1882), 352.

Michigan, John Fisher wrote home, "I bought one farm 80 acres and went to work on it but finding it had to much timber on it and I could not chop very well I bought 80 acres more clear openings similar to a pasture." [51] Many instances have been found of immigrants who added some grassland to their original land purchase or who bought prairie land in the first instance and used it, not for livestock as did the Americans, but as arable land for farming. [52] The Birkets wrote to their family in Lancashire to ask them to find out what prairie soil was, but most of the immigrants seem to have trusted in its fertility in the early days of their settlement. [53]

On prairie land an English farmer who had the necessary livestock, equipment, and labor could come closer to clearing ten acres a year. An inexperienced man like Eliza Courtauld's husband, who was a cabinetmaker by trade and had little equipment and unreliable labor, found that two acres were all that he could clear and break in a year, even on a patch of prairie near Gallipolis, in southern Ohio. [54] Edwin Bottomley, formerly a pattern designer in a woolen mill, also discovered that he could not reach his goal of ten acres a year on his prairie lands, because his plow was useless and he simply could not provide the fencing for the land he did manage to break. By the time of his death, nine years after his arrival in Wisconsin, he had succeeded in clearing and improving only thirty-five acres of land. [55] In con-

[51] John Fisher, Franklin, Mich., June 11, 1832, to his brothers, Fisher Letters.

[52] Robert Meatyard, Alton, Ill., March 22, 1836, to his mother, Meatyard Letters, Dorset Record Office, Dorchester, Eng.; Robert Shedden, Kane County, Ill., 1842, to Andrew Foulds, L.S.E.; Knight, *Important Extracts*, 27; Foreman, "English Settlers in Illinois," 311; Quaife, ed., *English Settler*, 34.

[53] John Birket, Peoria, Ill., May 6, 1833, to his brother, Birket Letters. The Burlends seem to have assimilated the American suspicion of the prairies after fifteen years in the United States (Quaife, *True Picture*, 84).

[54] *Courtauld Family Papers*, II, 910.   [55] Quaife, *English Settler*, 81.

trast, a Norfolk-born farmer's son, John Fisher, cleared twenty acres of prairie land in a single year with the aid of ten bullocks and at least two hired hands. Five years after he arrived in Michigan, he had cleared and improved seventy-five acres.[56] This was far and away the best achievement of any of the immigrants on prairie land.

Thus the immigrant letters support the view, expressed by Professor Gates many years ago, that English immigrants helped to dispel the American prejudice against prairie soils.[57] While prairie cultivation was still in its infancy, before 1840, English and Scottish immigrants were already acquiring prairie land as a means of saving labor.[58]

Apart from this readiness to believe in the fertility of prairie soils, one seeks in vain in the immigrant letters for differences in innovations in farming techniques. Allan Bogue is right in suggesting that the contribution of immigrant groups to the development of agricultural methods in the incipient cornbelt was marginal. What else could one expect? The English came from a country whose reputation for advancements in agriculture was largely due to methods which used labor intensively and which were quite unsuitable for American production conditions. Even immigrants from the English pastoral regions were accustomed

[56] John Fisher, Franklin, Mich., Oct. 7, 1835, Sept. 5, 1837, to his mother, Fisher Letters.

[57] Paul Wallace Gates, *The Illinois Central Railroad and Its Colonization Activities* (Cambridge, Mass., 1934), 12–13 n., 36.

[58] Recent research indicates that the reputation of prairies among the native-born was not so uniformly bad as was once thought and that New England immigrants were also settling on prairies at the edge of woodland in parts of Illinois before 1840 (Douglas R. McManis, *The Initial Evaluation and Utilization of the Illinois Prairies, 1815–1840* [Chicago, 1964], 32–34, 50, 56, 83–85, 92–93). In discussing the selection of land in Wisconsin, Eric Lampard maintains that the choice of timbered or prairie land was simply a matter of time of arrival and circumstance and followed no "ethnic principles" (*The Rise of the Dairy Industry in Wisconsin* [Madison, 1963], 17–20, 365 n.).

to a higher ratio of labor to land than was profitable in the United States.

Immigrants, especially nonfarmers, tended to criticize American farming methods for the lack of manuring, the poor standard of livestock care, the untidy and wasteful harvesting, the strange farm implements in use, and the absence of turnip cultivation.[59] Those who actually took up farming began to change their ideas about good farming, as English farmers on the east coast had already done by 1820.[60] We find immigrants telling their compatriots that in America manure was likely to injure the soil, that cattle were "inured" to fending for themselves, that they had not yet had time to turn their attention to turnip cultivation.[61] After five years in Michigan, John Fisher was ready to confess that he could not farm in the English fashion. His brother-in-law, formerly a shoemaker, who had less success than his brother as a commercial farmer in Michigan, wrote after twenty-five years in America that he was "still trying to get into the English way of farming," but that it did not seem to work."[62] Some immigrants became suspicious of newcomers with experimental ideas. When he had been in Athens County, Ohio, for thirteen years, James Knight hesitated to lease land to an English market gardener because the man "had too many new views—too many notions—which I knew he must have time to wear of."[63]

Among the English and Scottish immigrants a few were inclined to speculate in land and hoped to gain more from rising

---

[59] Jonas Booth, New Hartford, N.Y., March 20, 1829, to his brother and sister, typed copy, L.S.E.; H. Rose, near Lisbon, Ohio, Feb. 2, 1830, to his brother, Rose Letters; Henry Petingale, Newburgh, N.Y., Aug. 6, 1849, to his sister in Norfolk, Petingale Letters, L.S.E.

[60] Rodney C. Loehr, "The Influence of English Agriculture on American Agriculture, 1775–1825," *Agricultural History*, II (Jan. 1937), 3–15.

[61] Quaife, *True Picture*, 63, 106, 112; Corlett, *People of Orrisdale*, 54.

[62] John Fisher, Franklin, Mich., Oct. 7, 1835, to his mother; Robert Smith, Franklin, Mich., Oct. 22, 1860, to his brother-in-law, Fisher Letters.   [63] *Courtauld Family Papers*, IV, 1648–1649; V, 2193.

land values and high interest rates than from farming operations. Trempeleau County had a few British immigrants of this type.[64] Among them was John Birket. Son of a small tenant farmer of about a hundred acres in Westmorland, John Birket emigrated to Vermont in 1819 to join two uncles who had already settled there. In 1824 he set out alone for the West, paying his way by peddling tea, coffee, and calicoes. After a short stay in Ohio he arrived in Peoria, Illinois, then a village of six log cabins, in January 1826. There he claimed land ten years before it was possible to buy it under pre-emption privileges. During his early years in Peoria, he engaged variously in farming, orchard planting, carpentering, moneylending, and digging coal from surface outcroppings on his land. John Birket was always more interested in diversified development than he was in farming. But as Peoria's growth slackened in the late thirties, he moved out to Tazewell County, where his two brothers and his uncles had settled in 1831. His interest in industrial development and land prices continued unabated. Not until the 1850's did his town lands in Peoria (once the location of his farm) begin to sell profitably. Thus it took twenty-five years before his land investments began to pay off. Birket did not simply sell his town lands. He himself built residential additions to Peoria and sold land at more favorable prices to buyers who would undertake to build factories within a given period of time.[65]

Most of the immigrants intended from the outset to farm, either for a subsistence livelihood or as commercial farmers.

---

[64] Curti, *The Making of An American Community*, 418.

[65] A letter from John Birket and his son John C. Birket, July 31, 1856, to the former's brother describes terms of the sale (Birket Letters). Information on John Birket has also been obtained from census manuscripts, from Aaron Wilson Oakford, *The Peoria Story* (Peoria, Ill., 1949–1957), I, 35–36; and from *Portrait and Biographical Album of Peoria County*, III, 278. For similar, though less successful, speculators, see a letter from Joseph Hirst, Equality, Gallatin County, Ill., Aug. 29, 1829, to his son, L.S.E.; and James Knight Letters in *Courtauld Family Papers*, vols. III–VI, *passim*.

Though they did not arrive quite so long in advance of settlement and the sale of government lands as John Birket did, they were likely to appear in thinly populated regions where much government land was still unsold. There can be little doubt that those who came with some experience in farming, either as farmers or laborers, were the most likely to succeed in wresting farms from the wilderness. Experienced farmers did buy improved farms if they had the capital.[66] When their means permitted them to buy only unimproved or slightly improved lands, the men with experience in farming were more inclined to keep some of their capital for purchasing livestock.[67] Agricultural laborers from the west and north of England also placed considerable emphasis on livestock. For example, John Griffiths, who came from a laboring family in Shropshire to Hancock County, Illinois, in 1840, had by 1860 added 80 acres to his original purchase of 80 acres. He reported in that year that all of his land had been improved. He was growing very little wheat, but estimated his livestock, including cattle and pigs, to be worth $1100. Not many miles away to the south, in Monroe County, lived Thomas Whittaker and his family. They had been petty provision dealers in Leeds before they arrived in Illinois at about the same time as Griffiths. Thomas Whittaker had acquired 280 acres of land by 1860, but had succeeded in improving only 70 acres of it. He had six hundred dollars' worth of livestock and as many horses as swine, and was still devoting much more of his land to wheat than to corn and other animal foods.[68]

John Fisher, the Norfolk farmer's son, was also more inclined to continue to grow wheat than a man experienced in west-

[66] E. Nudham, William Corlett, and John Birchal (Morris Letters) fall into this category.

[67] John Fisher, Tecumseh, Mich., July 12, 1831, to his mother, Fisher Letters; Edward Gilley, Union, Rock County, Wis., Sept. 28, 1845, to his sister in Northumberland, L.S.E.

[68] Based upon Whittaker and Griffith Letters and U.S. Census Manuscripts, Agriculture Schedules, 1860, T. 2 S.R. 9W, Monroe County, Ill., 65, and Appanoose Township, Hancock County, Ill., 70.

country farming. Yet Fisher was careful to treat his land with manure, though he did not practice rotation. In contrast, in southeastern Ohio, the Morris brothers and their brothers-in-law, most of whom had been weavers in Lancashire, noted that they did not use manure for their scant livestock. When their yields declined, instead of treating the soil, the Morrises imitated some of their neighbors in turning to another soil-exhausting crop, tobacco.[69] Robert Pollock, an immigrant from the town of Ayr in Scotland who was farm-making in Dane County, Wisconsin, in the 1850's, remarked that the chinch bugs had been reducing his wheat yields since 1856. Yet four years later he was still planting wheat as his main grain crop.[70]

These few case histories suggest that the most successful men in farming among the English and Scottish immigrants were those who had some experience in farming but also empirically minded, not wedded to a particular scheme of farming. When these qualities were reinforced by a location near a growing city or by the appropriate timing of emigration, success was probable and the family likely to be firmly established on the land. Some of the children of John Griffiths, Walter and William Birket, and William Corlett remained on farms close to their fathers' land.

Those who did not succeed in commercial farming, or who found their image of a subsistence idyll dissolving after they had struggled for a time with farm-making, are equally interesting. The industrial workers and other urban people often purchased land in the southern counties of Illinois, Indiana, and Ohio that was rolling country affected by water erosion. Within twenty

---

[69] Andrew Morris, Aurelius, Ohio, Feb. 5, 1844, Feb. 21, 1846, to his brother, Morris Letters; Paul C. Henlein, *Cattle Kingdom in the Ohio Valley*, (Lexington, Ky., 1959), 73; Weisenburger, *The Passing of the Frontier*, 65.

[70] Robert Pollock, Cambridge, Wis., April 16, 1858, to his brother, Collection of Regional History; U.S. Census Manuscripts, Population Schedules, 1860, Cambridge, Dane County, Wis., 7; Agriculture Schedules, 1860, Cambridge, Dane County, 171a.

years of settlement, most of them found themselves in counties or townships which were losing population. Even immigrants who had for a time profited from a market of new settlers as population swelled in their neighborhood now found many of their neighbors leaving for new areas. This experience, as Bogue has pointed out, was a common one, since most counties attracted more farmers during their early burst of settlement than could possibly continue to make a living there in farming. Thus at some point immigrants who had settled in the river valleys, in particular, found local markets weakening and their lands declining in fertility.[71]

What did the English immigrant do when he met such reverses? Curti and Bogue found that the English-speaking foreign-born were slightly more "persistent" in Trempeleau County, Wisconsin, and Bureau County, Illinois, between 1850 and 1860 than the native-born, and considerably more so than immigrants from the Continent.[72] The statistical differences were

[71] Bogue, *From Prairie to Corn Belt*, 20.

[72] In a sample of five townships to which these letter writers came (Union and Porter, Rock County, Lake Mills, Jefferson County, and Christiana, Dane County, Wisconsin; Aurelius, Washington County, Ohio; and Appanoose, Hancock County, and Washington, Tazewell County, Illinois, the rate of departure from the township of English, Scottish, and even Irish-born farm operators was significantly lower than Curti found in Trempeleau County, Wisconsin, and Bogue recorded for Bureau County, Illinois.

Percentage	Trempeleau County, 1860 base		7 townships (males only) 1850 and 1860 base		
	All	ESF	English	Scottish	Irish
Farm operators leaving in less than 10 years	68	66	49	29	34
All gainfully employed leaving in less than 10 years	73	75	74	57	75
Total sample	662	160	174	84	233

ESF = English-speaking foreign born. See Curti, *The Making of an American Community*, 69–71; Bogue, *From Prairie to Corn Belt*, 25–26. The seven-township sample is based on census manuscripts, both population and agriculture schedules.

so slight, however, as to be insignificant. Yet an attitude of persistence is expressed in most of the letters. For example, the restless John Birket wrote of his brother, "I thought for us all to sell here and buy again near Bishop Chase, but Walter thinks it so much trouble to begin again that he will die where he now lives." [73] The common feeling against mobility was also expressed by a farmer from Kent: "[Mr. Pound] is quite a Yankee in respect to moving. I hope, my dear friend, if you come here you will not catch the disease." [74] He wrote with particular feeling because his own son had caught it.

Mobility continued until the immigrant actually bought land.[75] Only one instance has been found in the letters of an English or Scots family who, having once bought land, sold out in order to move farther west. Edward Gilley, who had been a farm servant in Northumberland, emigrated with his brother George in 1843 to Rock County, Wisconsin. Edward had a hundred sovereigns, but his brother had less. They both married and began farm making. Whereas Edward married an English-woman who died childless, George soon acquired a large family of children by his Michigan-born wife. When Edward remarried in 1853, George sold his eighty-acre farm to him in order to move to Minnesota. After twenty-five years on a farm there, George Gilley eventually returned with his four youngest children to spend his last years on his brother's flourishing farm in Wisconsin.[76]

[73] John Birket, Mount Pleasant, Ill., Dec. 25, 1841, to his brother, Birket Letters.

[74] Hugh Nudham, Monroe Township, Adams County, Ohio, Feb. 16, 1834, to a friend in Staplehurst, Kent, L.S.E.

[75] *Courtauld Family Papers*, V, 2042, 2230–2231; Smith, *Twenty-four Letters*, 27; Conway, *The Welsh in America*, 98; Quaife, *English Settler*, 169; John Fisher, Franklin, Mich., Nov. 30, 1836, to his mother, Fisher Letters; Clarence S. Paine, ed., "Edward Hawkes: The Diaries of a Nebraska Farmer, 1876–1877," *Agricultural History*, XXII (Jan. 1948), 1–3.

[76] Edward Gilley, Sept. 28, 1845, Union, Wis., to his sister, L.S.E.; *Portrait and Biographical Album of Rock County, Wisconsin* (Chicago, 1889), 1900.

The English and Scots immigrants seem to have hesitated to repeat the process of farm making because many of them looked on farming rather than on rising land values as their source of livelihood. If they could not achieve their social and economic aims on one farm, they were unlikely to realize them on another. Robert Bowles, living in the hinterland outside Cincinnati in the early 1820's, considered looking for some prairie land in Indiana, but his wife, who had suffered through the process of farm making and had just found some suitable English friends, firmly vetoed the project.[77] Similarly, the Morris brothers in Washington County, Ohio, watched their neighbors sell out in the early forties but decided not to follow the trek to the Illinois prairies.[78] The English and Scots on the plains after 1860 were probably recruited not so much from immigrants who had failed as farmers in the Great Lakes states as from new arrivals, men who had not yet bought land, and from immigrants' British-born children, who were unable to buy land in the neighborhood of their fathers' farms.

Once having bought land, the English and Scots immigrants tried first to adjust to the difficulties of farm-making or low incomes where they were. Rural areas in the Old Northwest acquired many industrial craftsmen in these Britons who had been originally attracted by the prospect of farming. Thus Robert Smith, in Lenawee County, Michigan, found that he could earn thirty shillings a week at his craft of shoemaking in 1836 and hire a man to run his farm.[79] A blacksmith from Lancashire discovered that he could do better at his trade than by tilling his soil in Washington County, Ohio.[80] A Cornish carpenter in Racine County, Wisconsin, at first leased his prairie land for

[77] Robert Bowles, Harrison, Hamilton County, Ohio, Aug. 10, 1823, to his brothers, Bowles Manuscripts.
[78] Andrew Morris, Aurelius, Ohio, Feb. 5, 1844, to his brother, Morris Letters.
[79] John Fisher, Franklin, Mich., Nov. 30, 1836, to his mother, Fisher Letters.
[80] William Morris, Aurelius, Ohio, Dec. 30, 1838, to his brother, Morris Letters.

three years in return for breaking and fencing, but by the end of that time he was doing so well as a carpenter and undertaker in the village of Yorkville that he continued to hire someone to run his farm.[81]

Others turned to other occupations to supplement their incomes from farming: Thomas Morris erected a horse-drawn flour mill when, after six years of effort, he still had only about eight acres of his timbered land under cultivation.[82] Some immigrants used skills they had brought with them, in a struggle to keep their original farms. None of these men had distinctive abilities born of the industrial revolution. Most of their skills—in the making of clothes, the building trades, and textile manufacture, as well as in blacksmithing and flour milling—were pre-industrial ones that could be found in most country villages in England. During the early industrial revolution England had drawn upon this diversity of skills in her rural population to make engineers of carpenters and other craftsmen. The society of the Old Northwest in its early development gained a great variety of knowledge of industrial crafts from British immigrants, as well as from Germans and New Englanders.

The immigrants in the Old Northwest before 1850 did not apply their skills there at anything like the level of specialization common in their homeland. Robert Bowles, who had been a farmer in England, found that he had other rudimentary skills which he could employ in a new territory. "I now find," he wrote, "my mechanical knowledge of great use to me, and it often enables me to earn many dollars in an easy way. . . . I am now a tolerable proficient in the smith way. . . . I have likewise made several vessels in the cooper's line."[83] A Lancashire

[81] "Autobiography of Hannibal Lugg, as told to Frances Green," 7-8, typescript, *c.* 1909, Wisconsin State Historical Society Library.

[82] William Morris, Aurelius, Ohio, Dec. 30, 1838, Morris Letters. See also Quaife, *English Settler,* 58, 63, 69; R. H. Kinvig, "Manx Settlement in the U.S.A.," *Isle of Man Natural History and Antiquarian Society Proceedings,* V (1955), 7.

[83] Robert Bowles, Harrison, Hamilton County, Ohio, April 20, 1823, to his brothers, Bowles Manuscripts.

weaver who had saved to purchase land in Fall River found that he could do better by using his elementary knowledge of coopering in Manitowac, Wisconsin, as a supplementary occupation to farming.[84]

To English immigrants, including those from rural communities, the lack of specialization among craftsmen in the United States stood out as a remarkable fact relevant to their adaptation. Thus many immigrants who were not craftsmen in the British sense of the word saw opportunities to practice rudimentary crafts in developing regions of the West. One immigrant advised a young relative to pick up a little information on the tanning business before emigrating; others counseled women to "get a sketch of the tailoring trade" if they did not already have it. A tailor from North Shields told his brother to keep his eyes open around the potteries. John Rochester asked George Courtauld to send some surveyor's instruments and a book on surveying. A family asked for a "recipe for making fire bricks." [85] In the early days of settlement skills could be bartered; later they could make a contribution toward keeping a farm enterprise afloat.[86] Probably more English and Scots immigrants adapted to reverses by diversifying their occupations than by moving to new farming regions.

The impetus toward diversification of the midwestern economy came also from immigrants who gave up their farms altogether. The only unmarried member of the Morris family finally sold his unimproved land in eastern Ohio to seek full-time employment as a weaver. He, like many others, drifted into western towns.[87] After a few years' experience of American farming,

[84] Mabel Kalmach Spencer, "Sketch of John Spencer," typescript, Wisconsin Historical Society Library.

[85] John Muir, Lisbon, Ohio, Oct. 3, 1842, to David Moore, L.S.E.; Quaife, *English Settler*, 87, Foreman, "English Settlers in Illinois," 311, 318; *Courtauld Family Papers*, II, 844; Samuel Mearbeck, Beverley, Randolph County, Va., Feb. 6, 1820, to his sister in Sheffield, typed copies, Mearbeck Letters, Sheffield Central Reference Library.

[86] Bogue, *From Prairie to Cornbelt*, 266.

[87] John Hale, ed., *Settlers . . .* (London, 1950), 97–98; Foreman, "Eng-

many immigrants warned relatives in industrial occupations in England against contemplating farming as a way of life. "If you come to this country," wrote William Morris (with some disregard for spelling) to his brother, "I think you would not like to go to the back countrey and go to clearing land and farming but you might do well in or near some of the Eastern Cittyes working at your trade. Or you could start a machecne shop of your own in some of the western towns . . ."[88] By 1870 the English and Welsh inhabitants of the midwestern states were strongly concentrated in mechanical occupations.

Immigrants who did not have a trade were not quite so easily absorbed into the economy. Schoolteaching, as Morris Birkbeck noted with reference to his son, was "only too often the refuge of the indigent and the failures." The sons and daughters of George Courtauld found it a poorly paid alternative to farming.[89] Even storekeeping and innkeeping were hazardous in the constant environment of change, of weakening local monopolies and a sudden melting away of population.[90] An immigrant farmer with a good education but no mechanical skills or aptitudes was likely to give up and return to the East or to England if he failed to make a livelihood from farming commensurate with his expectations. To succeed at farming he had to have resources of his own or from his family if he was unable to realize the cost of his investment in land and improvements.[91]

---

lish Settlers in Illinois," 308, "English Emigrants in Iowa," 413 n.; Ingleheart, "Coming of the English to Indiana," 176; Horn, *An English Colony in Iowa*, 31; Quaife, *English Settler*, 163; *Courtauld Family Papers*, II, 914, III, 931–934, 1020–1022; Flower, *History of the English Settlement*, 135.   [88] Barnsville, Ohio, July 14, 1841, Morris Letters.

[89] Thomson, *A Pioneer Family*, 84; *Courtauld Family Papers*, III, 1019.

[90] Flower, *History of the English Settlement*, 123, 359. This was also the experience of James Knight (in the Courtauld series) and of Robert Pollock.

[91] See, for example, Rebecca Butterworth, Outland Grove, Ark., July 5, 1846, to her father in Rochdale, Lancs., L.S.E.; Thomson, *A Pioneer Family*, 71; *Courtauld Family Papers*, II, 844; and Flower, *History of the English Settlement*, 150.

The ordinary immigrant could not so easily change his occupation once he had made the investment. While he was trying to establish himself on a western farm, he was unlikely to earn enough cash to return home. Because of his predicament, the states of the Old Northwest gained industrial skills and commercially minded people from among British immigrants who had failed as farmers but who were flexible enough in the face of adversity to turn to industrial occupations, either on the land or in the growing towns of the region. For many who hoped to escape from the uncertain results of industrialization in England, a period on the land in the Middle West was simply a detour back into industrial occupations, though probably, in their generation, with more of the "independence" they valued so highly.

Whether they came from agriculture or from industry and commerce in England, these immigrants had to change their ways of gaining a livelihood as well as their standards of living if they sought to enter either commercial or subsistence agriculture in the Old Northwest before 1860. The adaptability of individuals and isolated families who did not settle in assisted colonies to a new and different environment is a fascinating part of nineteenth-century history, especially when we think of the unwillingness of many twentieth-century people in more affluent societies to take such risks. In making their adaptation, the immigrants probably made little impact on American farming methods. Yet indirectly, despite their initial goals in farming, these English and Scots immigrants probably did make a contribution to the economic development of the region because of their drive toward diversification, for which their experience helped prepare them. Coming with preconceived ideas about the nature of good farming or about farming as a way of life, they sometimes revived those skills and attitudes they thought they had discarded by emigrating.

The Great Speculation:
An Interpretation of
Mid-Continent Pioneering

⌒~◊~⌒

LESLIE E. DECKER

In American mythology there is no more persistent legend than the one that holds that most of the hordes who poured toward the frontier were hardy pioneers who, like the boll weevil, were "just a-lookin' for a home." It was these homeseekers who provided the very touchstone of American democracy and inventiveness and morality and justice. In the West a man's homestead was his castle, and on it he could live and raise his family and be self-reliant and ingenious and independent and free. Every man in America with spunk and imagination could provide himself a farm: could wage his own war on poverty and win it. So the legend goes.

Historians have known better for a long time. Spurred on by Frederick Jackson Turner, the godfather of the professional study of the frontier, the first generation of Western historians did set out to prove that the homeseekers were and accomplished everything that popular legend (and Turner and James Fenimore Cooper and Hector St. John de Crèvecoeur and other creative writers) said they were and did. But they found that the pioneer was beset on every side by the facts of life—that it cost more than poor folks could pay, once the Appalachians were breached, even to get to the frontier; that land was almost

357

nowhere free; that social and economic and religious and ethnic distinctions migrated too; that intelligence and perserverance had to be supplemented by skill and tools and capital; that in the end the markets and politics and appetites of people the world over determined whether the pioneer succeeded or failed. Sadly the historians concluded, by the 1930's, that the westering home-seeker had had the deck stacked against him from the outset, that pioneering was neither idyllic nor profitable, that the death of rural America had come with its borning.[1] From one extreme the historians, as is their wont, had leaped to the other.

But the second generation of Western historians was not scared off by the facts of life. That generation eventually accepted their existence and sought to understand them. It is true, of course, that some of the second generation started with lamentations, which was natural—they were taught by the first generation. Some, just as naturally, never got over them. So it is that the literature of Western history still is filled with eulogies to an ideal that somehow went awry. Nonetheless, beginning in the 1930's (with a few noteworthy precursors, to be sure) some historians did undertake to identify and enumerate the nonhome-seekers in the westering, and when they did that they opened the door to understanding the pioneering process.

---

[1] See especially the arguments against democratization and the safety valve in Benjamin F. Wright, Jr., "American Democracy and the Frontier," *Yale Review*, XX (Dec. 1930), 349–365; Carter Goodrich and Sol Davidson, "The Wage Earner and the Western Movement," *Political Science Quarterly*, L (June 1935), 161–185, and LI (March 1936), 61–116; Fred A. Shannon, "The Homestead Act and the Labor Surplus," *American Historical Review*, XLI (July 1936) 637–651; Murray Kane, "Some Considerations on the Safety Valve Doctrine," *Mississippi Valley Historical Review*, XXIII (Sept. 1936), 169–188; and Clarence H. Danhof, "Farm Making Costs and the 'Safety Valve,' 1850–1860," *Journal of Political Economy*, XLIX (Dec. 1941), 317–359. See also Earle D. Ross, "Squandering Our Public Land," *American Scholar*, II (Jan. 1933), 77–86, and Curtis P. Nettels, "Frederick Jackson Turner and the New Deal," *Wisconsin Magazine of History*, XVII (March 1934), 257–265.

Chief among the nonhomeseekers enumerated was the speculator-capitalist, who sought, and sometimes got, great wealth from the frontier. His existence was, of course, not discovered by the historians. He already occupied a secure, if unenviable, place in the popular legend. In fact, the traditional heavy in the Western morality play was (and still is) the scheming speculator-capitalist, in the role of absentee landholder, loan shark, or political adventurer. What the historians undertook was to count and characterize the speculator-capitalists, and they turned out to be far more numerous and far different from what the legend makes them.

The historians of the speculator were paced by Paul Wallace Gates. In two notable articles—one on the relation of the Homestead Act to other means of acquiring land and one on the speculator as a force on the frontier—published in 1936 and 1942 respectively, Gates was instrumental in the founding of what for practical purposes became a "school" of Western historians dedicated to identifying, classifying, and assessing the role of capitalists on the frontier.[2] Gates himself, contrary to the usual practice, was one of the school's most prolific members. Ranging from Illinois to Wisconsin to Indiana to Kentucky and eventually to California, and dealing with everyone from public officials with their hands in the till, to railroad builders growing wealthy from government largess, to frontier landlords and bonanza farmers creating empires from the public lands, he sought out the capitalists wherever they were to be found. Nor did the plantation South escape his scrutiny. The result was an almost incredible collection of information on, and insight into, the workings of frontier capitalism.

To his output was added that of his allies (including some of his students), his challengers (including others of his students),

[2] "The Homestead Law in an Incongruous Land System," *American Historical Review*, XLI (July 1936), 652–681; "The Role of the Land Speculator in Western Development," *Pennsylvania Magazine of History and Biography*, LXVI (July 1942), 314–333.

and the independents (including still others of his students). In a little over two decades the literature on frontier capitalism grew mountainous. These historians, in their effort to discover how speculation tied in to government and society and pioneering, pushed ever further in their search for its limits and ever nearer to understanding the nature of pioneering.

Curiously, or so it seems at first glance, the study of the speculators was concentrated on the mid-continent frontier. One explanation may be that Gates started his pursuit there and that such great independents as Fred Shannon, James Malin, and Roy Robbins studied and taught there. Another might be that capitalist speculation seemed to have been most rampant there. In any event, well over two-thirds of all the studies in and around the frontier-capitalist school do have to do with the mid-continent frontier. In addition, and probably for the same reasons, more than half concentrate on the period between about 1840 and 1890. There are other studies of frontier speculation—ranging from the old Ohio Company to western lands in the Revolution, to Indian land swindles in the old South, to timber operations in the Pacific Northwest, to European mining, ranching, and grazing combines, and so on and on—but the fact remains that more is now known about the nature and extent of the drive for speculative profits on the mid-continent frontier than on any other.

So much has been brought to light about speculation on the mid-continent frontier, in fact, that a question can be raised that flies in the face of that part of the frontier legend that holds that pioneering was homeseeking, a question that none of the first and few of the second generation of Western historians ever seriously raised: namely, was mid-continent pioneering really homeseeking after all?

That such a question is raised does not, of course, mean that it can be answered. Western historical studies have a long way to go before either the store of knowledge or the degree of computerization will be great enough to provide an accurate estimate of which and how many of the pioneers were actually "a-lookin' for a home." Enough is known, however, and enough more can be easily discovered or interpolated to narrow the field considerably. It is already possible, in other words, to eliminate vast numbers from the running.

Some groups were never in the running, for legend had assigned them preparatory and service functions. No one ever claimed that the followers of the mule teams, ox trains, and camps, or the soldiers, Indian agents, and territorial officials intended to be or were home builders. Their role was to make it possible for others to build homes. Nor did anyone claim that the exploiters of the lowly fur bearer, the lordly pine, and the mother lode did anything but blaze trails, open up territories, and skim off the surface wealth. One special class of exploiters, the cattlemen, not only were not homeseekers in any usual sense but used every trick they could conjure up to prevent the building of homes in the West. What the capitalist school of historians has done with the exploiter has been to flesh him out by abundantly documenting his sharping, his unsavory stratagems, his willingness to corrupt. These historians have also revealed that in many instances the holders of public trusts and performers of public services, official as well as nonofficial, were equally preoccupied with the main chance, with recouping lost fortunes or making new ones.[3]

[3] For examples, see Paul Chrisler Phillips, *The Fur Trade* (2 vols.; Norman, Okla., 1961), II; Robert Glass Cleland, *This Reckless Breed of Men: The Trappers and Fur Traders of the Southwest* (New York, 1950); Robert Fries, *Empire in Pine: The Story of Lumbering in Wisconsin, 1830–1900* (Madison, 1951); Agnes M. Larson, *History of the White Pine Industry in Minnesota* (Minneapolis, 1949); Paul Wallace Gates, *The Wisconsin Pine Lands of Cornell University: A Study in Land Policy and Absentee Ownership* (Ithaca, N.Y., 1943); Anita Shafer Goodstein, *Biography of a Businessman: Henry William Sage, 1814–1897* (Ithaca, 1962), 66–134; John W. Caughey, *Gold Is the Cornerstone* (Berkeley, Calif., 1948); Rodman W. Paul, *Mining Frontiers of the Far West, 1848–1880* (New York, 1963); Raymond W. and Mary Lund Settle, *Empire on Wheels* (Stanford, Calif., 1949); Oscar

The homeseeking motive was long thought to have been somewhat greater among those who went west to perform more permanent transportation, commercial, and professional functions. There is not much evidence that it was. To be sure, the "permanent" builders were usually identified with specific corporate schemes or towns, or at least with locales. They did seek to build society on familiar lines. They also sought to make that society grow, and rapidly. It is this urge toward rapid growth and the means they used to produce it that reveals their motives. On close inspection it becomes apparent that they, like the skimmers, were looking for the main chance first, and, unlike the skimmers, for a home second, if at all.

That the transportation business on the frontier was a speculative one is no longer a subject for serious debate. It was risky, to say the least, to push into sparsely settled or unsettled areas with permanent, expensive transportation installations before there were population and freight enough to justify the investment. It was so risky, in fact, that even on the seaboard it was rarely undertaken until subsidies were offered to promoters as inducements, and on the mid-continent it was almost never undertaken without subsidies.[4] Because the risks were so great, promoters

Winther, *The Transportation Frontier, Trans-Mississippi West, 1865–1890* (New York, 1964), 1–74; Ernest Staples Osgood, *The Day of the Cattleman* (Minneapolis, 1929), especially ch. vi; Edward Everett Dale, *The Range Cattle Industry* (Norman, 1930); and Paul C. Henlein, *Cattle Kingdom in the Ohio Valley, 1783–1860* (Lexington, Ky., 1959).

[4] Carter Goodrich, *Government Promotion of American Canals and Railroads, 1800–1890* (New York, 1960); Carter Goodrich, "American Development Policy: The Case of Internal Improvements," *Journal of Economic History*, XVI (Dec. 1956), 449–460; Federal Coordinator of Transportation, *Public Aids to Transportation* (4 vols.; Washington, 1938–1940). See also W. Turrentine Jackson, *Wagon Roads West: A Study of Federal Road Surveys and Construction in the Trans-Mississippi West, 1846–1869* (Berkeley, 1952); John H. Krenkel, *Illinois Internal Improvements, 1818–1848* (Cedar Rapids, Iowa, 1958); Harry H. Pierce, *Railroads of New York: A Study of Government Aid, 1826–1875* (Cambridge, Mass., 1953); John B. Rae, "The Great North-

would accept the challenge and investors the stock only if prospective profits were large indeed. Except in the instances in which the subsidies included land that had windfall wealth on it, the only way to make the subsidies as well as the ventures pay was to attract the people and the goods. Furthermore, it all had to be done quickly, lest speculative profits be dissipated in capital and tax costs. Thus it was that the road builders, the canal builders, and the railroad builders had to become builders of society, promoters of towns, boomers of their territories, and colonizing agents. That some promoters chose the course of manipulating their subsidies or their companies and getting out quickly did not significantly alter the operation; it only increased the number of steps in the process of realizing profits by building society. Nor, conversely, did the existence of this process mean that it was the desire to build society that put transportation facilities on the mid-continent frontier. What put them there, and what kept them there, was the desire for speculative profits.[5]

---

ern's Land Grant," *Journal of Economic History*, XII (Spring 1952), 140–145; and Thomas C. Cochran, "Land Grants and Railroad Entrepreneurship," *ibid.*, X (March 1950), 53–67.

[5] Robert William Fogel, *The Union Pacific Railroad: A Case in Premature Enterprise* (Baltimore, 1960); Harry J. Carman and Charles H. Mueller, "The Contract and Finance Company and the Central Pacific Railroad," *Mississippi Valley Historical Review*, XIV (Dec. 1927), 326–341; Oscar Lewis, *The Big Four: The Story of Huntington, Stanford, Hopkins, and Crocker and of the Building of the Central Pacific* (New York, 1938); Henrietta M. Larson, *Jay Cooke, Private Banker* (Cambridge, Mass., 1936); James B. Hedges, *Henry Villard and the Railways of the Northwest* (New Haven, 1930); Paul Wallace Gates, *The Illinois Central Railroad and Its Colonization Work* (Cambridge, 1934); Richard C. Overton, *Burlington West: A Colonization History of the Burlington Railroad* (Cambridge, 1941); Morris Nelson Spencer, "The Union Pacific's Utilization of Its Land Grant, with Emphasis on Its Colonization Program" (doctoral dissertation, University of Nebraska, 1950); Vincent Victor Masterson, *The Katy Railroad and the Last Frontier* (Norman, 1952); L. L. Waters, *Steel Trails to Santa Fe* (Lawrence, Kan., 1950); William S. Greever, *Arid Domain:*

Town builders, too, were speculators, and only one group of modern writers—their descendants—still pretends otherwise. The townsman's first and key gamble was his choice of a location. Whether he was a town developer with thousands invested or a shopkeeper, lawyer, or newspaperman with only his life and a few dollars to lay on the line, if he was to prosper, his town must prosper; if he was to grow rich, so must his town. The odds were against him, the law of averages being what it is, so once a man committed his resources, large or small, to a town, he did everything in his power to assure that it would boom. He could not be satisfied with slow growth and slight profits. Both had to be commensurate with the risk inherent in the choice he had made.[6]

The Santa Fe Railway and Its Western Land Grant (Stanford, 1954); James B. Hedges, "Promotion of Immigration to the Pacific Northwest by the Railroads," *Mississippi Valley Historical Review*, XV (Sept. 1928), 183–203, "The Colonization Work of the Northern Pacific Railroad," *ibid.*, XIII (Dec. 1926), 311–342; Harold Peterson, "Some Colonizing Efforts of the Northern Pacific Railroad," *Minnesota History*, X (June 1929), 127–144, "Early Minnesota Railroads and the Quest for Settlers," *ibid.*, XIII (March 1932), 25–44; Edna M. Parker, "The Southern Pacific Railroad and the Settlement of Southern California," *Pacific Historical Review*, VI (June 1937), 103–119; Clyde C. Jones, "A Survey of the Agricultural Development Program of the Chicago, Burlington and Quincy Railroad," *Nebraska History*, XXX (Sept. 1949), 226–256; Stanley N. Murray, "Railroads and the Agricultural Development of the Red River Valley of the North, 1870–1890," *Agricultural History*, XXXI (Oct. 1957), 57–66.

[6] To the well-known town-prospecting and booming of such political figures as Stephen Douglas, Abraham Lincoln, "Long John" Wentworth, and Charles H. Van Wyck can be added the activities of a mass of lesser folk in all walks of life. For examples, see R. Richard Wohl, "Henry Noble Day: A Study in Good Works, 1808–1890," 153–192, in William Miller, ed., *Men in Business: Essays in the History of Entrepreneurship* (Cambridge, Mass., 1952); Anna Maury Bunting, *Our People and Ourselves* (Lincoln, Neb., 1909); Otham A. Abbot, *Recollections of a Pioneer Lawyer* (Lincoln, 1929); Victor Rosewater, "The Life and Times of Edward Rosewater" (a manuscript donated to the Nebraska State Historical Society by the Edward Rosewater Family); Alice E. Smith, *James Duane Doty, Frontier Promoter* (Madison, Wis.,

Town-booming, like any long-established game of chance, had rules and conventions, but these were suddenly and drastically altered when the frontier reached the mid-continent. Up to the eastern fringes of the mid-continent country, and before about 1840, the rules were somewhat more exacting, for the number of towns that could boom was strictly limited by certain locational factors. Only a town on a navigable stream, preferably at the head of navigation or, better yet, at the confluence of two or more such streams could hope to wax strong. Canals loosened things up a little, but with the coming of the railroad and the move beyond the Mississippi the possibilities multiplied astronomically. Now a railroad would function as a river, a junction as a confluence of rivers, and the courses could be laid almost anywhere. Great changes in the rules of the game necessarily followed, and the most vital was that political maneuvering replaced location as the key to success.

The principal political means by which towns sought to get railroads were two. Frontier townsmen could scarcely direct the location of the great federal land-grant roads or even the trunk-line feeders to them, for establishing their routes was the function of high-level political trading, memorializing, and lobbying. But if the projected route of a major road came at all close, mid-continent towns did have a political means of seeing that it ran through and not around them: designation as a county seat, a territorial or state capital, or the site for a penitentiary, normal school, agricultural college, or university. The fights for these

1954); Kenneth W. Duckett, *Frontiersman of Fortune: Moses M. Strong of Mineral Point* (Madison, 1955); Merle Curti et al., *The Making of an American Community: A Case Study of Democracy in a Frontier County* (Stanford, 1959), 17–24; and James C. Olson, *J. Sterling Morton* (Lincoln, 1942). Private papers regularly reveal such prospecting. For a classic example, see the letter of Alexander Sterrett to the Reverend John A. Anderson, Manhattan, Kansas, April 25, 1867, and Anderson's letters to his family discussing the prospects of Junction City, Kansas, March 14, 1868–March 23, 1869, Anderson Family Papers, Kansas State Historical Society, Topeka.

institutional guarantees of immortality became, on the mid-continent frontier, classic battles between small-town gladiators to whom defeat meant stagnation.[7]

Less important routes—though not less valuable subsidies—for junctions and feeder lines to fill out what came to be the most extensive railroad network in the world were determined at the county and town level. It was at this level that the townsmen could do most for themselves, and their efforts were herculean. The means was the voting of county, precinct, and municipal subscriptions to stock or gifts of bonds to prospective railroad builders, and becaue the nature of railroading was itself speculative, the towns had to bid against one another. The sums they poured into the railroaders' coffers were huge, even on the eastern fringes of the mid-continent (where earlier locational

[7] Paul Wallace Gates, *Fifty Million Acres: Conflicts over Kansas Land Policy, 1854–1890* (Ithaca, 1954), especially ch. iv; Robert R. Russel, *Improvement of Communication with the Pacific Coast as an Issue in American Politics, 1783–1864* (Cedar Rapids, 1948), 262–293; James C. Malin, *The Nebraska Question, 1852–1854* (Lawrence, 1953); James C. Malin, *Grassland Historical Studies: Natural Resources Utilization in a Background of Science and Technology*, I: *Geology and Geography* (Lawrence, 1950), 274–298; Henry F. Mason, "County Seat Controversies in Southwestern Kansas," *Kansas Historical Quarterly*, II (Feb. 1933), 45–65; Minnie Dubbs Millbrook, "Dr. Samuel Grant Rodgers, Gentleman from Ness," *ibid.*, XX (Feb. 1953), 305–349. The Nebraska Executive Papers (Nebraska State Historical Society, Lincoln) are sprinkled with the recriminations of county fathers over these and related questions. See, for example, the controversy over the organization of Holt County in the Garber Papers for February and March of 1876. An impressionistic estimate, derived from the author's reading, in another connection, of scores of Kansas and Nebraska newspapers and an equal number of county histories, would be that fully a third of the counties in these two states experienced some kind of protracted county-seat fight. That quarrels were often not resolved in favor of an existing town is clear from the large number of county seats established late, located in the exact center of the county, and given the same name as the county. Some of these fights and the battles for the other institutions in these two states are sketched in James C. Olson, *History of Nebraska* (Lincoln, 1955), and William Frank Zornow, *Kansas: A History of the Jayhawk State* (Norman, Okla., 1957).

factors had already determined in large measure which towns
would burgeon), but on the prairies and the high plains, where
the game was open to all comers, the sums paid reached fantastic
proportions. Between 1872 and 1890, Nebraska towns, for example, spent at least four million dollars to attract railroads. In the
same years Kansas towns spent over eighteen million.[8]

To the striving townsmen these figures, impressive as they are,
were as unreal as the rivalry among the great cities their towns

[8] The approximations given here are derived from the incomplete
listings of such bonds included in the state auditors' reports of the two
states, 1872–1890; from C. E. Tingley, "Bond Subsidies to Railroads in
Nebraska," *Quarterly Journal of Economics*, VI (April 1892), 346–352;
and from the fragmentary figures included in James E. Boyle, *Financial
History of Kansas*, University of Wisconsin Bulletin in Economics and
Political Science, V, no. 1 (Madison, 1909). There are discrepancies but
all sources agree on these general levels. Among the useful treatments of
the struggle for railroad connections through either state (a tiny fraction) or local (the lion's share) subsidies are Edwin L. Lopata, *Local
Aid to Railroads in Missouri* (New York, 1937); Charles N. Glaab,
*Kansas City and the Railroads: Community Policy in the Growth of a
Regional Metropolis* (Madison, 1962); John Wilson Million, "State Aid
to Railways in Missouri," *Journal of Political Economy*, III (1895),
73–97; Harry N. Scheiber, "Urban Rivalry and Internal Improvements
in the Old Northwest," *Ohio History*, LXXI (Oct. 1962), 227–242; Earl
S. Beard, "Local Aid to Railroads in Iowa," *Iowa Journal of History
and Politics*, I. (Jan. 1952), 1–34; Thomas M. Davis, "Building the
Burlington Through Nebraska—a Summary View," *Nebraska History*,
XXX (Dec. 1949), 317–347; Harold J. Henderson, "The Building of the
First Kansas Railroad South of the Kaw River," *Kansas Historical
Quarterly*, XV (Aug. 1947), 225–239; James J. Blake, "The Brownville,
Fort Kearney and Pacific Railroad," *Nebraska History*, XXIX (Sept.
1948), 238–272; Thomas LeDuc, "State Administration of the Land
Grant to Kansas for Internal Improvements," *Kansas Historical Quart-
erly*, XX (Nov. 1953), 545–552; Glenn H. Miller, "Financing the Boom
in Kansas, with Special Reference to Municipal Indebtedness and Real
Estate Mortgages" (master's thesis, University of Kansas, 1954); Herbert O. Brayer, *William Blackmore: Early Financing of the Denver and
Rio Grande Railway and Ancillary Land Companies* (Denver, 1949);
and Leonard J. Arrington, *Great Basin Kingdom: An Economic History of the Latter-Day Saints, 1830–1900* (Cambridge, Mass., 1958),
235–292.

were emulating. What was real to the townsmen was their rivalry with the towns around them, for a main rule of town-booming was that the really serious threat was the neighboring town that had won a spin of the wheel by gaining the county seat, the normal school, another railroad, or a factory. Life in frontier towns was dominated by county-seat fights (complete with disputed elections, viciously fought litigation, and on innumerable occasions, brawls and even gun battles between the champions of rival towns), railroad-promotion meetings (complete with padded estimates, threats and counter-threats, and not unusually, open bidding as crass and unprincipled as that received by any modern neutralist dictator), and guided tours and counter-tours for any passing stranger who might put capital or skill into the boom.

A single example will suffice. No less than nine towns bid for life in Adams County, Nebraska, an area twenty-four miles square. Natural circumstances narrowed the fight for supremacy by killing some, but four—Juniata, Ayr, Kenesaw, and Hastings —had a chance. Juniata got a running start, largely because the promoters of the Burlington Railroad chose the site for a water stop and acquired the surrounding land as a sideline speculation. They also established the first settlers and saw to it that the county seat was located there. But an independent group established Hastings, six miles to the east, bid hard for settlers, boomed its prospects, and worked to get another land-grant road, the St. Joseph and Denver City, to make its junction with the Burlington at their town. Juniata worked too, but Hastings outworked it, grew a little more rapidly, and began a campaign to move the county seat. In the classic fight that followed, every shady tactic was used. Hastings won, but not before it had successfully outbid both Juniata and Kenesaw for the junction point of the Burlington's Denver extension. Ayr, established on the Denver extension six miles south of Hastings, made its bid by acquiring the junction of the branch line to Colby, but Hastings aced Ayr by getting yet another junction, a feeder line to Grand Island, on the Union Pacific. Kenesaw finally got a junction too, the Burlington cutoff to Denver, but Hastings aced Kenesaw also, when it obtained still another junction, this one with the Missouri Pacific feeder to Concordia, Kansas. The fight had long since been won. Hastings had five railroads, half of the county's population, and bade fair to become the biggest city between Lincoln and Denver. It also had a municipal debt of over a quarter-million dollars, a county debt of over half that amount, and the booming habit. As a newspaper in a neighboring town put it, if the Hastings boomers' newspaper, the *Gazette Journal*, "should hear of a railroad projected from Behrings Straits to the North pole it would head the announcement in flaming head-lines, 'Another Railroad for Hastings,' and advocate voting bonds to aid in its construction." The booming habit led Hastings to bid for supremacy on a larger scale, even to entertain aspirations for acquiring the state capital, but that proved to be beyond the bounds of the possible. Meanwhile, residents of the other towns in the county either moved to Hastings, sought greener pastures elsewhere, or stayed in their own towns, defeated.[9]

That a town won in such competition did not, of course, guarantee that it would boom. Institutional and transportation facilities would come to naught if population did not follow. Thus another rule of town-booming was that the growth of

[9] *Grand Island Times* (Neb.), Aug. 4, 1887. The only lengthy second-ary account is in vol. I of William R. Burton and David J. Lewis, eds., *Past and Present of Adams County, Nebraska* (2 vols.; Chicago, 1916), a better-than-average county history. The struggle is best followed in the first volume of the "Proceedings of the Board of County Commissioners of Adams County, Nebraska," at the office of the county treasurer, Hastings, and in the local newspapers: the *Adams County Gazette* (Juniata), 1872–1880, and the *Juniata Herald*, 1876–1890, both at the Nebraska State Historical Society, Lincoln; the *Hastings Nebraskan*, 1883–1884, at the Hastings Museum; and the *Hastings Journal*, 1878–1880, and the *Hastings Gazette Journal*, 1880–1888, both at the offices of their successor, the *Hastings Tribune*. Indebtedness is figured from the *Nebraska State Auditor's Report*, 1873–1890, and from the "Proceedings of the Board of County Commissioners." See also Leslie E. Decker, *Railroads, Lands, and Politics: The Taxation of the Railroad Land Grants, 1864–1897* (Providence, 1964), 198–199, 209–212.

population had to be nurtured, that settlers had to be attracted by every possible means, especially by promotional advertising. Here, again, because the stakes were high, the townsmen went to extremes. Like all promotional advertising, their painted prospects large and failures small, saw great trends in minor accretions of population, and treated everything that was proposed as though it had been accomplished. Unlike the promotional advertising of such corporate speculators as railroads (which was usually careful to specify that there were risks),[10] theirs went so far as to suggest that their towns could offer something for nothing—wealth without work or, as one town's broadside put it, "beautiful homes for those in need."[11]

Three methods were used. One was to pad and glorify all reports to state fact-publishing agencies (and the federal census-takers too), which, in turn, printed the information in large quantity and sowed it broadcast.[12] The second was to organize their own, or hire outside, agencies to turn out and distribute

[10] For a discussion and examples of such advertising see Decker, *Railroads, Lands, and Politics*, 101–102.

[11] "Resources of Russell County, Kansas! Cheap Farms! Healthy Climate! Mild Winters! Best Soil in the World!" (broadside, [1887], issued by Russell County Immigrant Association, Russell, Kansas State Historical Society).

[12] Kansas, for example, had its State Board of Agriculture, an admittedly promotional organization, whose annual and special reports included boomer materials of many types, from essays by "authorities" on trade and agricultural potentials to optimistic land-sales, settlement, and price figures for all reporting counties. The state auditor's reports regularly included equally optimistic census figures for everything from capital invested in manufactures to acres of wheat planted. Other states and territories used similar tactics. See, for example, Livia Appel and T. C. Blegen, "Official Encouragement of Immigration to Minnesota during the Territorial Period," *Minnesota History Bulletin*, V (Aug. 1923), 167–203. For a study of misreporting in the federal census, see Edgar Z. Palmer, "The Correctness of the 1890 Census of Population for Nebraska Cities," *Nebraska History*, XXXII (Dec. 1951), 259–267. Public figures also often contributed boomer articles to eastern journals. See, for example, John A. Martin, "The Progress of Kansas," *North American Review*, CXLII (April 1886), 348–355.

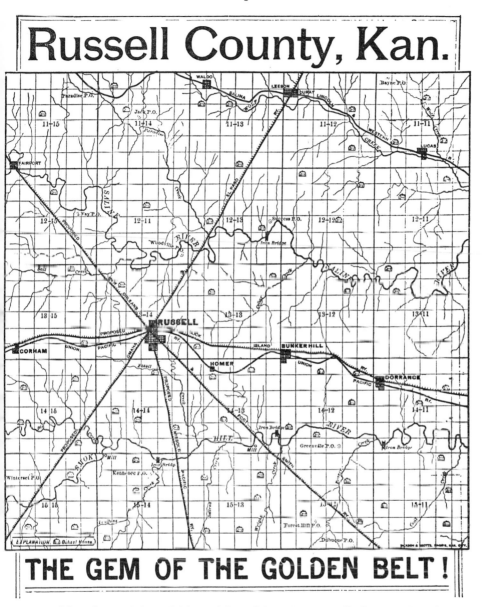

Russell County, Kan.

THE GEM OF THE GOLDEN BELT!

Map from a broadside published by the Russell County Immigrant Association, about 1889; by courtesy of the Kansas State Historical Society, Topeka.

broadsides, pamphlets, and business directories booming the town.[13] The third was to use the local newspaper as a primitive version of the modern press release. A good editor devoted his chief attention to booming the town and surrounding land, to reporting every promotional scheme ever talked of and proposing still others, and to spoofing the pretensions of neighboring towns. And he circulated his papers widely to the local weeklies in the older areas in the hope that some of his "exchanges" would print the good news from his town.[14]

[13] Some excellent examples of this outpouring are Warren, Keeney and Company, *Trego County, Kansas: Its Soil and Climate* . . . (Chicago, 1878); Pagett and Stinchcomb, immigration agents, *A Descriptive Review of Adams County, Neb., Showing the Resources, Climate, Water, Timber, Grasses, Grains, Towns, and People* . . . (Omaha, 1879); *The Leading Cities of Southeastern Nebraska* . . . (Chicago, 1883); *Handbook of Pottawatomie and Riley Counties, Kansas* (no imprint, [1883]); Ford County Immigration Society, *Handbook of Ford County, Kansas* (Chicago, 1887); and Sterling Land and Investment Company, *Sterling, Kansas: The Actual Advantages and Resources of a Grand Young Town Candidly Discussed* (no imprint, [1887]). That the business of publishing such items was in itself a booming one is illustrated by the facts that the C. S. Burch Company of Chicago alone published boomer directories for eighteen separate counties in Kansas, that the J. P. Edwards Company of Philadelphia published boomer atlases for fourteen separate counties in Kansas, and that as of 1955 the Kansas State Historical Society held 137 Kansas city and county directories published before 1900 (Lorene Anderson and Alan W. Farley, comps., "A Bibliography of Town and County Histories of Kansas," *Kansas Historical Quarterly*, XXI [Autumn 1955], 513–551).

[14] Some examples of these practices are in the *Ashland Times* (Neb.), under the editorship of J. G. Stockton, 1870–1873; the *West Point Republican* (Neb.), under the editorship of E. N. Sweet, also in the early seventies; the *Nebraska Herald* (Plattsmouth), under the editorship of C. P. R. Williams, 1873–1883; every newspaper in Adams County, Nebraska, no matter who the editor, but especially the *Hastings Gazette Journal;* the *Kearney County Gazette* (Neb.), under a succession of editors, but especially R. P. Stein, 1886–1887 (who also, incidentally, was the county treasurer for nine years); the *Russell County Record,* owned by the Dollison brothers until 1881 and by W. A. Lewis, 1881–1888, and edited by a succession of boomers; the *Junction City Union* (Kan.), under George Martin until 1873 and from 1881 to 1888, and under Noble Prentiss, 1873–1875; the *Junction City*

If enough people came to a town and the territory around it, land values in and around it rose, additional professional men, merchants, crop buyers, and other townsmen put in their appearance, and the boom was on. Sometimes it got out of hand, and there ensued booms and busts of the sort that were an old story in the gold camps. Ideally, and more commonly, the rise was fast enough to drive values up rapidly and steadily but not dangerously.[15]

The ideal was what the townsman hoped for. In fact, he hoped—and believed—so hard that he extended himself to his limit to get an interest in, and, if possible, title to, land around his town. In modern parlance, he was diversifying, adding to his investment in town lots and his profession or business an investment in land: becoming an absentee landholder (in the parlance of the frontier, a "land speculator") as well. Sometimes he bought lots from the local land-grant railroad. Sometimes he used such extralegal means as the claims association by which members bought and sold land claims in advance of government survey and land auction.[16] More commonly he secured land by pre-emption and, after 1862, by homesteading. At least half,

Tribune, under John W. Davis, 1878-1890 (who also, incidentally, became the Populist congressman from the district); and the *Wakeeney World* (Kan.), run by the company promoting the town. These practices were almost universal; the swiftly changing editors and the long succession of fly-by-night newspapers are effective testimony. For a chronology of these changes and eulogies of leading editors in one state, see William E. Connelly, ed., *History of Kansas Newspapers* (Topeka, 1916).

[15] See "Some Lost Towns of Kansas," *Collections of the Kansas State Historical Society*, XII (1911-1912), 426-490; James C. Malin, "The Kinsley Boom of the Late Eighties," *Kansas Historical Quarterly*, IV (Feb., May 1935), 23-49, 164-187; Herbert L. Glynn, "The Urban Real Estate Boom in Nebraska during the Eighties," *Nebraska Law Bulletin*, VI (May 1928), 455-481, and VII (Nov. 1928), 228-254; and Floyd Merle Farmer, "Land Boom of Southwest Nebraska, 1880-1890" (master's thesis, University of Nebraska, 1936).

[16] The use of the claims association in this fashion is discussed in Allan G. Bogue, "The Iowa Claim Clubs: Symbol and Substance," *Mississippi Valley Historical Review*, XLV (Sept. 1958), 231-253.

perhaps more, of the early comers to any town—from lawyers to doctors, to merchants, to just plain town developers—usually diversified in this fashion.[17]

In becoming absentee landholders, the townsmen were only emulating a technique that had been practiced since the days of Walter Raleigh. As the capitalist school of historians has abundantly shown, men of means in America speculated in western land almost as a matter of course, and such speculations reached their greatest heights on the mid-continent frontier. This was true partly because risk capital was available in greater amounts than ever before, partly because machinery for the investing of such funds had become institutionalized, and partly because the incongruous land system made the acquisition of large areas of land on long credit easier than it had ever been. Money poured westward in exchange for titles to railroad, Indian, state, agricultural-college, military-bounty, and various other kinds of vacant lands, and the new owners held the lands for the rise in value that an influx of population would bring. Like the townsmen who emulated them, these men chose their spots carefully, because they, like the townsmen and the railroaders, were gambling that the rise would be fast enough and high enough to justify the risk—a risk that in their operation was increased by their inability to do much directly to encourage a population rush or to do anything directly to supervise their holdings. Other absentees, some of them from not as far away and in other

[17] The basis of this estimate is the study of plats made from the numerical indices of land transfers (including original alienation) and some of the other title records of five scattered counties in Kansas and Nebraska. The counties involved are Saline and Trego, in Kansas, and Adams, Kearney, and Keith, in Nebraska; and the towns are the present county seats: Salina, Wakeeney, Hastings, Holdrege, and Ogallala respectively. These records are located at the office of the register of deeds of each county. In every area studied the majority of those identifiable from newspapers, county directories, and histories as early comers or leading citizens had, at one time or another, title to at least a quarter section and sometimes to several sections purchased from the railroad or acquired from the government, or both.

lines of work, joined the rush to speculate in western land values
—doctors, lawyers, politicians, railroadmen on their own accounts, colonizers, and those who aspired to landed estates.[18] Still
other absentees speculated at one step removed by investing in
western land mortgages, so that men without means could buy
and hold lands for their rise in value and in turn pay off the
mortgage holder (at a good profit to him) and make something
for themselves as well.[19]

There was one more group that, from yet another base, was
gaming at the same tables: the migratory settlers, those professional firstcomers who constituted the 50 to 80 per cent who, in

---

[18] In addition to his more than a dozen articles on aspects of these
speculations, see Paul Wallace Gates, *Fifty Million Acres, passim,*
especially 230–248; *Frontier Landlords and Pioneer Tenants* (Ithaca,
1945); and *The Farmer's Age: Agriculture, 1815–1860* (New York,
1962), especially 188–196. See also Joseph Shafer, *Four Wisconsin Coun-
ties: Prairie and Forest,* Wisconsin Domesday Book: General Studies, II
(Madison, 1927), 59–64, 69, 72–79; Fred A. Shannon, *The Farmer's Last
Frontier: Agriculture, 1860–1897* (New York, 1945), 51–75; Margaret
Beattie Bogue, *Patterns from the Sod: Land Use and Tenure in the
Grand Prairie, 1850–1900,* Collections of the Illinois State Historical
Library, XXXIV, Land Series, I (Springfield, 1959), Pt. I; Allan G.
Bogue, *From Prairie to Corn Belt: Farming on the Illinois and Iowa
Prairies in the Nineteenth Century* (Chicago, 1963), chs. ii and iii;
Gordon T. Chappell, "Some Patterns of Land Speculation in the Old
Southwest," *Journal of Southern History,* XV (Nov. 1949), 463–477;
and Robert P. Swierenga, "Land Speculator 'Profits' Reconsidered:
Central Iowa as a Test Case," *Journal of Economic History,* XXVI
(March 1966), 1–28.

[19] The only modern and dispassionate works on the subject are those
of the Bogues cited above, and Allan G. Bogue, *Money at Interest: The
Farm Mortgage on the Middle Border* (Ithaca, 1955). Not so modern
but as dispassionate is Arthur F. Bentley, *The Condition of the Western Farmer as Illustrated by the Economic History of a Nebraska
Township,* Johns Hopkins Studies in Historical and Political Science,
11 ser., nos. 7 and 8 (Baltimore, 1893). Eastern men of moderate means
and even the managers of family trusts invested heavily. See, for
example, the operations chronicled in the extensive Charles and Carter
Kingsley Papers and the Reuben Robie Papers, Collection of Regional
History and University Archives, Cornell University.

every new area, moved on within a decade.[20] These people usually had little money to invest. What they did have was ingenuity, generations of experience, and a sure sense of the value of being early. Given these—and given the land system, the system of government, the example of bigger operators, and the American dream—the migratory settlers necessarily played the game by first grabbing as much land as they could, then joining the railroadmen and townsmen in their efforts to increase its value by providing the trappings of society and attracting population.

The means of acquiring land on the modest scale required by these operators were many. In fact, by 1873 the land system was such that a homestead, a pre-emption, and a timber-culture claim —480 acres in all—could be acquired legally from the government for residence, some improvements, and just two hundred dollars in delayed cash payments. In addition, the small operator could acquire railroad land for no money down, no payments for one year, and installment payments for six to eleven years; and he, too, had potentially profitable access to the various other kinds of land.[21] Given these possibilities and the prospect of gain from increasing land values, it is not surprising that few of the settlers were satisfied to acquire only a farm-sized tract.

The amount of land that constituted such a tract increased as one moved westward. To take the central plains country as an example, in southeastern Nebraska and east-central Kansas, 80 to

[20] James C. Malin, "The Turnover of Farm Population in Kansas," *Kansas Historical Quarterly*, IV (Nov. 1935), 339–372; Peter J. Coleman, "Restless Grant County," *Wisconsin Magazine of History*, XLVI (Autumn 1962), 16–20; Bogue, *From Prairie to Corn Belt*, 25–28.

[21] Specific treatments of the public-land systems operating in two mid-continent states are Roy L. Lokken, *Iowa Public Land Disposal* (Iowa City, 1942), and Addison E. Sheldon, *Land Systems and Land Policies in Nebraska*, Publications of the Nebraska State Historical Society, XXII (Lincoln, 1936). For the sales practices of the railroads, see the works cited in n. 5, above, and Decker, *Railroads, Lands, and Politics*, 100–104. See also Agnes Horton, "Nebraska's Agricultural-College Land," *Nebraska History*, XXX (March 1949), 50–76.

160 acres usually sufficed; in south-central Nebraska and central
Kansas, 160 to 240 acres were usually enough; in the western
sections of both states, more than 320 acres were usually
needed.[22] In the light of these requirements the pattern of acquisition revealed in an analysis of the 112 townships in five counties
strung out across central and western Kansas and Nebraska is
instructive. The pattern was remarkably similar in all areas: only
25 per cent of the tracts were farm-sized or smaller; 50 per cent
were up to twice as large; 25 per cent were several times larger.[23]

And the settlers did not confine themselves to obtaining legal
titles. They often sought, obtained, and sold extralegal claims as
well. One way to do this was to join a claims association and sell
the claims obtained through it. Some of the claim associations in
Iowa served the function of obtaining and selling such claims for
what seems to have been a majority of their members. The
claims associations formed in Missouri and later in Kansas to
establish claims to Indian lands in Kansas served the same function, perhaps on an even grander scale.[24] Another way was to
locate pre-emption and homestead claims and sell relinquishments. To estimate the traffic in relinquishments it is only necessary to note that the discrepancy of 60 per cent between original
and final homestead entries at the local land offices cannot be

[22] In the process of adaption of both crops and techniques, these
requirements changed. See James C. Malin, *Winter Wheat in the Golden
Belt of Kansas: A Study in Adaption to Subhumid Geographical Environment* (Lawrence, 1944), and L. F. Garey, *Factors Determining Type
of Farming Areas in Nebraska*, Bulletin of the Nebraska Agricultural
Experiment Station, no. 299 (Lincoln, 1936). At the time, however,
these were the popular estimates. See, for example, John A. Anderson,
"Sketch of Kansas Agriculture," pp. 72–101 in *Annual Report of the
Kansas State Board of Agriculture, 1875* (Topeka).

[23] These conclusions are derived from an analysis of plats of the
original alienation of government lands and original sales of railroad
lands made from the numerical indices of Saline and Trego counties, in
Kansas, and Adams, Kearney, and Keith counties, in Nebraska. See n.
17.

[24] Bogue, "The Iowa Claim Clubs"; Gates, *Fifty Million Acres*, 54–57,
55n.

explained as an indication of failures among the original claimants. Original claimants regularly relinquished their claims for a fee.[25] Having done so, they could then move on and claim again or use their profits to obtain title to land, thereby climbing up the scale to become landowners.

The primary means by which the little operators sought to attract the settlers necessary to force up the value of the lands they owned or claimed was to use the borrowing power of precinct and county governments to finance as many desirable public improvements (schools, roads, bridges) and to attract as many desirable services (railroads, commercial centers) as possible to the lands' vicinity. Thus it was that schools with capacities far in excess of the need were immediately built, that county and precinct bonds for railroads and related promotions were voted by the firstcomers, that local debts mounted sharply during the first surge into any area.[26]

[25] For tables showing the annual and total discrepancies between original and final entries in two states, see Decker, *Railroads, Lands, and Politics*, 132–133. For patterns of alienation of public lands in two Nebraska counties, see Evan E. Evans, "An Analytical Study of Land Transfer to Private Ownership in Johnson County, Nebraska" (master's thesis, University of Nebraska, 1950), and John Arnett Caylor, "The Disposition of the Public Domain in Pierce County, Nebraska" (master's thesis, University of Nebraska, 1951). For some discussion of the complications in the land laws and their administration that made manipulation relatively simple, see George L. Anderson, "The Administration of Federal Land Laws in Western Kansas, 1880–1890," *Kansas Historical Quarterly*, XX (Nov. 1952), 233–251; George L. Anderson, "The Board of Equitable Adjudication, 1846–1930," *Agricultural History*, XXIX (April 1955), 65–72; and Decker, "The Railroads and the Land Office: Administrative Policy and the Land Patent Controversy, 1864–1896," *Mississippi Valley Historical Review*, XLVI March 1960), 679–699. See also Shafer, *Four Wisconsin Counties*, 74.

[26] For examples of newspaper testimony to this effect see the *Omaha Bee* (Neb.), Aug. 6, Sept. 3, 1873; the *Grand Island Times*, Aug. 20, 1873; the *Omaha Weekly Herald*, Aug. 23, 1873; the *Adams County Gazette*, March 6, May 1, 1872; the *Manhattan Nationalist* (Kan.), Jan. 13, 1871; the *Junction City Union*, May 3, 1873; and the *Russell County*

These things done, all anybody could do was to wait for the homeseekers to come. If they came, everyone already there had a home and a competence. If they did not come or came too slowly, there were two alternatives: to admit defeat, stay on, and make a home, or to move on and try again.

On the mid-continent frontier, then, almost all the early com-

---

Record, Nov. 18, 1881. If the testimony of railroadmen (who felt the pressure of high taxes on their holdings) can be credited, the majority of jurisdictions operated this way. See the testimony of Leavitt Burnham and Andrew J. Poppleton in *Sen. Ex. Doc. 51,* 50 Cong., 1 sess., 145, 2507–2511, 1888; and E. H. Talbott, *Railway Land Grants in the United States: Their History, Economy, and Influence upon the Development and Prosperity of the Country* (Chicago, 1880), 44–45. Somewhat less— or at least, differently—biased testimony to the same effect is in the report of D. H. Emery, superintendent of Dickinson County, in the *Annual Report of the Superintendent of Public Instruction* (of Kansas), 1873, 100–101; the *Kansas Auditor's Report,* 1874, 42–44, and 1888, iv; the *Message of Robert W. Furnas, Governor of Nebraska, to the Legislative Assembly, Tenth Regular Session, 1875* (Lincoln, 1875), 6; and the messages of Kansas Governors Osborne (1876), Martin (1885, 1887, and 1889), and Humphrey (1889 and 1891), bound together in "Messages of the Governors of Kansas," at the Kansas State Historical Society. The auditors listed such indebtedness by precinct or township and by county. School-district bonds are sometimes tabulated in the reports of the superintendents of public instruction. See also Bunting, *Our People and Ourselves,* 98–100; Abbot, *Recollections of a Pioneer Lawyer,* 126; Burton and Lewis, *Past and Present of Adams County,* I, 372; James C. Malin, ed., "J. A. Walker's Early History of Edwards County," *Kansas Historical Quarterly,* IX (Aug. 1940), 259–284; Alfred T. Andreas, comp., *History of the State of Nebraska, Containing a Full Account of Its Growth . . . , Description of Its Counties, Cities, Towns, and Villages . . .* (Chicago, 1882), 368; and Addison E. Sheldon, *Nebraska: The Land and the People* (3 vols., Chicago, 1931), I, 511. Boyle's *Financial History of Kansas,* published in 1909, proposed a thesis (pp. 79–80), based on local indebtedness, that explained many aspects of the political revolt of the nineties. Raymond C. Miller, in his excellent "The Economic Background of Populism in Kansas," *Mississippi Valley Historical Review,* XI (March 1925), 469–498, extended and refined Boyle's proposition in what is still the best single article on the origins of Populism.

ers to any area were speculators first and homeseekers second or not at all. Whether this is true of other frontiers it is impossible now to say for sure. But since Americans acquired habits quickly and almost never lose them, the nature of pioneering in the mid-continent may not have been very different from the nature of pioneering elsewhere in America.

The American West and Foreign Markets, 1850-1900

MORTON ROTHSTEIN

By 1850 the American conception of the West as the "granary of the world" had triumphed over two earlier competing ideas—of the West as an insulated "garden of the world" set apart from the complexities of modern civilization, and of the West as a vital component in a balanced, self-sufficient economy.

For generations intellectuals had envisaged the West as the garden of the world, which to them meant a wilderness haven where sturdy, self-reliant, and above all, self-sufficient farmers could claim a modest piece of land and practice the bucolic virtues. This vision persisted as a point of reference for political leaders, farm groups, and social critics. According to the Jeffersonian tradition, each settler in the American heartland was to be an island unto himself; each was to produce for his own needs, relying on the outside world only for simple necessities that were impossible to produce by the sweat of his brow. The society created by these settlers would be close to nature and to nature's God; it would be free of the corrupting influences of the marketplace and of the rude intrusions of industralization.[1]

---

[1] I use the term "garden of the world" in a more restricted sense than does Henry Nash Smith, in *Virgin Land: The American West as Symbol and Myth* (New York, 1957), 138–305, applying it only to the idea of an insulated agricultural heartland that could serve as a retreat. The phrase "granary of the world" began to appear in farm journals and

A second concept of the West envisioned the region as subservient to the older eastern seaboard. The men who held this vision, embodied in the pronouncements of Hamilton and Clay as the touchstone of the "American system," were leaders of a society already commercialized beyond redemption. They sought to restrain western settlement so that the region might be integrated, gradually and rationally, with the rest of the national economy. In their schema the farmer was to be a commercial producer who would find profitable markets in the industrializing East and thus remain independent of foreigners. Instead of the self-reliance of individual farmers, the notion stressed the interdependence of groups and regions within a self-reliant nation.

The third idea of the West, the West that was to become the granary of the world, envisioned an expanding, indeed an aggressive, commercialized agriculture, in which a farmer produced not only for himself and for the nation, but for the world as well. The bountiful resources of the Mississippi Valley basin, waiting for the advancing nation of farmers, would produce such abundant harvests that America could feed hungry masses everywhere and be rewarded with power and riches.

If there was ever a time that Americans seriously believed in the dream of the West as a garden, providing an escape into an isolated bucolic utopia, the vision was quickly subordinated to the more aggressive conception of the West as a center of commercialized agriculture. To be sure, intellectuals continued

---

the popular press with greater frequency in the 1850's. It was usually employed in discussions of the grain trade, but often was also used in a hyperbolic sense to include all western farm products, as I have used it here. For other discussions of these concepts, see Edward M. Burns, *The American Idea of Mission: Concepts of National Purpose and Destiny* (New Brunswick, N.J., 1957); Leo Marx, *The Machine in the Garden: Technology and the Pastoral Ideal in America* (New York, 1964); and Rush Welter, "The Frontier West as Image of American Society: Conservative Attitudes before the Civil War," *Mississippi Valley Historical Review*, XLVI (March 1960), 593–614.

to expound the old agrarian ideas, communitarian experiments thrived briefly in a host of wilderness settings, and from time to time such men as George Henry Evans saw hope for the American working man in an escape from the factories and cities of the East to an agrarian paradise in the West. Perhaps, too, some settlers felt that the hazards of their westward trek and the privations they endured while carving farms out of the virgin land had purged them and their work of worldly evil and had earned them a separate status as a chosen people. But the main goal of the vast majority of Americans who crossed the Appalachians was the re-creation of the kind of society they had known along the Atlantic seaboard, a society based on a commercial agriculture rather than a self-sufficient one.[2]

Therefore, when settlement of the West began to gain momentum after 1815, the real clash over public policy was between the notion of maintaining a balance between western agriculture and eastern markets, with the former restrained at the expense of the latter, and the ideal of an unfettered expansion that would open the potential farm lands of the West to all comers.

The advocates of the expansion of the Old Northwest had the example of the South to buttress their arguments. From South Carolina to Arkansas, cotton growers were creating a dynamic, thriving agricultural economy by responding to foreign demand, and the region seemed to be growing rich in the process. From time to time, planters glutted the market and suffered the consequences of overexpansion, but each downturn was followed by an even greater surge of development. If some cotton planters became discouraged in periods of low prices and tried other crops, they usually concentrated more on producing cotton for export when prices recovered. Few of them could find profitable alternatives to the crop which promised the greatest commercial

[2] Rodney C. Loehr, "Self Sufficiency on the Farm," *Agricultural History*, XXVI (April 1952), 37–41.

success, though the profits were based on a labor system rapidly becoming an abomination in the eyes of the world.[3]

The champions of the "American system," however, could point to the economic realities that confronted farmers in the Old Northwest. Settlers in that region had penetrated into the interior of a continental land mass, beyond the effective reach of markets. The climate restricted them to temperate-zone crops, and they could not grow the semitropical products possible for southerners. Furthermore, the overseas demand for their food products, which had lulled many early settlers into disregarding these limitations, dropped sharply after 1819. For the next twenty years the Atlantic-seaboard states alone would have food surpluses too great for either the traditional Caribbean markets or the newer ones in Europe.[4]

Between 1820 and 1840 the tension between the two opposing concepts was at its peak. While land hunger and the irresistible force of westward migration strengthened the drive for unfettered expansion, the twenty-year period marked a relatively low ebb in foreign trade in all agricultural commodities except cotton, a condition which weakened the support for the notion of the West as the granary of the world.

But the scales were tipped heavily in favor of the granary

[3] For a detailed study of the planters' difficulties in breaking away from cotton in one southern state, see John Hebron Moore, *Agriculture in Ante-Bellum Mississippi* (New York, 1958).

[4] During the 1820's several New York merchant houses were sending large quantities of beef, dairy products, and other provisions to New Orleans and Mobile. They purchased most of these items from New York and Philadelphia dealers, who in turn apparently purchased them locally (Leverich Family Papers, New-York Historical Society). From 1820 to 1840, Ogden, Ferguson, and Company, a New York exporting firm, shipped grain and flour to Britain during brief intervals of European demand, and purchased virtually all of it in Philadelphia, Baltimore, and even Virginia (Ogden, Ferguson Papers, New-York Historical Society). From the production estimates that we have it is probable that most of the grain, flour, and dairy products—which were far more valuable components of foreign trade from 1820 to 1840 than livestock or provisions—came from farms in the seaboard states.

concept by a series of developments in the 1840's. The canals and railroads that pushed into the Old Northwest began breaking down the old geographical barriers and diverted more and more farm products from the river routes going south to a direct eastward flow. The transportation revolution also began opening the prairies to settlement; farmers moving onto the level, rich land of Illinois and Iowa could bring their acres into cultivation quickly, without the old restrictive requirement of a lifetime devoted to clearing trees. Thus, the process of farm-making gathered speed. At the same time, the scope of commercial production on prairie farms was enlarging. The flat land was ideal for the adoption of the new farm machinery available for the first time in significant quantities. With a reaper, a farmer no longer had to limit the size of his wheat field to the amount he and his family, and hirelings if he could afford them, might gather with scythe and cradle during the brief harvest period. This single innovation removed a technical constraint on production that was as old as field cultivation. Western settlers in the 1840's could also improve their productivity with better plows, cultivators, and other implements that were coming into wider use. Technological innovation, both on and off the farm, was breaking down the old barriers to greater production in the West.[5]

[5] Marvin W. Towne and Wayne D. Rasmussen, "Farm Gross Product and Gross Investment in the Nineteenth Century," in *Trends in the American Economy in the Nineteenth Century*, National Bureau of Economic Research, Studies in Income and Wealth, XXIV (Princeton, 1962), 291–294, is the best source of data on the growth of farm output. For an excellent essay that attempts to separate the influence of westward expansion from the impact of technological change in measuring productivity increases, see William N. Parker and Judith L. V. Klein, "Productivity Growth in Grain Production in the United States, 1840–60 and 1900–10," in *Output, Employment and Productivity in the United States after 1800*, vol. XXX of the same N.B.E.R. series (New York, 1966), 523–580. Contemporaries had no fine devices for measuring productivity, but an article in the *Annual Report for the Commissioner of Agriculture, 1862* (Washington, 1863), which claimed that most of

In the political arena, too, the ideal of expansion emerged triumphant. Passage of the Pre-emption Act in 1841 marked a long step toward the reduction of all legal barriers to entry into western agriculture. The Mexican War and the Oregon Treaty added vast new territories to the public domain and reinforced the support, already implicit in the liberalized land policy, for continued rapid growth of the agricultural sector. Furthermore, the West was gaining in political strength, and her representatives had reached a position which enabled them to translate the popular, somewhat fuzzy notions about themselves into policy decisions.

Nowhere was this more evident than in the debate over the Walker Tariff of 1846, in which the proponents of the American system clashed directly with the advocates of unlimited expansion for agriculture. Whig spokesmen made an eloquent, last-ditch fight against the reduction in protection for domestic manufactures; in speeches and in pamphlets they warned against the consequences of seeking greater foreign markets for western farm produce and called for further development of a larger, dependable domestic market. The reply of those westerners who had abandoned their faith in that solution for the economic problems of their region was epitomized in the remarks of Representative Breese, of Illinois. "Illinois wants a market for her agricultural productions," he asserted, "she wants the market of the world. Ten counties of that State could supply all the home market." [6] When the final vote came, enough westerners had

---

the increase in the value of farm implements over the previous dozen years had been due to the purchase of reapers, also explained why: "Even if they were no speedier than the cradle, the fact that it substitutes horse-power for human labor is sufficient to insure their general use, for in this way harvest labor is doubled, and therefore the harvest crop may be doubled" (pp. 93–94).

[6] *Cong. Globe*, 29 Cong., 1 sess., XV, 1124, 1846. See also Thomas P. Martin, "The Upper Mississippi Valley in Anglo-American Anti-Slavery and Free Trade Relations, 1837–1842," *Mississippi Valley Historical*

turned from their flirtation with Clay's program to a temporary alliance with the South, on the side of freer trade and unlimited expansion.

Implicit in the concept of the West as the granary of the world was the assumption that Americans could not overproduce—that there would always be foreign markets, and profitable ones, for all that western farmers would raise. This simplistic version of Say's law—the classical dictum that supply creates its own demand—seemed to have been confirmed by the record of the southern cotton trade. At the beginning of the 1820's, cotton exports stood at an unprecedented half-million bales; in 1845 they exceeded two million bales. Britain's repeal of her Corn Laws in the mid-1840's, heralding a new era in which the European market would open to all foreign foodstuffs, seemed to confirm the westerners' faith that there would be an equivalent growth in demand for their own goods. The sharp increase in American grain and meat shipments to Europe during the "hungry forties," though it lasted little more than a season, held out a further hope that potential demand would grow as rapidly as western supply.

After 1850, westerners were fully committed to the ideal of rapid agricultural expansion and were continuously involved in a struggle to make the ideal a reality. The commitment rested on the assumption that in the long run the growth of foreign trade would match the output of farmers exploiting the magnificent resources of the upper Mississippi Valley. It was an expression of confidence that continuing technological and economic progress

---

Review, XV (Sept. 1928), 204–220; Thomas Stirton, "Free Trade and the Wheat Surplus of the Old Northwest" (master's thesis, University of Chicago, 1952); *Cong. Globe*, App., 29 Cong., 1 sess., XVI, 461–464, 1055, 1846; Edwin Williams, *The Wheat Trade of the United States and Europe* (New York, 1846). For an analysis of congressional voting patterns, see Joel H. Silbey, *The Shrine of Party* (Pittsburgh, 1967), 35–106.

would also bring western farmers the necessary markets for their growing surpluses. That confidence was rudely shaken by the sporadic record of food exports during the 1850's. Except for a brief surge during the Crimean War, which cut off some of western Europe's supplies from Russia and the Danube basin, shipments of grain and provisions grew at a relatively slow rate, overshadowed throughout the decade by the booming trade in cotton. During those ten years, cotton accounted for more than 53 per cent of the value of American exports, while grain and flour made up less than 13 per cent, and meat, provisions, and dairy products represented about 7 per cent. Furthermore, western foodstuffs made up a comparatively small proportion of British and western-European imports. Clearly, the outlying regions of Europe—primarily Russia, the Balkans, and the Baltic districts—were reaping the initial benefits from industrial Europe's growing demand for staple foods.[7]

Under these circumstances, opposition to an export orientation for western agriculture continued. The arguments of critics took a new tack. Many of them still emphasized the uncertainty of foreign markets and insisted that they would be profitable only in times of war or of extraordinarily poor harvests abroad. But more of them stressed the alleged danger to a farmer's resources of specialized production for export and the neglect of improved agricultural skills which heedlessly extractive farming methods invariably promoted. For the rest of the century, critics of the expansionist ideal were more likely to be agricultural reformers espousing better tillage and breeding techniques than advocates of a consistent program for balanced economic development. The increased pace of industrialization after 1850 and

---

[7] Olive Anderson, "Economic Warfare in the Crimean War," *Economic History Review*, XIV (Aug. 1961), 35–47; George R. Taylor, *The Transportation Revolution, 1815–1860*, Economic History of the United States, IV (New York, 1951), 451; *Annual Statement of Trade of the United Kingdom with Foreign Countries and British Possessions* (London, 1853–1860).

the ability of businessmen to recruit a labor force through immigration rather than by attracting it from the land, also helped to mute the traditional opposition to agricultural expansion.

Neither the warnings of agricultural reformers nor the widespread disappointment in the current state of the export trade dampened the general enthusiasm for the growth of the farm sector in the 1850's. Waves of settlers continued to pour into the West and turned their energies to the production of livestock and staple crops. Both corn and wheat acreage in the West doubled in the course of the decade, accounting for most of the increase in food production for the nation.[8] Obviously, for every farmer driven out of wheat production by frost, diseases, or low prices, and for every husbandman ruined by hog cholera, there were many others who eagerly engaged in production. Western farmers, on the whole, were following the advice given by a writer in 1854 to the grain growers of the developing frontier: "Work actively and cheerfully . . . with a perfect surety that, with the staff of life in your hands, you will ever be looked up to with interest, and always find willing buyers and remunerating prices."[9]

Finding those buyers for the mounting western surplus was the task of the hundreds of merchants and processors scattered throughout the developing agricultural districts. The drovers, millers, meat packers, and dairy processors in the smaller towns and villages usually sent their goods to the emerging primary markets—Cincinnati, St. Louis, Cleveland, Toledo, and Milwaukee—where entrepreneurs with greater facilities and resources stored and assembled shipments of incoming produce for transfer to the eastern seaboard. Processors in the larger western cities often dealt directly with eastern buyers. Both groups were heavily dependent on credit supplied by easterners and on a string of

[8] Parker and Klein, "Productivity Growth in Grain Production," 541–543.
[9] J. B. D. De Bow, *The Industrial Resources, Statistics, Etc., of the United States . . .* , I (3 vols.; New York, 1854), 91.

intermediaries associated with the system of consigning western produce to seaboard merchants. Both groups, too, received a constant stream of advice on the best ways to turn out products that would suit the requirements of foreign purchasers.

Some midwesterners felt themselves handicapped in their quest for a larger export trade by alleged deficiencies in the marketing system. Several entrepreneurs, impatient with cumbersome transportation on the Great Lakes–Erie Canal route and with the middleman's charges at transfer points on the seaboard, tried to make direct contact with the overseas market. Chicago and Cleveland packers and grain merchants promoted several experimental shipments from their ports direct to Europe via the St. Lawrence, but gave up when the route proved too difficult.[10] A group of Milwaukee flour millers, anxious to dispose of their rising surplus abroad, tried in 1853 to develop an alternate route to the seaboard by sending a few foreign-bound shipments down the Mississippi River to New Orleans, but with disastrous results. Daniel Wells, a Wisconsin congressman and one of the state's leading entrepreneurs, spent much of his time as a delegate to the Crystal Palace Exhibition in 1851 making contacts with people in the British grain markets and preparing for an ambitious export trade. But he, too, had no success.[11]

Railroad promoters establishing lines in the Old Northwest during the 1850's were confident that they could solve many of the problems facing westerners in search of easier access to overseas markets. The first roads in the West had been built as feeders to the waterways, but newer lines and the consolidation

---

[10] *Hunt's Merchants' Magazine*, XXXVI (April 1857), 437–440; *Introduction to Eighth Census of the United States, Agriculture*, III (Washington, 1864) cliii–clv; Thomas D. Odle, "The American Grain Trade of the Great Lakes, 1825–1873," *Inland Seas*, VIII (Winter 1952), 248–249.

[11] Charles Thomson and Co., Liverpool, to Daniel Wells, Jr., Milwaukee, Jan. 25, March 7, April 23, 1852, Horatio Hill to Daniel Wells, Jr., Jan. 25, 1852, Sept. 18, 1853, Daniel Wells Papers, Milwaukee County Historical Society, Milwaukee.

of older ones were designed to compete with water transportation for the growing volume of eastward-bound produce. Many of the railroad entrepreneurs had begun their business careers in foreign trade, were attuned to the possibilities of an expanding commerce and based their projects on expectations of its rapid development. A British visitor interviewed several western railroad executives in 1854 and received assurances that they would soon haul most foodstuffs at rates low enough to encourage a much larger volume of overseas trade.[12] Indeed, by that time railroads were already beginning to capture a significant proportion of the eastbound flour and livestock traffic.

The best efforts of farmers, middlemen, processors, and transporters were of no avail when a world-wide depression followed the conclusion of the Crimean War. The Panic of 1857 cut off the short boom in food exports and cast a pall of gloom over many parts of the West. Trade in provisions and dairy products held on to some of its gains over the next three years, but wheat and flour exports were little higher than they had been at the beginning of the decade. Gone were rosy predictions and proud boasts about the future course of trade between the "Great West" and Europe.[13]

Western confidence in the growth of a large, steady foreign trade returned with greater strength than ever during the Civil War. Exports of wheat and flour, which had never totaled more than about 30,000,000 bushels, averaged more than 50,000,000 for the three years from 1861 to 1863. The amount of ham and bacon sold abroad jumped from a modest 50,000,000 pounds in 1861 to 218,000,000 in 1864. Shipments of lard, butter, and

[12] Hugh S. Tremenheere, *Notes on Public Subjects, Made during a Tour in the United States and Canada* (London, 1852), 60–104.

[13] For two examples of the ebullient optimism generated by the brief Crimean War boom, see *Hunt's Merchants' Magazine*, XXXV (Nov. 1856), 597, and T. B. Thorpe, "Wheat and Its Associations," *Harper's Weekly*, XV (Aug. 1857), 301–313. They provide a sharp contrast to the gloomy discussion in Hunt's and other magazines, including the farm journals, in 1858.

cheese registered similar gains.[14] The growth of trade in northern grain and provisions partially compensated for the virtual stoppage of southern trade. Northerners exulted in the apparent victory of "King Wheat" over "King Cotton" and took special pride in figures showing that, for the first time in the century, the United States had outdistanced all competing nations in supplying Britain, the world's chief importer, with foodstuffs.[15]

The reasons for the abrupt wartime halt in cotton shipments are obvious—an increasingly effective blockade, strains on southern agriculture, and military devastation. It is not so easy to explain the spurt in northern farm exports. Part of the reason lies in the increase in available supplies. Despite the loss of manpower on many northern and western farms, grain harvests were unusually abundant in 1861 and 1863. Livestock production apparently kept pace. The loss of southern markets, though they were probably less significant than was formerly supposed, released additional foodstuffs. On the other hand, the military forces absorbed large quantities of flour and provisions, while transportation to the seaboard under wartime conditions was often uncertain and always expensive. Moreover, there were no unusual circumstances in Europe to stimulate the additional flow of produce. For the first time since the late eighteenth century, American grain and provision shipments to Europe increased sharply despite the absence of high prices occasioned by war or harvest failures. To be sure, British per capita consumption rose, primarily because American breadstuffs were more abundant. If Britain had not received a single cargo of American wheat or

[14] Paul W. Gates, *Agriculture and the Civil War* (New York, 1965), 224–228, 210–211.

[15] Louis B. Schmidt, "The Influence of Wheat and Cotton on Anglo-American Relations during the Civil War," *Iowa Journal of History and Politics*, XVI (July 1918), 400–439; Frank L. Owsley, *King Cotton Diplomacy: Foreign Relations of the Confederate States* (Chicago, 1931), 450–488, 567–572; Commissioner of Agriculture, *Annual Report*, 1862, 72–73, 548–549.

flour in the 1861–1863 period, her people would still have eaten as much bread as they had in the previous three years.[16]

Two additional elements must be considered in any discussion of Civil War foreign trade. First, shipping and mercantile services previously employed in the cotton trade were available at northern ports for other commodities. For example, many New York exporters who had concentrated on southern products turned their talents and energies to the search for profits in other kinds of produce.[17] The second element was the devaluation of American currency with the issuance of greenbacks. This step raised the price of imports but made American commodities cheaper for foreigners. David Dows, one of New York's leading grain dealers, noted in October 1862 that "for several years past wheat has not cost the exporter so little money as it is doing at present," since foreign exchange was selling at a price so high in terms of dollars that it meant a 30-per-cent discount on produce. Ironically, this advantage was greatest when northern military prospects were worst; news that northern armies had lost a battle in the first years of the war invariably sent up the price of gold and this in turn stimulated greater activity in New York's produce markets.[18]

[16] Eli Ginzberg, "The Economics of British Neutrality During the Civil War," *Agricultural History*, X (Oct. 1936), 147–156.

[17] Sheila Marriner, in *Rathbones of Liverpool, 1845–1873* (Liverpool, 1961), 74–84, describes the British firm that conducted the greatest amount of business in the foreign grain trade at New York. The papers of the Leverich family and of Richard Irvin and Company, in the New-York Historical Society, provide examples of two important New York firms in the cotton trade that turned to grain and provisions during the war.

[18] David Dows and Company, New York, to Daniel Wells, Milwaukee, Oct. 1 and Oct. 3, 1862, Daniel Wells Papers, Milwaukee County Historical Society. I wish to thank the Milwaukee County Historical Society for permission to quote from the Wells Papers. The same point is made at length in the *Eighth Census of the U.S., Agriculture*, III, xxxv–xxxvi.

As the war drew to a close, agricultural exports dropped. In part, this was due to the greater strength of the dollar once victory for the North seemed inevitable; in part, it reflected poorer harvests and the need for food supplies for relief programs in the occupied areas of the South. In 1864 shipments of breadstuffs and provisions were little higher than their best ante bellum levels. Only dairy products, of all the major categories, held their own in the general decline at the war's end. Predictably, there was disappointment in many western circles that the hold on the European market had again weakened, and there were grave warnings once more about the folly of competing with impoverished peasants in Europe and Asia.[19]

In a broader sense, the Civil War was more important to western farmers for the legislation it produced than for any short-term gains in foreign trade. The economic measures passed after the Republican electoral victory of 1860 were designed as much for the further development of agriculture as for business. Westerners bent on expansion had virtually all of their major demands satisfied: a homestead act that removed the remaining restrictions on the acquisition of land by potential farmers, a series of grants to railroad companies to provide badly needed transportation in areas beyond the reach of markets, and a federal Department of Agriculture to offer continuing government services. Aid of this magnitude assured the continuing rapid exploitation of the country's remaining farming resources and a continuing imbalance between the agricultural and industrial sectors. At the very least, the Civil War policies made the commitment to unrestrained expansion irreversible and consequently made the need for foreign markets more urgent.

The necessity for selling more and more farm products abroad served as the common point of reference for the growing antagonisms within the agricultural economy. Farmers and merchants

[19] *Eighth Census of the U.S.*, III, xliv; Commissioner of Agriculture, *Annual Report*, 1871, 297, 453.

attacked railroad companies on the ground that cheaper transportation from the West was imperative if America was to win "control," as some of them put it, of the European commodity markets.[20] Whether the attacks took the form of a movement for "Granger laws," pressures for refurbishing the waterways, or an insistence on rate structures that would spur competition among seaports, they were justified on the basis that costs of moving western crops to shipping points had to be lowered. In the mounting disputes over grading and inspection systems, as well as over other features of the new marketing methods in the grain exchanges, livestock yards, and dairy plants, each side presented its case in terms of impediments to the export trade. Much of the resentment against "monopolies," as in the Granger campaign against the grain-sack "ring" in California, the denunciations of implement manufacturers in the Midwest, and the outcry against the Buffalo grain-elevator "ring," was based on allegations that their "excessive" charges interfered with the flow of foodstuffs to Europe. To be sure, these conflicts were an understandable consequence of the onrushing commercialization of agriculture,

[20] In 1874, Lucius Fairchild, the United States consul at Liverpool, forwarded a copy of his report to the Windom Committee, created in the Senate at the behest of westerners anxious to get cheaper rates to the seaboard, to a friend in Wisconsin. Fairchild thought his information on rates would be valuable ammunition in the struggle against high railroad rates and pointed out that "the prices in our western states is [*sic*] controlled by the prices here, and here our grain comes in contact with that from other parts of the world, and must compete with it. The cheaper we can get it to the Atlantic the better we can control this market" Lucius Fairchild to G. W. Hazelton, April 13, 1874, Fairchild Papers, General Correspondence, Box 32, State Historical Society of Wisconsin, Madison. I wish to thank the State Historical Society for permission to quote from this letter. For other examples of the use of "control" and "command" in discussions of the export trade, and of the need for low freight rates, see Richard H. Edmonds, "Our Exports of Breadstuffs," *International Review*, XI (Nov. 1881), 450–462, and F. H. Morse (former consul general at London), "The American Export Trade," *ibid.*, VI (Jan. 1879), 39–53.

and the rhetoric may have exaggerated the reality. Yet the common appeal to the interests of foreign trade revealed a basic, pervasive concern.

The concern about foreign markets was heightened by growing regional specialization in western agricultural areas. From mid-century on, newer sections tended to specialize first in cattle or wheat, which required the extensive use of land, then shifted to more intensive practices after settlement became more concentrated and more capital was available. By the 1870's, cattlemen and wheat farmers were beginning to occupy their "last frontiers" and to adjust to the harsh new environment of the plains. Despite drought, grasshopper plagues, a lack of capital, and other handicaps, they were succeeding well enough in carving out extensive new areas for a range-cattle industry and new highly mechanized wheat belts in the Red River Valley, central Kansas, and California. Just as in the preceding generation the better farmers of the mid-Atlantic states had shifted their production to meet the competition from the cheaper livestock and grain of the Old Northwest, so the prairie farmers turned to new specialties when the agricultural frontier moved beyond the Missouri. Contrary to the advice of agricultural editors and other self-styled experts, farmers in all regions found their salvation in specialization rather than in "diversification." In region after region, the more successful farmers discovered greater profits and retained a community of interest with their neighbors by turning to the one or two items in which they had the greatest comparative advantage. The corn-hog farmers and cattle fatteners of Illinois and Iowa and the dairymen of Wisconsin and Ohio had perhaps found the best use for their skills and resources, but they, too, were producing surpluses and had to look to foreign markets for relief.[21]

[21] Two excellent studies of the process by which midwesterners made their shifts in specialization are Allan G. Bogue, *From Prairie to Corn Belt: Farming on the Illinois and Iowa Prairies in the Nineteenth Century* (Chicago, 1963), 148–168; and Eric E. Lampard, *The Rise of*

Fortuitously, western farmers did not have to look far or long for an outlet for their surplus. The same communications revolution that was unifying the American market was also drawing it closer to Europe. With trunk-line railroads vying for the western trade after 1873, freight rates between primary markets where crops and processed foods were assembled and the eastern ports where they were loaded onto waiting vessels began to drop sharply. The introduction of through bills of lading hastened the process, already well under way, of eliminating middlemen at the old intervening transfer points and placed westerners in more direct contact with exporters. The development of reliable transatlantic cable service put the exporter in more direct contact with the foreign buyer, reducing the risks of price changes and thereby lowering costs per unit. In no other major exporting country were marketing and processing, as well as basic farm production, so highly rationalized. It was natural, therefore, for more and more European importers to look to America to supply their markets. After the Civil War some of the more important European commodity importers established branches in New York and other major ports and began to deal directly with western merchants. In addition to the Rathbones of Liverpool, such British firms as Patterson Brothers, David Bingham and Company, and Fowler Brothers, Ltd. (which would later do business as the Anglo-American Provision Company) began conducting large-scale buying operations at New York. They were joined by the late 1870's by such cosmopolitan firms, doing business throughout Europe in a variety of commodities, as Ralli Brothers and Dreyfus et Cie.[22]

the Dairy Industry in Wisconsin: A Study in Agricultural Change, 1820–1920 (Madison, Wis., 1963), 23–32.

[22] Information about foreign firms specializing in the grain and provision trades at New York is contained in New York Assembly, Special Committee on Railroads (Hepburn Committee), *Proceedings* (8 vols.; Albany, 1879–1880) III, and New York Senate, *Testimony . . .* [on] *Making Corners and Dealing in Futures . . .* , Albany, 1882, in New York State Commerce Commission, *Report* (2 vols.; Albany, 1900),

When European demand leaped in the 1870's, the western farmer supplied virtually all the additional needs of the Old World. Wheat and flour exports from the United States rose from a little more than 50,000,000 bushels in 1870 to 180,000,000 in 1880. Indeed, for the only time in the century the value of breadstuffs sent abroad at the end of the decade was greater than the value of cotton exports. The trade in live cattle, sheep, and hogs for foreign markets, negligible before 1865 and amounting to a little more than half a million dollars in 1871, earned more than fifteen million dollars in 1881. British consumers bought 57,000,000 pounds of American cheese in 1870, and 148,000,000 pounds in 1881. Britain's requirements for meats were great enough to overcome consumer resistance to chilled beef, which began to move in large quantities from Chicago to London's Smithfield Market in the mid-1870's. In 1881, more than 100,000,000 pounds of refrigerated beef went abroad, almost all of it to British buyers. Of the major items, grain and provisions, the latter category had a more impressive rate of growth during the decade. Exports of bacon increased twentyfold between 1870 and 1880; lard shipments, sevenfold. The flood of food-stuffs was without precedent in the annals of international trade.[23]

The extraordinary surge of exports from the American West was all the more remarkable in view of the economic and financial situation in the 1870's. It was a decade of widespread busi-

---

V. Though located in New York, these firms did business at all the major Atlantic seaports and dealt directly with the large-scale grain and provisions firms of the interior. Thus, there was a growing decentralization of markets in a geographic sense at the same time that consolidation of marketing firms tended to centralize them in an organizational sense. This explains the continued concentration of marketing activity at Chicago and New York long after they had lost much of their relative position as commodity-assembling points.

[23] Edwin G. Nourse, *American Agriculture and the European Market* (New York, 1924), 16–27, 239–258; Robert E. Lipsey, *Price and Quantity Trends in the Foreign Trade of the United States* (Princeton, 1963), 45–52, 77–78.

ness depression at home and abroad, and the deflation in the United States was aggravated by the policy of specie resumption. Though absolute prices began to decline after 1873, relative prices of American products in international markets were rising. Ironically, the increased sales of western goods during the decade gave the United States a large favorable balance of trade and was the major factor in bringing gold into the country. The incremental shipments of western grain and meat earned the foreign exchange that made the Resumption Act work.[24] The western farmers who were joining the Greenback party movement at the end of the decade were themselves making feasible the policy against which they protested.

Such considerations were generally overlooked as the nation congratulated itself on the great export boom of the 1870's. Business leaders hailed the "capture" of Europe's markets and attributed the recovery from the depression to the sales of western products abroad. Farm journals and the general press cheered the phenomenon as evidence that after decades of struggle the nation had achieved its cherished goal, the permanent "command" of the expanding world market for agricultural products. The dream of the West as the granary of the world, the producer of vast surpluses for hungry masses abroad, seemed at last to be fulfilled. The remark made by a pioneer Chicago meatpacker was typical of the theme expressed over and over again in 1880. "Don't be afraid of over producing," he assured a farm gathering. "We cannot glut the markets for the 'old world' will take all our surplus." [25]

The irony of American agricultural history is that when the nation's farmers did achieve their goal and became the world

[24] James K. Kindahl, "The Economic Factors in Specie Resumption: The United States, 1865–79," *Journal of Political Economy*, LXIX (Feb. 1961), 30–48; U.S. Bureau of the Census, *Historical Statistics of the United States: Colonial Times to 1957* (Washington, D.C., 1960), 546–547.

[25] *Recollections of Gordon S. Hubbard: An Address before the Danville Old Settlers Association* (n.p., 1880), Chicago Historical Society.

market's major suppliers of food as well as fiber, the fruits of their success often proved bitter. Throughout their struggle to realize their ambition by turning the West into the granary of the world, Americans rarely perceived that what they could do, farmers in other lands could also do. During the rest of the century, western farmers watched one after another of the "empty" lands of the world—Australia, New Zealand, Argentina, Canada, South Africa—begin to fill with settlers as anxious as the Americans to earn a strong position in international commodity markets. During the rest of the century, western farmers discovered that they had to submit to the increasingly hard discipline of impersonal market forces beyond their control and to conform to the steadily rising standards of consumer tastes. They learned the same bitter lesson southern cotton and tobacco growers knew so well—that one can be imprisoned by the market he captures.

A major facet of the farmers' revolt in the late nineteenth century was the growing feeling that the idea of the West as the granary of the world had somehow been perverted. The trans-Mississippi regions were just coming into their own in 1880. Bonanza farms in the wheat belts and great cattle ranches on the high plains were adding greater momentum to continued expansion even as America reached a plateau in her foreign agricultural trade. Many of the farmers and ranchers who avidly seized the remaining easily exploitable land on the public domain felt that it offered the last opportunity to share in the dream of America as producer for the world, only to find that the reality was more demanding and less rewarding than the dream had promised. Many of them could not have abandoned the dream if they had wanted to, since their lands were relatively marginal and there were few alternatives to the export commodities in which they specialized.

Unable to face the possibility that the fundamental assumption of the century—the assumption that the West could not overproduce—might be fallacious, western farmers directed their protests against the middlemen, processors, and railroads, the agents that stood between them and the foreign consumer. The larger and better organized the target, the more vigorous were their attacks. To westerners, there was something basically wrong about a system that enabled giant meat-packing plants, flour mills, grain-elevator companies, and railroad corporations to flourish while many men who supplied them with basic goods could hardly make a living.

Yet the consolidation of marketing firms and the growth of giant processing plants helped American farmers retain their hold on export markets. After 1880, a larger proportion of western wheat went abroad as flour, most western meat arrived in Britain as chilled or tinned beef, and larger hog-packing factories accounted for more and more of the growing trade in provisions. None of the small mill owners could have been more aggressive than the St. Louis and Minneapolis flour makers in the quest for markets abroad.[26] None of the livestock shippers could have had greater determination than the Swifts and Armours to supply Europe with American beef.[27] None of the local butchers in the corn-hog belt could have taken greater care in preparing hams and bacons for British consumers that John Morrell or George Hammond.[28]

Indeed, farmers who produced commodities for middlemen less well organized than the grain or livestock business, or for processing industries less consolidated than flour or meat packing, fared worse in overseas markers. Dairy farmers refused to

[26] Charles B. Kuhlmann, *The Development of the Flour-Milling Industry of the United States* (Boston, 1929), 288–294; John Storck and Walter D. Teague, *Flour for Man's Bread: A History of Milling* (Minneapolis, 1952), 268–274; George Plant Papers, Missouri Historical Society, St. Louis.

[27] Rudolf A. Clemen, *The American Livestock and Meat Industry* (New York, 1923), 269–298; Louis F. Swift, *The Yankee of the Yards* (Chicago, 1927).

[28] Charles W. Towne and Edward N. Wentworth, *Pigs: From Cave to Corn Belt* (Norman, Okla., 1950), 179–181; Lawrence O. Cheever, "John Morrell and Co:," *Palimpsest*, XLII (April 1960), 145–192.

accept reforms of market standards for their butter and cheese and were served by a highly decentralized processing industry. They lost their foreign trade after 1880 as rapidly as they had gained it earlier.[29] The increasingly melancholy condition of cotton and tobacco farmers, though largely due to the persistent heritage of overexpansion and the continuing burdens imposed by the Civil War, was accentuated by the decentralized nature of the textile and cigar-making industries, as well as by anachronistic market structures.[30]

Both farmers and middlemen wanted to keep and to enlarge the foreign trade in western products, but they disagreed on the best means of conducting that trade and on the distribution of its costs and benefits. Farmers tended to regard the increasingly complex functions of middlemen and processors as interfering with the increase of exports. Grain and livestock producers, especially, were convinced that they could do better if they could sell their output directly to the foreign consumer. Both groups were aided and abetted in their campaigns against middlemen by the commission merchants who were being squeezed out through consolidation. Livestock owners, for example, gained support from old buying firms in the attack against the "beef trust." The cattlemen were particularly incensed by the regulation, imposed in 1880, that required all live cattle landing in Britain to be slaughtered within ten days, since it precluded the possibility of direct sales of range cattle to British feeders and placed the western rancher wholly at the mercy of American fatteners and packers. Throughout the 1880's and 1890's western cattlemen demanded diplomatic pressures to force open the European market and make possible a direct trade that would

[29] Lampard, *Wisconsin Dairy Industry*, 141–144.

[30] James E. Boyle, *Cotton and the New Orleans Cotton Exchange* (Garden City, N.Y., 1934); Harold D. Woodman, "King Cotton and His Retainers: A Study of Cotton Marketing in the South," doctoral dissertation, University of Chicago, 1964; Nannie May Tilley, *The Bright-Tobacco Industry, 1860–1929* (Chapel Hill, N.C., 1948), 201–202, 341–342.

circumvent the middlemen.[31] Hog raisers, too, felt frustrated by
the even tighter restrictions and prohibitions on the trade in
pork, for many of the same reasons.[32] Wheat growers came to
regard the line-elevator companies, the grain exchanges, and the
flour-milling industry as barriers between the farmer and the
foreign consumer. From time to time groups of northwestern
wheat growers sought to establish direct contact with British
millers, claiming that they could provide better grades at lower
prices if they could avoid dealing with a corrupt market system.[33]

On the other hand, the processors and middlemen had their
own complaints. They inveighed against the allegedly declining
quality of western produce, the failure of farmers to turn out
commodities geared to foreign tastes, and, most of all, the dishonest practices of farmers who disguised the poor quality of
goods they delivered. Moreover, few Populists could match the
bitterness of feeling against railroads that was held by some of
the leading flour millers and meat packers. The source of the
millers' unhappiness was the higher freight rates for flour as
compared to grain—a disadvantage which they claimed not even
a milling-in-transit privilege could overcome—and the refusal of
railroads to accept liability for damage or late delivery of this
perishable item.[34] The main thrust of these charges was that the
railroads prevented the flour millers from building a larger foreign trade. The meat packers, too, had a long standing grudge
against the railroads, charging that the trunk-line roads in partic-

[31] James Louis Erlenborn, "The American Meat and Livestock Industry and American Foreign Policy, 1880–1896" (Master's thesis, University of Wisconsin, 1966).

[32] John L. Gignilliat, "Pigs, Politics and Protection: The European
Boycott of American Pork, 1879–1891," *Agricultural History*, XXXV
(Jan. 1961), 3–12.

[33] Stories of these efforts were reported throughout the 1880's and
1890's in the *Northwestern Miller* (Minneapolis) and the *Evening Corn
Trade List Supplement* (London).

[34] Kuhlmann, *Flour-Milling Industry*, 89–92, 172–175, 184–187,
310–315.

ular had refused to provide refrigerated cars and that even when the packers furnished their own, the roads charged much higher rates for chilled beef than for live cattle.[35]

The barrage of charges and countercharges made by almost every group in the American agricultural economy rose to a crescendo in the 1890's, with the onslaught of another severe depression. Hard times sharpened the divisions within the farm sector and pitted one group against another. For a generation, as agriculture was drawn more firmly into the commercial nexus, the number of special interests had been increasing and the points of conflict multiplying. This time, unlike the 1870's, the depression was marked by a decline of foreign trade in foodstuffs. There was no adequate vent either for the surplus or for emotional frustrations.

Never before had the idea of the West as the granary of the world been in such jeopardy as in the 1890's. The European market seemed to be saturated and the surpluses were still growing. Competition from other parts of the world was stronger than ever. Never before had the future of the western farmer seemed so bleak. Shaken by overwhelming political defeat in 1896 and by the scarring experience of the depression, western adherents of Populism could find hope only by redefining the old concept of the granary of the world or by abandoning it in favor of an up-to-date version of national self-sufficiency.

Populist support for America's imperialist ventures at the end of the century was part of the effort to recast the definition of "world" to include Asia and Latin America. Indeed, some western farm interests had been moving in that direction since the 1880's. Flour millers and cattlemen, in particular, had pressed for diplomatic action to open Latin America to their products soon after the export boom of the 1870's subsided. By the late 1880's, they had gained additional supporters, including the influential James J. Hill, and had extended their vision to embrace Asia as

[35] Harper Leech and John C. Carroll, *Armour and His Times* (New York, 1938), 123–167.

well.[36] The belief that the West could continue to find outlets for its surpluses and at the same time free itself of an unhealthy dependence on the British market only by finding buyers across the Pacific persisted throughout the 1890's. Even the recovery from the depression and a resurgence of trade with Europe did not wholly diminish the thrust of that belief. Virtually every farm leader appearing before the Industrial Commission in 1899 agreed that the basic solution to the problems confronting American farmers could be summed up in two words: Asiatic markets.[37]

The new departure in agrarian rhetoric may have contributed to the expansionist impulse of Washington policy makers, but it had no foundation in the realities of international economics. Instead, Europe continued to serve as the major buyer of foodstuffs from America and from other overseas suppliers. America's relative share of the European trade was diminishing: no longer did she furnish 60 per cent of the breadstuffs, all of the beef, and most of the pork products that Britain and some of the Continental countries imported, as she did in 1880. But the absolute amounts of meat, provisions, and breadstuffs that western producers sent abroad in 1900 were greater than ever and represented roughly the same high proportions of total output in each case. The western farmers were getting better prices for their great "bargain counter" of foodstuffs, but Europeans were still the only customers of any consequence.

After the crisis of the 1890's had passed, cotton and tobacco farmers, still trapped in the glut of their own making, continued to struggle against their century-long bondage to foreign markets. In contrast, most western farmers began to take a more

[36] My colleague William A. Williams has been conducting research on the influence of agrarian interests in American foreign policy during the late nineteenth century. I am indebted to him for sharing his knowledge with me.

[37] Report of the Industrial Commission, *Agriculture and Agricultural Labor*, X (Washington, D.C., 1900), 267–269, 287–290, 626–627, 718–722.

tolerant view of their own continued dependence. They could, indeed, look back over the preceding century with some satisfaction. They had apparently reached the limit of expansion in the American West and, true to the old dream of the "granary," had transformed the West into the world's largest, most commercially minded, and most successful producer of agricultural commodities. From the perspective of the "golden age" in American farming, the vision of the West as the granary of the world still had merit. It was a far more complex world than anyone had envisaged at the beginning of the century, but if any country could lay claim to being its granary, it was America.

Works by
Paul Wallace Gates

~~◊~~

GOULD P. COLMAN

Books

The Illinois Central Railroad and Its Colonization Work. Cambridge: Harvard University Press, 1934. 374 pp.

The Wisconsin Pine Lands of Cornell University: A Study in Land Policy and Absentee Ownership. Ithaca, N.Y.: Cornell University Press, 1943. 265 pp. Reprinted by the State Historical Society of Wisconsin, 1965.

Frontier Landlords and Pioneer Tenants. Reprinted from *Journal of the Illinois State Historical Society,* XXXVIII (June 1945). Ithaca, N.Y.: Cornell University Press, 1945. 64 pp.

Fifty Million Acres: Conflicts over Kansas Land Policy, 1854–1890. Ithaca, N.Y.: Cornell University Press, 1954. 311 pp. Reissued with Foreword by Robert W. Johannsen. New York: Atherton Press, 1966.

The Farmer's Age: Agriculture, 1815–1860. New York: Holt, Rinehart, and Winston, 1960. 460 pp.

Agriculture and the Civil War. New York: Alfred A. Knopf, 1965. 383 pp.

California Ranchos and Farms, 1846–1862. Madison: State Historical Society of Wisconsin, 1967. 288 pp.

History of Public Land Law Development. Washington: United States Public Land Law Review Commission, 1968. 828 pp.

Works by Paul Wallace Gates

Other Selected Publications

"The Disposal of the Public Domain in Illinois, 1848–1856," *Journal of Economic and Business History*, III (Feb. 1931), 216–240.

"The Promotion of Agriculture by the Illinois Central Railroad, 1855–1870," *Agricultural History*, V (April 1931), 57–76.

"The Land Policy of the Illinois Central Railroad, 1851–1870," *Journal of Economic and Business History*, III (Aug. 1931), 554–573.

"The Campaign of the Illinois Central Railroad for Norwegian and Swedish Immigrants," *Norwegian-American Historical Association Studies*, VI (1931), 66–88.

"Large Scale Farming in Illinois, 1850 to 1870," *Agricultural History*, VI (Jan. 1932), 14–25.

"The Railroads of Missouri, 1850–1870," *Missouri Historical Review*, XXVI (Jan. 1932), 126–141.

"The Struggle for the Charter of the Illinois Central Railroad," *Illinois State Historical Society Transactions for the Year 1933*, XL, 55–66.

"Historical Periodicals in the College Libraries of Pennsylvania," *Social Studies*, XXV (Jan. 1934), 10–11.

"Official Encouragement to Immigration by the Province of Canada," *Canadian Historical Review*, XV (March 1934), 24–38.

"American Land Policy and the Taylor Grazing Act," in U.S. Resettlement Administration, *Land Policy Circular* (Oct. 1935), 15–37.

"Recent Land Policies of the Federal Government," in National Resources Board, *Certain Aspects of Land Problems and Government Land Policies*, in *Report on Land Planning*, Pt. VII (1935), 60–91.

"The Homestead Law in an Incongruous Land System," *American Historical Review*, XLI (July 1936), 652–681.

"A Fragment of Kansas Land History: The Disposal of the Christian Indian Tract," *Kansas Historical Quarterly*, VI (Aug. 1937), 227–240.

"Land Policy and Tenancy in the Prairie Counties of Indiana," *Indiana Magazine of History*, XXXV (March 1939), 1–26.

"Southern Investments in Northern Lands before the Civil War," *Journal of Southern History*, V (May 1939), 155–185.

"Federal Land Policy in the South, 1866–1888," *Journal of Southern History*, VI (Aug. 1940), 303–330.

"Land Policy and Tenancy in the Prairie States," *Journal of Economic History*, I (May 1941), 60–82.

"Western Opposition to the Agricultural College Act," *Indiana Magazine of History*, XXXVII (June 1941), 103–136.

"The Role of the Land Speculator in Western Development," *Pennsylvania Magazine of History and Biography*, LXVI (July 1942), 314–333.

Introduction, in *The John Tipton Papers*, Nellie A. Robertson and Dorothy Riker, eds. Indiana Historical Collections. Indianapolis: Indiana Historical Bureau, 1942. I, 3–53.

"Hoosier Cattle Kings," *Indiana Magazine of History*, XLIV (March 1948), 1–24.

"Cattle Kings in the Prairies," *Mississippi Valley Historical Review*, XXXV (Dec. 1948), 379–412.

"The Land System of the United States in the Nineteenth Century," in *Proceedings of the First Congress of Historians from Mexico and the United States*, Mexico, 1950. 222–255.

"The Struggle for Land and the 'Irrepressible Conflict,'" *Political Science Quarterly*, LXVI (June 1951), 248–271.

"From Individualism to Collectivism in American Land Policy," in Chester McA. Destler, ed., *Liberalism as a Force in History: Lectures on Aspects of the Liberal Tradition*, Henry Wells Lawrence Memorial Lectures. New London: Connecticut College, 1953. III, 14–35.

"The Railroad Land-Grant Legend," *Journal of Economic History*, XIV (Spring 1954), 143–146.

"Research in the History of American Land Tenure," *Agricultural History*, XXVIII (July 1954), 121–126.

"Weyerhaeuser and Chippewa Logging Industry," in O. Fritiof Ander, ed., *The John H. Hauberg Historical Essays*, Augustana Library Publications, no. 26. Rock Island, Ill.: Augustana Book Concern, 1954. 50–64.

"Private Land Claims in the South," *Journal of Southern History*, XXII (May 1956), 183–204.

"Frontier Estate Builders and Farm Laborers," in Walker D. Wyman and C. B. Kroeber, *The Frontier in Perspective*. Madison: University of Wisconsin Press, 1957. 143–164.

"Adjudication of Spanish-Mexican Land Claims in California," *The Huntington Library Quarterly*, XXI (May 1958), 213–236.

"Charles Lewis Fleischmann, German-American Agricultural Authority," *Agricultural History*, XXXV (Jan. 1961), 13–23.

"California's Agricultural College Lands," *Pacific Historical Review*, XXX (May 1961), 103–122.

"California's Embattled Settlers," *California Historical Society Quarterly*, XLI (June 1962), 99–130.

"Tenants of the Log Cabin," *Mississippi Valley Historical Review*, XLIX (June 1962), 3–31.

"The Morrill Act and Early Agricultural Science," *Michigan History*, XLVI (Dec. 1962), 289–302.

Free Homesteads for all Americans. Washington, D.C.: Civil War Centennial Commission, 1962. 11 pp.

"The Homestead Act in Operation," *Farm Policy Forum*, XV (1962–1963), 19–23.

"The Homestead Act: Free Land Policy in Operation, 1862–1935," in H. W. Ottoson, ed., *Land Use Policy and Problems in the United States.* Lincoln, Neb.: University of Nebraska Press, 1963. 28–46.

"Charts of Public Land Sales and Entries," *Journal of Economic History*, XXIV (March 1964), 22–27.

"The Homestead Law in Iowa," *Agricultural History*, XXXVIII (April 1964), 67–78.

"Land and Credit Problems in Underdeveloped Kansas," *Kansas Historical Quarterly*, XXXI (Spring 1965), 41–61.

Foreword, in Benjamin Horace Hibbard, *History of the Public Land Policies.* Madison: University of Wisconsin Press, 1965.

"Ulysses Prentiss Hedrick, Horticulturist and Historian," Introduction, in Ulysses P. Hedrick, *A History of Agriculture in the State of New York.* New York: Hill and Wang, 1966. Reprinted in *New York History*, LXVII (July 1966), 219–247.

"Pre–Henry George Land Warfare in California," *California Historical Society Quarterly*, XLVI (June 1967), 121–148.

"Changing Agriculture," in the University of the State of New York, *The Challenge of Local History.* Albany, 1968. 39–59.

Contributors

Lee Benson	University of Pennsylvania
Robert F. Berkhofer, Jr.	University of Minnesota
Allan G. Bogue	University of Wisconsin
Margaret Beattie Bogue	University of Wisconsin
James L. Clayton	University of Utah
Henry Cohen	California State College at Long Beach
Gould P. Colman	Cornell University
Leslie E. Decker	University of Maine
David M. Ellis	Hamilton College
Charlotte Erickson	London School of Economics
Frederick Merk	Harvard University
Irene D. Neu	Indiana University
Morton Rothstein	University of Wisconsin
Harry N. Scheiber	Dartmouth College
Robert W. Silsby	Kenmore West Senior High School
David C. Smith	University of Maine
Mary E. Young	Ohio State University

Index

Index

Railroad land grants, xi; federal, 47–73; major, 49, 60; indemnity lands withdrawn, 49; adjustment of, 50; forfeiture movement, 60; congressional debates over, 87–90, 97–100; Maine, 127, 132–134; on mid-continent frontier, 365; *see also* Northern Pacific, Oregon and California, *and* Union Pacific *railroads*

Railroads, xi; Pacific-railroad act, 20, 33–46, 49, 51, 53; foes, 50, 53, 98, 99, 403–404; companies with grants, 52–73; Maine lines, 113, 127, 132-134; public aids to, 365–367; town promotion, 365–369; Nebraska lines, 368–369; expansion in 1850's, 390–391; rate wars, 1870's, 397; *see also individual companies*

Ray, Gov. James, 285

Relinquishments, sale by squatters, 377–378; *see also* Squatters

Republicanism, tenet of congressional spokesmen on liberal ideology, 91ff

Republican Party, 20–46 *passim*

Republican River, 41

Review of Reviews, 15

Rice, Sen. Henry M., 29

Richardson, William, 340–341

Rights of occupancy, xxiii–xxv; *see also* Squatters

Roads: in Maine, 116–117, 125; transappalachian, 278

Robbins, Roy, x, 360

Roberts, Justice Owen, 71

Robinson, Rix, 317

Roman Empire, land monopoly deplored, 91, 92, 100

Ross, Earle, 20

Rural decline, in Old Northwest, 349–351

Russell County, Kan., 371

Safety-valve theory, 80, 81, 101–103, 358n, 383

St. Clair, Arthur, governor of Northwest Territory, 268, 269, 271

St. Joseph, Mo., 40

St. Mary's Canal Mineral Land Company, 179–180; policies, 180–183; land sales and profits, 184–186, 188–190; reorganized in 1901, 191

St. Mary's Falls Ship Canal Company, 169–179; charter, 169; land selection, 169–175 *passim;* sales, 176–179; absorption by St. Mary's Canal Mineral Land Company, 180

St. Mary's Mineral Land Company, 191

Sandusky: Indian council, of 1783, 258–259, of 1793, 273–274

Sanford, John G. X., 313

Sargent, Rep. Aaron, 89

Saulsbury, Sen. Willard, 36

Sault canal: need, 162, 164, 167; federal grant to Michigan, 164–166; grant to promoters, 167–169; St. Mary's Falls Ship Canal Company, 169ff

Sault Ste Marie, 162–164, 167, 170–174

Schulenburg v. Harriman (1875), 59–60

Schurz, Carl, Secretary of Interior, 60, 61

Schuyler, Gen. Philip, 262

Scioto Valley, Ohio, trade of, 281–283, 285

Scott, Julia Green: early life, 219–220; administration of farms, 221–245; quoted, 229–230

Scott, Matthew T., operation of farms, 217–223

Scott farms, 217–245; administration, of Matthew T. Scott, 217–223, of Julia G. Scott, 221–245; extent of holdings, 218; agents, 220–222, 227–229, 231–233, 235–239; value, 224, 242–245; tenants, 225, 228–243; leases, 240–244

Scottish immigrants in Old Northwest, 325, 329, 331, 334, 340–342, 351, 352, 354, 356; *see also* British immigrants

Sectionalism, 20–46, 383–384

Senate, U.S.: resolution against payment of traders' claims, 318; agreement with Menominee Indians, 321; *see also* Congress *and individual treaties with Indians*

Seneca Indians, *see* Iroquois Indians

Settling lands: Maine area defined, 118; sale policies, 118–121; Swedish settlement, 130–131; remainder, 134

Seymour, John F., 169, 175

Shallenberger, Aston C., in favor of Reclamation Act, 104–105

Shannon, Fred, 360